below.

Road lighting for safety

Dr Ir D. A. Schreuder

Translated by Adriana Morris
Illustrations: J. Kosterman

ThomasTelford

Published by Thomas Telford Publishing, Thomas Telford Ltd, 1 Heron Quay, London E14 4JD.
URL: http://www.t-telford.co.uk

Distributors for Thomas Telford books are
USA: ASCE Press, 1801 Alexander Bell Drive, VA 20191-4400, USA
Japan: Maruzen Co. Ltd, Book Department, 3–10 Nihonbashi 2-chome, Chuo-ku, Tokyo 103
Australia: DA Books and Journals, 648 Whitehorse Road, Mitcham 3132, Victoria

First published 1996 in Dutch as *Openbare Verlichting voor Verkeer en Veligheid* by Kluwer Bedrÿfs Informatie b. v., Deventer
First published in English 1998

A catalogue record for this book is available from the British Library

ISBN: 0 7277 2616 1

This book is published on the understanding that the author is solely responsible for the statements made and opinions expressed in it and that its publication does not necessarily imply that such statements and/or opinions are or reflect the views or opinions of the publishers.

Although all possible care is taken with regard to accuracy, neither the author nor the publisher accepts any liability for any damage resulting from any possible errors in this publication.

Typeset by MHL Typesetting, Coventry, UK
Printed and bound in Great Britain by Redwood Books, Trowbridge, Wiltshire

Preface

The Netherlands have long played an important part in the development of public highway lighting. This started with the development of lamps and luminaires suitable or specifically intended for street lighting. The low pressure sodium lamp, eminently suitable for road lighting, was first used in the Netherlands. To this technological pioneering work was subsequently added much research relating to visual observation on the road, and the way this observation can be promoted by quality lighting. The name of Philips in particular is associated with this research. The research, which covers decades, has been summarised in a number of standard works; the most important were compiled under the aegis of De Boer (De Boer, ed., 1967; Van Bommel & De Boer, 1980). Other companies and organisations also contributed to a considerable extent, in particular KEMA; one should also mention a number of large Dutch local authorities, as well as a number of manufacturers of lighting products.

Changes in the structure of industry in Holland and the changing division of labour between industry and government led to a shift in the main players during the years following 1975; but this did not affect the prominent position occupied by the Netherlands on the stage of street lighting. Gradually, less research was carried out by industry, and more by independent research institutions. This was usually commissioned by government (specifically the Ministry of Transport and the Department of Trade and Industry). These changes naturally led to a different point of view with regard to street lighting: whereas in the past the emphasis was on 'product', and the considerations were mostly economic, later the concept of 'process' moved into the limelight and considerations became more policy-oriented. The focus shifted towards functional aspects, led by safety and quality of life, and away from technology, where use of space and traffic flow had been in the forefront.

Primarily, the responsibility for carrying out policy fell to the Ministry of Transport, Public Works and Water Management, in particular the Regional Boards, the Transport Research Centre (AVV) of the Directorate-General for Public Works and Water Management, but also to the local authorities. The Ministry was largely responsible for policy planning; the Institute for Road Safety Research SWOV, the main research institute for traffic safety established by the government, played a decisive role in the research required for the planning and execution of the policy. Much of the commissioned research was carried out by institutes with direct or indirect links with government, in particular the TNO institutes, such as the Human Factors Institute (TM), the former Institute for Perception (IZF) in Soesterberg, and university institutes.

The past few years have seen another shift in the way street lighting is considered. Questions of policy obviously continue to play an important role, as long as research is funded by government, but the policy objectives have again been changed. Traffic safety is, and continues to be, the central point of interest, but a sustained safe solution is especially looked for; the aim is to design highway facilities relating to infrastructure, as well as vehicles, in such a way that safe conduct follows naturally. It should be noted that street lighting does not play an important part in these considerations. In addition, thought turns increasingly to crime prevention and the fight against crime. Finally, street lighting is accorded an important role in improving the quality of life.

Environmental considerations are becoming increasingly important. Here we are concerned with a reduction in energy consumption, and generally of more or less scarce, irreplaceable raw materials; the reduction of CO_2 and other greenhouse gases and a reduction in the discharge of waste (in the form of gases, fluids or solids) – all this in accordance with the environmental policy outlined by the Dutch government.

A special role has always been accorded to the Netherlands Institution of Illuminating Engineering (NSVV). The Institution is an independent foundation associated with KEMA, the industry and research and also, but to a lesser extent, with policy bodies, architects and road users. NSVV, the national organisation which combines all knowledge and experience relating to lighting science in the Netherlands, serves as the National Committee of the Commission Internationale de l'Eclairage (CIE) – the International Lighting Commission. The aim of the Institution is promotion of the science and application of lighting science. Education relating to lighting science is also listed among its official aims.

The work of NSVV is carried out in committees, in particular the Committee for Public Lighting, in addition to the recently established Committee for Light Nuisance. The former has set out the Recommendations for Public Lighting. These recommendations have been very important – still are, in fact – for the practical application of lighting science and for the promotion of the installation of quality lighting. The first edition dates from 1957, the second is dated 1974/75 (supplemented in 1977), while the third now finalised (NSVV, 1975; 1974/75; 1977; 1990; 1993; 1995; 1997).

This book is the result of the more recent approach to street lighting, where, as indicated above, the emphasis is less on the technology and the 'product' and more on use, function and 'process'. Developments in the Netherlands obviously play a large role; in view of the leading role which the Netherlands still play in the world of lighting science, and in view of the international character of the research mostly carried out in the Netherlands, this book also reflects the situation world-wide. In addition, the Dutch edition played a role in Part III (Design) of the already mentioned NSVV Recommendations for Public Lighting. That volume concentrates very much on the practice of lighting and in particular on the practice of designing lighting installations. A number of points are raised, which bear on the design, but whose nature is too theoretical for the Recommendations. Part III of the Recommendations was published in 1996 (NSVV, 1996). I should point out, however, that these are two totally independent publications.

The book is aimed at a broad readership and not primarily at experts in the field of public lighting. Experts will find more suitable material in the books by Baer (1990), Eckert (1993) and Hentschel (1994), as well as in the books mentioned earlier. Lighting is presented as a system, as a part of the public highway system in a more general sense, which in turn is seen as an important aspect of society. This is the reason that much attention is paid to subjects which are not, or hardly, raised in the specialist literature, such as aspects of the environment, problems relating to traffic safety and the prevention of, and fight against, crime and to the possibilities and the limitations which older and disabled persons experience in traffic. The book particularly deals with the role which lighting can play in all this. Likely readers are in the first instance those who are professionally interested in the lighting of public spaces and particularly in the lighting of the public highway. The book could also be used in education.

This book is mostly based on the studies carried out by the author as a Senior Scientific Officer for the Institute for Road Safety Research (SWOV) in Leidschendam (formerly in Voorburg), and before that in the (then) Lichttechnisch Laboratorium of Philips Gloeilampenfabrieken in Eindhoven. This research took place over a period of more than 35 years. Most of the material has been published earlier, mostly in the form of SWOV reports; partly also in the form of journal articles and conference papers. I have given references to original publications where this could be of interest to the reader. I am grateful to SWOV for their willingness to co-operate in the realisation of this book; and I should mention that I have also used results of SWOV research in areas other than lighting. References to original publications are also supplied here. In the first instance this concerns studies which relate to road safety in general, and which have been used as a basis for many considerations relating to visual observation.

Finally I would like to thank Mr G. C. Ederveen in Bilderdam, who has contributed significantly to the realisation of this book.

Dr Ir D. A. Schreuder
Leidschendam, January 1998

Bibliography

Baer, R. (1990). *Beleuchtungstechnik; Grundlagen.* Berlin, VEB Verlag Technik, 1990.
De Boer, J.B. (ed). (1967). *Public lighting.* Eindhoven, Centrex, 1967.
Eckert, M. (1993). *Lichttechnik und optische Wahrnehmungssicherheit im Strassenverkehr.* Berlin – München, Verlag Technik GmbH., 1993.

Hentschel, H.-J. (1994). *Licht und Beleuchtung; Theorie und Praxis der Lichttechnik.* (4. Auflage). Heidelberg, Hüthig Buch Verlag, 1994.

NSVV (1957). *Aanbevelingen voor openbare verlichting* [Recommendations for public lighting]. Den Haag, Moormans Periodieke Pers, 1957 (Year estimated).

NSVV (1974/1975). Richtlijnen en aanbevelingen voor openbare verlichting [Guidelines and recommendations for public lighting]. *Elektrotechniek* **52** (1974) 15; 53 (1975) 2 and 5.

NSVV (1977). Het lichtniveau van de openbare verlichting in de bebouwde kom [The level of light in public lighting inside city limits]. *Elektrotechniek* **55** (1977) 90–91.

NSVV (1990). *Aanbevelingen voor openbare verlichting* [Recommendations for public lighting]; Deel I. Arnhem, NSVV, 1990.

NSVV (1993). *Aanbevelingen voor openbare verlichting* [Recommendations for public lighting]; Deel II, Meten en berekenen [Measurements and calculation]. Arnhem, NSVV, 1993.

NSVV (1995). *Aanbevelingen voor openbare verlichting* [Recommendations for public lighting]; Deel IV, Financiîle aspecten [Financial aspects]. Arnhem, NSVV, 1995.

NSVV (1997). *Aanbevelingen voor openbare verlichting* [Recommendations for public lighting]; Deel III, Ontwerpen [Design]. Arnhem, NSVV, 1997.

Van Bommel, W.J.M. & De Boer, J.B. (1980). *Road lighting.* Deventer, Kluwer, 1980.

Contents

1   Introduction

1.1   Transport and lighting quality

The transport of people and goods plays a vital role in the structure of society. It becomes increasingly important to ensure that this transport can take place 24 hours a day. It is not possible for transport to take place at night without artificial light. The obvious answer is to carry artificial light and this has been the practice for thousands of years. Along with the rise of mass motoring, lighting evolved into what we now call vehicle lighting and this has been developed to a high degree.

The 'quality' of transport in darkness is important. The assessment of quality is based on two criteria

- access
- traffic safety.

A number of other criteria are added to these, some of which are unrelated, or only indirectly related to transport, rather they concern the use of public spaces in darkness in a more general sense

- travelling speed
- comfort
- public safety (crime prevention)
- quality of life (subjective security)
- aesthetics and the economy (trade and tourism).

With regard to the quality of transport in darkness, we see that access hardly seems to be affected compared with the situation during the day; neither is there a significant change in the travelling speed. Traffic safety, however, is considerably reduced: the risk of being involved in an accident is much greater. The remaining criteria are also affected. There is clear evidence that more crimes are committed in darkness than in daylight. Comfort, quality of life, aesthetics and the economy all diminish in darkness, for obvious reasons. However, quantitative data are scarce.

1.2   Organisation of this book

The organisation of this book is based on the fact that street lighting practice may differ greatly for different categories of application. Motorway lighting differs from lighting in a residential street, a pedestrianised shopping precinct, or a tunnel. However, they also have much in common. People using the various lighting systems have the same kind of eyes, and much of the theory is similar, and this is reflected in the book's approach.

In the preface I indicated that the emphasis in this book is less on the product and the associated economic factors than on the functional aspects of the process, amongst which safety and quality of life are foremost. In addition, environmental aspects play an increasingly important role. I therefore present lighting in this book as part of the transport system, which in turn is seen as an important aspect of society. I deal in particular with the role which lighting can play in this. This approach means that this book deals with subjects which normally do not appear in technical literature on lighting. Each chapter starts with a brief preamble on how that chapter fits into the overall approach, to give the reader an overview.

A number of general aspects relating to transport and lighting are discussed in the first part. 'Visual' and 'manual' bases for traffic are discussed in chapter 2. A number of social assumptions are brought up in chapter 3, including the right to travel, for older and disabled people, and the freedom to choose the means of participation in traffic, as well as legal aspects and factors relating to international standardisation and regulation. In addition, some visual aspects are considered, as well as the function and the purpose of lighting. Chapter 4 touches on the physical aspects of light and optics. Chapter 5 deals with photometry and the way photometric units are measured. Particular attention is paid to the newer developments in this area.

The second part of the book relates to visual observation. Chapter 6 discusses the anatomy of the visual organ and the physiological operation of the visual system. The psycho-physiology of the visual system is described in chapter 7. Some attention is paid to the methodological and statistical aspects of psycho-physical measurements, which of course form the basis for the specifications of the lighting equipment. Chapter 8 examines the most important psychological aspects of visual observation; as this deals with the way people observe in traffic, some more general psychological aspects are also considered.

The third part mostly deals with the application of the knowledge, gathered in the previous parts with regard to visual observation, to public lighting. The principles of the main recommendations and guidelines are described in chapter 9. The way in which these recommendations and guidelines are applied, is dealt with in chapter 10. The extent to which lighting fulfils its purpose is considered in the next two chapters. Chapter 11 relates to the effectiveness of public lighting, particularly the contribution public lighting can make to traffic safety and civic security. Appropriate conditions for efficient lighting are discussed in chapter 12; this relates to the conditions under which expenditure can be recouped via the reduction in accidents. The design of lighting systems is discussed in chapter 13. Only the outline of the design and the principles on which a proper lighting design should be based are examined; details are not considered.

Two subjects, which occupy a somewhat separate place in public lighting, are looked at in the fourth section. Aspects of the burden on the environment and environmental protection, of energy consumption and energy saving, but also of light nuisance and 'light pollution' are dealt with in detail in chapter 14. Finally, lighting in tunnels and underpasses is described in chapter 15. Here aspects of observation are raised, as well as a number of practical, more specifically technical lighting aspects, such as entrance lighting, quality of observation, lighting of transitional zones, the interior and the exit.

Naturally, lamps feature extensively in this book. In many cases it is useful to indicate the various types of lamps by way of an abbreviation. Until recently, codes introduced by the various manufacturers were used for types of lamps; presently an international coding system is used (IEC, 1993). The codes for the main types of lamps are shown in table 1.1.

Table 1.1 *Common abbreviations and those introduced by the IEC for types of lamps according to ILCOS (International Lamp Coding System; see IEC, 1993)*

Type of lamp	Common abbreviation (after Philips)	ILCOS abbreviation
Standard filament	GL(S)	I
Halogen filament	-	H
Fluorescent	TL	F
Compact fluorescent	CFL; SL; PL	FS; FB
High-pressure mercury-vapour	HP	Q
High-pressure fluorescent	HPL	QE
Metal-halide	HPI	M
High-pressure sodium	SON	S
Low-pressure sodium	SOX	L

A bibliography is given at the end of each chapter. This relates primarily to references made in the chapter, but at the same time gives a good overview of the technical literature relating to lighting for the past few decades. The following abbreviations are used:

Anon. Anonymous: no author given

CBS Centraal Bureau voor de Statistiek (Central Bureau for Statistics), Voorburg

CEN Centre Européenne de Normalisation, Brussels

CIE Commission International de l'Eclairage, Vienna

CROW Centrum voor Regelgeving en Onderzoek in de Grond-, Water- en Wegenbouw en de Verkeerstechniek [Centre for the Regulation and Research into Land, Water and

	Road Construction and into Transport Technology], Ede
OECD	Organization for Economic Co-operation and Development, Paris
IES (IESNA)	The Illuminating Engineering Society of North America, New York
ILE	The Institution of Lighting Engineers, Rugby
LITG	Lichttechnische Gesellschaft, Berlin
LRI	Lighting Research Institute, New York
NOVEM	Nederlandse Maatschappij voor Energie en Milieu [Dutch Association for Energy and the Environment] bv, Sittard
NSVV	Nederlandse Stichting voor Verlichtingskunde [Netherlands Institution of Illuminating Engineering], Arnhem
PAOVV	Orgaan voor postacademisch onderwijs in de vervoerswetenschappen en de verkeerskunde [Organ for post academic teaching in transport science and traffic science], Rijswijk/Delft
ROA	Richtlijnen bij het ontwerpen van autosnelwegen [Guidelines for the design of motorways], Rotterdam, Rijkswaterstaat
RONA	Richtlijnen bij het ontwerpen van niet-autosnelwegen, [Guidelines for the design of non-motorways], Rotterdam, Rijkswaterstaat
SCW	Stichting Studiecentrum Wegenbouw [Foundation Study Centre Road Construction], Arnhem (now CROW)
SVT	Stichting Studiecentrum Verkeerstechniek [Foundation Study Centre Traffic Technology], Driebergen (now CROW)
SWOV	Stichting Wetenschappelijk Onderzoek Verkeersveiligheid SWOV [Institute for Road Safety Research], Leidschendam
TRB	Transportation Research Board, Washington, DC
TRRL	Transport and Road Research Laboratory (now Transport Research Laboratory), Crowthorne

Bibliography

IEC (1993). *ILCOS; International Lamp Coding System*. Report IEC 1231:1993.

2 The lighting of public spaces

The transport of people and goods plays a vital role in our society. Lighting is required to ensure that this transport can take place 24 hours a day. Lighting is therefore a transport measure with a strong social aspect. Vehicle lighting is insufficient; public lighting is essential. The specifications for this lighting are derived from the demands on the quality of transport. Access and traffic safety are paramount, complemented by public security, quality of life and subjective security. The basis for the considerations is the functional approach, which objectively determines the requirements which lighting must satisfy.

2.1 Public lighting

The transport of people and goods plays a vital role in the structure of our society. More information on this is provided in this chapter. As many transport facilities, not only roads and vehicles, but also loading systems etc., risk becoming overloaded, it becomes increasingly important to ensure that transport can take place 24 hours a day. Transport cannot take place in darkness without artificial light.

Lighting evolved, along with the rise of mass motoring, into that which we now call 'vehicle lighting'. As far as motor vehicles are concerned, this vehicle lighting has developed to a high degree of perfection; although developments have been introduced recently (ellipsoid reflectors, high-pressure gas discharge lamps, plastic lenses), further improvements are not expected. See Schreuder & Lindeijer (1987).

Vehicle lighting can be used in two ways. The high beam may be used when there are no other road users in the vicinity. It throws the light straight ahead and it enables us to look ahead over a reasonable distance, usually sufficient for an average high speed. However, when other road users are nearby, and especially with oncoming traffic, the high beam causes an unacceptably strong dazzle, so that we must switch to dipped lights. The low beam aims a considerable amount of light straight ahead and (for right-hand traffic) especially towards the right kerb, which affords a reasonable observation at low speed, while the light which can cause dazzle is much reduced. Low beams are a not always successful compromise between 'adequate illumination' and 'little dazzle'. The high beam can only be used occasionally in present busy traffic conditions.

2.2   The quality of transport

The quality of transport, when using vehicle lighting, is to some extent lower than in daylight, even when allowing for high beam.

If we restrict ourselves to transport, and in the first instance to fast motorised traffic, as by far most traffic accidents are related to this, one may wonder how the 'additional' risk at night may be reduced. In view of the fact that transport nowadays is based completely on 'on line' and 'real time' availability of visual information, only lighting remains as a factor. Naturally, we think of public lighting in the first instance, lighting which has been used for centuries, albeit for a different reason. No real alternatives exist for the time being, although the application of retro-reflecting materials can clearly support vehicle lighting. So-called telematics, which at present features prominently in the compilation of designs for 'computerised traffic' (in any case an utopia for the distant future) does not yet seem ready for a complete replacement of visual input, and therefore of lighting.

2.3   Public lighting

The terms 'highway lighting' and 'public lighting' are often used indiscriminately. This is undesirable, for two reasons. The first, mentioned above, is that vehicle lighting is also highway lighting; and secondly, the term 'public lighting' itself is used in three different ways

- in relation to public spaces. This means spaces which are controlled by the authorities; not necessarily streets, they include some parks
- in relation to lighting paid for out of public funds; in this case it can include the illumination of buildings ('floodlighting'), but not the lighting of many public access parking spaces
- in relation to lighting of public access spaces, in particular lighting of all spaces to which road users (motorists, cyclists and/or pedestrians) have access.

Normally we mean the last when talking about 'public lighting'. As a collective term we also use 'roads'; sometimes 'roads and streets'. In addition to car parks, this includes roads or parts of roads such as mini roundabouts, bridges, tunnels and viaducts and also shopping centres, public parks etc. In this book, we will use mostly 'road lighting'. As the lighting requirements for all these areas vary considerably, it is imperative that roads be divided into categories.

2.4   The classification of roads

Roads and streets can be divided into categories. The method depends on the purpose of the classification, as well as on the way it is used. Different categories are required for determining the boundary of areas for ambulances, for waste collection, or for street maintenance, and for determining speed limits. A different system again is required for determining the specification for lighting in the various areas. It is not surprising, in view of the multitude of fashionable classification systems, that this gives rise to some discussion on the question as to which is the 'right' classification. This would not seem to be a very sensible question. However, we can look for the best approach for setting up the classification. This approach may then be used to find the classification which best suits certain objectives. On this basis I intend to follow the philosophy of the Dutch Institute for Road Safety Research (SWOV). This is set out in a number of publications by SWOV and CROW. This approach also forms the basis for the classification used by NSVV.

The category of a road is governed by three factors

- the place of the road in the road network
- traffic on the road (intensity, type, distribution)
- civil-engineering features.

The NSVV has chosen a simple classification for the general part of the new edition of the *Aanbevelingen voor Openbare Verlichting* [Recommendations for Public Lighting], based on two factors, i.e. location (roads within or outside the built-up area), and traffic destination (roads with a traffic or a destination function; NSVV, 1990). Section 9.3 gives greater detail to the classification used for lighting.

2.5   The functional approach to public lighting

Highway facilities are necessary for traffic. This applies not only for motorised traffic, but also for other ways of participation in traffic. The following question is central in the modern approach to the traffic processes and safety: 'what is required?'; or, more precisely: 'what is the function of the facilities in question?'. Based on this functional approach, we can determine objectively the requirements the facilities in question must satisfy. The functional approach is contrasted with the various methods for making decisions in the past, which are still used sometimes, such as an economic or a legal approach, where the emphasis is on the cost aspects of transport or the legal aspects of highway management. One also encounters the approach where aesthetic arguments are paramount. However, these should be subordinate to the functional requirement. This point often crops up in public lighting.

Above I indicated that the requirements for lighting can be determined objectively, based on the functional approach. The method is objective to an extent, but the criteria used are always, at least partially, based on subjective considerations. In addition to flow and safety, driving comfort, quality of life and a reduction in the fear of crime also play an important role.

Bibliography

NSVV (1990). *Aanbevelingen voor openbare verlichting* [Recommendations for public lighting]; Part 1. Arnhem, NSVV, 1990.
Schreuder, D.A. & Lindeijer, J.E. (1987). *Verlichting en markering van motorvoertuigen; Een state-of-the-art rapport.* [Lighting and marking of motor vehicles; A state of the art report R-87-7]. Leidschendam, SWOV, 1987.

3 Fundamental issues

Transport is social intercourse: it concerns the exchange of goods and particularly of information. Transport is communication. Lighting must keep up with the enormous increase in the number of journeys, so that it can continue to fulfil its function. As it forms part of society, we must pay attention to a number of different fundamental issues. Not just traffic and perceptual issues, but also social, legal and ethical aspects. It is not possible to define the function of lighting properly, without getting to grips with these points.

3.1 Transport issues

3.1.1 Transport terms

A number of transport terms are explained in this section, to aid the discussion on public lighting. These are mostly translated from the recent CROW (1995) publication. Further details on terminology can be found in CIE (1987), SCW (1986) and the so-called RONA-Richtlijnen van de Rijkswaterstaat (Anon., 1989) amongst others.

- *Travel*
  Travel is the element, the 'raw material' of transport. This relates to the transport of goods or people by means of vehicles, according to CROW (1995, page 123) 'A change in the location of persons or goods'. Journeys always have a starting point (origin) which is separated in space from the destination. The (travel) purpose of the journey is, of course, to arrive at the destination; the travel motive is the reason the journey is undertaken. Usually we assume that people are driven by the principle of profit; this means that the journeys must render some advantage (profit), which at least compensates for the trouble (cost) taken to effect the journey.
- *Traffic*
  The concept of traffic is used in two senses. The first is, according to CROW (1995, page 119): 'A collection of travelling units, either moving

or not moving, which use the road'. By travelling unit we mean: 'Vehicle, pedestrian or animal, accompanied or ridden by a person' (CROW, 1995, page 120).

- *Road (roadway)*
  By road we mean here: 'Metalled part of the terrain for the benefit of transport on land, bordered by road boundaries in the direction of the length and of the width' (CROW, 1995, page 131). The second sense matches the association among people. See e.g. ENSIE (1950) and Schreuder (1973).

- *Vehicle*
  A vehicle is an object made or used by persons in order to facilitate travel and to make it faster or more efficient. Vehicles are nearly always controlled by people; the drivers participate in traffic and belong legally to 'traffic'. Pedestrians are a separate case: here we are concerned with people who 'transport themselves', in other words, they are their own vehicle. The collective term 'participants in traffic' is often used.

- *Transport*
  By transport we mean the movement of goods or people with the aid of vehicles.

- *Road (highway)*
  The transport of 'material' units by road takes place in different ways. This may include land, water or airways. The first two are fundamentally two-dimensional; the third is three-dimensional. Only one dimension is essential: travel from the starting point to the destination, which is separated from it by space. Often the use of the second or third dimension is impossible, due to material restrictions or the law. These could be e.g. canal walls, rails or flight regulations. In the traffic to which we are accustomed, the 'road' in question would also seem to have such physical limitations in the form of kerbs etc., but those limitations are of minor importance in respect of normal traffic. The driver and the pedestrian are more or less free to select their speed in a forward direction, as well as their crosswise position on the road. In an emergency, this may turn out not to be so: a considerable number of accidents consist of collisions between vehicles and fixed objects alongside the road.

- *Information and communication*
  Transport concerns the exchange of information. See e.g. Bok (1958, page 181) for definitions in classic information theory. The exchange of information is called communication. Communication means the transmission and receipt of messages; these are usually converted into symbols. Symbols represent coded information (Bok, 1958; Schreuder, 1972).

- *Traffic safety*
  The concept of traffic safety is difficult to define. This difficulty is shared with other concepts which concern welfare or well-being. Ideally a person is happy and healthy and feels safe. In traffic also we speak of an ideal situation when people feel safe on the street. It is important to note that public lighting can contribute significantly to traffic safety, but also

to civic security and quality of life. In practice we often use a much simpler, but theoretically less pure description, i.e. that safety is the absence of danger, the latter being quantified by the number of accidents (collisions).

3.1.2   Traffic, information and communication
In the previous section traffic was defined as a collection of travelling units, or the association of people. In the course of human development, society has expanded. As the locations of production and consumption are becoming ever more removed from each other, there is an increasing flow of goods, services and, of course, people. Schreuder (1994) has pointed out the consequences of this for human welfare.

Much of the information exchange in the last few decades has taken place via electronic data transmission (EDT). The ever-increasing flow of people, goods and parcels which are transported show, however, that the idea that the explosive increase of EDT would lead to a reduction in the transport of persons and goods, is a fallacy. The role of telematics in traffic will be discussed later on.

3.1.3   Travel
This whole system of factors of influence leads to a gigantic increase in the number of journeys. Table 3.1.1 shows some data on the development of the volume of traffic in the Netherlands between 1970 and 2010.

The greatest proportion of this traffic occurs on public roads. Other means of transport (rail, water and air) contribute only to a small extent to the total volume, as far as the number of journeys, the number of articles transported and the volume, particularly in relation to the number of transported persons are concerned. Road traffic consists for the most part of private cars, as far as the number of vehicles and the kilometres per vehicle and per traveller are concerned. Lorries are, of course, significant in relation to the volume of goods transported. Table 3.1.2 shows some data relating to the manner in which people participate in traffic. It shows that the car accounts for the largest share (30.8 + 13.8 = 44.6% of journeys, and 44.7 + 27.1 = 71.8% of length of journeys). We also see that the bicycle and the pedestrian contribute significantly: together they account for 28.2 + 19.3 = 47.5% of journeys and 13.3% of the length of journeys. The relative contribution by cyclists and pedestrians will probably increase, if we include children under twelve years of age.

These figures apply to the Netherlands. In most other industrial countries the contribution of pedestrians and cyclists to the total traffic is considerably

Table 3.1.1: *Development of traffic volume in The Netherlands in billions of vehicle kilometres (according to Bovy, 1991)*

	1970	1980	1986	2010
Cars	37.5	61.4	67.9	115.0
Lorries	5.7	8.4	9.0	18.0

Table 3.1.2: *Number of journeys per hundred inhabitants in The Netherlands on average during weekdays. Average weekly length of journeys. Persons over twelve years of age, only during 1982. (Source: CBS.) Taken from SVT, 1984, table 4.4/2*

Means of travel	Number	Percentage	Length	Percentage
Car driver	94	30.8	1185	44.7
Car passenger	42	13.8	717	27.1
Public transport	16	5.3	314	11.9
Moped	5	1.6	31	1.2
Bicycle	86	28.2	269	10.1
Walking	59	19.3	85	3.2
Other	3	1.0	49	1.8
Total	305	100	2650	100

Table 3.1.3: *Accidents involving injury, depending on the nature of the light, the weather and the road situation (deaths plus hospital admissions, 1991). Data from CBS (1992)*

Weather	Road surface	Daylight	Darkness (not illuminated)	Darkness (illuminated)	Total
Dry	dry	27075 (77.4%)	1350 (58.2%)	5188 (57.0%)	6538 (57.3%)
Rain	wet	3125 (8.9%)	313 (13.5%)	1572 (17.3%)	1885 (16.5%)
All	wet	7240 (20.7%)	820 (35.3%)	3666 (40.3%)	486 (39.3%)
Total		35003 (100.0%)	2319 (100.0%)	9098 (100.0%)	11417 (100.0%)

less, while in the developing countries the bicycle often plays a dominant role in traffic.

The distribution of traffic during the day and during darkness differs, according to the manner of participation in traffic and the type of road. It is, for example, thought that more professional transport and less private transport takes place during the hours of darkness. However, total travelling is less. Motorways carry 15–20% of the total traffic between 7 pm and 7 am, whereas traffic in residential streets only accounts for 2 to 3% during these hours.

In darkness the accident rate per vehicle-kilometre is considerably greater than during the day; accidents at night are also usually considerably more serious than those taking place during the day. Darkness, rain and wet roads form an additional risk factor. See table 3.1.3.

3.2   Changes: prognoses

3.2.1   Prognoses relating to traffic

Society – and with it, most aspects of human existence – is always changing. Prognoses are required to plan measures. Below are a number of forecasts which have been taken from sources generally considered to be reliable. The data are partly taken from Bovy (1991) and are based on the *Structuurschema voor Verkeer en Vervoer* [Structural Plan for Traffic and Transport] (SVV-II, see

Table 3.2.1: *Road and traffic characteristics for the national road network in The Netherlands in 1986 and 2010; scenario 'at policies unchanged' (based on Janssen, 1988; the data are rounded)*

Type of road	Length (km × 10³)			Traffic motor vehicles per × km (×10⁹)		
	1986	2010	%	1986	2010	%
Motorways	1.9	2.7	138	27.4	52.3	191
Non-motorways	52.5	55.9	106	28.8	50.7	176
Outside built-up areas	54.5	58.6	108	56.2	103	183
Within built-up areas	45	46.8	103	26.6	40.3	152
Total	99.5	105.4	106	82.7	143.1	173

Anon., 1990) among others. These prognoses are not expected to be still significant in 1997; they are only quoted because certain trends can be expected to remain relevant. They are valuable as an illustration, rather than as a basis for policy.

Firstly the demographic changes. Taking the Netherlands as an example, between 1986 and 2010, the number of households is expected to increase significantly (+18%) and the number of cars to grow explosively (+74%), for a population which is only expected to increase a little (+4%). The economy is expected to improve: the number of workers is forecast to increase by 30% and household income by 80%. It is not surprising that transport is expected to increase by 57%, of which nearly 85% will occur by road, for the inland goods transport. An even larger increase is expected for international traffic; there growth is greatest, with a doubling in transport by road.

3.2.2   Prognoses relating to the road network and traffic performance

Prognoses have also been made in relation to the road network and traffic performance. The data are taken from Janssen (1988). These prognoses differ to some extent from those by Bovy (1991), as they were compiled at a different time. The 1986 data and the prognoses for 2010 are shown in table 3.2.1.

Table 3.2.1 shows that only a minimal expansion of the road network is foreseen (+6%). The rate of growth for motorways may be somewhat greater, but they only represent a few percentage points of the total road network. However, traffic is forecast to grow considerably (+73%). The prognoses for the growth of traffic equals that for the fleet of cars (see section 3.2.1). This is to be expected, as in the end everything is based on the SVV. The occupation of the road network is predicted to become much heavier; it is expected that the requirements for highway facilities, including lighting, will also grow considerably. We can already see a trend for roads outside the built-up areas to be increasingly provided with lighting. I will deal with the problems which this entails for nature reserves in section 14.5.

3.2.3   Prognoses relating to traffic safety; sustainably safe traffic

Koornstra et al. (eds.) (1992) have supplied prognoses which are based on the introduction of sustainably safe traffic. Current traffic conduct is presently not

Table 3.2.2: *Statistics for The Netherlands by road function for 1986 and prognosis for 2010, variation I (according to Koornstra et al., (eds.), chapter 5, tables 2 and 4, 1992)*

Function	Road length: km	Intensity: days	Injury accidents	Injury: 10^6 vehicle km	Fatal accidents	Deaths: 10^8 vehicle km
1986						
Flow	4308	21073	2633	0.08	237	0.71
Distribution	18308	4824	29005	0.90	756	2.35
Residential	76903	619	11943	0.69	536	3.09
Total	99519		43581	0.53	1529	1.95
2010 variation 1						
Flow	7827	26264	6526	0.09	562	0.75
Distribution	13906	5431	18683	0.68	619	2.25
Residential	78080	310	6107	0.69	262	2.96
Total	99813		31316	0.28	1444	1.30

adequate for today's traffic conditions. The principle of sustainable safety is based on an improvement in behaviour by means of highway facilities, i.e. the design of infrastructure as well as vehicles in such a way that safe behaviour follows naturally.

Variation I consists of traffic performance increased by 35%. This additional traffic mostly ends up on motorways. The risk per type of road remains the same. Even for these moderate objectives, where only part of the aims of 'sustainable safety' are included, a considerable improvement in traffic safety can be achieved: a reduction of 24% in the number of victims and of 6% in the number of traffic fatalities; compare this with an increase in traffic performance of 35%. An additional reduction is possible with more advanced measures.

Most striking is that neither the installation nor the improvement of public lighting as a measure for the promotion of sustainable safety are included.

3.3   Social issues

3.3.1   The right to travel; freedom of choice for transport

Participation in traffic is not an objective in itself; participation in traffic is an essential prerequisite for participation in most social and economic aspects of society. The right to participate in these social and economic aspects is part of the Basic Human Rights, as laid down by the United Nations.

Modern society, therefore, no longer accepts discrimination in relation to the right to travel. Children, older and handicapped people must be able to participate in traffic. However, restrictions in the choice of transport, based on practical considerations, are commonly accepted. Restrictions in the choice of mode of transport for 'normal' people are normally tolerated in The Netherlands. Complete freedom in a small and full country is not acceptable. But in practice there are no limitations for the pedestrian and the cyclist. Car drivers too usually do not have to do more than pass a driving test and pay taxes. Only in extreme cases are people's licences taken away. We should therefore take into account the fact that people with limited eyesight are allowed to and do take part in traffic. We will return to the effects of this statement in section 7.5.

3.3.2   Ethical considerations

Considerations relating to traffic safety and also to many aspects of civic security and the prevention of crime are often based on a statistical point of view. Priorities are set on the basis of the number of accidents or the number of victims which may be 'saved' by a particular traffic safety measure. Traffic safety policy in The Netherlands has been based on a quantified objective for a number of years. This is usually called a task-setting policy. Koornstra et al., (eds) (1992) discusses this issue in detail. The first step has been taken with the National Safety Plan in 1985 (Anon., 1985) with the objective of a reduction of 25% in the number of victims. See Wegman (1987).

It would seem that the objectives have not been attained in all aspects (Mulder, 1994). Nevertheless, the associated Structural Plan for Traffic and Transport (Anon., 1990) goes further still. We quote Koornstra et al., (eds.) (1992, page 23): 'by 2010 we must mourn 50% fewer traffic fatalities and 40% less seriously injured traffic victims than in 1986'.

Such a quantified objective differs considerably from an ethical point of view from the much more quantified objectives set in the past. See, for example, SWOV (1965). A society which calls itself civilised should not ignore nearly 2000 deaths and many tens of thousands of injured, many of whom are permanently disabled, annually. This apart from the fact that the risk of an accident for each individual inhabitant is relatively small. It would not be appropriate to say: 'As the individual risk is so infinitely small, we won't do anything about it'.

3.4   Legal issues

3.4.1   The management of lighting installations

By 'management' we mean the execution of policy goals, within the means available. Management includes amongst others the translation of the policy aims into technical and economic requirements; preparation of the design; planning and compiling estimations of cost; supervising the execution and the planning, preparation and execution (possibly contracted-out) of maintenance.

This comprises much more than previously, when management consisted of the replacement of lamps, the cleaning of the luminaires and the carrying out of incidental repairs. There are a number of reasons for this expansion of the task of the manager

- A social aspect
  There has been a trend among western European countries to reduce the power of central government. Two routes were typically taken: decentralisation and privatisation. Decentralisation assigned many of

the responsibilities to lower authorities, although the required financial scope and the accompanying authority often remained limited. Privatisation has led to the hiving off of many government tasks. These were often taken over by private bodies, but market forces frequently played a considerable role, so that the level of the services often was reduced. In some cases privatisation caused the services in question to be discontinued. Privatisation took place in many areas which previously were considered to be government tasks, including public lighting. This led to a broadening of the management task, particularly in the area of energy provision, design and maintenance.

- *An economic aspect*
  Decentralisation and privatisation resulted in economic repercussions on the management of lighting installations – for good as well as bad. Experience has shown that a 'modern' management, considering the installation as integral, can lead to considerable cost savings and also to better quality.
- *An aspect relating to liability*
  A new Civil Code became effective in 1990 in The Netherlands, describing responsibilities and liabilities in a manner which is important for the management of public lighting. See below for further details.

3.4.2   Liability: the 'new Civil Code'

This section describes the situation for The Netherlands, but the implications are similar for most countries, particularly those within the European Union.

In the past, questions of responsibility and liability relating to public lighting were quite simple. Although the former Civil Code also laid down that every one is responsible for the persons and matters they manage, a road user had little chance to recover any damages from the authorities (the managing institution). The infamous 'hatstand clause', clause 25 in the Wegen-verkeerswet [Road Traffic Law] always applied.

Much has changed with the introduction of the new Civil Code. Renckens (1993) gives an overview of the consequences. See also Van der Lugt & Albers (1995). The basis of the new Civil Code is that everyone is responsible for their own damages, whether insured or not. Exceptions are contractual and civic liability; that is to say, liability based on a contract or in law. The latter case relates to an unlawful deed. Unlawful is more than just against the law; an unlawful deed may also mean that it is against the rights of another person, or not in accordance with 'appropriate care in social interaction'.

Persons suffering damage are not obliged to bear the cost themselves in the case of an unlawful deed. The damage may be claimed from the person doing the unlawful deed. The liability remains, even when the actual work is contracted out or conferred to an agent. The 'leasing' of lighting does not discharge the liability of the manager, nor the contracting out of design, installation or maintenance.

Such an unlawful deed is termed 'culpable liability'. 'Culpable' here means that blame is attached to the deed or that there is a question of accountability. We could call the accountable unlawful deed an 'error'. A causal connection must of course exist between the error and the damage; the damage must reasonably be attributable to the error. As we are dealing here with culpable liability, the injured party − in this case the road user − must be able to prove the unlawfulness, the culpability and the causal connection.

The main change in the introduction of the new Civil Code is in the way these concepts are handled. Among others, Book 6 of the Civil Code was introduced on 1st January 1992. Liability is further extended in section 6:174. The first sub-section creates the risk liability for dangerous 'erections'. Sub-section 2 indicates that this includes the public highway and that the liability rests with the highway managers, who must ensure that the roads are 'in good condition'. According to sub-section 5, the highway includes the body of the road as well as the fittings and road furniture; public lighting is also included.

Instead of culpable liability, risk liability applies. For this, it is sufficient to prove the relation between the condition of the highway or of the road furniture and the danger. Of course the causal relation between the condition and the damage must still be demonstrable; the damage must be reasonably attributable to the condition.

3.4.3   European Directives

In 1992 the single market in Europe became reality. European Directives have been laid down for many product groups. One of the results is that the products offered on the European market must carry the CE mark, in accordance with these directives. The extent of the requirements for carrying the mark depends on the danger which the product in question carries. The requirements with regard to safety, health, environment and consumer protection at least should be met. The safety and health of the user are often paramount. At present the 'user' of the lighting also includes the road user.

The ultimate goal of the EU for all these activities is to exclude trade restrictions and to improve safety in the member states. This is achieved by setting out European Directives and making them binding by the European Commission. This means that in the case of a conflict between the national law and the supranational European legislation, European regulations prevail. But the risk of such a conflict is small, as the member states are compelled to adapt their national laws and regulations to the European Directives.

At present it is expected that the European Directives will say that lighting installations, when new, must demonstrably meet the harmonised European standards, e.g. by type tests. In addition, this should apply at any moment during the whole of the service life.

This means three things for public lighting

- all lighting installations must be designed and produced in accordance with the norms
- all installations must be maintained in such a way that they continue to meet them
- it is important for the regulation of the liability in case of any accidents

or crimes that it can be demonstrated clearly that maintenance has been carried out 'properly'.

Bibliography

Anon. (1985). *Nationaal plan voor de Verkeersveiligheid II* [National plan for Traffic Safety II]. Tweede Kamer, session year 1985–1986, 18 195, nrs 18–19. October 1985.

Anon. (1989). *Richtlijnen voor het ontwerpen van niet-autosnelwegen buiten de bebouwde kom; Voorlopige richtlijnen* [Guidelines for the design of non-motorways outside the built-up areas; Preliminary guidelines]; Hoofdstuk IV Alignement. Den Haag, Rijkswaterstaat, 1989.

Anon. (1990). *Tweede Structuurschema Verkeer en Vervoer; Deel D: Regeringsbeslissing* [Second Structural Plan Traffic and Transport. Part D: Government Decision]. Ministerie van Verkeer en Waterstaat. Den Haag, SDU, 1990.

Bok, S.T. (1958). *Cybernetica (Stuurkunde)*. Het Spectrum, Utrecht, 1958.

Bovy, P.H.L.(1991).'Mobiliteit in cijfers, modellen en scenario's [Mobility in figures, models and scenarios']. In: PAOVV (1991).

CBS. *Statistiek van de verkeersongevallen op de openbare weg* [Statistics on traffic accidents on the public highway]. Annual publication. Den Haag, SDU.

CIE (1987). *International Lighting Vocabulary*. 4th Edition. Publication No. 17-4. Paris, CIE, 1987.

CROW (1995). *Van A-nummer tot Zweepmast*. Publication 91. Ede, CROW, 1995.

ENSIE (1950). *Eerste Nederlandse Systematisch Ingerichte Encyclopaedie Deel VII* [First Dutch Systematically arranged Encyclopaedia Part VII]. Amsterdam, ENSIE, 1950.

Janssen, S.T.M.C. (1988). *De verkeersveiligheid van wegtypen in 1986 en 2010* [Traffic safety related to types of roads in 1986 and 2010]. R-88-3. Leidschendam, SWOV, 1988.

Koornstra, M.J. et al. (eds.) (1992). *Naar een duurzaam veilig wegverkeer* [Towards sustainable safe road transport]. Leidschendam, SWOV, 1992.

Mulder, J.A.G. (1994). *Het stimuleringsplan Actie −25% geëvalueerd; Een totaaloverzicht van de resultaten van de verschillende deelonderzoeken* [The priming plan Actie −25% evaluated; a comprehensive overview of the results of the various research subjects]. R-94-28. Leidschendam, SWOV, 1994.

NSVV (1995). *De NSVV op weg naar 2000; Congresdag 19 mei 1995* [The NSVV on the way to 2000; One-day conference 19 May 1995]. Arnhem, NSVV, 1995.

PAOVV (1991). *Verkeer en milieu; Van woorden (NEMP + SVV) naar daden (de uitvoering)* [Traffic and environment; From words (NEPM + SVV) to deeds (the execution)]. Course 16–18 April 1991. Delft, PAOVV, 1991.

Renckens, M.L.M.(1993). *'Wettelijke aansprakelijkheid jegens de weggebruiker'* [Civil liability towards the road user]. In: Syllabus Van knelpunt tot lichtpunt in de openbare verlichting [From obstacle to light in public lighting] Conference day NSVV, ANWB and CROW, 13 May 1993, Arnhem, 1993.

Schreuder, D.A. (1972). *The coding and transmission of information by means of road lighting*. In: SWOV (1972).

Schreuder, D.A. (1973). *De motivatie tot voertuiggebruik* [The motivation to use vehicles]. Haarlem, Internationale Faculteit, 1973.

Schreuder, D.A. (1994). *Sick cities and legend analysis as therapy*. International Workshop in Kumamoto on Urban Design and Analysis of Legends, July 26–28, 1994. Leidschendam, Duco Schreuder Consultancies, 1994.

SVT (1984). *Aanbevelingen voor stedelijke verkeersvoorzieningen* [Recommendations for urban traffic facilities] ASVV 1984/85. Driebergen, Studiecentrum Verkeerstechniek, 1984.

SWOV (1965) *Bijdragen voor de Nota Verkeersveiligheid* [Contributions to the Traffic Safety White Paper]. Den Haag, SWOV, 1965.

SWOV (1972). *Psychological Aspects of Driver Behaviour.* Symposium Noordwijkerhout, 2–6 August 1971. Voorburg, SWOV, 1972.

Van der Lugt, D.B. & Albers, H. (1995). *The art of lighting.* Brochure handed out during the conference: De NSvV op weg naar 2000 [The NSvV on its way to 2000](see NSVV, 1995)

Wegman, F.C.M. (1987). *Stimuleringsplan 'ACTIE-25%'; Een voorstel voor een evaluatie-onderzoek* [Stimulation plan 'ACTIE-25%'; A proposal for an evaluation study]. R-87-29. Leidschendam, SWOV, 1987.

4   Physical aspects

*Participation in traffic requires a considerable input of visual infor-
mation. The importance of this visual information relates in particular to the driving task; the 'input' relates to the decision-making
processes required to carry out the participation in traffic adequately. In order to understand the function of lighting properly and
to optimise the technology, a detailed understanding of the visual system is required. The visual system is therefore described in detail;
first with regard to the role played by visual observation, followed by
the anatomical, physiological, psycho-physical and psychological aspects of the human visual system.*

*Visual observation, in the final analysis, is the interpretation of mes-
sages which are transmitted via light. The way in which detection and
the interpretation of visual information takes place is closely related
to the physical aspects of light. But the generation of light is also closely
bound up with these physical aspects. Some understanding of the physical aspects of light is required for the practical appliance of lighting
science. In addition to the phenomena related to the wave and particle
properties of light, and the combined properties, this chapter discusses
the optical image. In practice, one often deals with cases which cannot
be described as ideal optics; 'turbid' media are also of interest. This
chapter deals with the physical aspects of light.*

4.1   The significance of the visual system

An analysis of the participation in traffic (the analysis of the traffic task,
discussed a little in chapter 3, and which will be discussed in detail later on)
results in three important points

- participation in traffic, as a driver, but also as a cyclist or pedestrian, is in
  the final analysis a decision-making task

- decisions are, for a large part and often for the most important part, taken on the basis of information gathered in situ and in real time from the external world
- this information is largely visual.

The participation in traffic can be considered from a number of different points of view. In all cases decision-making aspects are involved, but in many matters relating to traffic safety the emphasis is on the results of this decision-making process, i.e. on output. We are not so much concerned with the process, as with the product. In matters relating to traffic education and training, the emphasis is on the decision-making process itself; particular attention is paid to the skills which the participant in traffic must have, and the way these skills may be acquired. Considerations relating to the mode of transport involve adaptation of the person to the machine, or conversely, the adaptation of the machine to the human being, i.e. the ergonomics. This is called visual ergonomics, when relating to the realisation of visual aids.

This book deals with public lighting. Public lighting is a measure in support of visual information. The driving task, therefore, is considered from the point of view of visual input to the decision-making process. The visual system plays a decisive role in all considerations with regard to public lighting. The next chapter contains a description of the visual system from an anatomical and a physiological point of view; this is followed by an explanation of the function of the visual organ, the visual system. This involves particular psycho-physical and psychological aspects. As already mentioned, the driving task aspects will be considered as part of the visual input system. First though, some preliminary remarks about light will be made in this chapter.

4.2 Light

4.2.1   Duality; light as a wave phenomenon
Light can be described in two, mutually exclusive, ways

- as an electromagnetic wave phenomenon
- as a stream of fast-moving energy packets (photons); these photons may be considered to be particles, but we can also regard them as having a sort of 'wave character'.

This discussion will be restricted to the main points, as far as they relate to the science of lighting. For a more detailed discussion I refer to standard works relating to optics, e.g. Van Heel (1950) and Longhurst (1964). An extensive, mathematically well-founded treatment can be found in the classic work of Feynman et al. (1977).

Firstly let us look at light as an electromagnetic phenomenon. This is a partial description

- firstly, there is 'nothing' which can vibrate (a 'field' is 'nothing')
- secondly, there are many phenomena, which can only be described in terms of a stream of fast-moving particles (projectiles, particles of light, the above-mentioned photons). However, this particle description (the

'corpuscular model') entails the problem that it cannot explain the clearly wave-like properties, which follow from the many interference phenomena, without artificial tricks.

It is usually sufficient to consider light as an electromagnetic wave, as far as the science of lighting and photometry (see chapter 5) are concerned; light forms part of the electromagnetic spectrum. As the propagation speed of all electromagnetic waves, irrespective of the wavelength, is the same, they can be described in terms of wavelength and of frequency; these two terms are interchangeable. In a vacuum, the propagation speed is approximately 300,000 km per second, the 'speed of light'. Electromagnetic phenomena can be quantified by their wavelength or by their frequency. The equation is

$$f = \frac{\lambda}{c} \qquad\qquad [4.2.1]$$

in which

f	is the frequency
λ	the wavelength
c	the speed of propagation (in electromagnetic radiation always equal to approximately 300,000 km/s). See also figure 4.2.1.

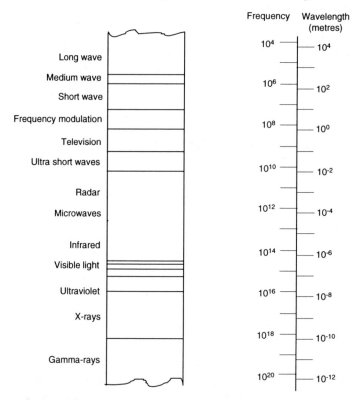

Figure 4.2.1: *The electromagnetic spectrum*

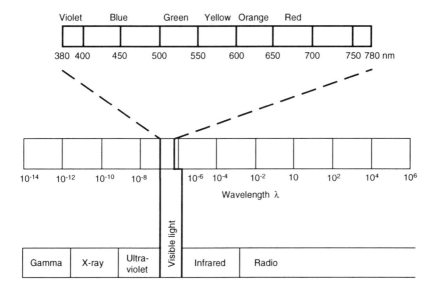

Figure 4.2.2: *Visible light as part of the electromagmetic spectrum*

The visible light only occupies a small part of this electromagnetic spectrum: the wavelengths from approximately 400 to a little under 800 nanometres, i.e. 10^{-9} metres. See figure 4.2.2.

To use a musical analogy, this corresponds to a little less than an octave. The nanometre, abbreviated to nm, is the internationally established ISO unit. The formerly often used Ångström (10^{-10} metres) has been largely dropped.

Each wavelength has a single colour. Thus light with a wavelength of 600–700 nm is red; 550 nm light is yellow, 500 nm light is green and 400–450 nm light is blue. These are the 'colours of the rainbow'. The rainbow *is* light dissected into successive wavebands. I will return to the topic of colours and seeing colours in section 7.4.

Longer waves, or lower frequencies, constitute infrared, or heat, radiation (often incorrectly called 'infrared light'), TV, radar and radio waves. Shorter waves, or higher frequencies, constitute ultraviolet radiation ('light'), X-rays, gamma rays, cosmic rays, etc.

The corpuscular or photon model, is used to describe a number of other phenomena, such as the operation of photoreceptors, gas discharge and fluorescence. This is based on the fact that light can be described as a stream of fast moving photons. Photons are characterised by their energy. This energy cannot be subdivided infinitely; the energy is quantified. This minimum energy is called a light quantum. Quantum mechanics is a relatively new branch on the tree of physics. See the work by Feynman et al. (1977) mentioned above, for a detailed description. A simple description is given in a number of popular science books (e.g. Gribbin, 1984). The well-known gamma DTV series deals with the matter briefly, but thoroughly (Breuer, 1994). See also the extensive and well-documented course published by Philips (1989).

The frequency of visible light is very high; and although the propagation velocity of light is also very high, the wavelengths are so small that they are not significant for the practice of lighting engineering. Usually the phenomenological description, which is the basis for geometric optics, suffices.

Waves are characterised by their direction of vibration and their direction of propagation. These two may coincide, in which case we call it longitudinal oscillation – a well-known example is sound. Waves can also be at right angles to the direction of propagation, in which case they are called transverse vibrations. Light waves are of the latter, transverse type. In principle we can define infinitely many directions of oscillation which are all perpendicular to the direction of propagation. Usually light vibrates simultaneously in all these directions. But it can also occur that light only vibrates in a single plane. The light is then said to be 'polarised' in that plane. This makes no difference to visual perception, but it is significant in the case of refraction, as discussed in section 4.5.3.

4.2.2   Phenomenological optics; thermal radiators

The frequencies we are dealing with are very high, and the corresponding wavelengths are very small. Furthermore, the dimension of atoms and their components are so small that matter and energy could, for many theoretical and practical investigations, be considered as a continuum. The phenomenological description given above suffices. We may still use the overview produced by Helbig (1972) for a short description of phenomenological optics. A discussion of the main aspects important for the science of lighting can be found in the classic work by Moon (1961). A clear summary can be found in Breuer (1994).

The physical Law of the conservation of energy leads us to conclude that the light emitted equals the light absorbed, for a certain temperature and for a certain wavelength of the light, per unit of surface and of spatial angle, in a state of equilibrium with the surroundings. A body which absorbs nothing does not emit anything either. It follows that a body which absorbs all energy which falls on it, has the highest possible emission The emission only depends on the temperature, and not on the substance, the model, or the dimensions of the body. Such a body is therefore used as the radiation standard. It is called a black emitter or 'black body radiator'.

The emission of radiation by a black body is not equal for all wavelengths. A wavelength can be found for each temperature for which the relative radiation is at a maximum. The relative radiation gradually diminishes for longer as well as shorter wavelengths to approach zero asymptotically. This maximum shifts to shorter wavelengths as the temperature increases. According to Wien's Law, the product of wavelength and absolute temperature is constant; there is therefore a hyperbolic relationship between both. See Breuer (1994, page 181):

$$\lambda_{max} = \frac{b}{T}$$

[4.2.2]

where

λ_{max} is the wavelength at which emission is at maximum intensity
b a constant
T temperature (in Kelvin)

The wavelength grows to extremely high values at decreasing temperatures; the wavelength continues to shorten with increasing temperatures. Figure 4.2.3 shows a number of examples.

'Ideal' black bodies do not exist. However, there are many materials in everyday life which are similar to them. Most formulae derived for black bodies may be used for such substances without large errors; coal, cast iron, stone and tungsten, for example. However, the reflection or absorption of such materials should be borne in mind. In general, the dependency on the temperature for most substances is, relatively speaking, similar to that of a black body, but the absolute power emitted is proportional to the absorption; or, more accurately, to the total spectral radiance factor. And that can make

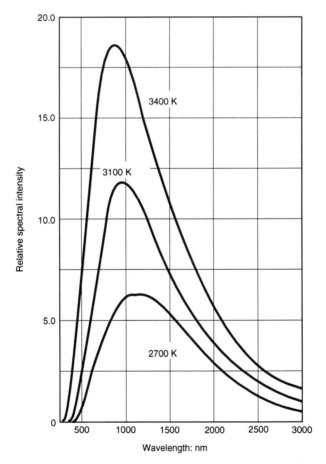

Figure 4.2.3: *Maximum itensity moves to shorter wavelengths at increasing temperatures*

quite a difference in practice. This is shown by Stephan Bolzmann's Law, which reads (in the form given by Moon, 1961, page 125):

$$J = e_t \times 5.709 \times 10^{-12} \times T^4 \qquad\qquad [4.2.3]$$

in which

J is the emitted power (in Joules)
e_t the total spectral radiance factor (without dimensions)
T the absolute temperature (in Kelvin)

e_t is a material constant. This factor is by definition equal to the unit for the black body. Astronomers often use the effective temperature (T_{eff}), instead of the total spectral radiance factor. The effective temperature is the temperature of a black body which has a similar luminance to the respective light source or star. T_{eff} is, of course, not without dimensions (Weigert & Wendtker, 1989, page 79). For most metals the value of e_t lies around 0.5. This means that the total emitted power of a practical material can never amount to much more than half of the theoretical value of the black body. An example is given in figure 4.2.4.

This figure is drawn to scale; however, the scale is not given. Finally, it should be noted that the radiance factor depends on the wavelength; this factor decreases for most metals as the wavelength increases, so that the specific light beam sometimes differs less from the value of the black body than the total emitted power.

Wien's Displacement Law has a number of consequences which are important for practice. The first is important for so-called thermal radiators. If one uses a light source similar to a black body, then the light becomes shorter-waved as the temperature increases. A body which is not very hot, emits mainly infrared radiation and only a little visible light, which is mainly red. Coal in a barbecue glows red. If the temperature is increased, then the maximum intensity of the radiation moves in the direction of the visible light.

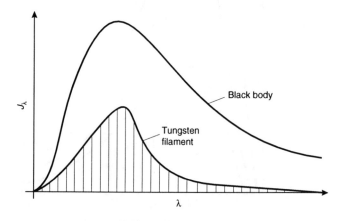

Figure 4.2.4: *The emitted power of tungsten compared to that of the black body for T = 3038K; according to Moon, 1961, fig. 5.10*

Ever more energy is emitted in the visible area, and also at shorter wavelengths, to an increasing extent. The light becomes orange and finally yellow. At even higher temperatures, solids melt. Tungsten is the solid with the highest known melting point, 3653 K. Carbon, like some ceramic materials, is heat-resistant at extremely high temperatures. This point will be returned to in the discussion of the construction and operation of filament lamps (section 13.3.1). Stars, however, can attain a much higher temperature without losing their shape; the sun emits 'white' light because the maximum intensity of the radiation lies approximately in the centre of the visible part of the spectrum. This corresponds to approximately 500 nm at an effective temperature of approximately 6000 K (Weigert & Wendtker, 1989, page 104). Some stars are considerably hotter; Sirius, for example, is blue-white. This corresponds with a surface temperature of approximately 11,000 K (Thomas, 1944, page 452). The temperature may reach 50,000 K in class O5 stars; the colour is blue (Weigert & Wendtker, 1989, page 89). There the maximum intensity of the emission has passed the centre range of the visible spectrum. A second consequence of Wien's Law affects a different subject: the hothouse effect mentioned in section 14.3.

When we look closer at the graphs in figure 4.2.3, we can see that, as well as a shift to a shorter wavelength by the maximum intensity of the relative energy emission, the surface 'under' the curve increases, in accordance with Stephan Bolzmann's Law. The emitted power increases by T^4, in accordance with equation 4.2.3.

The practical implication of this is clear. When using a thermal radiator as a light source its temperature must be increased as much as possible. The method of making the incandescent body glow is irrelevant. The most common method is to use an electrical current, but gas, petrol or oil may all be used. The incandescent bodies cannot reach a high temperature due to the low flame temperature, so the yield of such light sources is much lower. Even lower is the yield of light sources where coal particles accidentally present in the flame, must function as incandescent bodies, as is the case with oil lamps or candles. When ceramic elements are used, with carbide lamps or carbon bodies, 'mantels' with gas lights, the yield can become reasonably high. Even the electrical arc light, often used in the past, is a thermal radiator. The arc discharge, which is created between the two carbon points when the electrical current is sufficiently high, loosens carbon particles from the carbon points, which in turn start to glow as a result of the high temperature of the arc discharge. These lamps were often used in public lighting during the second half of the last century, because of their high light yield. The brightness of the light source rendered them especially fit for projection purposes, particularly film projection. These arc lamps have been replaced by filament lamps and later by gas discharge lamps, for practical reasons.

The maximum feasible yield of thermal radiators as light sources is limited, for three reasons

- The substances used on 'earth' as incandescent bodies do not allow for incandescent temperatures of more than approximately 2600 to 2850 K (see Philips, 1989, part 8, sec. 4.2). As figure 4.3.3 shows, the maximum intensity of the relative emission at this temperature is still well into the infrared, so that the source does not make an efficient 'light source'. However, it does make an efficient 'heat source'.

- The relatively low incandescent temperature also results in a restricted total emitted power.
- The radiation spectrum of thermal radiators is quite broad. Even if most of the relative radiation is within the spectrum to which the eye is most sensitive, as is the case with the sun, a considerable proportion of the radiation is still emitted at wavelengths to which the eye is not sensitive.

These three reasons led to the development of light sources turning in another direction over the past 50 years towards gas discharge lamps. The process of gas discharge light radiation is completely different. These lamps are not thermal radiators and cannot be described in terms of phenomenological optics. In order to explain their operation, a quantum mechanical description is required.

4.3   Quantum optics: gas discharges

Gas discharge is rather a complicated physical phenomenon, so this section will give just a brief description, in large part based on the classic book by Oranje (1942). Details can be found in similar books edited by Elenbaas (Elenbaas, 1959, 1965). The more recent books by De Groot & Van Vliet (1986) and Meyer & Nienhuis (1988) are of interest for the large amount of detail covering the technology, and especially on the use of modern gas discharge lamps.

In construction, all gas discharge lamps are similar in principle. The lamps consist of a glass tube filled with the gas in question. Only two gases are used in public lighting: mercury and sodium. As mercury is a fluid at room temperature and sodium a solid, we may also speak in terms of the vapour phase to characterise the gas in gas discharge lamps.

Apart from the vapour, the tube contains two electrodes: a negative cathode and a positive anode. The cathode gives off negative electrons, which move towards the positive anode under the influence of the difference in voltage between the cathode and the anode. The difference in voltage causes the velocity of the electrons to increase; the energy of the electrons is derived from the voltage supply of the cathode and the anode, i.e. from the discharge.

On the way, they collide with the vapour molecules. As mercury, as well as sodium vapour, are single atom gases, the terms atom and molecule are interchangeable. Three different effects may occur during such collisions, depending on the energy the electrons derived from the discharge (see also Oranje, 1942, paragraph 3).

1. An elastic collision occurs; the electron and the vapour atom remain unchanged; only their velocity and direction, their 'impulse', may change. These elastic collisions do not contribute to the generation of

light. As a part of the displacement energy is changed into heat, elastic collisions are important for the heat exchange system of the discharge.

2. There is such a large transfer of energy between the electron and the vapour atom, that one of the electrons of the atom enters a 'higher' trajectory round the nucleus. This is called the excited state. Here the atom absorbs a particular amount (a quantum) of energy. After a short time – approximately 10^{-7} seconds – the electron returns to its original condition, the stable state. The quantum of energy which was absorbed is then emitted. The radiation has a particular frequency, which is proportional to the energy of the quantum in question, and the following equation applies

$$E = h \times f \hspace{4cm} [4.3.1]$$

in which
   E is the energy of the quantum
   h the so-called Planck's Constant
   f the frequency, which, as we know, relates to the wavelength

3. Here we find an even greater transfer of energy between the electron and the vapour atom. As a result, one or more electrons of the vapour atom are torn loose. This is called ionisation because the remaining incomplete atom is called an ion. A particular amount of energy is required for ionisation, as is the case for the 'excitation' of an atom. The 'remains' carry an electrical charge, and move therefore just like the original electrons from the cathode to the anode (the electrons) or, conversely, from the anode to the cathode (the ions). On the way, further collisions may take place, but often ions combine with a free electron after a short time. The atom is then complete again. Exactly the same amount of energy is released on recombination as was required for the ionisation.

In all these cases (a part of) the displacement energy of the electrons is converted into energy quanta with a particular frequency, which represents a particular wavelength. A number of specific energy transfers are characteristic for each type of atom; these transfers correspond to absorption lines and emission lines in the spectrum of the atom in question. As the size of each quantum always remains the same during the absorption and the release of the energy, the corresponding spectral lines are very sharp at a low vapour pressures. The spectrum is a kind of fingerprint of the substance used. Spectral analysis, used often in physics research, makes use of these fingerprints.

In principle, we should be able to construct a gas discharge lamp from any material, i.e. from any type of atom. In practice, however, only the above-mentioned mercury and sodium prove to be suitable for use in light sources. This depends, in the first instance, on the wavelengths characteristic of the energy transfers during excitation and ionisation. In addition, a number of practical points are involved relating to the practicality of manufacture, use, service life and cost.

Figure 4.3.1 shows how, for mercury atoms, each energy transfer corresponds, as already mentioned, to a spectral line. The associated wavelengths are indicated in the then current Ångström units. These wavelengths are dispersed over the whole of the visible range, as well as over the infrared and the ultraviolet. Which spectral lines are most pronounced, depends in particular on the temperature and the vapour pressure. In particular the lines in the ultraviolet are significant for low-pressure mercury lamps (the 'TL'-lamps; see section 13.3.1). In order to produce a source of visible light it is necessary to influence the wavelength by means of fluorescent substances. High-pressure mercury lamps also have spectral lines in the visible range, so these can be used directly as a light source. The provision of fluorescent substances in high-pressure mercury lamps is particularly useful for affecting the colours produced.

Figure 4.3.2 shows the energy transfers characteristic of the sodium atom. It shows many spectral lines distributed over a large part of the spectrum. However, in contrast with the mercury atom's energy transfers, the sodium atom lines are directly 'usable'. The greatest part of the energy is radiated in two closely neighbouring lines, especially at low vapour pressures. The wavelengths are 589.0 nm and 589.6 nm (see e.g. Meyer & Nienhuis, 1988, plate 8). This wavelength is situated close to the wavelength of 555 nm, where photopic eye sensitivity is at a maximum (see section 6.2). This is why the

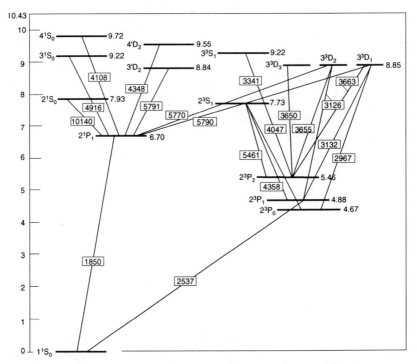

Figure 4.3.1: The energy transfers characteristic of the outer electron of the mercury atom; according to Elenbaas ed., 1965, fig. 1.10

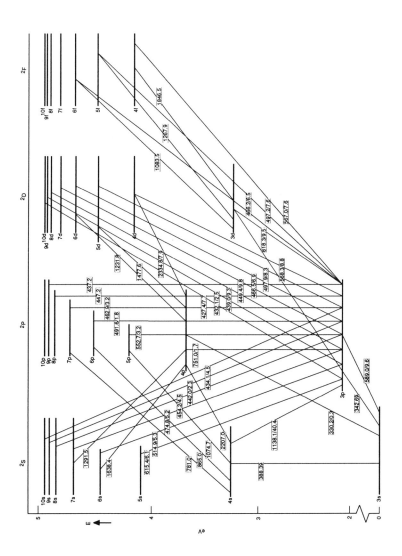

Figure 4.3.2: *The energy transfers of the sodium atom; according to De Groot & Van Vliet, 1985, fig. 3.6*

luminous efficacy of low-pressure sodium lamps is so high. The two lines are situated so close together, that they correspond to one 'colour' only, i.e. yellow. Low-pressure sodium lamps are therefore also called monochromatic.

When, as is common in public lighting, the lamps are operated with an alternating current, the cathode and anode change functions 50 times per second. This gives the light a frequency of 100 Herz. A number of points should be mentioned at this time relating to the practical operation of gas discharge lamps.

Firstly, the narrow spectral lines mentioned above become wider when the vapour pressure increases. This applies to all gas discharges. The reason for this is that the elastic and, in particular, the partial elastic collisions between electrons and atoms play an increasingly important role. As a result, high-pressure sodium lamps have a more or less continuous spectrum, instead of the virtually monochromatic spectrum of low-pressure sodium lamps. Something similar can be seen in mercury lamps. As the vapour pressure for mercury and sodium is closely related to the temperature of the gas discharge, the heat exchange system of these discharges is paramount. An important part of the acumen of lamp designers is aimed at optimisation and maintenance of the heat exchange system. See the texts by De Groot & Van Vliet (1986) and Meyer & Nienhuis (1988).

The second point relates to luminescence. Short-wave radiation is absorbed with luminescence, which leads to an excited condition in the atoms of one of the materials. The absorbed energy is subsequently emitted again, but not at the same frequency, in contrast to the description above for the operation of gas discharge lamps. Some is converted into heat during the processes of energy absorption and radiation, so that less energy is available for radiation. Less energy means a lower frequency light quantum and therefore a longer wavelength. This increase in the wavelength is called luminescence. There are two kinds of luminescence: fluorescence, where the emission of light stops the moment the light incidence is halted; and phosphorescence, where the material continues to glow. Only the first is of interest for light sources. For example, the two most important lines of the low-pressure mercury discharge have wavelengths of 253.7 nm and 185 nm, both situated in the invisible ultraviolet. This emission is converted into longwave light, e.g. red or yellow, when suitable fluorescent materials are selected. This renders low-pressure mercury discharge useful for lamps – the well-known 'TL' tubes (see section 13.3.1.).

Another characteristic of gas discharge that should be mentioned here is that it can be described as a negative resistance. This means that an external current restriction, termed the ballast, is required for all gas discharges.

4.4 Turbid media

The propagation of light in turbid media is a subject which has hardly any theoretical basis and yet is paramount in practice. As mentioned above, phenomenological optics may be used when the 'objects' which can be found in the light path are very large, compared with the wavelength of the light (a factor 1000 or higher). Conversely, Rayleigh set out a theoretical model for the interaction between light and a substance for a case in which the substance particles are 'infinitely small'; this model is suitable for particles which are smaller than the wavelength of the light by at least a factor of 10. Minnaert (1942) described Rayleigh's Law thus

$$s = K \frac{(n-1)^2}{N \cdot \lambda^4}$$ [4.4.1]

where

s	is the scattering per volume unit
K	a constant
n	the refraction index
N	the number of particles per cm^3
λ	the wavelength of the light.

Van de Hulst (1981) has set out very detailed models for the interaction of light and spherical particles with arbitrary dimensions. The well-known Lorenz–Mie Theory also offers several clues, again only for spherical particles. See, for example, Mie (1908). An overview of this material can be found in CIE (1995).

It has not proved possible to set out a strict mathematical treatment for particles with arbitrary shapes which absorb light, either selectively or not, and whose dimensions are not distributed normally. Only numerical approximations can be applied. An overview is provided in CIE (1995). In addition, field measurements are often used. Overviews can be found in Douglas & Booker (1977) and Middleton (1952).

The most relevant aspect of light propagation in turbid media is fog. This has been the subject of much practical research. Overviews are given in a number of OECD studies (1972, 1976) and CIE (1995). See also Schreuder (1991). A number of more general studies have been conducted. See e.g. Kocmond & Perchonok (1970) and Spencer (1960). Here also the above-mentioned publications by Douglas & Booker (1977) and Middleton (1952) are particularly relevant.

A special case of interaction between light and 'unordered' material is light reflection on rough surfaces. Most efforts to achieve a general analytical description have foundered in this area too. Light reflection on road surfaces is of particular relevance to traffic; this subject has been tackled completely empirically, due to the lack of mathematical or physical 'models'. See also section 5.4.8.

4.5 Geometric optics

4.5.1 Light

Light propagates uniformly in a vacuum, i.e. in a straight line and with a singular velocity. The propagation of light is affected by any material which it encounters. This material may consist of solids, fluids or gases; it can be transparent or opaque. As long as we are dealing with 'objects', including gas bubbles etc., which are at least a thousand times larger than the wavelength of light, particle-wave duality is not relevant: light may be understood with the aid of straight 'light rays'. The use of light rays is also called geometric optics: all phenomena are studied with the aid of the exclusive application of geometrical laws, drawings and constructions. The basis for geometric optics was laid by Newton. A modern discussion is given in Feynman et al. (1977), while the material is dealt with in a somewhat simpler manner by Van Heel (1950) and Longhurst (1964). See also Breuer (1994).

The method of geometric optics is used for the design and construction of nearly all optical equipment and of the light paths in them. This means that these light paths in a mathematical sense can be calculated strictly; the results are totally determined and predictable, down to even the smallest detail. In many cases the actual calculations and/or constructions are extremely simple: the operation of plane mirrors and 'lenses' can be described completely by means of the simple laws relating to reflection and refraction. We should mention that these simple laws can be derived 'rigorously' from the Maxwell Laws. They can also be applied to non-plane surfaces. The simple laws relating to reflection and refraction continue to apply in principle; they are only a little more difficult to handle. The laws relating to reflection and refraction suffice to determine the path of the rays for the design of luminaires, with or without cover plates, with reflectors and/or refractors.

The basic rule for reflection is the principle which is commonly ascribed to Huygens. This principle says that the angle, which is formed by the incident ray with the vertical (the 'normal'), equals the angle which the reflected ray of light forms with the normal. The 'angle of incident' therefore equals the 'angle of reflection'. See figure 4.5.1.

Readers should refer to Van Heel (1950, page 53) for the derivation of the principle. This 'principle' applies as long as the dimensions of the mirror are large in relation to the wavelength of the light. In approximation, this law also applies to mirrors which are curved. Instead of the mirror itself, the tangent to the mirror is chosen. This approximation is, of course, only valid if the curvature of the mirror is not too large. Here also one can say that this principle applies when the dimensions of the part of the mirrors which can be considered to be in a plane, are large in relation to the wavelength of the light. The limit of application cannot be indicated precisely, but it would seem that

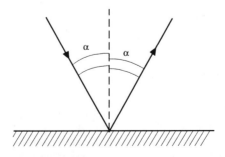

Figure 4.5.1: *Huygens' Reflection Principle*

the principle of reflection cannot be used for dry road surfaces. In principle, it should be possible to divide road surfaces into plane facets, but the micro-crystalline character of the common aggregates means that the facets are no longer 'large' in relation to the wavelength. The reflection principle cannot be used for these facets. A road surface, therefore, has the character of a 'turbid' medium. In addition, many of the natural aggregates show double refraction, which leads to a further complication of the facet models.

4.5.2   Reflection

By reflection we mean, as a collective term, all phenomena where light is reflected by a surface. The luminance of a non-luminous object is proportional to the incident light, and to the reflection factor, as indicated in section 5.2.3. This reflection factor depends on the surface condition of the object and on the method of lighting.

Three types of reflection can be defined, including hybrids

1. *Mirroring or regular reflection*
   The light follows the so-called Huygens' reflection principles: the angle on the surface between the incident rays and the normal equals the angle of the reflected light rays and the normal. Examples include metal surfaces such as mirrors and non-crystalline substances such as glass and water; etc. See figure 4.5.1.
2. *Diffuse reflection*
   Light is reflected equally in all directions, irrespective of the manner of incidence. This is the case for all surfaces with a grainy structure, whose grains are randomly oriented. Some examples are talcum powder and snow. See figure 4.5.2.
3. *Retro-reflection*
   We use the term retro-reflection when the light is reflected in the direction from which it originated. This form of reflection only occurs exceptionally in nature. There are two forms of retro-reflection: 'genuine' with angled mirrors, and 'false' with lens collimators. See figures 4.5.3 and 4.5.4.

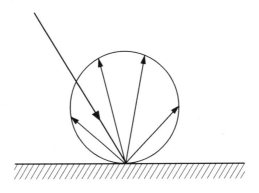

Figure 4.5.2: *Diffuse reflection*

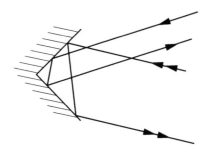

Figure 4.5.3: *Retro-reflection with angled mirrors*

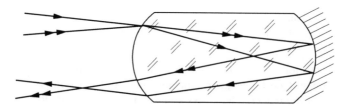

Figure 4.5.4: *Retro-reflection with so-called lens collimators*

In practice, especially with regard to highway lighting and traffic safety, retro-reflection has become very important for marking and signalling purposes.

Only in the case of diffuse reflection can we speak of a single reflection factor, which is then a 'scalar'. In all other cases the intensity of the reflected light, and therefore the reflection factor, depends on the direction of the incident light as well as on the direction of the reflected light. Two independent variables are required to determine the direction for the incident as well as for the reflected light; they are both therefore types of reflector. The quantities, however, do not meet exactly the mathematical definitions of a vector. In particular, the vector addition does not apply for the light rays described here. A total of four variables are required. This means that reflection can only be described by an expression which, although it has much in common with a tensor, does not precisely meet the mathematical criteria of a true tensor.

4.5.3   Refraction

The second important law is that relating to refraction, which is usually ascribed to Willebrord Snell (often called 'Snell's Law'). Light rays, which move from a medium with a refraction index n_1 to a refraction index n_2, do not move in a straight line; they are 'broken'. If the light moves from a medium with a small refraction index, e.g. air, to a 'denser' medium with a greater refraction index, e.g. water or glass, then the light is refracted towards the normal. See figure 4.5.5.

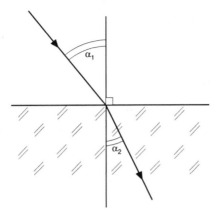

Figure 4.5.5: *Snell's Law; from air to glass*

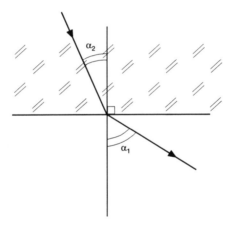

Figure 4.5.6: *Snell's Law: from glass to air*

However, if the light moves from a denser to a less dense medium, e.g. from glass to air, then the light is broken away from the normal. See figure 4.5.6.

We will return to this for the discussion of total reflection in section 4.5.4. The formula for Snell's Law is

$$n_1 \sin \alpha = n_2 \sin \alpha_2 \qquad\qquad [4.5.1]$$

where n_1 and n_2 are the refraction indices of the two media, and α_1 and α_2 the angles which the light rays form before and after refraction with the normal on the surface. For the derivation of the formula refer to Van Heel (1950, page 61). The law is based on Fermat's Principle, which indicates that each light ray selects the 'shortest' route. The shortest route is really the route which takes least time; as the propagation velocity is in inverse proportion to the refraction index of the medium, the shortest route is 'refracted'. By stating

$n_1 = 1$ (vacuum or air) and $n_2 = -1$ (also vacuum or air, with a minus, due to the inversion of the direction) the law of refraction switches to the law of reflection.

4.5.4   The total reflection

Although light moving from a denser to a less dense medium is generally refracted away from the normal, the maximum angle of refraction is 900. If the angle of incidence increases any further the light cannot 'escape'; it is reflected within the first, denser medium. This is called total reflection. See figure 4.5.7.

The total reflection is characterised by the threshold angle. It follows from the law of refraction that this threshold angle, also called Brewster's angle, is represented by

$$\sin g = \frac{n}{n'} \qquad\qquad [4.5.2]$$

in which

g	is the threshold angle
n and n'	the refraction indices of the 'first' and the 'second' medium, where $n' > n$

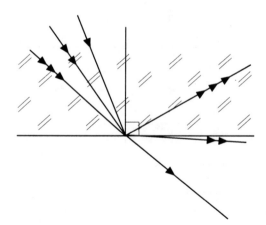

Figure 4.5.7: *Total reflection; Brewster's angle*

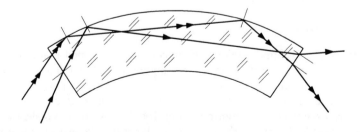

Figure 4.5.8: *Total reflection in a wave conductor*

The total reflection is relevant for the dimensioning of prisms, for example as used in luminaires. The operation of fibre optics and other wave conductors is also dependent on total reflection. See figure 4.5.8.

4.5.5   Double refraction

The refraction law, of course, only applies if the second medium is transparent. Different laws apply to metals. In a number of cases, materials occurring in nature prove to be doubly refracting.

The reflection of those materials as described by Fresnel is

$$a_n = -\frac{\sin(i - i')}{\sin(i + i')}; \quad a_p = \frac{\tan(i - i')}{\tan(i + i')} \qquad [4.5.3]$$

where

a_n is the amplitude of the reflected light, polarised in the incidence plane

a_p the amplitude of the reflected light polarised at right angles to the plane of incidence

i and i' the angles of incidence and refraction.

This relationship applies to an amplitude of the incident light equal to one. The angle i' follows from the angle i with Snell's Law when the refraction indices n and n' for the light polarised in the incidence plane and the light polarised at right angles to the incidence plane are known. The derivations of Fresnel's Laws are given by Van Heel (1950, page 65). As mentioned above, the fact that many natural aggregates are doubly refracting leads to complications in the facet model for road surfaces.

Bibliography

Breuer, H. (1994). *DTV-Atlas zur Physik, Band 1*. 4. Auflage. München, Deutsche Taschenbuchverlag DTV, 1994.

CIE (1995). *Road visibility in fog conditions*. 8th Draft. Vienna, CIE, 1995.

De Groot, J.J. & Van Vliet, J.A.J.M. (1986). *The high-pressure sodium lamp*. Deventer, Kluwer, 1986.

Douglas, C.A. & Booker, R.L. (1977). *Visual range: Concepts, instrumental determination, and aviation applications*. NBS Monograph 159. Washington D.C., National Bureau of Standards, 1977.

Elenbaas, W., (ed.) (1959). *Fluorescent lamps and lighting*. Eindhoven, Philips Technical Library, 1959.

Elenbaas, W., (ed.) (1965). *High-pressure mercury vapour lamps and their applications*. Eindhoven, Philips Technical Library, 1965.

Feyman, R.P.; Leighton, R.B. & Sands M. (1977). *The Feynman lectures on physics*. Three volumes. 1963; 6th printing. Reading (Mass.), Addison-Wesley Publishing Company, 1977.

Gregory, R.L. (1965). *Visuele waarneming; De psychologie van het zien* [Visual observation; the psychology of seeing]. Wereldakademie; De Haan/Meulenhoff, 1965.

Gribbin, J. (1984). *In search of Schrödinger's cat.* London, Bantam, 1984.

Helbig, E. (1972). *Grundlagen der Lichtmesstechnik.* Leipzig, Geest & Portig, 1972.

Kockmond, W.C. & Perchonok, K. (1970). *Highway fog.* NCHRP Report 95. Washington D.C., Highway Research Board, 1970.

Longhurst, R.S. (1964). *Geometrical and physical optics.* Fifth impression. London, Longmans, 1964.

Middleton, W.E.K. (1952). *Vision through the atmosphere.* University of Toronto Press, 1952.

Mie, G. (1908). *Beitrage zur Optik trüber Medien, speziell kolloidaler Metallösungen.* Annalen der Physik. 25 (1908) 377–452 (cit. CIE, 1995).

Minnaert, M. (1942). *De natuurkunde van 't vrije veld.* [The physics of the free field]. Derde druk. Zutphen, Thieme, 1942.

Moon, P. (1961). *The scientific basis of illuminating engineering.* Revised edition. New York, Dover Publications Inc., 1961.

Meyer, Chr. & Nienhuis, H. (1988). *Discharge lamps.* Philips Technical Library. Deventer, Kluwer, 1988.

OECD (1971). *Road lighting and accidents.* Paris, OECD, 1971.

OECD (1976). *Adverse weather, reduced visibility and road safety.* Paris, OECD, 1976.

Oranje, P.J. (1942). *Gasontladingslampen [Gas discharge lamps].* Amsterdam, Meulenhoff, 1942.

Philips (1989). *Correspondence course light application.* Eindhoven, Philips Lighting B.V., 1989.

Schreuder, D.A. (1991). *Motorway lighting in fog conditions.* R-91-72. Leidschendam, SWOV, 1991.

Spencer, D.E. (1960). *Scattering functions for fog.* J. Opt. Soc. Am. **50** (1960) 584–585.

Thomas, O. (1944). *Astronomie; feiten en problemen* (Astronomy; facts and problems). Amsterdam, Strengholt, 1944.

Van de Hulst, H.C. (1981). *Light scattering by small particles.* New York, Dover, 1981.

Van Heel, A.C.S. (1950). *Inleiding in de optica* [Introduction to optics]. Derde druk. Den Haag, Martinus Nijhoff, 1950.

Weigert, A & Wendker, H.J. (1989). *Astronomie und Astrophysik – ein Grundkurs.* 2. Auflage. Weinheim (D), VCH Verlagsgesellschaft, 1989.

5 Photometry: describing and measuring light

The creation of images is dependent on the optical aids used to create them based on the properties of the illumination. Illumination is essentially the creation of images from sources of light in the proximity of the objects to be rendered visible. The act of rendering something visible is relevant to both vehicular and pedestrian traffic and their safety.

In order to describe illumination or lighting, especially in the context of optimising lighting design, it is essential to quantify light. Light must be measured in order to ascertain whether a lighting design meets its requirements. The field of photometry comprises the description and the measurement of light, and both of these depend on the quantification of light.

5.1 The quantification of light

5.1.1 The history of photometry

Section 4.2.1 discussed light as an electromagnetic phenomenon which in many contexts can be treated as a wave phenomenon, but can often also properly be described as a collection of extremely fast-moving particles (photons). Proper discussion of the subject of 'public lighting' requires the ability to quantify and measure the action of light. The discipline which concerns itself with this, is called photometry. Photometric units and variables form part of the system of variables and units established by the International Organization for Standardization, ISO. In practice, however, the ISO approach is rather cumbersome. Here, a method which is better suited to the practice of handling photometric units and variables will be used.

Photometry is an old branch of applied physics. Bouguer and Lambert laid the foundations for photometry as early as the eighteenth century. Keitz (1967) offers a brief overview of the history of photometry. See also CIE (1932). This chapter will only address those aspects of photometry which are relevant to the practice of public lighting. Suffice to say that CIE has played an important role throughout. Not for nothing was its original name 'International Commission on Photometry'. This interest came to the fore again recently when CIE was charged with setting out draft standards relating to photometry. It is the CIE's drafts which are ratified by ISO.

Refer to the thorough textbooks and manuals by Helbig (1972), Keitz (1967), Moon (1961), Reeb (1962) and Walsh (1958) for greater detail. A classic, but nearly completely forgotten, work in this field is the study by Gershun (1939), which outside Russia is only known in translation by Moon and Timoshenko.

5.1.2 Radiometry and photometry

Radiometry concerns the way radiation propagates in space and how the effects of radiation are shown in radiometric units and variables. Hentschel (1994, par. 2.2) and Moon (1961, Chapter 1) offer overviews, similarly Feynman et al. (1977), in much greater detail.

The operation of the human visual system and how the action can be described are discussed in more detail in chapters 6 and 7. Here, the focus is on the spectral response of photoreceptors. This indicates the part of radiometric ability which can generate an impression of light. It is important to note that there are two different types of receptors: cones, which operate during the day and rods, which operate at night. Later on we will see that both types operate in twilight.

The visual system is not equally sensitive to all colours. Sensitivity in different conditions depends on whether cones, rods, or both are involved. There are three types of cones, each with their own spectral sensitivity, and these are linked to each other by nerve cells in a complicated manner.

It is certainly not impossible to determine the spectral response of the visual system as a whole, despite these complicating factors. However this book is not the place to discuss the rather complicated way in which this response is determined, nor the fact that the result depends on the method of determination. For further information, see e.g. CIE (1932; 1978; 1989).

5.1.3 The V_λ curve

Usually, the total spectral response is shown in a graph. This is the so-called V_λ curve, when related to cones. This curve shows the sensitivity in a relative scale against the wavelength of the light used. This sensitivity is indicated with V and the dependence of the wavelength with λ. See figure 5.1.1.

Photometry as generally practised – and in particular the practical variables such as lumen and candela discussed later in this chapter – are all based on this V_λ curve. The curve is defined by the international body which controls measures and weights, the Commission Internationale des Poids et Mesures, established in Paris in the early 1900s. The curve was determined at the 1932 CIE congress in Cambridge on the basis of recommendations by the Commission Internationale de l'Eclairage (CIE, 1932). As a result the curve is also called the CIE Cambridge curve.

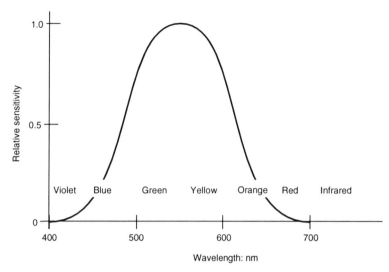

Figure 5.1.1: *The V$_\lambda$ curve*

The curve is essentially empirical. This means that different measurements could result in a different curve, and therefore in different photometric variables. Later data have shown that the curve depends on the extent of the field of vision deployed during the measurements. The usual curves are based on a measuring field of two degrees diameter. More recent research has shown that the values for a field with a diameter of ten degrees differ in essential aspects. This discrepancy probably relates to the distribution of the rods and cones across the retina, discussed in section 6.1.5; as the *fovea centralis* is approximately two degrees in diameter. The discrepancies can usually be discounted. But figure 5.1.2 shows that in the wavelength area around 500 nm, around the colour green, the ten degree values result in values for V$_\lambda$ which are nearly 30% above the two degree values.

The measuring method also influences the result. The use of a flickering photometer, with which two fields of a contrasting colour are presented continuously in quick succession, leads to essentially different results than the use of the step-by-step method, where fields which only show a slight difference in colour, are presented next to each other. Physiological and chemical measurements result in different values again. The research relating to this subject is summarised in a CIE report (1978).

It is strongly suspected that the CIE values for blue are too low. The 'normal' eye is more sensitive to blue than the CIE curve leads one to suspect. In other words, the present photometric variables underestimate blue light. This is attributed to the fact that no blue light sources with sufficient 'intensity' to allow accurate measurements existed at the beginning of this century. This assumption is supported by the difference shown in figure 5.1.2 between the V$_\lambda$ curves for measuring fields of between ten and two degrees.

Any revision of the CIE curve is still under discussion; the consequences are immense. Not only would all measurements and calibrations have to be

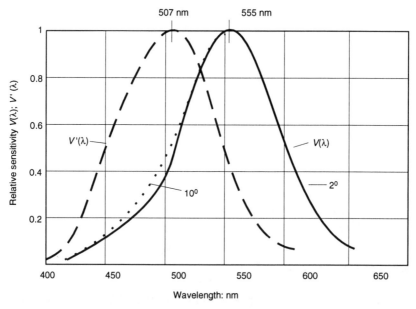

Figure 5.1.2: V_λ *curves for photopic perception. The* V_λ *curves for measuring fields of between 10 and 2 degrees are shown for photopic perception. After Baer, 1990*

changed, but the higher spectral light yield which is so often cited as an advantage of low-pressure sodium lamps compared with high-pressure mercury lamps, would also be less than is often supposed. In addition, the Purkinje effect described in section 6.2.1 would be weaker than is commonly thought.

The V_λ curve reflects the results of psycho-physical measurements with humans as observers. Consequently, the characteristics of these humans are reflected in these results. Important differences exist between individuals, as well as significant variations in results by the same observer at different times and/or under different conditions. The V_λ curve, therefore, cannot be a mathematical or a physically fixed relation. CIE has defined a 'standard observer', so as to be able to derive a photometric standard from the plurality of data. All perceptions are thus ascribed to one single hypothetical observer. The V_λ curve associated with this standard observer forms the basis of the total system of photometric units and variables. This also shows why the adaptation of the V_λ curve to the results of recent research, in order to eliminate a number of imperfections, would be so drastic.

In the end it was agreed that in nearly all cases photometry is based on the spectral response associated with cones. See section 6.2.1. 'Current' photometry therefore means photopic photometry. But the eye also possesses a system of rods, whose sensitivity varies in an absolute sense as well as in relation to the relative spectral distribution of sensitivity. As well as the photopic V_λ, there is a scotopic V'_λ curve, which characterises the sensitivity of rods. See figure 5.1.2.

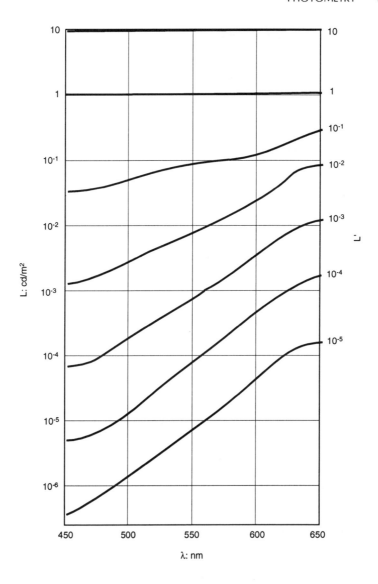

Figure 5.1.3: *The relative eye sensitivity for mesopic perception*

As will be explained in section 6.2.1, a number of families of V_λ curves exist. In addition to the curves mentioned, for photopic vision, or vision in daylight, and scotopic vision, or night vision, there exists also a host of curves for the various mesopic areas. If necessary, a completely parallel scotopic photometry, or even a system of mesopic photometrics could be defined. On practical grounds however, the photopic system is nearly always the one used, even in situations where eye sensitivity can be much better described with the aid of the scotopic relation. See figure 5.1.3.

5.2   The photometric units

5.2.1   The luminous flux

Although the ISO system is structured differently, we will start our discussion with the most simple variable, the luminous flux, for reasons of clarity. Like the definition of all photometric variables, the definition of the luminous flux is based on the above-mentioned V_λ curve. The V_λ curve is a relative curve, which shows the relation between the power emitted in wavelength bands and the associated visual impression. V_λ is a ratio, i.e. without dimensions. The dimension of the power emitted in these wavelength areas is the watt. The dimension of the corresponding visual impression therefore is also the watt; it is sometimes called 'luminous watt' or 'light watt'.

It can also be expressed in other terms. We speak of 'energy flux' which is propagated by means of the electromagnetic field. This flux causes a visual perception, which is termed the luminous flux expressed in lumen (lm). A lumen therefore is a watt 'weighted' in accordance with the V_λ curve. In practice, the lumen is used as the basic unit in photometry. All other units and variables are derived from the lumen. It should be mentioned again that the V_λ curve is incorporated in all photometric units and variables; should one wish to use a different V_λ curve for one reason or another, then all the photometric units and variables must be adapted accordingly.

If the total energy of a light source could be converted into visible light, then it would be seen that 1 watt corresponds to 683 lumen (Hentschel, 1994, page 38). This necessitates all the energy being emitted at a wavelength at which V_λ has a maximum value; this occurs at 555 nm. These 683 lumen per watt (lm/W) indicate the 'maximum efficiency' of a light source. In practice this value is not attainable, in particular as the spectral energy distribution of practical sources of light deviates from the ideal. In addition, we must reckon with a whole series of losses. The maximum efficiency, the specific luminous flux, found in practice is the low-pressure sodium lamp; this amounts to approximately 200 lm/W. See also section 13.3.1, where the characteristics of the lamps used in public lighting are discussed.

5.2.2   Illuminance

Light is propagated in a straight line in homogenous media. But light is only effective if it falls on a surface. This effect is quantified by the illuminance. The measure for this is the lux, sometimes abbreviated to Lx. Illuminance in lumen per square metre (lm/m²) is usually indicated in formulae by E. In practice, one often uses 'illumination' instead of 'illuminance'. I will follow this usage as long as there is no risk of confusion. It is, of course, possible to determine the E for a mathematical plane through which light shines, if only in theory. No physical phenomenon can be detected at all in that case, and the term illuminance is here rather misleading. This variable is sometimes used for theoretical considerations; it is also called the 'density' of the luminous flux, also expressed in lm/m².

Moon & Spencer (1981) made, based on the approach of the earlier-mentioned Gershun, a number of attempts to arrive at a general lighting theory where the problem of the difference between the illuminance and the density of the luminous flux is solved, as well as a number of other problems. These attempts came to nothing, partly because Moon and Spencer were of the opinion that they had to introduce a completely new terminology. The proposals are commonly discarded as 'amateurish' in applied lighting technology; however, they deserve more attention than they receive presently, due to their theoretical importance.

The illumination is in the first place a measure for the quantity of light which incidents on something. But illumination is often also used in public lighting as a measure of the quality of the lighting. The reason for this is that the effect of public lighting is usually proportional to the amount of light, the 'light level', or, as is explained in section 9.1.1, the state of adaptation of the visual system of the observer. The illumination can be simply calculated and measured; it also represents a variable which is easy to picture. This is the reason why illumination is used as the main variable in most applications relating to lighting. In itself this is a curious matter, as illumination cannot be 'seen'. Further details on this will be given in the discussion of the concept of luminance. As indicated in section 9.1.4, horizontal illumination, in particular, is used as the main quality criterion in public lighting in most recommendations and directives.

The concept of horizontal illumination is self-evident: it relates to illumination on a horizontal plane. Usually this refers to the plane of the road surface; sometimes horizontal illumination is measured or calculated at a height of 1.5 metres above the road surface. A different convention is sometimes adhered to in relation to special applications.

The orientation of the plane on which the light incidents should always be determined when specifying illuminance. That is not a problem with horizontal illumination, as only one horizontal plane can be defined through each point. The horizontal plane, or the normal on it, is always the same and no further specification is required. In all other cases the orientation of the plane should be indicated.

This is the case for vertical illuminance, which is often used in public lighting, in addition to horizontal illuminance. When the visibility of objects is to be determined or researched, vertical illuminance is usually specified on a vertical plane which is at right angles to the central lengthways road axis or the direction of vision, and facing the observer. The height above the road surface is determined according to the purpose; usually a height of 10 cm is chosen for 'Small Target Visibility', to be discussed in section 9.2.2. Values of 15 or 20 cm can also be seen. The height is particularly significant when taking into consideration the effect of the indirect light reflected from the road surface. This reflected light can significantly contribute to vertical illuminance. See also sections 10.1.2 and 15.4.5 where counterbeam lighting in tunnels is discussed.

In addition to horizontal and vertical illuminance, we also may encounter semicylindrical illuminance in public lighting. This variable is often used to describe the recognition of other road users, in particular in relation to their facial expression. Semicylindrical illuminance is defined as the average value of

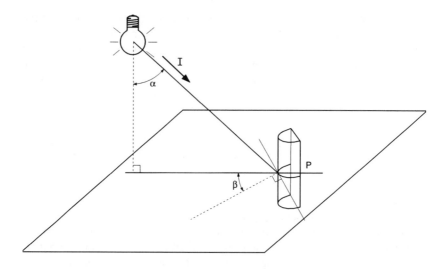

Figure 5.2.1: *Semicylindrical illuminance*

illuminances on the surface of a cylinder. As we can see only one side of a cylinder at a time, the definition is limited to half a cylinder. Semicylindrical illuminance can be described in formula form as follows

$$E_{semicyl} = \frac{I}{\pi \cdot h^2} \sin \alpha \cos^2 \alpha (1 + \cos\beta) \qquad [5.2.1]$$

Figure 5.2.1 illustrates this formula. It also gives the meaning of α, β and h.

A different measure is used in some areas of application, in particular for characterising brightness which is perceived with optical systems that have a retiring pupil which is smaller than 'the normal' human eye pupil. Baer (1990, page 18) calls this measure the 'Pupillenlichtstärke'; the term illumination on the retina' is also used. The unit is the Troland

$$I_p = L \times A_p \qquad [5.2.2]$$

in which

I_p is the illuminance on the plane of the observer, in Troland
L the luminance, in cd/m^2
A_p the surface of the pupil, in mm^2

The Troland, abbreviated to Trol, has the dimension: cd m^{-2} mm^2 (after Baer, 1990); expressed thus, it is obviously not an ISO measurement.

5.2.3 Luminance

Light only has a perceivable effect when the visual system is activated in one way or another. In other, simpler, words: light is only visible once it falls on the eye. Wright (1967) has written an interesting little book, in which he describes this phenomenon in a rather philosophical fashion.

Light is seen as the brightness of the observed object. In order to arrive at a better definition, as well as a concept which is easier to measure, luminance, indicated by L, was introduced. Luminance can be said to be the objective, measurable measure of brightness. The concept of brightness is used in two ways in the discipline of lighting. The first is the colloquial equivalent of the concept of luminance. The second is the subjective experience of the light impression. This is also called 'lightness'. Section 7.4 discusses colour and returns to the matter of lightness.

It only makes sense to speak of the luminance of an object if the object itself emits light. Otherwise it is just dark and the luminance will be zero. However, the use of luminance, and therefore the definition of the concept of luminance itself, requires a distinction between an object only reflecting any incidenting light and an object which itself emits light. These two cases will be discussed separately and I will start with that of a body which does not itself emit light.

A surface which does not itself emit light is invisible when no light falls on it, and the illuminance is zero. However, it is also invisible when all the incidenting light is absorbed, i.e. when no light is reflected. Only if part of this reflected light falls on the eye of an observer, can the surface be observed. It is therefore obvious that the brightness of the surface is proportional to the illuminance on the surface and to the reflection of the surface. This results in the following simple relation

$$L = R \times E \qquad\qquad [5.2.3]$$

When the usual measure for the reflection, the dimensionless number ρ, the ratio between the incidenting and reflected luminous flux, is used (the reflection factor; see later), this formula then becomes

$$L = \frac{\rho}{\pi} E \qquad\qquad [5.2.4]$$

The factor π in the formula is related to the standardisation introduced by ISO. When we assume that has no dimension, then L and E have an identical dimension, i.e. [lm/m^2]. When discussing the solid angle (section 5.2.4) it will be shown that this is not the whole story.

A more formal definition based on the CIE standard curves is illustrated in the following relations

$$L_v = K_m \int_{360nm}^{830nm} L_{e,\lambda a} V_{\lambda a} d\lambda \alpha \qquad\qquad [5.2.5]$$

$$L_v' = K_m' \int_{360nm}^{830nm} L_{e,\lambda a}' V_{\lambda a}' d\lambda \alpha \qquad\qquad [5.2.6]$$

in which

L_v and L_v'	is the photopic and scotopic luminance
$L_{e,\lambda a}$	the spectral radiance
$V_{\lambda a}$ and $V_{\lambda a}'$	the CIE eye sensitivities for photopic and scotopic perception

$$K_m \qquad = 683 \text{ lm/W}$$
$$K' \qquad = 1699 \text{ lm/W}$$

This expression basically corresponds to the one used by Hentschel (1994, page 29).

The luminance of a surface which does not itself emit light, is easy to define in this way. The definition of a surface which itself does emit light is based on luminous intensity.

5.2.4 Luminous intensity

The luminous intensity of a light source is defined as the intensity from the source itself. The ISO stipulated that the luminous intensity in a certain direction, which causes a radiation intensity of 1/683 watt per steradian via a monochromatic emitter with a frequency of $540 \ 10^{12}$ Hz (or in ISO units c/s), equals the unit of luminous intensity. According to ISO, the unit of luminous intensity is called the candela, abbreviated to cd. This definition is taken from Hentschel (1994, page 37) and is based on the international conference of measures and weights (Anon, 1979). The definition only applies to point sources of light. This restriction carries considerable consequences for practical applications, to which we will return several times. The concept of the steradian will be returned to later in this section.

The luminous intensity can be described as the luminous flux which is emitted within a spatial area. This spatial area is indicated with a solid angle, which in turn is defined as the surface, expressed in square metres, which is intercepted at the centre of a unit sphere with a radius of 1 m, by the limits of the spatial range, around the light source. This definition can be written as follows

$$I = \frac{\Delta\Phi}{\Delta\Omega} \qquad\qquad [5.2.7]$$

The solid angle is expressed in steradians (abbreviated to sr). See figures 5.2.2 and 5.2.3. In formulae, the solid angle is usually written as a capital omega (Ω). The surface cut out of the sphere is proportional to the square of the radius of the unit sphere. If the radius of the unit sphere measures 1 m, then the dimension of the solid angle is expressed in steradian [square metres] per metre squared. In practice, this means that the solid angle is a number without dimensions. In theory, however, it is dubious whether the square metre cancels the metre squared. In other words, it is an open question, and according to some a question of taste, whether a crosswise metre has the same dimension as a lengthways metre.

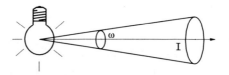

Figure 5.2.2: Single angle ω as a cone

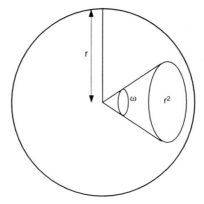

Figure 5.2.3: *Solid angle ω as a part of the 'unit sphere'*

Practical light sources do not emit the same amount of light in all directions. In order to describe the effect of the light source, the direction effects should be taken into consideration. This is done by considering the luminous intensity of the light source as a vector. A vector is a variable which is dimensional as well as directional; we should note that luminous intensity does not meet with the mathematical definition of a 'real' vector in all aspects.

As indicated before, the luminous intensity can only be defined, according to the ISO definitions, for a point source of light. The solid angle is the 'cone-shaped' section with the top in the point, where the light source is also situated as illustrated in figure 5.2.2. If the light emission is homogenous within this solid angle, then the luminous intensity can be defined as the luminous flux which is emitted within the solid angle, divided by the surface which is cut' from the unit sphere. The luminous intensity therefore is

$$I = \frac{\Delta\Phi}{\Delta A} \qquad\qquad [5.2.8]$$

A transition to an infinitely small solid angle offers the formal definition of luminous intensity *I*

$$I = \frac{d\Phi}{\Delta A} \qquad\qquad [5.2.9]$$

The luminous intensity as indicated above is expressed in candela, abbreviated to cd. The problem with this definition is that there is no possibility to come to a strict agreement on the luminous intensity relating to non-point sources of light. Practical measurements have shown that the deviation from 'pointedness' may be ignored when the distance between the source of light and the measuring location exceeds 10 to 15 times the largest dimension of the source of light. This distance might be called the photometric threshold distance. This is usually the case in the practice of public lighting, so that we are usually able to work with the candela as the unit of luminous intensity. But this condition is certainly not met by line lighting in tunnels, nor by most applications of light in interior spaces, especially in office spaces; here it is not possible to work with the definition of luminous intensity. Usually this problem is solved by breaking the large light sources down into many smaller light sources, which each satisfy the photometric threshold distance. This problem can easily be overcome with computers, but the calculations become much more complicated. Here, a solution is not expected.

5.2.5   The luminance of light-emitting bodies

According to ISO, the luminance is derived from luminous intensity, see section 5.2.4. This is based on a light emitting surface, which is divided into small particles dA , which are so small that we can use the luminous intensity as per the definition given. The luminance of that particle is defined as the quotient of luminous intensity and surface, i.e.

$$L = \frac{dI}{dA} \qquad\qquad [5.2.10]$$

Now it is clear why we write the luminance as candela per square metre (cd/m^2).

5.3   Relations between photometric variables

5.3.1   The inverse square law
The distance law

From the definition of the luminous flux, given in section 5.2.1 and from the definition given in section 5.2.2 for luminance, we can derive that the illuminance decreases with the square of the distance for a point source of light. The luminous flux which is emitted by the light source, must be distributed over a larger surface when the incidence plane is further removed. This relation is called the inverse square law.

$$E = \frac{kI}{r^2} \qquad\qquad [5.3.1]$$

in which
       E is the illuminance
       I the luminous intensity
       k a proportional constant (dependent on the units used)
       r the distance

This formula is taken from Breuer (1994, page 175) where details can also be found on the distance law. See also figure 5.3.1.

As is indicated by Helbig (1972, para. 5.2), the distance law only applies in this form for diffuse emitting ('Lambertian') sources. Later in this section this point will be returned to in the discussion on bundled lights. See also section 5.3.2.

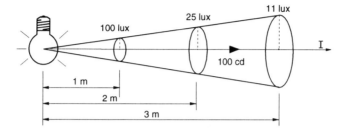

Figure 5.3.1: *The inverse square law*

Large light sources

Two important cases exist where the inverse square law does not apply. The first is the case already mentioned in section 5.2.4 for large light sources. As the definition for luminous intensity only applies to point light sources, the inverse square law must be adapted. We can theoretically break down the light source into many small sources of light, where the inverse square law applies to each light source. This is done in the calculations for the design for installations for tunnel lighting. According to the derivation which Helbig (1972, pages 47–48) has given, the ratio between actual luminous intensity *I* and the approximated (measured or calculated) luminous intensity *I'* is

$$\frac{I}{I'} = \frac{(r^2 + R^2)}{r^2}$$
[5.3.2]

in which

I and I'   is the above-mentioned actual and approximated luminous intensity
r   the distance between light source and measuring point
R   the radius from the theoretically circular source of light

Based on this relation, we can find out at which distance the deviations from the inverse square law are still 'acceptable'. See also figure 5.3.2.

Table 5.3.1 shows some values, also taken from Helbig (1972, page 48).

This table shows that the deviations very soon become 'acceptable'. At R/r = 1/10 (the measuring distance × five times the dimensions of the light source), the deviation is already reduced to 1%. This distance is also called the photometric threshold distance. Sometimes different values of this ratio are used, depending on the accuracy required. Helbig (1972, pages 48, 49) gives formulas, with which the photometric threshold distance for light sources of a different shape may be determined. Keitz (1967, page 187) indicates how the

Table 5.3.1: *Deviations from the inverse square law. The meaning of the letters corresponds to those in formula [5.3.2]; after Helbig, 1972, page 48*

R/r	1/2	1/4	1/6	1/8	1/10
I/I'	1.250	1.062	1.028	1.016	1.010

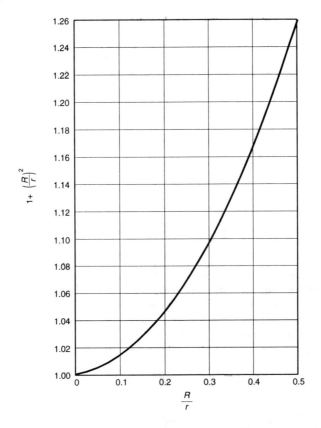

Figure 5.3.2: *Deviations from the inverse square law. The meaning of the letters corresponds to those in formula [5.3.2]; after Helbig, 1972, page 48*

photometric threshold distance can be determined for optical systems with lenses.

Bundled lights

A second case where the inverse square law does not apply, is light sources with a strong bundled character, such as car headlights, traffic lights, lighthouses and floodlights for sport field lighting. The illuminance is not reduced at all when the distance is increased, if the combination of light source and optics produces a perfectly parallel bundle. See figure 5.3.3.

The inverse square law would seem not to apply here. However, this is not true: it is better to say that the virtual light source lies very far (in our example an infinite distance) behind the actual light source/optics combination. With bundled lights, such as dipped headlights with a convergent bundle, a real image is formed at some distance in front of the combination, so that the illuminance is reduced more rapidly than the square of the distance. See figure 5.3.4

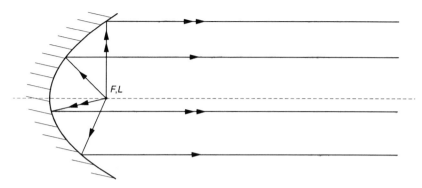

Figure 5.3.3: *A bundled light with a nearly parallel bundle. F is the focus of the parabola; L is the the light source*

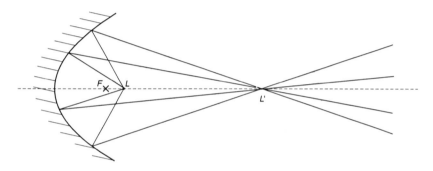

Figure 5.3.4: *A bundled light with a convergent bundle. F is the focus; L is the image of the light source*

5.3.2 The cosine law

A second important law in photometry is the cosine law. By this we mean the rule that the illuminance at a point in a flat plane is proportional to the cosine of the angle made by the normal on the plane at the point in question, and the line between the point in question and the light source. This law is derived directly from the definition of the cosine; the size of the illuminated area increases as the angle becomes greater. The illuminance will therefore be reduced if the luminous flux remains the same. The law can be written as follows

$$E = \frac{I}{d^2} \cos\gamma \qquad\qquad [5.3.3]$$

in which

E	is the illuminance
I	the luminous intensity
d	the distance
γ	the angle with the normal

The law is expressed in the diagram in figure 5.3.5.

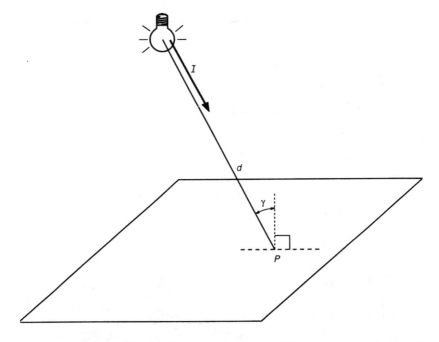

Figure 5.3.5: *The cosine law. I is illuminance; d is distance; P is the point to be illuminated;* γ *is the angle made by the two planes*

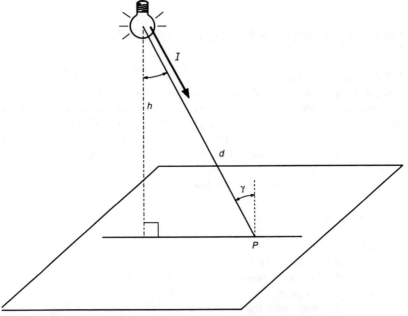

Figure 5.3.6: *The cosine to the third power law. I, d and P are as in figure 5.3.5; and h is height (length of the perpendicular)*

5.3.3   The cosine to the third power law

A combination of the inverse square law and the cosine law produces the third main law in photometry: the cosine to the third power law. See figure 5.3.6.

This law says that the illuminance on a flat plane at different distances from a light source (rather, of the projection of the light source on the plane) is proportional to the third power of the cosine of the angle between the normal on the plane in the point in question and the line between the respective point and the light source. In the formula

$$E = \frac{I}{n^2} \cos^3 \gamma \qquad\qquad [5.3.4]$$

in which

E	is the illuminance
I	the luminous intensity
h	the mounting height (analogous to d, the distance, in formula [5.3.3];
γ	the angle to the normal

This can be explained as follows. One cosine derives from the cosine law and the other two derive from the inverse square law. This law is important for street lighting. Imagine a lighting designed with light points which possess the same luminous intensity in all directions (emit an equal amount of light in all directions; this is not unusual in opal sphere lamps), then the illuminance on the road surface is inversely proportional to the cosine to the third power of the angle made by the normal and the line 'lamp–road surface point' for each light point.

5.3.4   Absorption, transmission and reflection

Part of the light is usually reflected when light falls on a material body, while often another part of the light is let through (transmission). The law relating to the conservation of energy poses that energy cannot 'disappear'. This law is usually represented in thermodynamics as follows (Breuer, 1994, page 109)

$$Q = \delta U + A \qquad\qquad [5.3.5]$$

in which

Q	is absorbed energy (e.g. heat)
δU	the increase in internal energy
A	energy delivered externally ('work')

Any energy not reflected and not transmitted, must therefore be absorbed by the body. The law in question can be written as follows

$$I = R + T + A \qquad\qquad [5.3.6]$$

in which

I	is the energy from the incident light
R	the energy from the reflected light

T the energy from the transmitted light
A the energy from the absorbed light

5.4   Measurements

5.4.1   Principles of light measurements

In the past only relative photometry was used. Two planes are compared visually; when one is known, we can say something about the other. This is called visual photometry and was the only method before the existence of photocells. Visual photometry is still required for the determination of the V_λ curve mentioned in section 5.1.3, as we are here dealing with the 'calibration' of the human visual system. An overview of the historical development can be found in Hentschel (1994, page 66–73).

Presently only objective measurements are made in practice and a photocell (detector) can be used for this. The detector determines the total energy of the incidence photons per unit of time. The energy flow is converted into electric energy. Light measurements are therefore measurements of power.

A number of different principles exist to realise this conversion. Philips (1989, part 5, pages 18–20) and Baer (1990, pages 154–156) offer overviews. Details can be found in Hentschel (194, pages 73–84). Three of these are presently used in practice

1. *Photoresistors*
   These are resistors made of cadmium-sulphide (CdS) and sometimes cadmium selenide (CdSe). The resistance changes when the amount of incidence light changes. They are easy to use but are not accurate, especially as the resistance also depends on other ambient factors, such as the temperature. They are not used for accurate measurements.

2. *Photodiodes*
   Diodes are in fact rectifiers: they let the electric current through in one direction, while the current is completely or partly blocked in the other, blocked, direction. This occurs in a *p-n* transition. In photodiodes, the current let through in the blocked direction is affected by the incidence light. The relation between the incidence light and the photoflux depends on the source of the current and on the external resistance. See Hentschel (1994, pages 77–79) for a fairly complete theoretical explanation. Photodiodes used to be mostly made of selenium but presently silicium is used almost exclusively. The spectral response of detectors of these materials is pictured in figure 5.4.1. Silicium cells are used extensively, either separately in current measuring instruments, or in groups, e.g. in CCDs. These are used in videocameras, but presently also as detectors in measuring instruments. See e.g. Rossi etc. (1996).

3. *Phototransistors*
   Just like all transistors, phototransistors are also amplifiers, in addition to the blocking effect they share with diodes. They are usually made of gallium arsenide (GaAs). Their non-linearity renders them especially suitable as an element in electronic switches. The most common

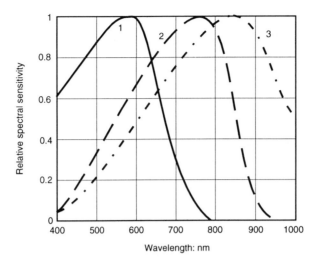

Figure 5.4.1: *The spectral response of Se-, Si- and GaAs-detectors. (After Baer (1990) fig. 1.159) 1: Se; 2: GaAs; 3: Si*

application is as a detector in CD players; they are used less often for light measurements.

All sorts of other detectors are used for light measurements, in addition to these three main groups. Many are only of historic interest (TV camera tubes; gas-filled and vacuum photocells; Se-blocking layer cells; see Hentschel 1994, page 73 ff.). Sometimes photo-multiplier tubes are used for very small quantities of light. These use amplification based on secondary emission. In the past this was the only possibility to measure the small luminous flux available in luminance measurements on roads. The equipment, however, is complicated and very sensitive to interference and external influences. See Schreuder (1967a). They belong to history as far as practical photometry is concerned. This also applies to photographic photometry, which was used in astronomy in particular. It has been almost completely replaced by measurements with electronic detectors, and in particular by CCDs. See e.g. Budding (1993, pages 116 132) and Sterken & Manfroid (1992, Chapters 3, 4, 13 and 14).

5.4.2 Measuring luminous intensity and the luminous flux
Luminous intensity

Luminous intensity is simple to measure in principle. Making use of the relation that the illuminance on a plane depends on the square of the distance between the light source and the plane (the inverse square law, see section 5.3.1), the luminous intensity of the light source can be derived directly from the illuminance on that plane and the distance between the plane and the light source. A few complications were pointed out in that section, in particular when large light sources or bundled lights are involved.

The distribution of the luminous intensity (the luminous intensity distribution or light distribution for short) is particularly relevant to applied illuminating engineering. This is determined by measuring the luminous intensity in a number of directions. The number and the distribution of these directions depend on the characteristics of the light distribution and of the area of application. The graphic representation of the result sometimes causes difficulties: we are dealing with a two-dimensional representation, the projection, of three-dimensional data. CIE has suggested a number of conventions: the problem is that different conventions are adhered to in different areas of application (CIE, 1977; see also CIE, 1973, 1990). This is of minor importance in public lighting. The most common representation is the *I* table; see Van Bommel & De Boer (1980, pages 202–205). This representation is required for the calculation of luminance; see section 13.1.3. Figure 5.4.2 shows a result in diagrammatic form.

In order to obtain an overall impression of the performance of any lamp, polar diagrams are sometimes used. Figure 5.4.3 shows an example.

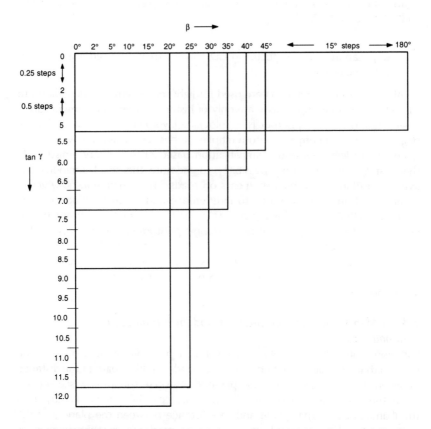

Figure 5.4.2: *Presentation of an I table in diagram form; after Van Bommel & De Boer, 1980, fig. 14.6*

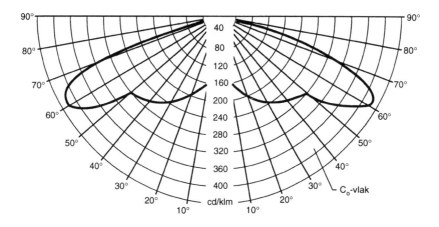

Figure 5.4.3: *An example of a polar diagram; after Hentschel, 1994, fig. 4.29*

Formerly the so-called 'onion diagram', the ISO candela diagram was also used sometimes. See Hentschel (1994, page 90).

The luminous flux
The luminous flux is also easy to measure in principle. The most common method is based on the definition of the luminous flux (see section 5.2.1). The light source is placed in a diffuse reflecting hollow sphere. The whole interior of the sphere has the same luminance, due to multiple reflections; this can be drawn off at any point by placing a photocell in the wall of the sphere. See Keitz (1967, pages 303–319). There are, of course, sources for possible errors. The theory is discussed extensively in Hentschel (1994, page 94).

A variant is to determine the total luminous flux by integrating the luminous intensity distribution. This is often done to determine the total light yield of lamps, for which the luminous intensity distribution must be determined in any case. See Hentschel (1994, pages 91–96).

5.4.3   The purpose of measurements and calculations in public lighting
In principle, calculations in public lighting are used at the design stage. Installations for public lighting are required to meet the requirements; in The Netherlands these are laid down in the Recommendations by the NSVV (NSVV, 1990). The calculations are described in section 13.1.3.

Following the design, the installation is erected. It is necessary to check that the realised installation actually complies with the requirements and a test is required on completion. This involves measurements. The completion test is carried out by measuring the illuminance in streets where that is the basis for the design. See section 10.5. The luminance must be measured in roads where the luminance is the basis for the design. A number of methods exist for measuring the luminance on roads. Most of these are cumbersome and often not sufficiently accurate. Better methods are badly needed. In addition, the various methods often produce results which can differ to a considerable extent. A system of certification relating to measuring methods is therefore also desirable. The luminance measurements are dealt with further in section 5.4.7, and measurement of the reflective properties of road surfaces, in addition to the measurements of the illuminance and the luminance, in section 5.4.8.

As long as a direct completion test cannot be carried out for luminance measurements, NSVV recommends measuring the horizontal illuminance as an intermediate step (NSVV, 1993). This is clearly an undesirable situation; a good, generally accepted method for measuring luminance on roads is therefore urgently required. This necessity is underlined by the recent developments relating to liability and responsibility. European legislation requires that the installation complies with the requirements, not only when new, but also during the whole service life (see sections 3.4.2 and 3.4.3). Measurements during the period when the installation is in use are therefore urgently required.

5.4.4 Point measurements: the measuring grid

Most measurements are point measurements. This means that a point is marked on the road where the illuminance, the luminance or the road reflection is measured. It should be remembered that in practice a 'point' is not infinitely small. The 'dimensions' of the points are not negligible in luminance and reflection measurements. A measuring grid is required for point measurements. One tries to select a measuring grid which is equal to the grid used in the calculations, for obvious reasons. This point will be looked at again when discussing lighting calculations (section 13.1.3). There are also integral measurements where any dimensions of 'points' produce no problems. I will deal with this more fully later.

The results of the measurements depend on the density of the grid. A considerable number of points is required to determine the average illuminance. But for determining the uniformity, the grid often needs to be considerably more 'dense'. The number of points, and the pattern of distribution across the road surface, is still the subject of discussion. CIE has established a number of guidelines, which do not always produce the 'correct' answer and which are not always consistent (CIE, 1976, 1990). NSVV (1997) therefore proposed to review the definitions of points and grids (see section 5.4.6).

The grid is usually set out on the road surface. This causes no problems when measuring the illuminance. It is necessary to ensure that the photocell is horizontally placed; sometimes a correction needs to be made for the fact that the photocell sticks out above the road – even if only a couple of centimetres. However, one should certainly take into consideration the characteristics of the measuring grid for luminance measurements. Section 5.4.7 on luminance measurements deals with this further.

5.4.5 Measuring illuminance

We can be brief with regard to the measuring of horizontal illuminance on the road surface. This subject is one of the classics in the discipline of lighting; the principles can be found in the textbooks by De Boer, ed., (1967); Helbich (1972); Keitz (1967) and Reeb (1962). In particular the old, but not yet obsolete, book by Walsh (1958) is recommended. A recent overview can be found in Part II of the new NSVV recommendations (NSVV, 1993) which deals with this subject. See also CIE (1990). The measurement of horizontal illuminance, particularly in public lighting, is discussed in Schreuder (1967a, section 8.1).

The measuring equipment is subject to great demands, in four respects

- Firstly, the light levels to be measured can be very low. A minimum of 0.1 lux or even less in residential streets is not exceptional. In order to assess the uniformity, the minimum values in particular must be well-known; the equipment must be very sensitive to measure such a value reasonably accurately at least up to 0.01 lux. However, this is not a problem with the modern digital luxmeters. Regular calibration is necessary. Usually an annual calibration is recommended.
- Secondly, the angle dependence of the photocell must correspond properly with the cosine distribution (the cosine correction or angle correction). The reason for this is that a considerable proportion of the luminous flux to be measured falls on the road surface at a striking angle while the light may come from many directions simultaneously. Even modern luxmeters do not all perform equally well in this respect; special attention should be paid to the selection of the photocell. See Schreuder (1967a). The cosine correction is particularly important when measuring horizontal illuminance, but the correction in other illuminances should also be correct.
- Thirdly, the photocell, in combination with the meter, must be very accurately geared to the eye sensitivity curve. The colour correction must satisfy strict requirements. The reason for this is that light sources with narrow spectral lines (SL, PL, SON) and often even monochromatic light sources (SOX) are used in street lighting. In addition, lamps of various types are used in many installations simultaneously, so that the traditional trick to deploy conversion factors can no longer be applied. Modern luxmeters do vary in this respect also, and special attention is required here (see Baer, 1990, page 161).
- Fourthly, the top surface of the detector should be exactly horizontal, in particular when measuring horizontal illuminance. The same characteristics which demand a very accurate angle correction (striking and multidirectional light incidence) demand a very accurate horizontal setting. A cardan mount is required, and regular adjustment is necessary, even with this.

A number of factors should be monitored, or otherwise also measured, after which the results should be corrected. This relates to dampness, meteorological visibility, the flatness of the road, the constancy of the mains voltage, any stray light present etc. A comprehensive list of all possible types of fault factors is supplied in Part II of the NSVV Recommendations. See NSVV (1993).

As well as the common horizontal illuminance, other types of illuminance are used in special cases. Vertical illuminance plays an important role in road lighting, but particularly in the lighting of entrances to traffic tunnels. Semicylindrical illuminance is sometimes used in residential streets as a criterion. See chapter 9. The definition is given in section 5.2.2. However, the definition can be interpreted differently and the measurement itself is difficult. Some companies supply accessories for their equipment with which this value can be measured directly, but the accuracy is not always exactly known. This is due to the difficulty of calibrating semicylindrical illuminance. Finally, the sporadically applied hemispheric illuminance: measurement of which does not produce any special difficulty. All types of illuminance suffer from the fault factors mentioned above, although of course not all to the same extent.

5.4.6   The definition of luminance in road lighting
The measuring distance
As will be explained in section 9.1.2, luminance is the most important quality criterion for road lighting. This relates, of course, to luminance as seen by the participant in traffic; on the road this implies the driver of a motor vehicle. This means that we are concerned with the luminance of part of a road, which is a considerable distance away from the driver. As described by Schreuder (1967), the relevant area is usually taken to be 60 to 160 metres. This distance is based on the consideration that a driver must be able to stop when encountering an obstacle on the road. The stopping distance can be determined with the aid of the well-known formula

$$s = \beta v + \frac{v^2}{2a} \qquad\qquad [5.4.1]$$

in which

s	is the stopping distance in m
v	the speed in m/s
a	retardation in m/s^2
β	the reaction time in s

Table 5.4.1 shows the stopping distance for a number of combinations of these variables.

One can deduce from this table that the stopping distance depends on the reaction time, but even more on the starting speed and the retardation. See also section 8.2.2. We also see that the distance of 60 to 160 metres, as given

Table 5.4.1: *Stopping distances (metres) in relation to reaction time β in seconds), the starting speed (ν, in m/s and the retardation (a, in m/s²)*

β	a	v	s	v	s	v	s	v	s
1	2	10	35	20	120	30	255	50	675
3	2	10	55	20	160	30	315	50	775
1	5	10	20	20	60	30	120	50	300
3	5	10	40	20	100	30	180	50	400
1	7	10	17	20	48	30	94	50	229
3	7	10	37	20	89	30	154	50	328

by Schreuder (1967), and certainly the average value of 100 metres, is rather arbitrary, but it corresponds with reasonable assumptions with regard to traffic. The convention that the measuring distance lies between 60 and 160 metres with the focus on 100 metres would therefore seem to correspond well with road traffic practice. I will return to the relation between the observation distance and the stopping distance in section 8.2.2, when discussing the preview, in particular for higher speeds. I will also discuss there the various manoeuvres relating to traffic and the relevance of the stopping manoeuvre.

The angle of perception

The angle α between the measuring direction, which by convention coincides with the direction of sight is, again by convention, set to 1° with the horizontal. This angle is also used for the R tables to be discussed in section 10.4.1. See figure 5.4.4.

It is also agreed that the luminance of a point on the road is always measured and/or calculated with the position of the observer at a height of 1.5 metres above the road surface. These two basic assumptions together imply that the observation distance is always 85.935 m. The observation distance of 85.935 m is rounded up to 86 m. This value lies between the previously mentioned values of 60 and 160 m, and not too far removed from the 'focus' which has been set to a distance of 100 m. As point measurements are always measured with $\alpha = 1^{\circ}$, this is also called the co-moving observer. Further details are given in CEN (1995) and CIE (1995, 1995a). See figure 5.4.5. It should

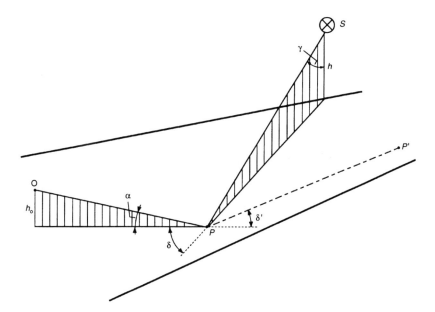

Figure 5.4.4: The geometry for measurements and calculations in public lighting. Line P– P' is parallel to the road axis/direction of movement. O is the observer; S is the light source; P is the measuring point

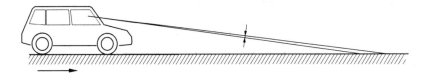

Figure 5.4.5: *The co-moving observer*

be noted that, resulting from the fact that all luminance meters have an aperture angle greater than zero, a 'point' on the road is not a mathematical point but rather a small area. See table 5.4.2 on page 69.

The following may help to explain this. The definition of the co-moving observer presently applies to the calculation of the road surface luminance in points and for the average luminance derived from the point values, as well as for the uniformity, as this is always based on the reflection of the road surface for which α is constant. The co-moving observer also applies to a number of methods for calculating 'disability glare' (see section 7.3.2). However, it does not apply to all methods, nor does it apply to the 'discomfort glare' discussed in section 7.3.3. In addition, a different height is used for the observer, e.g. 1.2 or 1.25 m. The most common measuring instruments, however, for integral measurements as well as for spot measurements can only be used from a fixed observation position at a constant measuring height; this implies that α is variable.

An exception is formed by the measuring method, where a moving measuring installation and a meter with a 'line scan' CCD chip is used. Here α is constant; the observer in fact co-moves (Schreuder & Van de Velde, 1995;

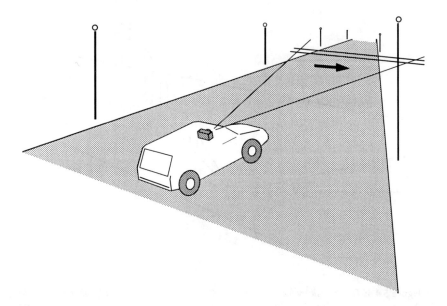

Figure 5.4.6: *The 'line scan' luminance meter*

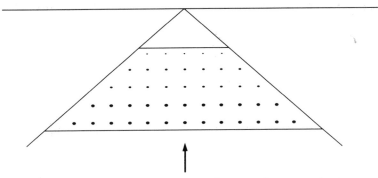

Figure 5.4.7: *Measuring points distributed equally across the perspective image, seen perspectively*

Schreuder, 1996). See figure 5.4.6.

As indicated above, the convention is, that the point from which the measurements are taken is situated at a height of 1.5 m. This value is supposed to represent the eye level of the driver. This no longer applies to modern cars, nor does it apply to trucks. The consequences of a change in this convention, however, are so great that the value is maintained (CIE,1995; NSVV, 1996).

Most methods commonly used for measuring luminance use fixed observation positions. This means that the measurement in fact takes place in a part of the perspective road image. The luminance is measured at a number of points which are distributed on the road surface in the form of a grid. The points may be distributed evenly across the perspective image. See figures 5.4.7 and 5.4.8.

The measuring points may also be distributed evenly across the road. See figures 5.4.9 and 5.4.10.

The distribution across the perspective road image is suitable when using an integrating meter. Both distributions can be used with a spotmeter, but usually an even distribution across the road is used, as this suits the calculations better. However, it is not perfect. This is due, firstly, to the variations in the observation angle α, mentioned above, and secondly to the fact that the measuring points become larger as the points are further

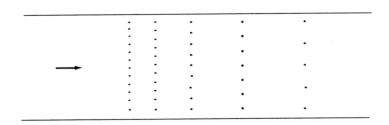

Figure 5.4.8: *Measuring points distributed equally across the perspective image; top view*

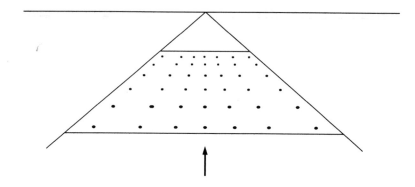

Figure 5.4.9: *Measuring points distributed equally across the road; seen perspectively*

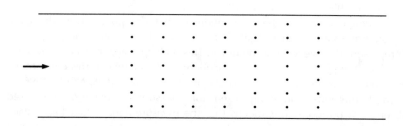

Figure 5.4.10: *Measuring points distributed equally across the road; top view*

removed from the observation position (see table 5.4.2).

As mentioned before, this means that the observation angle is not constant; it varies, in fact, from approximately 40 to approximately 100 arc minutes. It is therefore not possible to compare the results of a measurement with a fixed observation position with the calculations which have been produced with the aid of a co-moving observer. But in practice it would seem that the discrepancies are small for common street lighting installations, and they can usually be ignored. This applies to measurements with an integrating meter as well as to those carried out with a spotmeter.

The measuring point

As already mentioned, the measuring points become larger the further they are from the observation position. This is shown in figure 5.4.11 (vertical view).

The dimensions of the measuring point in current geometry are given in table 5.4.2. This table shows that the measuring point is quite large, and that in particular the length increases considerably when the distance is increased. This gives rise to one of the advantages of the co-moving observer defined above, as not only α (or its complement β) remains the same, but also the dimensions of the measuring point. Also, the measuring point for asphalt and concrete roads is large in relation to the unevenness which can occur as a result of the dimensions of the stone aggregate, but not compared with other

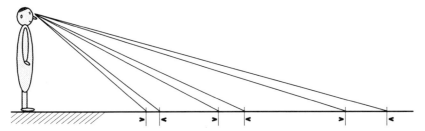

Figure 5.4.11: *The measuring points became larger when the distance to the observation position increases*

Table 5.4.2: *Dimensions of the measuring point*

	Distance to measuring point (m)		
	60	**100**	**160**
Measuring height (m)	1.5	1.5	1.5
β (90 - α) (degrees)	88.568	89.141	89.463
$\delta\beta$ (2') (degrees)	0.033	0.033	0.033
$\beta - \delta\beta$ (degrees)	88.535	89.108	89.430
length δx (m)	1.35	3.70	9.34
δ (δ) (20') (degrees)	0.333	0.333	0.333
width δy (m)	0.349	0.582	0.931

irregularities such as repair patches. Nor is the measuring point in streets large in relation to the street elements (clinker or concrete stones). This is important for the determination of the reflective properties of road surfaces; see section 5.4.8. The determination of the measuring area given here applies to a measuring area of 2′; as will become clear, this is approximately the minimum which can still be managed easily. Point measurements with a fixed location are not therefore a very happy compromise.

Problems with the more common definitions

There are several drawbacks associated with currently common definitions of luminance, respectively the illuminance in public lighting. The main drawbacks are

- the definitions are themselves not always consistent
- the definitions for the averages, non-uniformities and glare are not always mutually consistent
- the definitions for luminance and for illuminance are not geared to one another
- the definitions used for the measurements and those for the calculations sometimes conflict with each other.

The three most important reasons for these discrepancies are discrepancies in the definition of the observation position, the difference in systems used to define grid points and the cross-wise position of the observer for different conditions. Presently a proposal has been offered for discussion in the appropriate working parties of NSVV, CIE and CEN. The purpose of the proposal is to eliminate a number of these problems. See also CIE (1995) and NSVV (1997).

5.4.7 Measuring the luminance of the road surface

Theoretically it is not very difficult to measure the luminance of light sources. I indicated in section 5.4.2 that the luminous intensity, the illuminance and the distance can be determined with the use of the inverse square law (section 5.3.1). When the surface, or 'area' of the light source is known, the luminance can be determined by dividing the luminous intensity by this area. The measurement of the illuminance was discussed above (section 5.4.5).

Current luminance meters all use basically the same method. As indicated in section 5.4.1, the detector determines the total incidence energy (or 'power'). This energy corresponds with the average luminance within the measuring area, after proper calibration. The measuring area is quite large for simple meters, such as photo exposure meters, which in fact are also luminance meters; the measuring area is usually 1 degree for the commonly termed 'spotmeters', for the more expensive types this is 0.25 degrees. As follows from section 5.4.6, this measuring area is much too large for street lighting applications. Table 5.4.2 shows, that even a measuring area of two arc minutes (2') can lead to quite large measuring points on the road.

The problem only arises when measuring the luminance of very small or very weak light sources, or of planes which reflect light, and which can be considered as indirect sources of light. In public lighting we are dealing with both problems at once, in particular when determining uniformity. The luminance of very small parts of the road must be determined, which in addition have a very low luminance. Moreover, the measuring instrument must be aimed very precisely. Some typical values: a point is often characterised by a solid angle which is 2' high and 20' wide, viewed from the position of the luminance meter. Section 5.4.6 showed that even such a small measuring area as this can lead to an unhappy compromise. As regards the light level, the lowest value for the minimum luminance in common lighting installations often amounts to 0.01 cd/m^2; or even less for wet roads.

In integrated measurements, the average of the road surface luminance is determined with one measurement. These measurements are in principle a little less difficult, as the luminous flux, which falls on the detector in the instrument, is considerably larger than in point measurements, so that the demands in relation to sensitivity are a little less strict. However, the average luminance is not sufficient to describe the quality of an installation for public lighting – uniformity remains one of the requirements.

Until recently, the combination of these requirements meant that measurements of luminance in road lighting were impossible. Although an instrument with which the average road surface luminance could be measured was developed, and even marketed in a limited series, some 30 years ago, this instrument was very difficult to operate and the accuracy was not perfect. Moreover, point luminance cannot really be measured. See e.g.

Schreuder (1967a). The instrument has long been taken out of production. A number of companies produce luminance meters, sometimes of very good quality and with a sufficiently small measuring area. These meters are very expensive – £30,000 or more – and difficult to operate, making them impractical for routine measurements on roads.

Another problem relates to the difficulty in finding the correct grid point and to ensure that the meter is accurately aimed at this point. As is clear from figure 5.4.8, the alignment must be accurate to one or two arc minutes – not an easy task on roads! In addition, these measurements can only be used to check the requirements relating to light level and uniformity. It is not possible to compare the actual glare with the glare requirements.

The application of television techniques seemed to promise an improvement, but practical problems, especially the afterglow of the cathode-ray tube, rendered routine applications impossible. See Dalderop (1986).

Modern micro-electronics also offer a number of possibilities with which luminance measurements in road lighting can, in principle, be carried out. Here CCDs (charge coupled devices; in fact a very large number of microscopic tiny photocells which are grouped on a single chip) are used. The relevant photofluxes can be captured very easily with a CCD; the available software for image processing allows us to derive the luminance patterns from the relevant photofluxes (see Serres (1990) and Frank & Damasky (1990)). CIE sponsored a symposium in Liège (Belgium) in 1994, where the 'state of the art' with regard to luminance measurements was presented (see Rossi, ed., 1996). On that occasion a system using a 'line scan CCD', was presented. Section 5.4.6 mentioned that the 'co-moving observer' can be realised with such an installation. The method is described in Schreuder & Van de Velde (1995) and Schreuder (1996). See also figure 5.4.6.

5.4.8   Measuring the reflective properties of road surfaces
For a meaningful application of the methods for the calculation of the luminance of a lighting installation, the reflective properties of the respective road surface must be known. The measurement of reflective properties of road surfaces will be briefly touched on in this section.

The reflection of road surfaces is determined by measuring the luminance of a point on the road, which is illuminated in a known way. A decisive factor is the dimension of the measuring area of that point. Road surfaces, and in particular asphalt roads, have rather a coarse structure. It should be noted at this point that the structure of a road surface should not be confused with its texture. Usually, the grit in the aggregate used is approximately 1 cm in diameter, but sometimes even larger stones are used. In order to arrive at a representative value for the reflection, the measuring area should, of course, be large in relation to the diameter of the pieces of grit. A comprehensive study has shown that a sufficiently large measuring area is obtained by using five drill cores 15 cm in diameter, the effective diameter being approximately 12 cm, and that these should each be measured twice, for common asphalt road surfaces in The Netherlands (SCW, 1974, page 67). This corresponds to a surface area of approximately 1100 cm^2. Usually a good approximation can be obtained by taking three cores, each measured twice (SCW, 1974, page 71). Sometimes the cores are only measured once, and from this the often mentioned minimum surface area of approximately 400 cm^2 stems. If this were done with one measurement, then the sample should measure at least 20 × 20 cm.

It is questionable whether modern road surfaces such as porous asphalt ('ZOAB') or profiled concrete still satisfies this requirement (see also section 10.3). One suspects, although there is no proof, that the 'sample' should be considerably larger for such road surfaces. The same applies to other countries, e.g. in Belgium and the UK, where road surfaces with a much coarser aggregate are commonly used.

It should also be remembered that the reflective factors are defined based on the assumption that the beams of incident light and the light which is measured, are parallel. These conditions impose strict limitations on the measuring conditions, in particular on the dimensions of the measuring installation. It is difficult to say exactly how large the deviation from the parallel may be. This can be estimated, based on the fact that the end of an R table (see section 10.4.1) includes angles with a tangent of 11.5 and 12. This corresponds with angles of 85.03° and 85.23°. The difference is 0.20° or 33'. The resolution of the measuring instrument must therefore be considerable larger. We cannot say exactly how much larger.

Complete R tables are measured in laboratory installations. The method is described in SCW (1974). The principle is simple: a light source is moved around a road surface sample in a goniophotometer; the luminance is recorded and read as often as is required. Usually, the distance from the light source to the road surface sample is at least a couple of metres. Sometimes the goniophotometer is replaced by a straight rail. See Schreuder (1967a). The measurements are complicated and costly. Only a small number of measuring installations have been constructed, of which most are no longer used. The results of these measurements are published in several atlases. The most complete one is by Erbay (1974). See also Erbay (1973) and Erbay & Stolzenberg (1975).

Measurements have been produced in Canada based on the same principle (Jung et al., 1983). The photometer expressly constructed for this, however, is considerably smaller: the light source was only 68 cm above the road surface. This height lies only just within the photometric threshold distance, but it is questionable whether this is sufficient for a reflective surface like that of a road. The core is 15 cm in diameter; each core was measured three times. In total, 400 cores were measured, taken from 100 road surfaces across the whole of Canada. The final conclusion was that the $Q_0 - S_1 - S_2$ classification, described in section 10.4.2, is useful.

As this method is cumbersome and costly, a method for measuring on roads has long been sought. The limitations mentioned above apply to an even greater extent. An instrument was developed in Denmark a number of years ago, where the R table was approximated by measuring the luminance factor in eight directions (Anon, 1979a). The device is no longer considered to be up-to-date; it is only used for lack of a better one. One problem is that the eight directions are not exactly known. More recently Schreuder (1991) described a method whereby the measuring area is only a couple of centimetres square; much smaller than what we called a 'point' above. In order to realise the measuring area of 400 cm^2, many of these 'micropoints' must be measured sequentially. Section 10.4.2 returns to this method and details some results.

Bibliography

Anon. (1979). *16. Generalkonferenz für Mass und Gewicht.* Paris, 1979 (cit.: Hentschel, 1994, page 37).

Anon. (1979a). *Instruction manual; Portable road surface reflectometer LTL 200.* The Danish Illuminating Engineering Laboratory, 1979.

Baer, R. (1990). *Beleuchtungstechnik; Grundlagen.* Berlin, VEB Verlag Technik, 1990.

Breuer, H. (1994). *DTV-Atlas zur Physik, Band 1.* 4. Auflage. München, Deutsche Taschenbuchverlag DTV, 1994.

Budding, E. (1993). *An introduction to astronomical photometry.* Cambridge University Press, 1993.

CEN (1995). *Lighting applications and road equipment; Road lighting, calculation of performance* (Draft 4, January 1995) CEN/TC 169/226 JWG 'road lighting', 1995.

CIE (1932). *Receuil des travaux et compte rendue des scéances, Huitième Session Cambridge – Septembre 1931.* Cambridge, University Press, 1932.

CIE (1973). *Photometry of luminaires for street lighting.* Publication No. 27. Paris, CIE, 1973.

CIE (1976). *Glare and uniformity in road lighting installations.* Publication No. 31. Paris, CIE, 1976.

CIE (1977). *Road lighting lanterns and installation data: Photometrics, classification and performance.* Publication No. 34. Paris, CIE, 1977.

CIE (1978). *Light as a true visual quantity: Principles of measurement.* Publication No. 41. Paris, CIE, 1978.

CIE (1989). *Mesopic photometry: History, special problems and practical solutions.* Publication No. 81. Paris, CIE, 1989.

CIE (1990). *Calculation and measurement of luminance and illuminance in road lighting.* Publication No. 30/2. Paris, CIE, 1982 (reprinted 1990).

CIE (1991). *Proceedings 22th Session, Melbourne, Australia, July 1991.* Publication No. 91. Paris, CIE, 1992.

CIE (1995). *Road lighting calculations* (Revision of CIE Publication No. 30.2). First draft. Vienna, January 1995.

CIE (1995a). *Recommendations for the lighting of roads for motor and pedestrian traffic.* Technical Report. Publication No. 115-1995. Vienna, CIE, 1995.

Dalderop, R. (1986). 'The video luminance system'. *The Lighting Journal* 1986 (year estimated).

De Boer, J.B. (ed.). (1967). *Public lighting.* Eindhoven, Centrex, 1967.

Erbay, A. (1973). *Verfahren zur Kennzeichnung der Reflexionseigenschaften von Fahrbahndecken.* Dissertation Technische Universität Berlin, 1973.

Erbay, A. (1974). *Reflective properties of road surfaces.* Atlas published by the Technical University Berlin, 1974.

Erbay, A. & Stolzenberg, K. (1975). Reflexionsdaten von allen praktisch vorkommenden trockenen Fahrbahnbelägen. *Lichttechnik* **27** (1975) 58–61.

Feynman, R.P.; Leighton, R.B. & Sands, M. (1977). *The Feynman lectures on physics*. Three volumes. 1963; 6th printing 1977. Reading (Mass.), Addison-Wesley Publishing Company, 1977.

Frank, H. & Damsky, J. (1990). Entwicklung eines mobilen Messsystems zur Untersuchung der lichttechnischen Eigenschaften des Strassenraumes bei Dunkelheit. In: *NSVV*, 1990a.

Gershun, A. (1939). The light field (original title 'Svetovoe pole', Moscow, 1936). Translated by Moon & Timoshenko. *Journal of Mathematics and Physics* **18** (1939) No. 2, May, pp 51-151.

Helbig, E. (1972). *Grundlagen der Lichtmesstechnik*. Leipzig, Geest & Portig, 1972.

Hentschel, H.J. (1994). *Licht und Beleuchtung; Theorie und Praxis der Lichttechnik*. 4., neubearbeitete Auflage. Heidelberg, Hüthig Buch Verlag, 1994.

Jung, W.; Titishov, A.I. & Kazakov. A. (1983). *Road surface reflectance measurements in Ontario*. Preprint TRB Annual Meeting 1984. Washington, D.C., TRB, 1984.

Keitz, H.A.E. (1967). *Lichtmessungen und Lichtberechnungen*. 2. Auflage. Eindhoven, Philips Technische Bibliotheek, 1967.

Moon, P. (1961). *The scientific basis of illuminating engineering*. (Revised edition). New York, Dover Publications, Inc., 1961.

Moon, P. & Spencer, D.E. (1981). *The photic field*. Cambridge (Mass.), The MIT Press, 1981.

NSVV (1990). *Aanbevelingen voor openbare verlichting*; Deel I [Recommendations for public lighting; Part I]. Arnhem, NSVV, 1990.

NSVV (1990a). *Licht90. Tagungsberichte Gemeinschaftstagung, Rotterdam, 21–23 Mai, 1990*. Arnhem, NSVV, 1990.

NSVV (1993). *Aanbevelingen voor openbare verlichting*; Deel II: Meten en berekenen [Recommendations for public lighting; Part II: Measurements and calculations]. Arnhem, NSVV, 1993.

NSVV (1997). *Aanbevelingen voor openbare verlichting*; Deel III: Ontwerpen [Recommendations for public lighting; Part III: Designs]. Arnhem, NSVV, 1997.

Philips (1985). *Correspondence course lighting applications*. Eindhoven, Philips International B.V., 1985.

Reeb, O. (1962). *Grundlagen der Photometrie*. Karlsruhe, Verlag G. Braun, 1962.

Rossi, G. (ed.) (1996). *International workshop and intercomparison of luminance CCD measurement systems*. Liège, Belgium, 23 September 1994. CIE, 1996 Draft.

Schreuder, D.A. (1967). Theoretical basis of road-lighting design. Chapter 3 in: De Boer (ed.), 1967.

Schreuder, D.A. (1967a). Measurements. Chapter 8 in: De Boer (ed.), 1967.

Schreuder, D.A. (1991). A device to measure road reflection in situ. In: CIE (1991).

Schreuder, D.A. (1996). A CCD line-scan system for road luminance measurement. *Traffic Engineering and Control* **37** (1996) 208–209.

Schreuder, D.A. & Van de Velde, A. (1995). *A CCD line-scan measuring system for road surface luminance*. In: Rossi, ed. (1995).

Serres, A.-M. (1990). *Les images pour les études de visibilité de nuit*. Bull. Liais. Labo. P. et Ch. 165 (1990) jan-fév. 65–72.

Sterken, C. & Manfroid, J. (1992). *Astronomical photometry*. Dordrecht, Kluwer, 1992.

Walsh, J.W.T. (1958). *Photometry* 3rd Edition. London, Constable, 1958.

Wright, W.D. (1967). *The rays are not coloured*. London, Adam Hilger, 1967.

6 The anatomy and physiology of the visual system

Participation in traffic requires a large amount of information which is collected on line and in real time in today's traffic conditions and relates to one's channel of visual perception. The role which public lighting can play in supporting the collection and processing of visual information necessitates a rather detailed discussion, starting with the anatomy and the physiology of the visual system.

6.1 The structure of the human visual system

6.1.1 The general structure

This section offers an outline of the anatomy and the physiology of the visual system which is very complex in both people and most animals. The traditional anatomy is described in detail in the anatomical textbooks such as, e.g. Davies, ed., (1969). For the present discussion I have used the recent publication by Crick (1994). This publication discusses the visual system for illustrative purposes, based on theories which are not relevant here. See also Gregory (1965) and Philips (1989).

The human visual system consists of five main parts

- the optical parts of the eye
- the retina with the photoreceptors
- the nerve cells or neurones in the eye
- the visual nerve trajectories
- the cortex.

The first three are situated in the eyeball; the latter two are located in the brain within the skull. The parts and their location in relation to each other are illustrated in figure 6.1.1.

The eyeball is, as the word indicates, a more or less spherical organ, which contains – in addition to the 'active' parts – many elements that are not directly related to vision. One of these relates to the iris, which is important for adaptation (see section 7.2.3), and the aperture of the pupil.

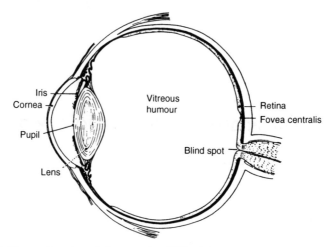

Figure 6.1.1: *The construction of the eye; after Philips, 1989*

6.1.2   Optical parts: the eye lens

The optical parts of the eye create an optical image of the external world on the retina. The optical parts comprise

- the cornea
- the lens
- the pupil
- the retina.

As far as the optical image is concerned, the eye is almost exactly rotationally symmetrical. The rotational axis is the symmetry axis or optical axis of the eye. The fovea centralis discussed below (section 6.1.5) is situated on the optical axis. We achieve the sharpest focus when we look straight ahead.

The eye as an imaging instrument may be compared with a video camera. The optical image is mainly created by the cornea. The eye lens also contributes, particularly in so far as the focusing of the image is concerned. This accommodation can be compared with the distance regulation or focusing in a camera. See figure 6.1.2. This focusing deforms the eye lens, see figure 6.1.3. As the eye lens hardens with age, accommodation becomes more difficult over the years; this is called presbyopia.

Finally, the retina may be compared with the light-sensitive part of the video camera – the CCD. In essence, both produce a digitised image. See section 6.1.3.

In common with all optical image instruments, the eye also has its imaging errors. See Van Heel (1950) for the theory and for the detailed discussion of this in respect of optical instruments. The errors in the visual system can sometimes be even greater than for optical instruments, due to the non-ideal construction of the optical parts, but sometimes also less, as the visual system possesses certain psychological facilities for correction. These may partly compensate for monochromatic imaging errors. This subject will be returned to in chapter 7.

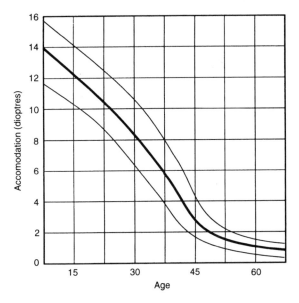

Figure 6.1.2: *Accommodation related to age*

Heterochromatic imaging errors in particular are important in public lighting. These are created because the refraction index of all optical media, including those of the cornea and the eye lens, depend on the wavelength of the light. This results in the fact, that the focusing distance of a lens for blue light, with a small wavelength, is smaller than for red light, with a larger

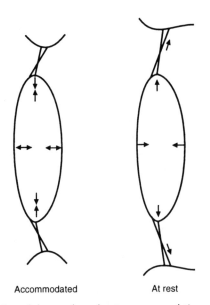

Accommodated   At rest

Figure 6.1.3: *Deformation of the eye lens due to accommodation*

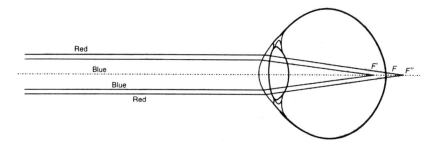

Figure 6.1.4: *Heterochromatic imaging errors – F': the focus for blue light, F'': the focus for red light. F: the 'average' focus*

wavelength. The dimensions of the image for blue light are different, usually smaller, than for red light. These errors are not affected by the dimensions of the pupil opening. Other correction facilities are also hardly or not at all effective. See figure 6.1.4.

However, they are not present in the monochromatic light in low-pressure sodium lamps. This means that visual performance for this type of lamp is consistently better than for light sources which emit more or less white light. This point plays a large role in the preference which is given to low-pressure sodium lamps in road lighting. Van Bommel & De Boer (1980, page 59) state as their conclusion that for equal visual acuity (see section 7.2.3) the road surface lighted by high-pressure mercury lamps must have a luminance which is 50% higher than for light in low-pressure sodium lamps; the figure for high-pressure sodium lamps is 25% higher. Van Bommel & De Boer (1980, chapter 4) offer an overview of the available literature in this field. See also De Boer (1967) and, for much of the original research, De Boer (1951).

Additional advantages of monochromatic light have also been mentioned. One of these is less sensitivity to psychological glare (see section 7.3.3). It is not certain whether this is the result of the monochromatic character or of the geometry of the lamp. Other advantages, especially concerning the subjective evaluation of lighting installations, have not always been confirmed by other researches.

Another advantage of low-pressure sodium lamps is that the greatest part of the light is emitted in a wavelength to which the eye is very sensitive; the sodium line is situated close to the top of the eye sensitivity curve (see section 5.1.3). This leads directly to a possible disadvantage: as a result of the Purkinje effect described in section 6.2.1, the sodium light is less effective than white light at very low luminances.

6.1.3   The retina: photoreceptors
Photoreceptors capture the light and convert it into electrical impulses. The visual pigment serves as an intermediary step. These are protein-type substances which are activated by the energy of the incidenting light quanta. The chemical aspects of this activation will be touched upon in the discussion on adaptation (sections 6.4, 7.2.4 and 7.2.5).

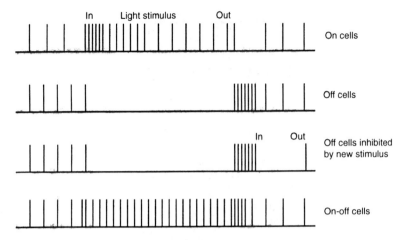

Figure 6.1.5: *Some examples of bursts in so-called 'on' and 'off' receptors; based on Hentschel, 1994, fig. 1.10*

The receptors are, in fact, neurones or nerve cells. This means that they can convert certain chemical signals into electrical signals. Several types of receptors exist, i.e. rods and cones. These are explained in section 6.1.4. Part of the light quanta which fall on a photoreceptor are absorbed. Only 3 to 4 light quanta incidenting on the receptor within the required time of some milliseconds suffice to cause a reaction for rods; sometimes even less light quanta are required (Weale, 1968, page 27). The quantum efficiency of cones is considerably less.

The energy of the light quantum, the stimulus, initiates a neuronal reaction which consists of 'firing' spikes, these are short electrical impulses, which are conducted along the nerve trajectories. A short flash of light causes a short series of spikes, a 'burst'. When the light is extinguished, the receptor returns to the rest condition. If the light continues, the delivery of spikes will also continue for some time, usually no longer than a few seconds. The frequency of the spikes is subsequently reduced, and returns to the rest level, even when the illumination continues. Figure 6.1.5 shows some examples.

6.1.4 Rods and cones
The image is formed on the rear of the eye. This rear wall is covered by the retina. The retina contains two types of photoreceptors: rods and cones. They are so-called because of their shape. Figures 6.1.6 and 6.1.7 show a diagram of the retina. The light in these illustrations comes from below.

Rods have only one type of visual pigment, rhodopsin. This means that all light quanta with sufficient energy in the frequency band within which the quanta are absorbed cause the same reaction, irrespective of the frequency of the light. It was shown in chapter 4 that different colours are associated with different frequencies; apparently, rods cannot distinguish between colours. However, they are not equally sensitive to each colour, see the discussion on the eye sensitivity curve (sections 5.1.3 and 6.2.1).

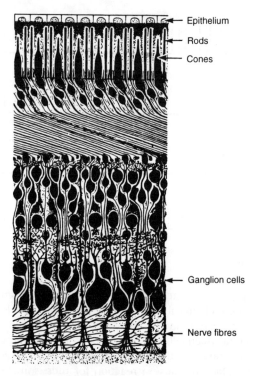

Figure 6.1.6: *The retina; after Philips, 1989*

Cones show a more complicated picture. There are at least three types of cones, each with its own, specific type of visual pigment and sensitivity curve. As the three types of cones are each sensitive to a different colour light, colours can be distinguished based on the collaboration of the cones. This characteristic is used in the fact that nearly any colour can be made by mixing three appropriately selected basic colours. This fact, on which all types of colorimetry are based, will be returned to in section 7.4. The three basic colours, however, are not equal to the sensitivity curves of the three types of cones. In order to derive the three basic colours from the sensitivity curves, complicated summation and difference rules come into play. However, it is not impossible to determine an aggregated eye sensitivity curve for the cones.

6.1.5 Spatial distribution of photoreceptors

The human eye contains a very large number of photoreceptors, some hundreds of millions per eye: by approximation 1.2×10^8 rods and approximately 6×10^6 cones! The rods are distributed across the whole of the retina, with the exception of the centre, the yellow spot, also called macula or fovea centralis. The fovea has no rods; however, in the fovea the cones are packed closely together, so that sharp vision is possible through this area. Cones do appear in the periphery of the retina, but they are less

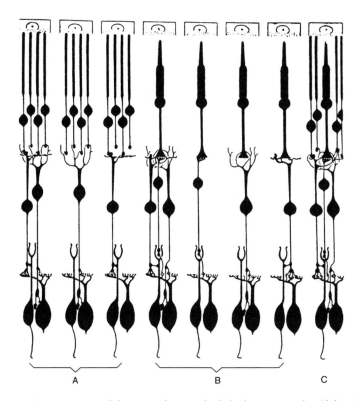

Figure 6.1.7: *Representation of the retina showing the linked receptors; after Philips, 1989*

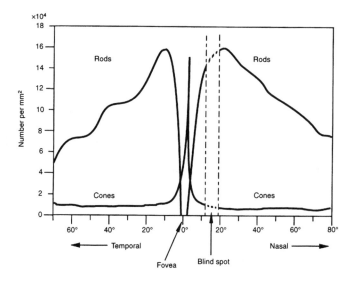

Figure 6.1.8: *Spatial distribution of photoreceptors*

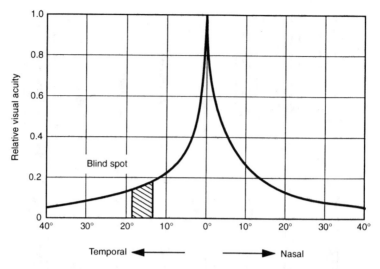

Figure 6.1.9: *The relation between viscual acuity and the retina location; after Hentschel, 1994, based on data from Wertheim*

dense, so that peripheral vision is less sharp than foveal vision (see figure 6.1.8).

As a result, the sharpest vision can be found in the area of the yellow spot located at $0°$ in figure 6.1.9. The 'blind spot' in figures 6.1.8 and 6.1.9 is the place where the optical nerve leaves the eye-ball.

6.2   Eye sensitivity

6.2.1   Photopic and scotopic eye sensitivity: the Purkinje effect

The visual system is not equally sensitive to all wavelengths. Furthermore, the sensitivity depends on whether the cones, the rods, or possibly both at the same time, are active. Moreover, there are three types of cones, each with their own sensitivity. See the discussion on colour in section 7.4 for further details.

It is common practice to depict this total spectral response in graphical form. This is the V_λ curve discussed in section 5.1.3. There, I described how this curve is determined – and its limitations – and showed that there is a separate curve for night vision, the scotopic curve, also called the V_λ' curve. Finally, the existence of a family of mesopic V_λ curves for the intermediate area, twilight vision, was indicated.

The sensitivity curves for rods and cones are similar in shape; there is, however, a shift along the wavelength axis. As a result, red and blue sources of light, which photopically appear to possess a similar brightness, appear to have a completely different brightness in the field of scotopic vision. The blue source of light seems to be much brighter than the red one. This is also called the Purkinje effect, after the researcher who described it initially. Details are given in Helbig (1972, page 25). It should be mentioned that, although as far as scotopic vision is concerned, the blue source of light may appear to be brighter, it is, however, not possible to see the blue colour.

6.2.2   Consequences for practice

In most cases the light level on main roads is higher than approximately 0.1 cd/m^2. This means that we are in the first instance dealing with photopic vision, as well as with the area of mesopic vision, which is immediately adjacent to the photopic area, 'high mesopic' vision. Practice shows, that high mesopic vision is little different from photopic vision, so that we may assume that photopic photometry applies.

This is different for residential areas. As will be explained in section 10.5, lighting is normally considered sufficient when the average illuminance amounts to 2 to 3 lux, as long as the uniformity, i.e. the minimum illuminance divided by the average illuminance, is at least 0.1. The minimum illuminance can therefore be 0.2 lux; this corresponds to approximately 0.01 cd/m^2 for commonly used road surfaces. This level of light is situated in the mesopic area. The Purkinje effect, described in section 6.2.1, allows the light of the yellow low-pressure sodium lamps to cause a relatively low brightness perception in residential streets. The specific luminous flux, see section 13.3.1, is therefore lower in the mesopic area than in the catalogue value, which is based on the photopic value, the photopic lumen. The reverse can be expected for blue tinted mercury lamps. Based on the definition of luminance given in section 5.2.3, and on the information supplied by CIE (see CIE, 1978, 1989), it should be possible to estimate this effect. An unpublished study was conducted in 1984, in which such calculations have been produced. For a luminance of 0.01 cd/m^2, the 'mesopic specific luminous flux' (which has been set at 100% for photopic lumens) amounts to 34% for low-pressure sodium lamps and 68% for high-pressure sodium lamps. The mesopic specific luminous flux is higher in mercury lamps than the photopic luminous flux: 107% in high-pressure mercury lamps with enhanced colour reproduction and 138% in mercury halogenide lamps. The question remains, to what extent these values are significant in practice; they apply to a complete adaptation to the levels in question, which cannot be expected in residential streets, with glare and additional light sources. However, the results are in line with results gathered from evaluations by residents.

6.3   Depth and movement

6.3.1   Depth perception: eye movements

In normal cases, both eyes are used for perception. However, the final conscious process of vision is a single phenomenon; the images of the two eyes are integrated into a single picture in the cortical part of the visual system. Information relating to distance is deducted from the two images on the retina. Both eyes are therefore required to perceive depth. See also Gregory (1965, fig. 4.10); Hopkinson (1967, fig. 2.1 and 2.2) and Crick (1994, chapter 7).

The eye muscles ensure that the eye axes are aimed correctly. Each eye is controlled separately. The eye muscles also take care of changes in the direction of sight. It is not necessary to turn one's head completely in order to look at a certain object. We can turn the eyes, but it proves to be easier to turn the head at an angle of more than approximately 10 to 15 degrees. At an angle of more than 30 degrees, the whole upper body is usually turned. These values are important when siting traffic signals. See also Bunt & Sanders (1973) and Sanders (1967).

6.3.2   Perception of movement
The perception of movement is complex and can only be partially explained. It is clear how the movement of an object is seen when the eyes remain in the

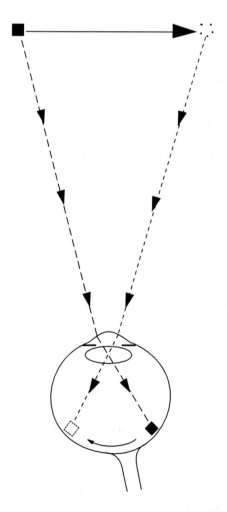

Figure 6.3.1: The perception of movement with the eyes remaining in place

Figure 6.3.2: *The perception of movement when the eyes are moving*

same place: the images of the moving object move across the retina and occupy different places at each moment (see figure 6.3.1). If the object is traced with the eye, the eye muscles are activated. The retina image remains still, but the eyes themselves move (see figure 6.3.2).

The visual system seems to be able to relate the movement of the eyeball and the movement of the retina image to each other. How this is done is only partially known, but constancy plays a role. By this is meant the phenomenon whereby the world seems to remain still when the eyes move, or the body. It would seem that there are feedback systems, where the information from the retina and from the movement muscles of the whole body are related to each other. Gregory (1965, chapter 7) describes a number of simple, but convincing tests. The Gestalt psychologists conducted much research into a number of visual phenomena, including movement phenomena, at the beginning of the century. Overviews can be found in the well-known works by Koffka (1963) and Köhler (1929). Metzger (1953) provides an interesting overview of the possible significance of Gestalt psychology for research into perception. However, very little of this research has been carried out.

6.4   The visual nervous system

6.4.1   Neurones: nerve tracts

Neurones are the building blocks of the nervous system. The construction and the operation of neurones is extremely complex; neurophysiological research has explained much during the last couple of decades, but many unanswered questions remain. A brief overview is given here of a number of aspects which are important for lighting. Further details can be found in the specialist literature; readers can also refer to a number of works which are more accessible, but still reflect the state of the science well. First and foremost, these include the books by Nobel prize winners Crick (1989, 1994) and Edelman (1992). See also Damasio (1994), Dennett (1993), Hubel (1988) and Maturana & Varela (1992).

The anatomy of neurones is reasonably well-known. A neurone or nerve cell is a single cell with a cell body, containing among other things a cell nucleus, just like any cell. A nerve cell is characterised by a 'spur', the axon. Some axons can be as long as a metre. They are, however, extremely thin; the thickness is usual between 10^{-4} and 10^{-3} mm. Both sides of the cell – the cell body and the end of the axon – have smaller protuberances, the dendrites. There are, therefore, two groups of dendrites, one at each side of the cell. The dendrites ensure the contact with other neurones. See figures 6.4.1 and 6.4.2.

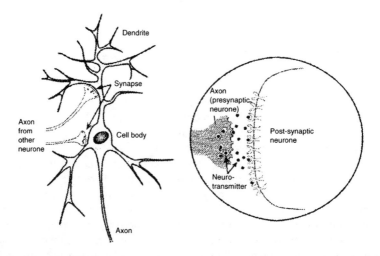

Figure 6.4.1: *Representation of the anatomy of neurones; after Edelman, 1992, fig. 3.2*

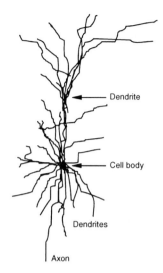

Figure 6.4.2: *Anatomy of a neurone; after Damasio, 1994, fig. 2.6*

The function of neurones is to transmit information. Information arrives at the dendrites on the side of the cell body; they are conducted along the axon and passed on by the dendrites to the dendrites belonging to the next cell. In this way, chains are created; as most neurones on both sides possess a large number of dendrites, which each are in contact with other neurones, a complicated network is created. The information transmission in the neurone itself is of an electrical nature; the information is coded in series of electrical impulses, usually indicated with the term 'spikes'. The intensity of the signal determines the frequency of the spikes; it is therefore a type of frequency modulation. Spikes are also fired at rest. Contact with other neurones is essential for the operation of neurones in a chain or a network.

The location, where the information is transmitted from one cell to the next, is called the synapse. This is the place where the dendrites in one cell are in contact with the dendrites from the next cell. There is a very narrow gap with a width of approximately 25×10^{-6} mm, the synaptic gap. See also figure 6.4.1. The contact itself is very complex, and presently not all details are completely known. Further details can be found in the books by Crick (1994) and Edelman (1992), mentioned above.

Neurones are usually bundled in nerve tracts. The nerve tracts relevant for vision – the eye nerve, optical nerve or nervus opticus – start with the retina and run to the visual cortex. The course of the nerve tract is rather complex. A clear overview is supplied by Voorn (1995) in the introduction to the important Dutch standard opthalmology work by Stilma & Voorn, eds. (1995).

6.4.2   The cerebral cortex
The eye nerve ends in the cerebral cortex which forms the outer part of the large brain. It is a layer, a few millimetres thick, which lies directly below the skull. See figure 6.4.3.

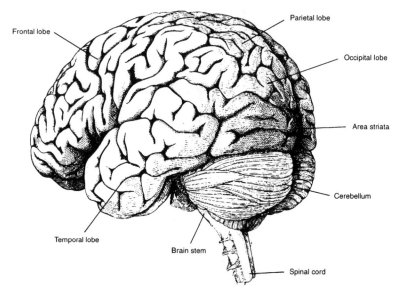

Figure 6.4.3: *The brain seen from the outside; the cortex; after Hubel, 1988, page 3*

Generally speaking, certain bodily or mental functions are linked to certain areas in the cortex. The brain functions related to vision are located in the rear part of the cortex. This section is therefore called the visual cortex. The allocation of functions to areas of the brain, however, is not very strict. It is better to speak of systems, according to Damasio (1994, page 15).

Awareness of visual perception is located at the end of the visual system. Although some progress has been made, described in the books mentioned above, the nature of human consciousness is still essentially unknown. It is certain that the cortex plays an important role. Other parts of the brain also affect consciousness, but there are also indications that other factors besides the operation of the brain also play a role in awareness. This awareness is relevant to a number of aspects in road lighting and will be further discussed in later chapters. I will pass over the difficult philosophical question relating to the nature of consciousness.

Bibliography

Bunt, A.A. & Sanders, A.F. (1973). *Informatieverwerking in het functionele gezichtsveld; Een overzicht van de literatuur* [Information processing in the functional range of vision; an overview of the literature]. Report No. IZF-1973 C-8. Soesterberg, IZF-TNO, 1973.

CIE (1978). *Light as a true isual quantity: Principles of measurement.* Publication No. 41. Paris, CIE, 1978.

CIE (1989). *Mesopic photometry: History, special problems and practical solutions.* Publication No. 81. Paris, CIE, 1989.

Crick, F. (1989). *What mad pursuit; A personal view of scientific discovery.* London, Penguin Books, 1989.

Crick, F. (1994). *The astonishing hypothesis; The scientific search for the soul.* London, Simon & Schuster, 1994 (Touchstone Books, 1995).

Damasio, A. (1994). *Descartes' error: Emotion, reason and the human brain.* New York, Avon books, 1994.

Davies, D.V., (ed.) (1969). *Gray's Anatomy.* Thirty-fourth edition, Second impression. London, Longmans, Green and Co. Ltd., 1969.

De Boer, J.B. (1951) *Fundamental experiments of visibility and admissible glare in road lighting.* Stockholm, CIE, 1951.

De Boer, J.B. (1967). *Visual perception in road traffic and the field of vision of the motorist.* Chapter 2 in: De Boer, ed., (1967).

De Boer, J.B. (ed). (1967). *Public lighting.* Eindhoven, Centrex, 1967.

Dennett, D.C. (1993). *Consciousness explained.* London, Penguin Books Ltd., 1993.

Edelman, G. (1992). *Bright air, brilliant fire; On the matter of the mind.* London, Penguin, 1992.

Gregory, R.L. (1965). *Visuele waarneming; De psychologie van het zien.* [Visual observation; the psychology of seeing.] Wereldakademie; De Haan/Meulenhoff, 1965.

Hentschel, H.J. (1994). *Licht und Beleuchtung; Theorie und Praxis der Lichttechnik.* 4. Neubearbeitete Auflage. Heidelberg, Hüthig Buch Verlag, 1994.

Hopkinson, R.G. (1969). *Lighting and seeing.* London, William Heinemann, 1969.

Hubel, D.H. (1988). *Visuele informatie, Schakelingen in onze hersenen.* [Visual information, Links in our brains]. Wetenschappelijke Bibliotheek, deel 21. Maastricht, Natuur en Techniek, 1988.

Koffka, K. (1963). *Principles of Gestalt psychology.* New York, Harcourt, Brace & World, Inc., 1963.

Köhler, W. (1929). Gestalt psychology. New York, London, 1929.

Maturana, H.R. & Varela, F.J. (1992). *Der Baum der Erkenntnis.* München, Goldmann, 1992.

Metzger, W. (1953). *Gesetze des Sehens.* Frankfurt a/M, Waldemar Kramer, 1953.

Philips (1989). *Correspondence course light application.* Eindhoven, Philips Lighting B.V., 1989.

Sanders, A.F. (1967). *De psychologie van de informatieverwerking.* [The psychology of information processing.] Arnhem, Van Loghum Slaterus, 1967.

Stilma, J.S. & Voorn, Th. B., (eds.) (1995). *Praktische oogheelkunde.* [Practical ophthalmology.] First edition, second imprint with corrections. Houten, Bohn Stafleu Van Loghum, 1995.

Van Bommel, W.J.M. & De Boer, J.B. (1980). *Road lighting.* Deventer, Kluwer, 1980.

Van Heel, A.C.S. (1950). *Inleiding in de optica* [Introduction to optics]. Derde druk. Den Haag, Martinus Nijhoff, 1950.

Voorn, Th.B. (1995). 'Inleiding'. ['Introduction'] Chapter 1 in: Stilma & Voorn, eds., 1995.

Weale, R.A. (1968). *From sight to light.* Edinburgh and London, Oliver and Boyd, 1968.

7 The psycho-physiology of the visual system

As the information required for participation in traffic is of a visual nature, and has to be gathered 'on line' and in 'real time', a considerable amount of knowledge of the visual system is essential in order to gain a proper understanding of the role of public lighting. The anatomy and the physiology of the visual system were discussed in the last chapter. These serve as the basis for a better comprehension of the functions of the visual system in perception. The discussion of these functions is based on the psycho-physiological characteristics of the visual system.

Besides physiology, also psychology, psycho-physics and psycho-physiology are at the centre of research into the visual system. In order to be able to apply the results from this research to road lighting, an understanding of the characteristics and possibilities, but in particular of the limitations of this type of research is required. This relates to the research methods and, in particular, the role which paradigms and models play, as well as the limitations of the usual statistical methods when one is interested in causal relations.

The visual functions are interdependent. Being able to distinguish certain objects is especially important when participating in traffic. The ability to distinguish and, in particular, to be sensitive to contrasts and visual acuity, are central in this context. The operation of the visual system can vary from one moment to another; adaptation is therefore important too. The ability to see colour also deserves attention, in view of the significance of coloured signals in traffic. But the importance of being able to see colours well should not be overestimated. As being able to participate in road traffic. at least as a pedestrian, is considered to be a fundamental right, attention should be paid to visual handicaps and to measures which public lighting can offer to reduce these handicaps.

7.1   Research methods

7.1.1   Physiology and psychology

By physiology one commonly means the study of the functioning of the organism, from a chemical and biological point of view. This used to be called the study of the phenomena of life, such as breathing, metabolism and reproduction. The visual system is part of the nervous system, but also belongs to the brain, viewed from a physiological aspect. Much of the material in chapter 6 belongs to physiology.

By psychology one usually means: the science of human behaviour. This description gives rise to some problems. The concept of science is subject to different interpretations. Studies must meet with a number of conditions before they can claim to be scientific. The main conditions are that

- they should be based on a hypothesis
- the conclusions should be based exclusively on either logic or mathemetics.

People often mean experimental science, when they speak of science. As this method was first used in physics, one can also speak of the natural sciences. This leads to a number of additional conditions

- the research should be replicable (by the same researcher)
- the research should be capable of being duplicated (by other researchers).

Sometimes the stipulation is added that the hypothesis may only be falsified. This condition is not generally accepted in physics: physicists often verify hypotheses.

7.1.2   Psycho-physiological measurements, statistical processing
Statistics

Psychological measurements are often simpler than physical or physiological measurements. The problems concern the processing of the data in particular, besides the interpretation of the results. Often many measure-ments are required which must be processed with the aid of statistical methods. I will touch on a few aspects of statistical methods, as they are important for the application of the science of lighting in public lighting. For the background and for a more thorough discussion on statistics, readers should refer to one of the 'classics' in applied statistics, the well-known book by Moroney (1990) and to the recent book by Buijs (1995), which is often used in higher education in The Netherlands. The mathematical foundation can be found in the no longer recent but very clear book by Dixon & Massey (1957). For the application of statistical methods refer to the older but very comprehensive work by Krech et al. (1969) and the book by Gleitman (1995), presently often used in higher education, which, although more modern, is also less thorough.

I will not go into the collection and the pre-processing of empirical data here. See Moroney (1990). The sample should be quite large. Determination of the minimum sample size is discussed in Dixon & Massey (1957). As psychological and psycho-physiological research relates to a reaction by a living system, which is subject to noise, one does not always see the same reaction. Therefore a threshold value is determined in measurements; by this is meant that value of the stimulus, at which a perception takes place in a set percentage of cases. The concepts of noise and threshold value are explained in detail in Bok (1958, page 159). The percentage for the definition of the threshold value is usually set at 50%. The noise characteristic sometimes causes a stimulus which is weaker than the threshold value, to be followed by a perception, while conversely no perception may occur after a stimulus which is stronger than the threshold value. The dispersion is often characterised by chance.

Normal distribution
Phenomena which are subject to chance are studied in statistics. It can be shown that chance phenomena, also called normal distribution, can be described with a Gaussian distribution, as long as the number of cases is large enough. The derivation is rather difficult; even Dixon & Massey (1957) decline to give it. Figure 7.1.1 shows the normal distribution.

The width of the curve is called the dispersion, mathematically characterised by the standard deviation. See figure 7.1.2.

The data must satisfy a number of conditions for the results to be able to be represented by a normal distribution. In practice this often proves to be the case. And theoretically different distributions, e.g. the binomial distribution and the Poisson distribution, both of which are often seen in traffic safety research, can also often be approximated by a normal distribution. Sometimes a transformation is required. See Buijs (1995, chapters 6 and 7).

Statistically significant differences
Most psychological and psycho-physiological research relates to differences. So it is important for applied lighting to know whether the visual acuity for

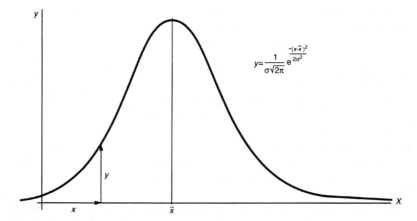

$$y = \frac{1}{\sigma\sqrt{2\pi}}\, e^{\frac{-(x-\bar{x})^2}{2\sigma^2}}$$

Figure 7.1.1: *The normal distribution*

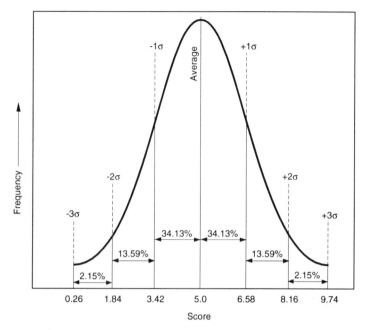

Figure 7.1.2: *The Gaussian normal distribution; σ is the dispersion or standard deviation*

light from low-pressure sodium lamps is better than for light from high-pressure sodium lamps, or to what extent and how far visual performance diminishes with increasing age. A difference is called statistically significant when the averages diverge more than twice the standard deviation. The risk that a difference is concluded erroneously is then lower than approximately 5%. This is sometimes called a significance level of 5%. The higher level of significance of 2% or 1% is often selected when an error could have serious consequences. It should be remembered, however, that this level is solely a convention; no other meaning should be attached to the statistical significance.

In many cases, it proves to be useful to represent the data in a cumulative distribution. The cumulative distribution is created by adding the numbers of the second measuring value to those of the first measuring value, etc. A cumulative distribution starts by definition at zero (0%), and ends, also by definition, at 100%. The 50% value of the cumulative distribution is also called the median; there are as many values below as above it. The cumulative distribution is useful for determining the threshold value. See figure 7.1.3.

Interdependence of variables
The previous section discussed how the difference between two groups of phenomena, also called 'universa', can be determined in a statistically sound manner. Another question, often encountered in research, is whether there is a relation between collections of phenomena. Here two different problems may be involved: how does a variable depend on a given factor or what is the

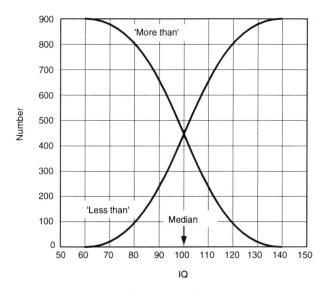

Figure 7.1.3: *The cumulative distribution for determining a threshold value. After Maloney, 1990, fig. 9. The distribution of the intelligence quotient IQ is used in this example*

relation between pairs of data. The first case deals with a regression problem and the second with a correlation problem.These statistical problems will not be discussed in detail here; for this refer to Buijs (1995, chapter 12). The main reason to pay attention to them is the fact that in practice we are usually not interested in the correlations, but rather in causal relations. Often these two are used indiscriminately, which may lead to incorrect conclusions.

7.1.3 Research in practice
As will be explained in chapters 11 and 12, the importance of traffic safety measures is expressed in their effect with regard to efficacy or efficiency. In practice, a certain measure is often compared with a different measure. The research is then concerned with the difference in effect between these two measures. One therefore often speaks of difference studies. Difference studies may be conducted in various ways. Here they are briefly described, based on an example: research into the relation between the level of public lighting and traffic accidents (see section 11.2).

Before-and-after studies
A section of the road is selected, the accidents are counted and the lighting is altered. Subsequently the accidents are again measured. The differences in accident patterns are ascribed to the change in lighting. It is a simple method, but the drawback is clear. There may be many differences between the before and after period which have nothing to do with the lighting, but which may affect the pattern of accidents. Another drawback is that the process usually takes a long time: the before and after period must obviously run subsequently.

Comparative studies

Two similar stretches of road are selected; the lighting in one part is changed, the other is left untouched (the 'control group'). The differences in the pattern of accidents are again ascribed to the change in the lighting. The problem here is also obvious: similar stretches of roads are almost impossible to find. However, the duration of the study is reduced, as the two sections of road may be studied at the same time.

Before-and-after studies with control groups

Here the two methods mentioned earlier are combined. Two reasonably similar stretches of road are selected. The lighting is changed in one of them, but not in the other. The second stretch of road is used as a control group. A before-and-after study is carried out in both stretches of road. Thus the effects of time as well as the differences between the stretches of road may be largely eliminated. One drawback remains: it is a before-and-after study, which means a longer duration of the research.

Relation studies

The lighting and the accident patterns of a large number of road stretches are determined, as well as the relation between the two. As the data are collected simultaneously, time-dependent effects are not significant.

Meta-analysis

The meta-analysis method can be considered as a variant on the relation study. As Elvik (1995) has indicated, several forms of meta-analysis are possible; the simplest is probably the one called 'voting'. Those studies, which resulted in a positive effect of the lighting on safety, are selected from all known studies, as well as those, where the result was neutral or negative. The statistical processing is rather complex, as there are corrections for all sorts of systematic and arbitrary effects. As indicated in section 11.1.1, the results of the meta-analysis carried out in Norway showed a considerable reduction in accidents as a result of the presence of public lighting (Elvik, 1995).

7.1.4   Paradigms and models

A particular paradigm is used for each piece of research. By this one means the framework used in the research, which often is based on theoretical foreknowledge. The hypothesis to be tested may be derived from the paradigm. Often a model, based on a number of assumptions, is used. This facet will be explained in a rather simple example, i.e. the optical image with the aid of a lens. See figure 7.1.4.

Take a red-coloured object 'to be grasped'. This object is situated in the object space. Through the lens an image is formed, which is also red, in the image space. Now the object can be manipulated. The object is painted green in the example. Now we want to know what happens to the image. The lens portrays the red object as well as the brush; the model-based principle says, that if the red object has been rendered green by the brush in the object space, then the image is also rendered green by the brush in the image space.

The model allows us to make the following prediction: objects also turn green in the image space when they are painted green. This is shown in figure 7.1.5. The optical image in this illustration runs from top to bottom and the model runs from left to right.

The usefulness of these seemingly complex model contemplations lies in the fact that there is no need to actually carry out all the tests, when one has a useful model. One can limit this to carrying out the manipulations in the image space and can then conclude what would happen in the object space, in reality, when a corresponding manipulation would be carried out. This can be very important. Reality is often inaccessibly far removed, too large or too small, or the manipulations might be too costly, too complicated, or take to long, or they might give rise to unacceptable ethical objections.

Or, reality does not exist, or not yet, or no longer! In all these cases a useful model is very important. Obviously, it is better to speak of a useless rather than of a wrong model.

For the discussion of behaviour in traffic, a certain model is relevant. Here I am concerned, as explained in section 8.2, with decisions with regard to the selection of the most appropriate manoeuvre. In order to make the correct choice, the participant in traffic requires an image of the environment, i.e. of the actual state of the situation, but also of future conditions. The future situation can, of course, only be estimated. This estimation is based largely on the extrapolation of the actual immediate situation. The model used says that extrapolation from the present may provide a useful image of the future.

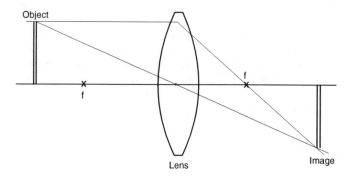

Figure 7.1.4: *The optical image with the aid of a lens*

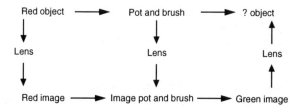

Figure 7.1.5: *The model illustration of the optical image by means of a lens*

7.2   The visual functions

7.2.1   The primary visual functions

A number of visual functions are important for road traffic; not only in isolation, but also in respect of their reciprocal relations. These will be discussed in detail in the sections below. A brief explanation of the reciprocal relations will be given in this introductory section.

As the visual organ is an organ with which light is perceived, we can defend the assumption of the perception of light as the basis function, and start the discussion of the visual functions with this, as well as with the accompanying phenomenon of adaptation. But in addition to this, participation in traffic also requires being able to detect, and in particular being able to distinguish, certain objects. This requires us to start with the ability to distinguish, in particular, sensitivity to contrasts and visual acuity. Of these two, sensitivity to contrast is the most fundamental one, as objects can only be seen when there is a contrast between the object and the background. Our discussion will begin with sensitivity to contrast (section 7.2.2), based on the significance of the latter. This is followed by visual acuity in section 7.2.3, not least because this matches the day-to-day practice of optometrists and ophthalmologists to measure performance based mainly on visual acuity. Two objects may have a contrasting brightness, as well as a contrasting colour; therefore the ability to distinguish colours is important (section 7.4). The working may vary at any moment. This is described by adaptation (sections 7.2.4 and 7.2.5). Furthermore, failures may also occur; one should therefore pay attention to glare (section 7.3). Further attention will not be given to the recognition of shapes, which in traffic especially plays a role in the legibility of traffic signs. For more details see, e.g. Gleitman (1995, pages 208–224) and Hentschel (1994, section 3.3).

A good overview, based on experimental psychology, of the field of visual perception in traffic is offered by Noordzij et al. (1993). The overview concerns a critical consideration of available research results. The conclusion summarized here is predictable: too many field studies are subject to methodological deficiencies. An aside worth mentioning is that the translation of laboratory research to practice often poses considerable problems. Some conclusions are important: it is indicated that pre-attentive perceptual processing is a global analysis which is carried out parallel across the whole field of vision, whereas attentive perceptual processing is a process, where the visual attention is directed serially at different locations in the field of vision. However, little attention is paid to the important pre-attentive perceptual processing. The visual demands imposed on participants in traffic and the effects of visual handicaps on traffic safety are also not discussed.

7.2.2   Sensitivity to contrast

The ability to see small differences in brightness is usually considered to be the most fundamental function of the visual system. The ability to do this is usually indicated with sensitivity to contrast. By contrast I mean

$$C = \frac{L_o - L_b}{L_b} \tag{7.2.1}$$

in which L_o is the luminance of the object and L_b is the luminance of the background. According to this definition, contrast may have positive as well as negative values, i.e. from -1 at $L_o = 0$ to $+$ infinitely at $L_b = 0$. The formula is asymmetrical, as both L_o and L_b appear in the numerator, but only L_b in the denominator. A contrast of zero corresponds with a situation in which $L_o = L_b$; the object is then invisible. For small contrasts at least, perception does not depend on the sign: a positive contrast of a certain size can be seen just as easily as a negative contrast of the same size. See for this Adrian (1961), Blackwell (1946) and Schreuder (1964). For larger contrasts, this assumption would not seem to hold (see Adrian, 1995 and Aulhorn, 1964). I cannot say whether this is due to a physiological aspect, or whether it is only the result of the asymmetry in formula 7.2.1. The relations given by Adrian (1995) are too complicated to check whether the difference is importance for practice.

In the past, sensitivity to contrast was measured with the aid of Landolt rings or other objects which are used in measuring visual acuity. The Landolt ring is shown in figure 7.2.4.

Visual acuity is what is called a confounding factor. In order to overcome this, a sinusoidal grid is often used nowadays. This is a screen, in which light and dark bands alternate; the luminance in each band varies with a sine function. There is no longer any foreground or background. The contrast therefore must obviously be defined differently

$$C^* = \frac{L_1 - L_2}{L_1 - L_2} \tag{7.2.2}$$

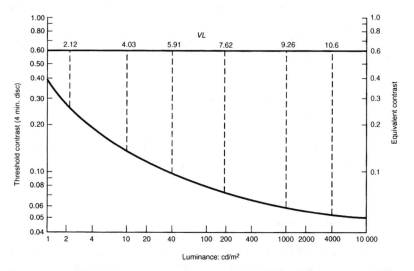

Figure 7.2.1: *The relation between sensitivity to contrast and adaptation*

in which L_1 is the maximum luminance of the bright bands and L_2 is the minimum luminance of the dark bands. Not only the contrast itself is used as a variable, but also the modulation depth, the frequency (to be expressed in periods per degree) and the orientation of the bands (vertical or horizontal in the field of vision). This method has the advantage that visual acuity is not relevant. It is, however, questionable whether the fact that there is no specific foreground or background corresponds with traffic conditions in practice. It is known from psychological research that the foreground/background effect ('figure and ground') is important for perception. See, e.g. Krech et al. (1969, page 152) and Gleitman (1995, page 213). Applications are given in Bourdy et al. (1987).

The sensitivity to contrast is the measure for the smallest luminance difference, which can still be perceived. It is therefore a threshold value. The threshold value for the contrast which can just be seen, depends on a number of factors; the most important is the general brightness (adaptation level; see section 7.2.4). CIE has established a standard curve which is based on the measurements by Blackwell (1946), combined with other measurements (CIE, 1981). See figure 7.2.1.

The threshold contrast at a very low adaptation level is quite high. It is gradually reduced with an increasing adaptation level, to reach an asymptote for luminances which correspond to daylight. The curve applies to luminances up to levels of 1000 to 2000 cd/m^2. But the threshold contrast increases again with considerably higher adaptation levels. See figure 7.2.2.

Something similar is also indicated in the classic measurements by König & Brodhun (1889). See also Helbig (1972) and Moon (1961). Public lighting, however, lies in the area where the threshold value of the contrast is reduced clearly with increased luminance. This is the reason that a relatively high luminance level is specified in nearly all recommendations and guidelines for roads, where perception is critical (see, e.g. CIE, 1965, 1977, 1995; NSVV, 1957, 1974/1975, 1977, 1990). All these recommendations are based in the final analysis on studies by Adrian, De Boer, Van Bommel and Schreuder. De Boer (ed.), (1967), Van Bommel & De Boer (1980), Schreuder (1981) and Adrian (1982, 1989).

For most people the threshold contrast, as determined in the laboratory, lies in the area of 0.5 to 1%. In practice, such a small contrast cannot be perceived in traffic, particularly when the observer is also the driver of a car or when he or she rides a bicycle. A field factor should be added to the lab value to arrive at a threshold value 'in the field'. The magnitude of this field factor depends closely on the driving task, and on the alertness and the motivation of the observer. Values of five to fifteen are not unusual. Values of about six have been found at tunnel entrances (Schreuder, 1990, 1991; see also section 15.2.2).

7.2.3 Visual acuity
A second important basic function of the visual system is visual acuity. By this, I mean the reciprocal value of the smallest object or the smallest detail which can still be perceived. Visual acuity is usually indicated with the angle measure

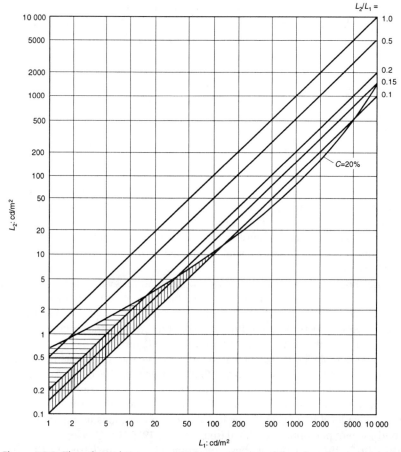

Figure 7.2.2: *The relation between sensitivity to contrast and the adaptation level for high luminances; L₁ corresponds to the background and L₂ to the object (After Schreuder (1964))*

for which this smallest detail occurs. For healthy adults with good eyesight or good glasses the smallest detail lies usually below one arc minute. This is also indicated with 100/100 or with 100% visual acuity (visus). This applies to the fovea. Figure 7.2.3 shows that visual acuity is reduced in the periphery.

Like sensitivity to contrast, visual acuity depends on the adaptation level. See figure 7.2.4.

In practice, detecting very small objects or minuscule details in larger objects is hardly ever necessary in traffic; visual acuity is therefore seldom a critical factor in visual performance in traffic. It is therefore incorrect that visual acuity is still considered to be an important criterion for determining driving ability.

Section 8.2 will show that participation in traffic, in particular as a car driver, requires making a large number of often complicated decisions. These decisions can only be made adequately if the traffic participant possesses the

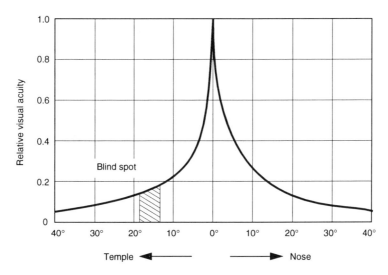

Figure 7.2.3: *The relation between visual activity and the location on the retina*

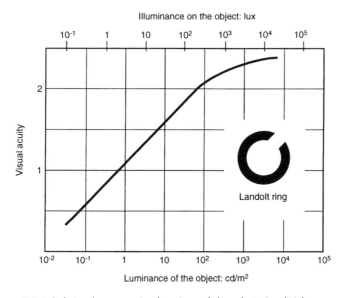

Figure 7.2.4: *Relation between visual acuity and the adaptation brightness*

relevant information. Relevant here relates to content as well as quantity. The information in normal traffic is largely of a visual nature. When visual information is missing, or is very bad, then normal participation in traffic is nearly impossible. Nevertheless, the decision-making process proves to be the limiting factor for safe traffic, rather than the visual process. One could say that the visual system is essential, but that the quality requirements are not very high, it is soon sufficient.

This conclusion is supported by research results. On the one hand Hofstetter (1976) has shown clearly that inadequate sight gives rise to a considerable increase in risk; poor visual performance is overrepresented in people who are frequently involved in accidents. On the other hand, Burg (1964, 1968; elaborated by Hills, 1975) showed clearly that there is no significant relation for the population as a whole between visual performance and involvement in accidents. These two results would seem to contradict each other. However, Hofstetter concentrates on the relatively very small group of people who are frequently involved in accidents, while Burg looks at the population as a whole. A possible explanation is that people are able to compensate to a large extent for physical handicaps, and in particular for visual handicaps (see Schreuder, 1988; 1994).

7.2.4   The state of adaptation

The total range of brightness, in which the visual system operates, is surprisingly large. Hopkinson (1969) gives an example. This example is slightly adapted in table 7.2.1.

At a particular moment, the range is much smaller. The sensitivity of the visual system is limited by two extremes: at the bottom by darkness, and at the top by dazzle. This is shown in figure 7.2.5.

Table 7.2.1: *Range of brightness; based on data by Hopkinson, 1969*

Luminance log (cd/m^2)	Brightness	Visual acuity
5		Dazzle
4.5	Sun on snow	Glare
4		
3.5	Average daylight	
3		Good perception possibilities
2.5		
2	Interior lighting	
1.5		
1	Dusk	
0.5	Lighting in main roads	Reading possible
0	Candle light	Reading difficult
−0.5	Lighting in residential streets	
−1		Colour perception impossible
−1.5	Moonlight on snow	
−2		
−2.5	Moonlit night	
−3		
−3.5	Clear moonless night	Only vague shapes
−4	Starlight on snow	
−4.5	Dark moonless night	
−5		Only vague light impressions
−5.5		
−6		Perception threshold

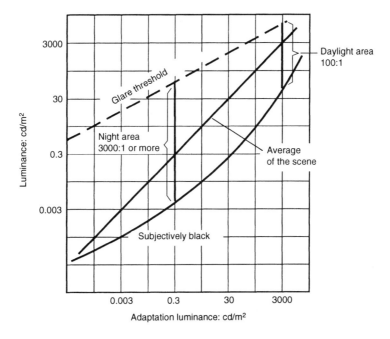

Figure 7.2.5: *The scene and its limits of darkness and dazzle*

At a particular moment one can speak of the sensitivity setting existing at that moment. This falls obviously between the two extremes mentioned. Figure 7.2.5 shows this with the average for the scene. This setting is called the state of adaptation. The luminance associated with this, is called adaptation luminance. In most cases, adaptation luminance equals the average luminance of the range of vision by approximation.

7.2.5 Time-dependent adaptation processes

When the luminance in the field of view changes, the visual system adapts. This process is called adaptation. These time-dependent effects are rather complex. Adaptation comprises three processes

- changes in the diameter of the pupil
- sensitivity adaptation of the receptors
- switching on and off of the receptors.

The contribution from changes in the pupil diameter to adaptation is quite small. Figure 7.2.6 shows how the diameter of the pupil opening depends on the luminance in the field of vision.

According to figure 7.2.6, the pupil diameter varies from 7 to 2.8 mm for adaptation luminances of 0.01 to 1000 cd/m^2, corresponding with a surface of 49 and 7.84 mm^2 – approximately a factor of six. In addition, the Stiles – Crawford effect should be considered, which means that the edge of the pupil allows less light to pass through than the centre (see Helbig, 1972 and Weale, 1961). Finally, the variability is reduced even further for older people, as the

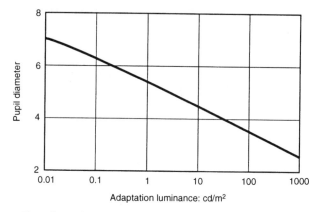

Figure 7.2.6: *The relation between the diameter of the pupil opening and the field of vision luminance*

elasticity of the pupil reduces with advancing age, like the elasticity of all bodily tissues.

The adaptation of the photoreceptors is much more important. The switching on and off of photoreceptors is also important. In all cases light adaptation from low to high is much more rapid than the adaptation to the dark in the reverse direction; in nearly all cases occurring in traffic the light adaptation can be ignored. In respect of dark adaptation two effects can be distinguished. According to Schouten (1937), this involves, on the one hand, neuronal interactions and on the other hand photochemical processes. There are indications that the neuronal interactions are the same as those which are involved in light adaptation. There is therefore no difference in this respect between light adaptation and dark adaptation. This is not the case in photochemical processes. According to Rushton, bleaching out is involved in light adaptation and the regeneration of visual pigment is involved in dark adaptation (Rushton, 1963; Rushton & Gubish, 1966; Rushton & Westheimer, 1962).

Figure 7.2.7 shows how the percentage of bleached out pigment depends on the adaptation level. The adaptation level in this illustration is shown by the measure described in section 5.2.2, the Troland.

When the starting level as well as the end level is above approximately 0.1 cd/m^2, i.e. both in the photopic area, bleaching and regeneration occurs quite rapidly and approximately at the same speed, but rather slower than the neuronal interactions in darkness adaptation. This involves seconds or dozens of seconds. Regeneration is accompanied by the disappearance of after images. These after images may interfere with visual perception. This immediately offers two possibilities to study the effects of darkness adaptation: it is possible to measure the ability to detect objects or determine the hindrance from after images. The first method has been used in Japan by Kabayama (1963). The results are shown in figure 7.2.8. See also Ohayama (1995).

Figure 7.2.8 shows the results from measurements by Kabayama in absolute measure. As the data are reproduced in a logarithm scale, the curves may be made to coincide by a translation. This is shown in figure 7.2.9.

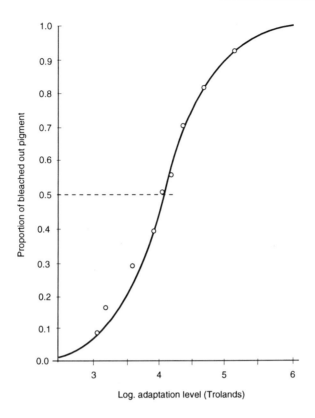

Figure 7.2.7: *The relation between the adaptation level (in Trolands) and the percentage of bleached out pigment; after Cornsweet, 1970, based on data from Rushton, 1963*

The second method has been developed by Schreuder (1964); the results have been incorporated in the CIE curve, which forms the basis for a number of national and international recommendations on tunnel lighting (CEN, 1997; CIE, 1984, 1990, 1995a; NSVV, 1990a). See also section 15.4.5. The subjective curve is also shown in figures 7.2.8 and 7.2.9. The two methods lead to analogue results.

When the starting level of luminance is much lower, some tenths of a cd/m^2 or even less, the speed with which darkness adaptation takes place is considerably slower. When adaptation continues right into the area of scotopic vision, then adaptation may take some minutes, even one hour, depending on the end level. See figure 7.2.10.

Figure 7.2.10 also shows another phenomenon. After several minutes the rods start to participate in the adaptation process. This is shown in the illustration by a kink in the curve. The degradation of the visual pigments proves to be much slower for the rods than for the cones. But we can also see a split: the branch representing the periphery continues to fall after the kink; the other branch, representing the fovea, no longer falls. This obviously relates

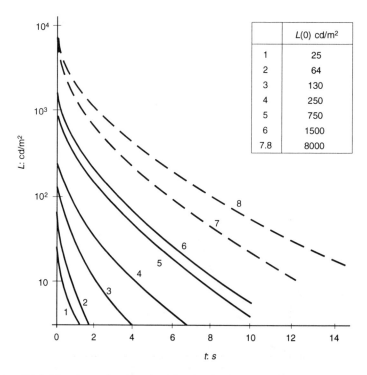

	L(0) cd/m²
1	25
2	64
3	130
4	250
5	750
6	1500
7.8	8000

Figure 7.2.8: *The time effect in adaptation in absolute measure. Curves 1 ... 6 after Kabayama (1963). Curves 7 and 8 after Schreuder (1964)*

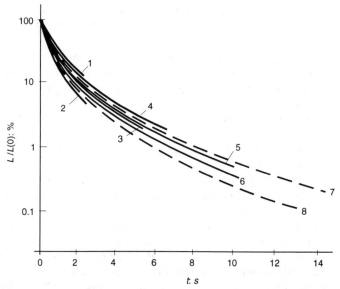

Figure 7.2.9: *The time effect in adaptation in relative measure. See figure 7.2.8 for the meaning of the numbers*

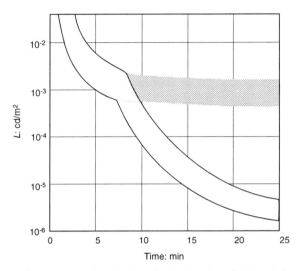

Figure 7.2.10: *Adaptation speed at low light levels. Top branch: (fovea). Bottom branch: rods (periphery)*

to the fact discussed in section 6.1.5, i.e. that rods are present in the periphery, but not in the fovea.

When changes in luminance take place rapidly, adaptation cannot keep up; an adaptation defect results. An idea of the adaptation defect can be obtained by reducing luminance in steps and by checking how long it takes before a certain object can again be perceived. Such measurements have been carried out by Schreuder (1964). Some results are reproduced in figure 7.2.11.

The adaptation defect is especially important for lighting during the day in tunnel entrances. See section 15.2.2.

7.3 Glare

7.3.1 Dazzle

Glare relates to the phenomenon where perception is rendered difficult or even impossible. Glare has three aspects

- dazzle (absolute glare)
- physiological glare
- psychological glare.

Dazzle occurs when the stimulus rises above the upper limit of the sensitivity area of the visual system: the stimulus in question does not contribute to perception but prevents the occurrence of relevant perception. The luminance at which dazzle occurs depends on the adaptation luminance. Damage to the eye may occur in extreme cases (Van Norren, 1995).

Dazzle is seen quite often in traffic

- when encountering a car which does not dip its headlights in darkness

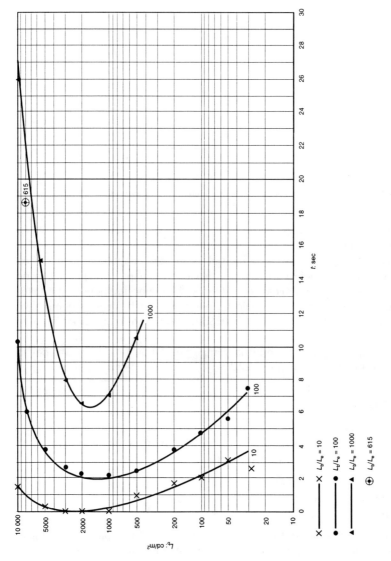

Figure 7.2.11: *The adaptation defect expressed in time units, depending on the starting level and the end level of the step.* L_b: *starting luminance;* L_c: *end luminance*

- leaving a tunnel in daylight
- driving on smooth, wet asphalt against a low sun
- driving on snow in full sun.

One cannot do much against dazzle: the use of sun-glasses may lessen the dazzle in some cases, but the relevant stimuli are further weakened.

7.3.2   Physiological glare

Physiological glare is called physiological because the effect is of a physiological nature. It is often indicated with the term 'disability glare' and occurs when a strong source of light appears in the field of vision, from a different direction than the object to be detected. The light from the glare source is dispersed into the eye media. This causes a light veil, which seems to spread over the whole field of vision.

In practice not just one, but a number of dazzling sources of light often occur at the same time. Moreover, many of these dazzling sources of light are not points. The total effect is equal to the sum of the separate effects when we are dealing exclusively with stray light in the eye; the glare phenomena are additive. A large glare source of light may be divided into parts in the imagination and the effects can be summed. The glare effects may be integrated (Vos, 1963). In some rather extreme cases, such as a tunnel entrances in surroundings with snow in sunlight, variations in additivity and in integrativity may occur.

The light veil has a negative effect on the perceptibility of objects, as all contrasts in the range of vision are reduced. According to section 7.2.2, the luminance contrast is usually defined as follows

$$C = \frac{L_o - L_b}{L_b} \qquad\qquad [7.3.1]$$

The light veil can be described with the equivalent veil luminance L_{seq}, to be discussed later. Veil luminance L_v applies when additional veil effects come into play. As can be seen from formula 7.3.2, all contrasts are reduced

$$C' = \frac{(L_o + L_v) - (L_b + L_v)}{L_b + L_v} = \frac{L_o - L_b}{L_b + L_v} \qquad\qquad [7.3.2]$$

C' is always smaller than C, as the numerator remains equal while the denominator is increased. C is usually called the intrinsic contrast, while C' is called the visible contrast.

The effect of the light veil is described by the illuminance on the eye, on a plane perpendicular to the direction of vision. Above I indicated that the glare depends on the angle made by the light source and the direction of vision. This angle is usually called the angle of glare θ. The glare does not depend on the azimuth angle φ; as far as glare is concerned, the visual system is rotationally symmetrical. See figure 7.3.1.

The veil luminance depends closely on the age of the observer. See Schouten (1972). I will return to this later in this section.

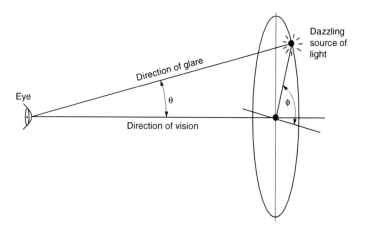

Figure 7.3.1: *The geometry in glare; θ glare angle, φ azimuth angle*

The θ dependence has been researched thoroughly. Overviews can be found in Vos et al. (1976) and Schreuder (1964, 1981). The first proposal which became known on a large scale stems from Holladay (1927). This proposal was very simple: the equivalent veil luminance is inversely proportional to the square of θ (measured in degrees; Stiles & Crawford, 1937; Adrian, 1961).

$$L_{seq} = k \frac{E_e}{\theta^2}$$ [7.3.3]

in which

L_{seq} is the equivalent veil luminance in cd/m²
E_e the illuminance on the eye in lux
k the proportional factor which depends on age, but is usually set to ten as a sort of average.

The relation, usually called the Stiles–Holladay formula, proves to be reasonably accurate for values of θ larger than 4° and smaller than approximately 60°. In particular the lower limit is important. In many practical cases, and particular in road traffic, the angle of glare is considerable smaller than 4°. Examples are: glare in oncoming traffic on a two-way, two-lane road; the entrance lighting in tunnels. However, for many applications, e.g. for sports and area lighting, the lower limit is not critical. Hence the Stiles–Holladay formula may be applied. See CIE (1994).

Many proposals have been made to select another value for the exponent of θ and so to relate it better to practice, particularly for smaller angles. Usually an exponent around 2.8 was found. (See, e.g. Hartmann & Moser, 1968; Hartmann & Ucke, 1974; Schreuder, 1981; Vos, 1963.) With this, glare could be described up to considerable smaller angles; often values of between 10 and 15 arc minutes are given. Vos (1983) has proposed a new formula based on data known at the time. See also Vos & Padmos (1983). This formula reads

$$\frac{L_{seq}}{E_e} = \frac{10}{(\theta + 0.02)^2} + \frac{10}{(\theta + 0.02)^3} + \frac{10^6}{\exp(\theta/0.02)^2} \qquad [7.3.4]$$

In this formula, E_e is the illuminance on the eye in lux and the angle θ is expressed in degrees. A computer program called 'SNAEFELL' has been written for the practical application of the formula in the design of tunnel lighting (see Swart, 1994, and also Schreuder, 1993; Schreuder & Swart 1993; Schreuder et al., 1994). CIE proposed a formula to calculate the veil luminance, which can be used to determine the physiological glare (disability glare) in public lighting in 1990

$$L_v = \sum 3 \times 10^{-3} \frac{E}{\theta^2} \qquad [7.3.5]$$

The veil luminance $L_v = L_{seq}$ is expressed in lux per radian (CIE, 1990a, page 121). As computer programs are now available, such approximation formulas are no longer required.

Fisher & Christie (1965) proposed to take account of the age dependence by writing the following for the proportional factor in formula 7.3.3

$$k = d + 0.2A \qquad [7.3.6]$$

in which A is the age in years and d a factor which depends on the configuration. In order to get an idea of the effect of age according to Fisher & Christie (1965), our approximation is based on the fact that, according to Adrian (1961), k has a value of 9.2 for 25 year olds. The factor d amounts then to $d = k - 0.2A = 9.2 - 5 = 4.2$. For 50 and 75 year olds there are similar findings

- for 25 years: $k = 4.2 + 0.2 \times 25 = 4.2 + 5 = 9.2$ (this was the basis)
- for 50 years: $k = 4.2 + 0.2 \times 50 = 4.2 + 10 = 14.2$
- for 75 years: $k = 4.2 + 0.2 \times 75 = 4.2 + 15 = 19.2$

The latter figure is therefore approximately double the value found for the 25 year olds. This relates to the average value; nothing is known about the dispersion. But I suspect that it is primarily the dispersion which increases with the advancing years.

In public lighting, physiological glare is usually expressed in the rise in the threshold value for the sensitivity to contrast. Normally the term 'threshold increment' (TI) is used. As a result of the veil, an object which is just visible can no longer be perceived with glare. Should we wish to see the object even with glare present, then the intrinsic contrast must be increased. The increment in the intrinsic contrast equals the above mentioned TI.

The relation between L_v and TI can be derived as follows. The contrast without glare is given in formula 7.3.1 and with glare in formula 7.3.2. From the two formulas we can say that

$$\frac{C'}{C} = \frac{L_2}{L_2 + L_v} \qquad [7.3.7]$$

From the definition of TI it follows that

$$C' = C(1 - TI) \qquad [7.3.8]$$

When formula 7.3.7 is joined with formula 7.3.8, two equivalent methods for expressing the relation between L_v and TI are found

$$TI = \frac{L_v}{L_2 - L_v} \qquad [7.3.9]$$

$$L_v = \frac{L_2\, TI}{1 - TI} \qquad [7.3.10]$$

From these two relations it would seem that TI is not exclusively a lamp variable; L_v, a lamp variable, as well as L_2, an installation variable, are entered in the relations.

Less complex formula are in use. These will become obsolete when computer programs become more common. Most models are either oversimplified or are not additive. Van Bommel & De Boer (1980, page 147; Appendix C) give the following relation

$$TI = 65 \frac{L_v}{L_{av}{}^{0.8}} \qquad [7.3.11]$$

in which

TI   is the well-known threshold increment
L_v the equivalent veil luminance
L_{av} the average road surface luminance

In CEN (1995) the following formula was proposed, which is clearly grafted onto the last formula:

$$TI = \frac{650\, E_e\, MF^{0.8}}{L_{av}{}^{0.8}\, \theta^2} \qquad [7.3.12]$$

in which

E_e is the illuminance on the eye of the observer, perpendicular on the direction of sight (1.5 m high; direction of sight 1° downwards and situated on a quarter of the road width; in lux per 1000 initial lamp lumen)
MF   the maintenance factor
L_{av} the average road surface luminance
θ the angle of glare.

Although not given, it may be assumed that MF is expressed as a number, L_{av} in cd/m^2 and θ as degrees. The same formula is proposed by CIE (CIE, 1995).

7.3.3 Psychological glare

The third type of glare is psychological glare, also called 'discomfort glare'. Psychological glare relates to some discomfort in perception, without detection being impeded in a way which can be measured directly. In the past, quite a lot of attention was paid to discomfort glare in public lighting (NSVV, 1957; 1974/1975; 1977; De Boer, ed., 1967).

In later recommendations, national as well as international, disability glare is exclusively mentioned (CIE, 1977; NSVV, 1990). The reason given is that car lights dazzle so much that there is no sense in trying to limit the discomfort glare in public lighting. There is also a rather close relation between the two: when physiological glare is limited, then psychological glare is also usually limited. In addition, combating psychological glare was sometimes seen as a luxury.

The relation between physiological glare and psychological glare is discussed by Adrian (1966). See figure 7.3.2.

However, often a more subtle view is seen. Thus both types of glare are mentioned in the recently published recommendations by CIE (CIE, 1995).

Several formulas have been proposed to determine psychological glare (De Boer, 1951). Schreuder carried out measurements several years later, in a scale model of a street lighting installation, where driving was also simulated (De Boer & Schreuder, 1967). Based on subjective appraisals, a formula was established to determine the glare level (De Boer & Schreuder, 1967). The formula is rather complex. The graphic method based on it is also cumbersome and computer programs which contain the formula are not generally available. Nevertheless, CIE has adopted this formula, albeit in an appendix, as psychological glare can be calculated for nearly all possible situations with this formula (CIE, 1995, Appendix B).

Over the years various simplifications have been proposed. NSVV (1957) has adopted a simple classification e.g., which is easy to operate in practice. See table 7.3.1.

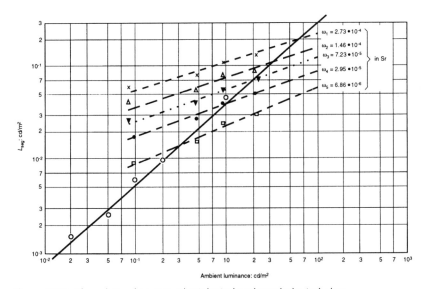

Figure 7.3.2: *The relation between physiological and psychological glare*

Table 7.3.1: *Classification of luminous intensity distributions; after NSVV, 1957, table 3.4.1*

Name	I_{max}	I_{hor}	θ for $\delta < 80°$
	per 1000 lamp lumen		(lumen)
Shielded deep emission	0–30	< 15	> 600
Shielded wide emission	50–70	< 15	> 500
Diffuse deep emission	0–30	30–50	550–650
Medium emission	45–65	50–150	450–600
Wide emission	60–75	100–300	450–550
Free emission	50–90	> 100	300–400

Table 7.3.1 uses the following symbols

I_{max}	is the direction of the greatest luminous intensity in degrees
I_{hor}	the luminous intensity in horizontal direction, in cd per 1000 lumen
ϕ for $\delta < 80°$	the luminous flux below 800 in lumen
δ	the downwards angle with the vertical through the lamp in degrees.

As no account has been taken of the dimensions of the lamps so that, in particular, deviations are found with concentrated light sources, and as no account has been taken either of asymmetrical luminous intensity distributions (the 'toe-in'), this classification has fallen into disuse. However, it is very suitable for residential streets and deserves to be introduced again.

CIE proposed a simplification in 1965 (CIE, 1965; 1977). Here the luminous intensity distributions are divided into three classes; only the maximum permissible luminous intensities below 80° and 90° per 1000 lamp lumen are given for each class. See table 7.3.2.

These recommendations are not very useful, as in practice nearly all lamps for roads fall into the class 'semi cut-off', even though there are large variations between them.

At present, the possible inclusion of psychological glare in residential areas in the standards is still the subject of discussion. The most suitable proposal stems from Einhorn, although no account is taken of the adaptation situation. This proposal has not yet been been published. The formula proposed by Einhorn reads

$$L_k = A < h^2 \qquad\qquad [7.3.13]$$

Table 7.3.2: *The CIE recommendations from 1965 and 1977*

Name	I_{90}	I_{80}
Cut-off	10 cd/1000lm	30 cd/1000lm
Semi cut-off	50 cd/1000lm	100 cd/1000lm
Non cut-off	—	1000 cd

in which

L_k is the threshold of the luminance of the luminaire in kcd/m^2
A the surface of the luminaire in m^2
h the mounting height in m

7.4   The perception of colours

7.4.1   Colours

The concept of colour is very important in life. In relation to traffic this concerns the colour of traffic lights and traffic signs, of fire engines and flashing lights on police cars. It is irrelevant for the impression of colour whether the light originates from a light source or is reflected by an object. But it is relevant for the types of colorimetry described in this section; light follows the rules of additive colour mixing while pigments on the other hand follow those of subtractive colour mixing. Additive colour mixing is characterised by the fact that three suitably selected produce white; in subtractive colour mixing, three different, appropriately selected colours produce black.

Colorimetry, or the science of colour, goes back a long way. MacAdam (1970) has compiled a very readable and thoroughly documented summary of this history. See also Bouma (1946). The basis of colorimetry is the previously mentioned fact that there are three types of cones in the retina, each with their own sensitivity curve. See figure 7.4.1. The curves are derived from measurements on observers with colour vision defects, i.e. protanopes, deuteranopes and tritanopes. This supposedly describes the sensitivity curves for the different types of cones. See also section 7.5.4.

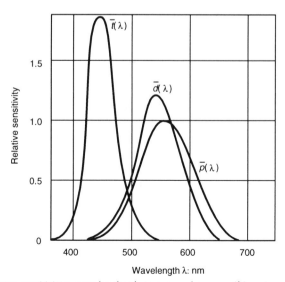

Figure 7.4.1: *The eye sensitivity curves for the three types of cones: p(λ) protanopes; d(λ) deuteranopes; t(λ) tritanopes; after Hentschel, 1994, fig. 4.40*

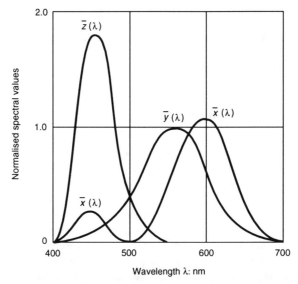

Figure 7.4.2: *The standard curves for the CIE system of colorimetry; after Hentschel, 1994, fig. 4.42*

CIE has defined a standard observer in 1931. Photometry is based on the eye sensitivity of the standard observer, as indicated in section 5.1.3. The same standard observer is used for determining colorimetry (CIE, 1932). A number of standard curves have been introduced for this. See figure 7.4.2.

7.4.2   Colour points: colorimetry

Any colour can be produced by mixing three arbitrary colours. Colorimetry is based on this. As additive colour mixing applies to light sources, but subtractive colour mixing to pigments, there are differences in colorimetry. The CIE trichomatric system is used for light sources, based on the colour space. Readers should refer to Bouma (1946) for the theory. The practical CIE system is based on three axes, x, y and z. The z axis represents the luminance. Leaving this out of consideration, any colour can be formed by a combination of x and y. This can be shown in a flat plane. The standard colours are selected in such a way, that the area in which existing colours occur is more or less similar to a triangle. We therefore speak of the colour triangle. See figure 7.4.3.

Points within that triangle are called colour points. The colour points for a number of important sources of light are also indicated

- C   incandescent lamp
- 2   fluorescent lamp colour 'daylight'
- 3   fluorescent lamp colour 'white'
- 4   fluorescent lamp colour 'warm white'
- 5   high-pressure mercury lamp without fluorescence
- 6 and 7   high-pressure mercury lamp with fluorescence
- 8 and 9   high-pressure xenon lamp

- 10   low-pressure sodium lamp
- 11   high-pressure sodium lamp

A colour impression is not always associated with just one colour point. The colour impression is also determined by the prehistory (colour adaptation) and the environment (colour contrast). Details and examples can be found in Walraven (1981, page 40; 142). The edge of the figure corresponds with the spectral colours, see section 4.2.1; the lower edge with the purple colours. In addition, figure 7.4.3. shows the spectral locus of the Planckian radiator (section 4.2.2). As the scale along the locus is the temperature, this temperature is called the colour temperature. See section 7.4.3.

The resolution of the visual system is not unlimited; it is possible to indicate areas in which the colours deserve just one name. CIE has established a

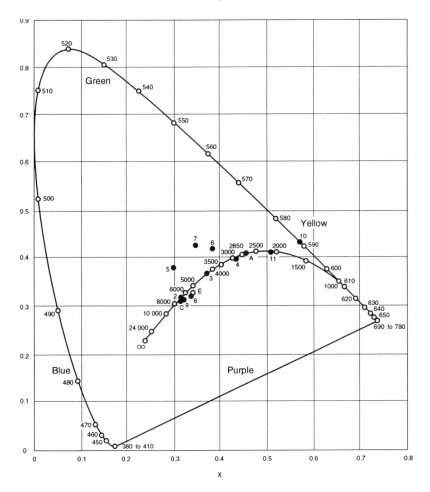

Figure 7.4.3: *The CIE colour triangle (explanation: see text; after Hentschel, 1994, fig. 4.43)*

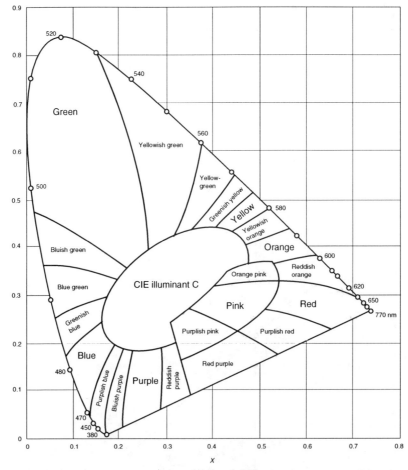

Figure 7.4.4: *CIE colour triangle showing areas with the same colour name (after De Boer & Rutten, 1974, fig. 3-21)*

number of practical rules which are explained in De Boer & Rutten (1974). See figure 7.4.4. These rules are based on the studies by MacAdam, hence the name MacAdam areas. An elliptical shape seems to correspond best with the experiments, see figure 7.4.5.

This coarsening of the colour triangle can have important consequences for practice, in particular for signal lights. It is impossible to devise a system for light signals in which at the same time red and orange and yellow light appear; if we can perceive the difference between red and orange, the difference between orange and yellow cannot be seen, and vice versa.

It was indicated above, that the subtractive colour mixing applies to surface colours, which may contain pigments. The colour which is perceived depends on the colour of the incidence light and the colour characteristics of the surface. The colour characteristics of the surface are established in the Munsell system. The Munsell system can be described along three axes, like the CIE system. These axes are

- the colour itself (the hue or chroma)
- the saturation
- the lightness or value.

These terms have the following meaning

- the hue is what is commonly understood by colour (red, yellow, green etc.)
- the saturation is its hardness: red can be pale and saturated and similarly all other colours
- the lightness finally represents the brightness.

In traffic, the colour of surface colours is less important than the colour of the lights. A clear, although brief, description of the Munsell system is provided in Walraven (1981).

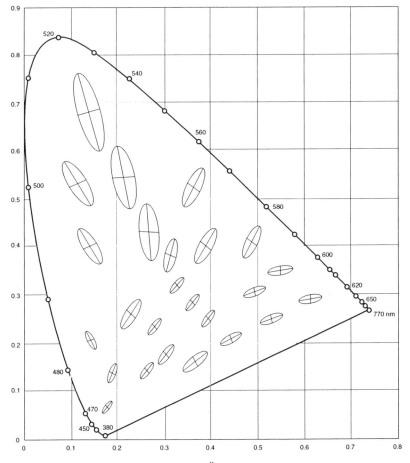

Figure 7.4.5: *The elliptical MacAdam areas. Not to scale (after De Boer & Fischer (1981))*

Table 7.4.1: *The colour temperature for a number of well-known sources of light (after Philips, 1989)*

Light source	Colour temperature (in K)
Candle	2000
Carbon filament lamp	2100
Incandescent lamp	2800
Halogen incandescent lamp*	3000
Carbon arc	3800
Sun	6000

* The halogen incandescent lamp is a tungsten lamp with the addition of halogen

7.4.3   Colour temperature, colour impression: dominant colours

There are two more important methods to describe the colour of a source of light. The first is the colour temperature. As established in section 7.4.2, this is the temperature in Kelvin of a Planckian radiator, whose light is similar to that of the source of light in question. See figure 7.4.3. Tungsten follows the spectral locus of the Planckian radiator reasonably well, so that the colour temperature is a good approximation of the colour of incandescent lamps. The colour temperature of a number of well-known sources of light is given in table 7.4.1.

The second method indicates the dominant colour. The spectrum of gas discharge lamps usually differs strongly from the spectrum of a Planckian radiator, as is indicated in section 4.3. The colour temperature is often only a crude approximation. In order to characterise the colour of gas discharge lamps by a simple method, the dominant colour is used. The colour point in the colour triangle is found, after which one tries to find the spectral colour nearest to that colour point. This spectral colour is called the dominant colour. Some examples are given in figure 7.4.3.

Sources of light, where the colour coincides with the same colour point, produce a light which gives the same colour impression, irrespective of the spectral distribution of the light. Thus the light from low-pressure sodium lamps is similar to the light from the yellow lights at traffic lights. In traffic, this similarity of the colour impression may give rise to confusion and misunderstandings. However, the problem can be overcome by simple means.

7.4.4.   The colour rendition of sources of light

Coloured surfaces reflect the incident light, but not to the same extent for different wavelengths. The colour impression of a surface, which does not emit light itself, depends on two things

- the spectral distribution of the incident light
- the spectral distribution of the reflection.

It is generally agreed that the colour impression of a surface can be considered normal in daylight. The definition of the colour rendition of light sources is based on this. The colour impression of a number of standard surfaces with very divergent colours is compared under the light of the light source to be investigated with the impression in daylight. The colour rendition of a light source is expressed in the colour rendering index. Usually $R_{a,8}$ is used, the colour rendering index for the eight standard colours

$$R_{a,8} = \frac{\sum_{i=8} \delta E_i}{8} \qquad [7.4.1]$$

in which $R_{a,8}$ is a dimensionless number which runs from 100 to a very low number. Conventionally, the reference light sources (the sun or incandescent light) have an index of 100. δE is the colour difference in arbitrary measure. The eight reference colours are taken from the 'Rectangular Uniform Colour Space (RUCS)'. For special applications sometimes an additional determination is used, where another six standard colours are added. This index is called $R_{a,14}$. Further details relating to the determination of R_a can be found in the standard work by De Boer and Fischer relating to interior lighting (De Boer & Fisher, 1981). See also De Boer & Rutten (1974).

Table 7.4.2 shows the colour rendering index for a number of current lamp types with, if relevant, different colour types. The specific luminous flux and the colour impression are added.

I have adhered to the type indications by Philips in the table, for the sake of brevity. Here are some explanations. Fluorescent lamp 36/40 W is the straight

Table 7.4.2: The specific luminous flux, the dominant colour (here approximated with the colour temperature) and the colour rendering index for a number of current lamp types; after Philips, 1989

Lamp type	Specific luminous flux (lm/W)	Colour temperature (K)	Colour rendering index $R_{a,8}$
Incandescent lamp 100 W	14	2800	100
Halogen lamp 500 W	19	3000	100
Fluorescent lamp 36/40 W			
Colour 29	83	2900	51
Colour 33	83	4100	63
Colour 57	45	7300	94
Colour 93	64	3000	95
Colour 94	65	3800	96
Colour 95	65	5000	98
SL 18 W	50	2700	85
Sodium lamps			
SOX-E 131 W	200	1700	–
SON-T 400 W	118	2000	23
High-pressure mercury lamps			
HP 250 W	47	6000	15
HPL C 250 W	56	3300	52
CSI	60	4200	80

tube lamp. The various colours are used for different applications. The compact fluorescent lamps discussed in section 14.2.3 have similar colour characteristics. The HP lamp is the old high-pressure mercury lamp without fluorescence powder. HPL C is the newer high-pressure mercury lamp with fluorescence powder and enhanced colour rendering (Comfort). These are little used in public lighting nowadays, due to their energy consumption rate. The CSI lamps are compact high-pressure mercury lamps, which are used particularly for lighting large sites, sport fields, halls and shop windows. They appear more and more in current street lighting.

Table 7.4.2 shows that the colour rendering index of current lamps can vary considerably. Detailed recommendations for the application of certain types of lamps in certain application areas apply to interior lighting. See, e.g. De Boer & Fischer (1981) and Hentschel (1994). In public lighting, there is usually less interest in the colour rendition than in the specific luminous flux. In road lighting, monochromatic low-pressure sodium lamps, in which no colours at all can be distinguished, are used in many countries. In residential areas higher requirements apply: high-pressure sodium and high-pressure mercury lamps with an $R_{a,8}$ of approximately 25 and 50 respectively are considered acceptable. The latest CIE recommendations read

> Monochromatic light sources should be avoided for areas where crime risk is high, that are environmentally sensitive, or where pedestrian activities predominate. (CIE 1995, clause 9.3.4).

Still greater demands apply to shopping centres and formal public spaces. In preference, fluorescent lamps with an $R_{a,8}$ of at least 85 are to be used here. CSI lamps with an $R_{a,8}$ of approximately 80 are increasingly used for larger outdoor spaces.

7.5   Functional defects

7.5.1   Causes and frequency of the occurrence of visual disorders

The previous chapters explained to what extent participation in traffic, either as a car driver or as a pedestrian, depends on the adequate functioning of the visual system. This is based on a type of average with regard to visual functions. Many people suffer to a lesser or greater extent from disorders of the visual system. This section discusses the disorders relevant to traffic in greater detail. A simple overview of disorders in the visual system is given in Anon (1970). This encyclopaedia, however, is no longer up-to-date for a number of points. A more detailed description can be found in the opthalmological literature. Reference is made in this respect in particular to the recent book by Stilma & Voorn, eds. (1995), which is considered a standard work in The Netherlands. Of interest is the clear, but quite old book by Mann & Pirie (1950).

Quite a number of diseases and defects exist in the visual system, but not all are important for the functioning. Table 7.5.1. shows an overview of the occurrence of the most common eye diseases and visual disorders in the

Table 7.5.1: *The most common eye diseases and visual disorders; Dutch population, reference year 1990; some patients suffer more than one disorder*

Disorder	Number of patients
1. Defects in the physical optical system	
– Refraction defects	6,000,000
2. Eye diseases	
– Cataracts	760,000
– Aqueous humor pathology	230,000
– Ditto + macula degeneration	480,000
– Glaucoma	90,000
– Ditto + ocular hypertension	400,000
3. Neurophthalmological defects	
– Accidents	50,000

Dutch population of about 15 million for the reference year 1990. The data are taken from Voorn (1995, table 1–3).

The most important causes for loss of function in the Western world are congenital defects and the effects of age, as well as degenerative loss of function. In the past, in particular in the developing countries, the lack of food and diseases have also been important causes. Readers should refer in this respect to the excellent, although presently less applicable to Western Europe, book by Mann & Pirie (1950), who devote a complete chapter to vitamins and also discuss other aspects of diseases. A modern Dutch book such as the one by Stilma & Voorn, eds. (1995) hardly pays attention to this. Loss of function as a result of accidents will not be discussed here, as this is a very specialised field. See, e.g. Stilma (1995b).

7.5.2   Congenital defects and trends

The highest visual acuity (section 7.2.3) is achieved when the optical image, which is formed by the cornea and the lens on the retina, is as sharp as possible. In many cases, the optical elements in the eye show some defect, which often results in a less sharp image. This is often the result of the fact that the focal length of the optical elements differs from the distance between lens and retina. The image may be sufficiently sharp but it does not fall on the retina. This is called a refraction defect. Table 7.5.1 shows that approximately 40% of the total Dutch population is affected. According to Mann & Pirie (1950), this relates in particular to short-sightedness (myopia); myopia is in most cases an inherited characteristic in which the eyeball is longer than the focal length of the cornea plus the lens. This characteristic increases with the advancement of age as a result of the hardening of the eye lens, to be discussed later. Myopia is also determined by other than inheritance factors; one therefore speaks of age trends. Something similar applies to the often occurring far-sightedness (hypermetropy or hyperopia). However, all this is not very important in traffic safety, as refraction defects are usually simply and very effectively corrected with spectacles or with contact lenses. See figure 7.5.1. Furthermore, it would seem that humans, particularly where the visual system is concerned, are able to compensate very well.

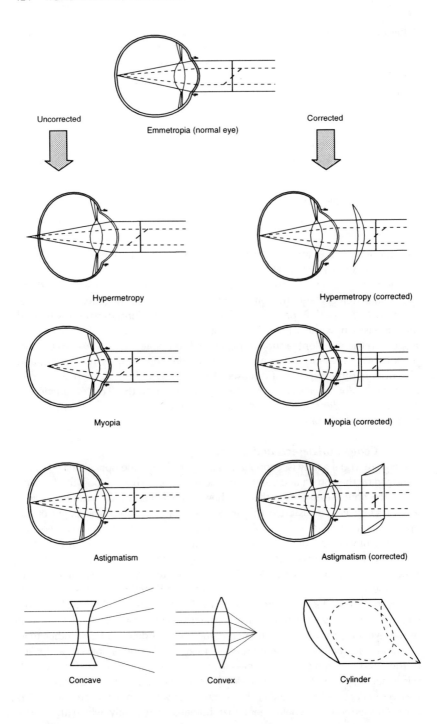

Figure 7.5.1: *Refraction defects and their correction*

It also often happens that defects occur in the rotational symmetry of the eye. The image is then sharp in a certain plane, but blurred in another; in such cases we speak of astigmatism. Van Heel (1950, chapter IXa) gives a very sound description of the optical phenomena relating to this. This defect can be corrected simply with a cylinder glass. See also figure 7.5.1.

Accommodation was discussed in section 6.1 where it was noted that the possibilities for accommodation are reduced with age, due to hardening of the eye lens. The most significant result is that it becomes ever more difficult for older people to read small letters; reading glasses are essential. This phenomenon is called presbyopia. Just like other refraction defects, it is easily corrected with spectacles. A side effect is that for a small extent of myopia or astigmatism it is less easy to compensate, due to lens hardening. It is not clear whether the myopia or the astigmatism become worse; it is clear, however, that they cause further difficulties and must be corrected even more.

7.5.3   Degenerative loss of function
Increasing spread
The most important cause of visual disorders, as far as traffic is concerned, is the degenerative loss of function. All physical and mental performance deteriorates with advancing age. A characteristic of this degeneration is that it varies considerably for different people in extent and seriousness. This means that the dispersion (or spread) of all sorts of functions increases sharply with advancing age. In practice, this often has more serious consequences than the average degeneration. The reason for this is that the measures, which one must take in order to ensure that older people can continue to participate in traffic, must have an ever wider area of application. These problems are discussed in detail by Schreuder (1994).

Table 7.5.1 shows that there are three diseases of the eye which affect a great number of people. These relate to cataracts, macula degeneration and glaucoma. All three occur increasingly with age and they relate to the less effective working of the physical functions. In addition, all three are associated with serious loss in respect of visual functions: often all three end with blindness. Finally, it may be expected that their frequency, as a result of the greying of The Netherlands, will increase considerably in future years. Thus Voorn (1995, tables 1–4) indicates that an increase in the occurrence of cataracts of 30% is expected between 1990 and 2005, for macula degeneration that figure is 26% and for glaucoma 50%. This is a considerable problem. Diabetes may indirectly lead to eye damage and the associated disorders. The fact, that diabetes is increasing rapidly is also relevant in respect of visual disorders (see Hendrikse, 1995).

Cataracts
Cataracts are the result of clouding, in particular, of the eye lens. The stray light within the eye mentioned in section 7.3.2 in the discussion on physiological glare, is increasing rapidly and so is the sensitivity to glare. In serious cases, even large contrasts can hardly be distinguished.

Light impressions, however, remain but visual acuity is reduced. Particularly with cataracts due to age, the reduction in visual performance is very slow and gradual and sufficient attention is not always paid to it. But cataracts also appear in young people. According to Mann & Pirie (1950, page 142) lens clouding to a small extent is very common

> at least 25 percent of normal people have some slight imperfections in their lenses which are, technically, cataracts.

The medical aspects of cataracts are described in detail in Stilma (1995).

As a result of the increased sensitivity to glare in people who suffer from cataracts, much attention is paid in public lighting and, in particular, in lighting of residential areas and pedestrian precincts to the reduction of physiological glare. This requirement may conflict with the designers of such installations, where, in order to achieve a certain sparkle, often non cut-off lanterns are used. The solution has to be found in producing luminaires which cause little glare and nevertheless look attractive, especially during the day.

Macula degeneration

According to Stilma (1995a), macula degeneration is a main cause of blindness in Western countries. By far the most frequent form of this is age-related macula degeneration. The cause is a decreased metabolism in the retina, especially in the macula. A comment on the terminology. According to Mann & Pirie (1950, page 48), the central area of the retina is called the macula lutea or yellow spot; the central part of this is called fovea centralis. The first symptom of macula degeneration is usually greater sensitivity to after images; this may be relevant to the requirements for transition lighting in tunnels (see section 15.4.6). Subsequently, deformations and other defects in the blood vessels in the macula occur, which may give rise to the formation of scar tissue which destroys the photoreceptors. Finally, the blood vessels affected may start to leak and fluid enters the eyeball. This causes serious clouding, which may lead to blindness.

The clearest symptom of macula degeneration is the fact that parts of the retina no longer function. In addition, deformation in the perceived image occurs, caused by the deformations in the parts of the retina which still function. Visual acuity in the foveal area is reduced dramatically; visual performance in the periphery, however, remains usually up to the mark. This fovea effect means that in the first place the critical perception of small details is affected–exactly the function which is so important for participation in traffic. As the photoreceptors are destroyed, no therapy exists; nor can glasses or contact lenses bring an improvement. As far as lighting is concerned, an increase in the level of light or increasing the contrast does not bring solace. The only possibility is the use of larger letters or signs. This measure is especially relevant to pedestrian areas. These include not only roads and streets, but also station platforms, shopping centres etc.

Glaucoma

As shown in table 7.5.1, glaucoma is a frequent phenomenon, especially in combination with increased eye pressure. Glaucoma is a result of decreased moisture circulation in the eye. The first symptoms are usually the result of the failure of the central peripheral part of the retina. Later the foveal part also often fails, which may result in total blindness. The risk of a cataract also becomes greater. The pathology is described in detail in Langerhorst (1995).

7.5.4   Colour blindness

Approximately 8% of all men and 0.3% of women has a malfunction in colour vision (Gleitman, 1995, page 194). This disorder has its origins in the malfunctioning of one or more of the types of cones in the retina (see section 6.1.4). People, in whom all three types of cones function properly, are called colour normals (trichromates).

It often happens, that one or more of the cone types no longer functions, or not properly. In most cases malfunction is limited to one type of cone. Two types remain; people who suffer from this disorder are therefore called dichromates. As there are three types of cones, there are also three types of dichromates. According to the somewhat oversimplified classification by Anon (1970; part II page 273), these three types can be characterised as follows

- protanopes are insensitive to red
- deuteranopes are insensitive to green
- tritanopes are insensitive to blue.

Deuteranopes occur most frequently; protanopes occur less frequently. The effect of these two disorders is rather similar: neither can distinguish between red and green. In addition, protanopes are almost insensitive to red light. Tritanopy is seldom seen; it applies more often to people in whom only one type of cone functions, or where the cones do not function at all. These people cannot distinguish colours at all; they are therefore called monochromates. In most cases this disorder is associated with other visual defects.

The effects of defects in perceiving colours is smaller than might be suspected from the description. There are no serious restrictions in daily life. See De Jong (1995). Only seeing traffic lights may pose problems. When the colours are selected carefully, neither deuteranopes nor protanopes will encounter many difficulties. In the past we used to think otherwise. Hopkinson (1960) and Mann & Pirie (1950) e.g., recommended that colour-blind people had to be kept out of many occupations.

7.5.5   Consequences for public lighting

Visual disorders can have significant consequences for the practice of public lighting. The most important ones are

- the large spread among people suffering from visual malfunctions makes it necessary to make any adaptations more drastic than would be required for the average of the group with disorders

- reduced visual acuity (refraction defects, macula degeneration) can, at least partly, be compensated for by producing letters, signs and signals which are larger, more evident, or with a larger contrast than would be required for 'normals'
- reduced sensitivity to contrast (cataract, glaucoma) can, at least partly, be compensated for by making the requirements for limiting glare stricter than would be required for normals.

7.6   Older and disabled people in traffic

Older people form a group which encounter additional problems in traffic. This is evident from, among other things, traffic accident statistics: older people are involved considerably more often in accidents than younger people, while the outcome of accidents is usually more serious (Wouters, 1991). Solutions and improvements are looked for, in particular in the area of adaptation to the infrastructure, that allow older people to participate in traffic as completely as possible. The problems of disabled people in traffic are, to a certain extent, similar to those of older people.

Usually the design of traffic facilities enables the normal traffic participant to make optimal use of them. The functional restrictions in older and disabled people may be in the area of visual perception, auditive perception, motor skills and cognition. A few examples: the letters on traffic and road signs are sufficiently large for normal people to be able to see and read them in good time; the announcements at public transport stops are loud enough for normal people to be able to hear them in a moving tram or bus; the steps at train doors are a sufficient height and width for normal people to be able to easily enter the train or leave it; machines for cancelling transport tickets are designed in such a way that normal people understand these and can deal with them. A standard person is defined, who serves as a measure for all those 'normal' people. See also section 8.3.2. However, there are many people in traffic who are not normal in the sense meant here and whose functioning is far removed from the norm.

A handicap is not an absolute indicator; it depends on the traffic task, whether an obstacle or a restriction should be considered a handicap. Car drivers are required to approximate the norm quite closely. See e.g. De Jong (1995). For pedestrians and cyclists, however, no legal minimum requirements exist, which they must meet in order to participate in traffic; nor for riding a moped or for the use of public transport. As far as public lighting is concerned, the main problems are found in the lighting of pedestrianised areas.

The problem with this is that not much research has been carried out into the epidemiology of handicaps. The approach is emotional, rather than statistical. An example of a rational approach by which disabled people are better served in the long term can be found in a study on the power which people can exert under certain conditions (Daams, 1994). A similar study in respect of visual ergonomics is not known.

Bibliography

Adrian, W. (1961). 'Der Einfluss störender Lichter auf die extrafoveale Wahrnemung des menschligen Auges'. *Lichttechnik* **13** (1961) 450–454; 508–511; 558–562.

Adrian, W. (1966). 'Neuere untersuchungen über die Blendung in der Strasseneleuchtung'. In: Anon., (1966).

Adrian, W. (1982). 'Investigations on the required luminance in tunnel entrances'. *Lighting Res. Technol.* **14** (1982) 151.

Adrian, W. (1989). *A method for the design of tunnel entrance lighting.* University of Waterloo, School of Optometry, Waterloo, Ontario, Canada (1989)

Adrian, W. (1995). 'The visibility concept and its metric'. In: Anon (1995a).

Anon. (1966). *The lighting of traffic routes.* Congress Amsterdam. 26–27 April 1966. Arnhem, NSVV. See also *Electrotechniek* **44** (1966) (22) 509.

Anon. (1970). *Visuele medische encyclopedie* (Two parts) [Visual medical encyclopaedia]. Utrecht, Uitgeverij het Spectrum N.V., 1970.

Anon. (1995). *Symposium on tunnel and motorway lighting congress,* Amsterdam. 25 September 1995. Express Highway Research Foundation of Japan, Amsterdam, 1995.

Anon. (1995a). *PAL: Progress in automobile lighting.* Technical University Darmstadt, September 26/27, 1995. Darmstadt, Technical University, 1995.

Aulhorn, E (1964). *Graefes Archiv für klinische und experimentelle Ophthalmologie* **167** (1964) No 1, 4.

Blackwell, H.R. (1946). 'Contrast threshold of the human eye'. *J. Opt. Soc. Amer.* **36** (1946) 624.

Bok, S.T. (1958). Cybernetica (Stuurkunde) [Cybernetics]. Utrecht, Prisma Aula, 1959.

Bouma, P.J. (1946). *Kleuren en kleurenindrukken* [Colours and colour impressions]. Amsterdam, Meulenhoff, 1946.

Bourdy, C., Chiron, A., Cottin, C. & Monot, A. (1987). 'Visibility at a tunnel entrance: Effect of temporal adaptation'. *Lighting Res. Technol.* **19** (1987) 35–44.

Buijs, A. (1995). *Statistiek om mee te werken* [Statistics to be employed]. Fourth, revised edition, third impression. Houten, Stenfert Kroese, 1995.

Burg, A. (1964). *An investigation of some relationships between dynamic visual acuity, static visual acuity and driving record.* Report No. 64–18. Dept. of Engineering, Univ. of California, Los Angeles, 1964.

Burg, A. (1968). *Vision and driving; A summary of research findings.* Annual Meeting Highway Research Board 1968.

CEN (1995). *Lighting applications and road equipment; Road lighting, calculation of performance* (Draft 4, January 1995) CEN/TC 169/226 JWG 'Road lighting', 1995.

CEN (1997). *Standard for the lighting of road traffic tunnels,* CEN/TC169/WG6, 10th draft.

CIE (1932). *Receuil des travaux et compte rendue des scéances,* Huitième Session Cambridge, Septembre 1931. Cambridge, University Press, 1932.

CIE (1965). *International recommendations for the lighting of public thoroughfares.* Publication No. 12. Paris, CIE, 1965.

CIE (1977). *Recommendation for the lighting of roads for motorized traffic.* Publication No. 12/2. Paris, CIE, 1977.

CIE (1981). *An analytic model for describing the influence of lighting parameters upon visual performance.* Volume I: Technical foundations. Publication No. 19/2. Paris, CIE, 1981.

CIE (1984). *Tunnel entrance lighting – a survey of fundamentals for determining the luminance in the threshold zone.* Publication No. 81. Paris, CIE, 1984.

CIE (1990). *Guide for the lighting of road tunnels and underpassses.* Publication No. 88.

Vienna, CIE, 1990.

CIE (1990a). *Calculation and measurement of luminance and illuminance in road lighting.* Publication No. 30/2. Paris, CIE, 1982 (reprinted 1990).

CIE (1994). *Glare evaluation system for use within outdoor sports and area lighting.* Publication No. 112. Vienna, CIE, 1994.

CIE (1995). *Recommendations for the lighting of roads for motor and pedestrian traffic.* Technical Report. Publication No. 115-1995. Vienna, CIE, 1995.

CIE (1995a). *Tunnel lighting; A design guide.* Revision of CIE Documents No. 61 and No. 88. First draft, 1995.

Cornsweet, T.N. (1970). *Visual perception.* London, Acad. Press, 1970.

Daams, B.J. (1994). *Human force exertion in user-product interaction; Backgrounds for design.* Delft, Delft University Press, 1994.

De Boer, J.B. (1951). *Fundamental experiments of visibility and admissible glare in road lighting.* Stockholm, CIE, 1951.

De Boer, J.B. (1967) 'Visual perception in road traffic and the field of vision of the motorist'. Chapter 2 in: De Boer (ed.) (1967).

De Boer, J.B. & Fisher, D. (1981). *Interior lighting* (Second revised edition). Deventer, Kluwer, 1981.

De Boer, J.B. & Rutten, A.J.F. (1974). *Algemene verlichtingskunde* [General lighting science]. Diktnr 7.815. Eindhoven, Technische Hogeschool, Afdeling der Bouwkunde, 1974.

De Boer, J.B. & Schreuder, D.A. (1967). *Glare as a criterion for quality in street lighting.* Trans. Illum. Engn. Soc. (London) 32 (1967) 117–128.

De Boer, J.B. (ed.) (1967) *Public lighting.* Eindhoven, Centrex, 1967.

De Jong, P.T.V.M. (1995). 'Ergoftalmologie' ['Ergophthalmology']. Chapter 20 in: Stilma & Voorn, (eds.), (1995).

Dixon, W.J. & Massey, F.J. (1957). *Introduction to statistical analysis.* 2nd Edition. New York, McGraw-Hill Book Company Inc., 1957.

Elvik, R. (1995). *Meta-analysis of evalutions of public lighting as accident counter-measure.* TRB, Transportation Research Rec. No. 1485 (1995) 112–123.

Fischer, A.J. & Christie, A.W. (1965). 'A note on disability glare'. *Vision Research* 5 (1965) 565–571.

Gleitman, H. (1995). *Psychology.* Fourth edition. New York, W.W. Norton & Company, 1995.

Hartmann, E. & Moser, E.A. (1968). 'Das Gesetz der physiologischen Blendung bei sehr kleinen Blendwinkeln'. *Lichttechnik* 20 (1968) 67A–69A.

Hartmann, E. & Ucke, C. (1974). 'Der Einfluss der Blendquellengrösse auf die physiologische Blendung bei kleinen Blendwinkeln'. *Lichttechnik* 26 (1974) 20–23.

Hendrikse, F. (1995). 'Retinale vasculaire afwijkingen: hypertensie en diabetes. ['Retinal vascular defects: hypertension and diabetes.] Chapter 15 in: Stilma & Voorn, (eds.), (1995).

Helbig, E. (1972). *Grundlagen der Lichtmesstechnik.* Leipzig, Geest & Portig, 1972.

Hentschel, H.-J. (1994). *Licht und Beleuchtung; Theorie und Praxis der Lichttechnik.* 4. Auflage. Heidelberg, Hüthig Buch Verlag, 1994.

Hills, B.L. (1975). *Visibility under night driving conditions.* ARR no. 29. Aust. Road Res. Board, Vermont South, 1975.

Hofstetter, H.W. (1976). 'Visual accuity and highway accidents'. *Journal of the American Optometric Association* 47 (1976), Number 7, July 1976, 887–893.

Holladay, L.L. (1927). 'Action of a light source in the field of view in lowering visibility'. *J. Opt. Soc. Amer.* 14 (1927) 1.

Hopkinson, R.G. (1969). *Lighting and seeing.* London, William Heinemann, 1969.

Kabayama, H. (1963). 'Study on adaptive illumination for sudden change of brightness'. *J. Illum. Engn Inst. Japan.* **47** (1963) 488–496 (in Japanese).

König, A. & Brodhun, E. (1889) *Experimentelle Untersuchungen über die psychophysischen Fundamentalformel in Bezug auf den Gesichtssinn.* Sitz. Ber. Preuss. Akad. Wiss. (1889) 641–644 (cit. Helbig, 1972).

Krech, D.; Crutchfield, R.S. & Livson, N. (1969). *Elements of psychology.* Second edition. New York, Alfred Knopf, 1969.

Langerhorst, C.L. (1995). 'Glaucoom' ['Glaucoma']. Chapter 14 in: Stilma & Voorn, (eds.), 1995.

MacAdam, D.L., (1970). *Sources of color science.* Cambridge (Mass.), MIT Press, 1970.

Mann, I. & Pirie, A. (1950). *The science of seeing.* Harmondsworth, Penguin books. Pelican A 157, 1950 (Revised edition).

Moon, P. (1961). *The scientific basis of illuminating engineering* (Revised edition). New York, Dover Publications, Inc., 1961.

Moroney, M.J. (1990). *Facts from figures.* Harmondsworth, Penguin Books Ltd. Pelican A236. (3rd revised edition). 1956. Latest edition Penguin books, 1990.

Noordzij, P.C.; Hagenzieker, M.P. & Theeuwes, J. (1993). *Visuele waarneming en verkeersveiligheid* [Visual perception and safety in traffic] R-93-12. Leidschendam, SWOV, 1993.

NSVV (1957). *Aanbevelingen voor openbare verlichting* [Recommendations for public lighting]. Den Haag, Moormans Periodieke Pers, 1957 (year estimated).

NSVV (1974/1975) 'Richtlijnen en aanbevelingen voor openbare verlichting' [Guidelines and recommendations for public lighting]. *Electrotechniek* **52** (1974) 15; 53 (1975) 2 and 5.

NSVV (1977). 'Het lichtniveau van de openbare verlichting in de bebouwde kom' [The level of light in public lighting in built-up areas]. *Electotechniek* **55** (1977) 90–91.

NSVV (1990). *Aanbevelingen voor openbare verlichting;* Deel I . [Recommendations for public lighting; Part I] NSVV, Arnhem, 1990.

NSVV (1990a). *Aanbevelingen voor de verlichting van lange tunnels voor het gemotoriseerde verkeer.* [Recommendations for lighting in long tunnels for motorised traffic]. Arnhem/Leidschendam, NSVV/SWOV, 1990.

Ohayama, T. (1995). 'Studies in lighting curves for dimmed tunnel entrances'. In: Anon (1995).

Rushton, W.A.H. (1963). Cited by Cornssweet, (1970).

Rushton, W.A.H. & Gubisch, R.W. (1966). 'Glare: its measurement by cone threshold and by the bleaching of cone pigment'. *J. Opt. Soc. Amer.* **56** (1966) 104–110.

Rushton, W.A.H. & Westheimer, G. (1962). 'The effect upon the rod threshold of bleaching neighbouring rods'. *J. Physiol.* (London) 1962: 164; 319–329.

Schouten, J.F. (1937). *Visueele meting van adaptatie en van de wederzijdse beünvloeding van netvlieselementen* [Visual measurement of adaptation and of the reciprocal effects caused by retina elements] Dissertation, Universiteit Utrecht, 1937.

Schouten, T.M. (1972). *Verblinding, enige fysiologische, leeftijdsafhankelijke oorzaken* [Glare, some physiological, age-dependent causes]. R-72-9. Voorburg, SWOV, 1972.

Schreuder, D.A. (1964). *The lighting of vehicular traffic tunnels.* Eindhoven, Centrex, 1964.

Schreuder, D.A. (1981). *De verlichting van tunnelingangen; Een probleemanalyse omtrent de verlichting van lange tunnels.* [Lighting in tunnel entrances; A problem analysis relating to the lighting of long tunnels] Two parts. R-81-26 I and II. Voorburg, SWOV, 1981.

Schreuder, D.A. (1988). *Gezichtsvermogen en verkeersveiligheid* [Vision and traffic safety]. R-88-9. Leidschendam, SWOV, 1988.

Schreuder, D.A. (1990). *De veldfactor bij de bepaling van de verlichtingsniveaus bij tunnelingangen; Verslag van experimenteel onderzoek.* [The field factor in determining lighting levels in tunnel entrances; Report on experimental research]. R-90-10. Leidschendam, SWOV, 1990.

Schreuder, D.A. (1991). *De veldfactor bij de bepaling van de verlichtingsniveaus bij tunnelingangen; Een nadere analyse.* [The field factor in the determination of lighting levels in tunnel entrances; a more specific analysis]. R-91-65. Leidschendam, SWOV, 1991.

Schreuder, D.A. (1993). *Contrastwaarnemingen in tunnels.* [Perceiving contrasts in tunnels]. R-93-36. Leidschendam, SWOV, 1993.

Schreuder, D.A. (1994). *Duurzame verkeersveiligheid voor ouderen en gehandicapten; Verslag van een pilot-studie ten behoeve van een onderzoekopzet.* [Sustainable traffic safety for older and disabled people; Report on a pilot study to determine a research framework]. Leidschendam, Duco Schreuder Consultancies, 1994.

Schreuder, D.A. & Swart, L. (1993). *Energy saving in tunnel entrance lighting.* Right Light, Arnhem, 1993.

Schreuder, D.A., Swart, L. & De Haan, H. (1994). *Gegenstrahlbeleuchtung in Tunneleinfahrten.* Paper presented at LICHT94, Interlaken, Switzerland, 14.9 - 16.9.1994.

Stiles, W.S. & Crawford, B.H. (1937). The effect of a glaring light source on extrafoveal vision. *Proc. Roy. Soc.* **122b** (1937) 255-280.

Stilma, J.S. (1995). 'Cataract'. Chapter 13 in: Stilma & Voorn, (eds.), (1995).

Stilma, J.S. (1995a). 'Visusdaling: acuut en geleidelijk' [Reduction in visus: acute and gradual'] Chapter 12 in: Stilma & Voorn, (eds.), (1995).

Stilma, J.S. (1995b). 'Oogletsels' [Eye injuries] . Chapter 16 in: Stilma & Voorn, (eds.), (1995).

Stilma, J.S. & Voorn, Th. B., eds. (1995). *Praktische oogheelkunde* [Practical ophthalmology]. First edition, second revised imprint. Houten, Bohn Stafleu Van Loghum, 1995.

Swart, L. (1994). *Tegenstraalverlichting in tunnels – wat is daar tegen?* [Contraflux lighting in tunnels – what is against it?] Congress day 12 April 1994. NSVV, Amsterdam, 1994.

Van Bommel, J.W.M. & De Boer, J.B. (1980). *Road lighting.* Deventer. Kluwer, 1980.

Van Heel, A.C.S. (1950). *Inleiding in de optica* [Introduction to optics] (Derde druk). Den Haag, Martinus Nijhoff, 1950.

Van Norren, D. (1995). 'Lichtschade' [Light damage]. Chapter 4 in: Stilma & Voorn, (eds.), (1995).

Voorn, Th. B. (1995). '1. Inleiding' [Introduction]. In: Stilma & Voorn, (eds.), (1995).

Vos, J.J. (1963). *On mechanisms of glare.* Dissertation, Universiteit Utrecht, 1963.

Vos, J.J. (1983). *Verblinding bij tunnelingangen I: De invloed van strooilicht in het oog.* [Glare in tunnel entrances I: The effect of stray light in the eye.] IZF 1983 C-8. Soesterberg, IZF-TNO, 1983.

Vos, J.J. & Padmos, P. (1983). *Stray light, contrast sensitivity and the critical object in relation to tunnel entrance lighting.* Amsterdam, CIE, 1983.

Vos, J.J.; Walraven, J. & Van Meeteren, A. (1976). 'Light profiles of the foveal image of a point source'. *Vision Research* **16** (1976) 215–219.

Walraven, J. (1981). *Kleur* [Colour]. Ede, Zomer & Keuning. 1981.

Weale, R.A. (1961). *Transactions of the Illuminating Engineering Society (London),* **26** (1961) No 2, page 95.

Wouters, P.I.J. (1991). *De veiligheid van oudere verkeersdeelnemers* [The safety of older participants in traffic]. R-91-77. Leidschendam, SWOV, 1991.

8   The psychology of visual perception

As the information required for participation in traffic is of a visual nature, and must be gathered 'on line' and in 'real time', knowledge of the visual system is essential in order to properly understand the role of public lighting. The anatomy and the physiology of the visual system were discussed in previous chapters. The psychological aspect of visual perception will be dealt with in this chapter. This forms the basis for a better understanding with regard to the interpretations of the functions which are part of the visual system, and which are used in traffic.

These functions must be interpreted in order to establish the requirements in respect of lighting to help promote safety in traffic and in public areas. The minimum requirements of awareness and alertness must be satisfied first. In addition, the ability to identify objects and, in particular, situations is essential, as the correct execution of manoeuvres in traffic is based on an accurate interpretation. Manoeuvres are selected on the basis of results from a decision-making process. Anticipation plays an important role in the decision-making process. The requirements in respect of lighting are very often based on the needs and requirements of the average person (John and Jane Average).

The quality of the decisions depends largely on whether the person in question is prepared. This is based on motivation. The latter leads us to the concept of aggression, which is also relevant to participation in traffic.

8.1   Visibility

8.1.1   Perception, detection and identification

The purpose of public lighting is to improve the visibility of objects. This involves the following concepts

- *perception* (visibility): by this I mean the general concept of gathering and processing information
- *detection* (detectability): this means the extent to which primary perception is satisfied, where the presence of an object is merely established. The word 'visibility' is normally used in relation to visual perception
- *conspicuousness*: by this I mean the extent to which an object is perceived in the real world, taking into consideration any interference present in the real world
- *identification*: this means the extent to which comparison of the object with the content of the memory is possible; the extent to which the object can be assigned to a class of known objects.

8.1.2   Arousal and alertness
Attention
Not only the visibility but also the observer is important in relation to two factors: attention and motivation. These two factors will be discussed briefly. By attention I mean a general, qualitative way of managing stress, representing the total of stimuli from the environment. Attention can be divided into arousal and alertness. Awareness and arousal relate to the general physiological state of the organism; attentiveness relates to the extent to which attention is focused. The distinction between the terms attention, attentiveness, awareness, arousal and alertness is not always clearly established. There is some overlap but they are not identical. Motivation represents the inclination or willingness of the observer to contribute to the perception process.

Arousal and alertness depend on the mental or perceptual load. An increase in the latter is generally accompanied by an increase in arousal, while attentiveness decreases. Different results may occur under extreme stress, but these are of minor importance for traffic. Summing these two relations results in a curve with a 'reverse U shape' (Brunia, 1979). See figure 8.1.1.

Arousal
Arousal is usually considered to have a physiological aspect and may be affected by physiologically active substances. A minimum degree of arousal is required for adequate functioning; the degree depends on the task. In traffic, there are few activities which can be undertaken while daydreaming, not even those which at first sight seem to be automatic. Schreuder (1985) points out that an inadequate level of arousal may play a role in many unexplained accidents.

Attention
Krech et al. (1969, page 186) describes attention as

> The focusing of perception involving a heightened awareness of a limited part of the perceptual field.

Awareness is in turn described as 'an emotional feeling' (page 606). And regarding emotions we read

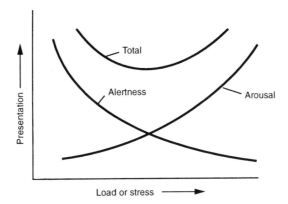

Figure 8.1.1: *The 'reverse U-shaped curve'; efficacy as a function of stress*

> The hormones of the adrenal gland, the thyroid gland and the pituitary gland are
> of special importance for emotional response (page 591).

Although these descriptions are rather vague, it is clear that attention has a
hormonal, as well as a motivational aspect.

Attention and arousal depend on stress in a further respect. Attention is
high at a very low level of stress; competition between different stimuli is
absent. When stress is increased, attention remains high, but arousal must be
distributed among several competing stimuli. In traffic, we continually meet
with objects which demand attention. The relative value of these objects is
important; a great many problems in traffic can be reduced to a less than
optimum allocation of perceptual priorities.

Perceptual priorities
As explained in section 8.2.3, not all visual objects are equally important. Most
objects in the field of vision are not relevant to driving. They only contribute
to the 'noise'. Other objects, however, are information carriers or risk carriers;
in other words, they are the visually critical objects (Padmos, 1984). The visual
task in traffic relates in the final analysis to detecting these visually critical
objects among irrelevant objects: setting correct priorities in perception. This
causes problems in practice, as only a minimum of research has been
undertaken into the type of objects that deserve priority.

The distribution of attention
In traffic, objects may compete for attention. It should be remembered that
attention is not a constant quantity which can be forced by a third party with
regard to focus and quantity. Research by Theeuwes (1992) shows that
focusing attention in traffic situations mostly takes place top-down, i.e. the
driver decides the object on which he or she will concentrate. This decision is
taken on cognitive grounds and is little influenced by chance characteristics in
the environment.

Consequently, objects which are meant to draw attention are not very effective. Research has shown that most road and traffic signs are not or hardly noticeable (Gundy, 1989). Additional measures are required where a message is essential and must not be missed, as in the case of warning signs. Public lighting plays a part in this. Another consequence is that the double task method is not very useful in traffic research. See also section 8.1.3.

Functional field of vision

As indicated in section 6.1.5 visual perception in the periphery is of a different nature than that in the foveal area. The functional field of vision can be divided into the following

- up to approximately 2° from the axis of the field of vision: foveal vision
- between approximately 2° and 25° from the axis: close peripheral vision (the stationary field)
- between approximately 25° and 85° from the axis: peripheral vision (the eye field)
- further than approximately 85° from the axis: remote peripheral vision (the head field).

Eye movement is not always required for foveal vision and in the stationary field, but it is needed in the eye field. In the head field, more than approximately 85° from the axis, movements of the head are also required (Bunt & Sanders, 1973, page 1a). Eye movements are required for an angle of more than 25°, for useful vision. Anybody will be able to discover that most people prefer eye movements and head movements at much smaller angles.

8.1.3   The communication channel

A channel is always required for transmitting information; the usual term used is communication channel. All channels have a limited capacity, expressed in an information measuring unit (e.g. bits). The message can never exceed the capacity of the channel. In formula

$$T \leq C \qquad\qquad [8.1.1]$$

in which T is the information in the message and C the capacity. The double task method mentioned in section 8.1.2, is based on the assumption that T is constant, so that the attention T_1 required in traffic can be determined by measuring performance T_2 for a secondary task. It is assumed that

$$T_1 + T_2 = T = C \qquad\qquad [8.1.2]$$

The method in question is described in Brown & Poulton (1961) and Michon (1964). However, C is not constant in living systems; it is co-determined by motivation. This does not mean that a concept such as 'overload of communication channels' (information overload) has no real meaning (Roszbach, 1972). As an example there is a pilot study relating to driving and visual conditions in traffic tunnels. The load is not measured in relation to a second task, however, but by means of a number of physiological parameters, including heartbeat, skin resistance and blinking (Verwey, 1995). The subsequent report (Verwey et al., 1995) mentions that eye movements may prove a more effective measure. Eye movements are used frequently for this purpose in other areas (Rockwell et al., 1967; Zwahlen, 1980; Hagiwara & Zwahlen, 1995).

8.1.4   Anticipation

Anticipation rates highly among aspects of perception. By anticipation is meant the extent to which the appearance of an object of a certain class can be foreseen. Unexpected objects are detected much less easily – later, to a lesser extent, or sometimes not at all – than expected objects. Anticipation itself depends

- on familiarity with the objects (general experience as a participant in traffic)
- familiarity with the situation (the local experience of the participant in traffic).

A great deal of research has been conducted in this area. See, e.g. Broadbent (1958) and Norman (1976). Griep (1971) has given a description of the effect of anticipation on perception in traffic which is still relevant. Anticipation is an important factor in the identification of road classes (Janssen, 1979), in particular in relation to sustainably safe traffic, discussed in section 3.2. (Koornstra et al., (eds.), 1992; Vis & Krabbendam, 1994).

Search behaviour is also relevant. When someone is placed in a familiar environment, he or she usually actively looks for stimuli which can be anticipated. But when the environment is unfamiliar stimuli can only be absorbed passively.

8.2   Driving, perception and decision-making

8.2.1   The driving task

By driving task is meant the extent to which demands in traffic can be met. This relates to behaviour characteristics of participants in traffic, traffic behaviour. Behaviour is based on the processing of information. This can also be called the visual task. A number of current models relate to the driving task (Schreuder, 1973; OECD, 1972; Janssen, 1986).

Frequently only the simplest psychological model is used in psychological and psycho-physiological research – the familiar behaviourist model, i.e. the stimulus – response model. This consists of a stimulus (S) and the subsequent response (R),which are characterised by a single, causal relation. In many cases this model suffices for the description of human or animal behaviour. But often, especially when analysing the driving task, the S–R model shows serious shortcomings. As this often relates to decision-making processes, a considerable improvement is achieved by introducing the decision (D) between the absorption of information and the performance of actions. This produces the decision model, or S–D–R model. This model proves to be satisfactory for traffic behaviour in most cases.

Table 8.2.1: *Levels in the hierarchical model; based on Schreuder, 1974, table 1*

Level	Need leads to:	
	Individual behaviour	Total behaviour
1a	Selection of travel motive	Trip generation
1b	Selection of destination	Trip distribution
2	Selection of means of transport	Distribution across travel modes
3	Selection of route	Distribution of the journey bundles
4a	Selection of compound manoeuvre	Travel
4b	Selection of elementary manoeuvre	Travel
4c	Selection of manoeuvre component	Travel

Behaviour described on the basis of the S – R model is also called automatic behaviour. This relates to reflexes which may or may not be learnt ('conditioned'). Behaviour which can be described with the S – D – R model is conscious behaviour, in contrast to automatic behaviour.

Traffic may be described as a succession of manoeuvres to be undertaken, each the result of a decision-making process. Manoeuvres can be ranked in a hierarchical system, with the selection of the destination, the route and means of transport at the top; at the bottom is managing the vehicle (Schreuder, 1970, 1972, 1974; Asmussen, 1972). Elementary manoeuvres are at the centre of the hierarchical model. Compound manoeuvres can be built up from these elementary manoeuvres. Elementary manoeuvres, on the other hand, may be split into their components. Table 8.2.1 shows the levels of the hierarchical model.

The function of traffic facilities is twofold, according to section 2.5

1. Arrival at the trip destination
2. Safe arrival at the trip destination.

Steering manoeuvres are required in order to reach the destination. Other manoeuvres are required in relation to safety: evasion manoeuvres. In terms of the afore-mentioned anticipation, steering manoeuvres relate to the avoidance of expected objects and evasion manoeuvres relate to the avoidance of unexpected objects.

8.2.2 Preview

Preview is the distance in time or in length, in which an object must be perceived to be able to carry out the respective manoeuvre to a reasonable degree. To a reasonable degree means without endangering oneself or other traffic. The minimum preview required for steering manoeuvres is usually smaller than for evasive manoeuvres, as they usually fall into the anticipated pattern. However, because of other traffic, the maximum permissible deceleration in steering manoeuvres is smaller than for evasive manoeuvres, where sometimes an emergency stop is necessary. This leads to an increased preview. A deceleration of more than 2.5 to 3 m/s^2 at speeds above approximately 30 km/hour is not desirable, from the point of view of driving comfort. A newspaper can slide from a car seat when braking at approximately 2 m/s^2 (Mortimer, 1971). This is also the limit which is adhered to for buses and trains; standing passengers can reasonably remain standing at this deceleration. 5 m/s^2, the minimum standard at which a car is permitted to be used in traffic, is set as a top limit for an emergency stop. A value of 7 to 8 m/s^2 is feasible in favourable circumstances (Schreuder, 1981). The minimal preview, which is equal to the stopping distance mentioned in section 5.4.6, can be determined with the aid of the familiar formula

$$s = \beta v + \frac{v^2}{2a}$$
[8.2.1]

in which

s	is the stopping distance in metres
v	the speed in m/s
a	the deceleration in m/s^2
β	the reaction time in s

Table 8.2.2 shows some values for the stopping distance as an illustration.

Large differences are found in stopping distance. Driving speed and reaction time have a considerable effect, but not as much as deceleration. Stopping distance becomes even greater when higher speeds are allowed, as in Germany on many roads and on certain new roads in Japan. See, e.g. Schreuder (1994).

As different reaction times, as well as different decelerations, apply to different manoeuvres, one must take account of considerable differences in the preview. Below the preview is given for three types of road

- class A: urban roads and streets; driving speed 15 m/s (approximately 50 km or 30 miles per hour)
- class B: rural main roads; driving speed 25 m/s (approximately 90 km or 55 miles per hour)
- class C: motorways; driving speed 35 m/s (approximately 125 km or 75 miles per hour).

Readers should refer to Schreuder (1991) for determination of the preview, as well as for an account of the parameter values used. See table 8.2.3.

There are clear differences between the values in table 8.2.3 and the values encountered in popular literature. The difference lies mainly in the more realistic

Table 8.2.2: *Stopping distances (metres) in relation to reaction time (β in seconds), the starting speed (v, in m/s) and the deceleration (a, in m/s^2) See also Table 5.4.1.*

β	a	v	s	v	s	v	s	v	s
1	2	10	35	20	120	30	255	50	675
3	2	10	55	20	160	30	315	50	775
1	5	10	20	20	60	30	120	50	300
3	5	10	40	20	100	30	180	50	400
1	7	10	17	20	48	30	94	50	229
3	7	10	37	20	89	30	154	50	328

Table 8.2.3: *Preview (in metres) for different manoeuvres and different speeds. For the manoeuvre 'overtaking with oncoming traffic', the results depend closely on the assumptions. This is not relevant for road type C (N/A) (based on Schreuder, 1991)*

Manoeuvre		Preview distance (metres) Road type		
		A	B	C
Maintaining crosswise position		45	75	105
Maintaining route		150	375	700
Overtaking (oncoming traffic)	from	450	600	N/A
	to	750	1250	N/A
Stopping		60	175	350
Evasion		45	125	250
Emergency stop		55	140	270

assumptions relating to reaction time and the deceleration on which they are based. Practice shows that sometimes accidents happen in fog, when the preview is indeed less than the values given here, and which remain unexplained in terms of popular values of the stopping distance. It would therefore seem sensible to use for purposes of information and education the values given in table 8.2.3, in particular in lighting by vehicle headlights (Schreuder 1991a). In the case of lighting by dipped headlights, the distance at which all details are clearly visible is of the order of approximately 50 metres. The preview, however, is considerably longer: other information, such as signalling lights, retroreflectors etc., can be detected from a much greater distance.

The image of the reality does not need to be complete. An overall picture suffices to select the correct manoeuvre. This overall picture is called tableau. A tableau is an image at a given moment in time. An impression relating to a future situation can only be obtained by extrapolation from the present situation to the future. Extrapolation can only be done when a number of situations in the recent past are known, as well as the actual situation. Such a succession of tableaux form a sequence. The minimum length of a sequence depends on the manoeuvre to be carried out. Several seconds usually are sufficient.

8.2.3   Objects relevant to traffic

The visual elements essential to the construction of tableaux are called visual critical elements. These elements must be visible even in darkness; they must therefore be illuminated. In relation to steering manoeuvres, this concerns objects which transmit information

- objects which are part of road furniture (light masts, road side reflectors, prewarning signs, traffic signs, warning lights, traffic lights
- objects belonging to the road itself (road markings) other participants in traffic (in particular, preceeding vehicles)
- objects which carry a risk, in the case of evasive manoeuvres
- stationary objects (obstacles; stationary cars; stones and boxes on the road; shed loads and lost car parts, but also light masts, bridge pillars, trees, holes in the road etc.)

Table 8.2.4: *Number of traffic accidents with injury and fatalities, by manoeuvres at the time of the accident, 1988; statistics and categories taken from CBS, 1989*

Manoeuvre		Injury	Fatal
1	vehicles same road, same direction	5201	82
2	vehicles same road, oncoming	3104	147
3 + 4	same road, turning off	8243	153
5 + 6	crossroads	12036	299
7	with parked vehicle	1307	25
8	with pedestrian	4054	192
9	object (exclusive of 931 and 951)	4308	254
931	crash barrier	549	28
951	loose object on or alongside road	240	5
0	accident involving no others (exc. 011, 021, 022)	847	48
011	skidding on the road	1749	21
021	off road, straight	120	3
022	off road, bend	101	1
Total		41859	1258

- moving objects (participants in traffic, in particular cyclists and pedestrians, but also crossing traffic and slow-moving preceeding vehicles).

These risk-carrying objects are obviously not encountered with the same frequency. Accident statistics offer an indication of the relative frequency of all types of objects in accidents. Table 8.2.4 shows a selection from the detailed Dutch data for 1988 (CBS, 1989). More recent data are of course available; however, they only differ in absolute measure, but not or hardly in their relative values.

Table 8.2.4 shows that more than two thirds of the accidents are related to collisions between vehicles participating in traffic; the majority relate to moving vehicles. Approximately 10% of the total relates to pedestrians, while more than 20% relates to stationary obstacles (trees, light masts) and accidents involving no others, such as leaving the road after skidding. Collisions with loose objects on or alongside the road, however, are very rare; this concerns just over half a percent (0.57%) of the total. This category includes obstacles such as stones and boxes. These are objects on which many of the considerations regarding visibility are based in classic literature relating to public lighting. See, e.g. Blaser (1990); CIE (1981, 1990, 1992), De Boer (ed.) (1967); Schreuder (1964). This preference would seem to contradict reality, considering the data in table 8.2.4. These small objects have been introduced as a standard, as they were supposed to represent the visual task.

8.3   Psychological factors

8.3.1   Motivation and aggression
A number of specific psychological factors can be raised in the discussion of traffic and the related traffic facilities, concerning both road users and

managers. Motivation is particularly relevant to the first group – the reasons people act the way they do, including aggression. The norm is of particular interest to the second group. The method by which standards are established is briefly touched on in the following section (John and Jane Average).

People as well as animals act; they are active. People usually have a reason to undertake an activity. Behaviour is seldom random; there is usually a motive. Motives need not always be reasonable or even conscious. The reasons or explanation stated after the activity, however, is usually just that. Often motive and explanation are summed up in the term motivation. An overview of a number of aspects of motivation in traffic is given by Schreuder (1973).

Tension-raising and tension-lowering motivations can be distinguished (Krech et al., 1969, page 498, where a different terminology is used; see also Maslow, 1954). In traditional psychology, only tension-lowering motivations are normally discussed. In practice, however, tension-raising motivations, which may incite risk-taking, are often seen.

Both types of motivation are present in the concept of risk homeostasis, which is sometimes used. The idea is that increasing the safety leads to an increase in risk-taking behaviour, in such a way that the end result of the measure is exactly zero (Wilde, 1982). Experience shows that there is indeed often an inverse relation. This inverse relation is already included in accident data, so that it is possible to see that an exact compensation is certainly not the rule. Many measures, including public lighting, have a proven net positive effect on traffic safety. However, the opposite also occurs. The net effect of anti-blocking devices in cars has been proven to be negative (OECD, 1990).

Finally, a comment on the concept of aggression. The act of deliberately harming others, sometimes accompanied by enjoyment, cannot be squared with rational decision-making. First the terminology. Aggression is often considered to be synonymous with violence and criminal behaviour (Hollin & Howells, 1992). Hence the attention paid to aggression in the traffic sector. Hollin & Howells (1992, pages 4–8) give an overview of current theories on aggression, surprisingly leaving out the politically tinged theories by Laing (1970). The instinct theories by Freud (1915) and Lorenz (1968) as well as the later learning theories by Box (1983) are not favoured, as they are not supported by experiments. According to Hollin & Howells (1992, page 5), the frustration aggression theory follows, however, from experiments. Aggression is always the result of frustration, and frustration always leads to aggression (Dollard et al., 1939). There are indeed signs that busy traffic and aggressive traffic behaviour are closely linked. This should be taken into consideration when traffic reduction measures are considered. The theory, however, has two drawbacks: in the first place it does not take account of any feeling of responsibility in the aggressor, and secondly, aggression is seen as an autonomous automatism. Results which better match reality may be expected from a more specifically psychological approach. See, e.g. Schreuder, (1973). Hollin & Howells (1992, page 15) also indicate that a more inclusive theory would be desirable. They refer to the study by Novaco (1978) as a likely approach.

8.3.2   John and Jane Average

Public lighting is installed in order to illuminate certain objects and to enable the carrying out of the traffic task; I have called this the functional approach with, at its centre, the functions of public lighting. However, it has been shown that there are large differences between the people using the road, and between conditions and situations under which people participate in traffic. In practice, it is not possible to keep on adapting public lighting; specifications for the design of public lighting must be based on a standard. I will call the people who satisfy the standard John and Jane Average. The question which must be asked is: 'What do John and Jane Average look like, and what do they do in traffic?' Initially, I will look at the motivation which causes them to act.

This concerns motivation in the first place. Section 8.3.1 indicated that stress-lowering and stress-raising motivations exist. Stress-lowering motivations often lead to automatic behaviour and, in particular, to conditional reflexes. As long as the environment does not give cause to adapt or change the behaviour, then there is no change. This is in contrast to activities which relate to stress-raising motivations; here new aspects may be added to the behaviour – there is scope for creativity. One of the more undesirable forms of this is aggression, which often crops up as a reaction to frustration. John and Jane Average, however, are considered not to suffer from creative action, nor from aggression, or from the fright reactions discussed in detail by Schreuder (1992). The design specifications for public lighting are based on a sensible and rational John and Jane Average.

John and Jane are average perceivers. It would be possible to describe them with the median discussed in section 7.1.2; 50% falls below the median, the remaining 50% above. This is not recommended for public lighting; it does not seem sensible to base lighting on specifications which half the population cannot satisfy. But neither is 100% realistic. In practice, the following is normally done: an arbitrary degree of performance is used as a measure; lighting is provided in such a way that people who satisfy this measure are able to accomplish the visual task in question; and an alternative solution is sought for the remainder (e.g. auditive or tactile signals instead of visual signals). These threshold values are laid down in the standards. Car drivers, e.g., are allowed to be colour-blind, and they must – possibly with correction – possess a visus of at least 0.5 in the best eye and 0.2 in the worst eye. One-eyed people are also allowed to participate in traffic if their visus is at least 0.8 (De Jong, 1995). It is usually assumed that John and Jane satisfy this condition.

There are additional characteristics which John and Jane possess. All of these will not be discussed in detail, but John and Jane fit the following description

- they are not very attentive, but they do not daydream
- their actions are mainly determined by automatisms, and anticipation plays an important role

- they react slowly to unexpected events
- they may react in a non-functional way in a suddenly occurring critical situation, which may lead to panic
- they limit aggressive behaviour
- their eyesight is 0.7 to 0.8
- they are not drunk
- they travel in good weather or in fog or snow
- the route is not familiar.

Design specifications in public lighting are usually based on a similar observer. This means that the lighting in many cases does not satisfy the requirements for even the average observer. It is hoped in such cases that John and Jane will be able to compensate by increasing attention, by slowing down, etc. As this is not always the case, frequent problems and accidents must be expected – which indeed often occur.

Section 7.5.1 stated that a considerable proportion of the population has a visual handicap. Although the number of blind people would seem to decrease, due to better diagnoses and treatment methods, there is a considerable increase in the number of visually impaired people, in particular among older people, who may also be disabled in other respects. As older and visually impaired people participate less frequently in traffic as car drivers there is a greater probability that they participate as pedestrians. The greater sensitivity to glare with increased age has already been mentioned. This carries consequences for the lighting of residential areas, consequences which are not taken into account by the lighting specifications for John and Jane Average.

Bibliography

Anon. (1974). *Wegontwerp en wegverlichting tegen de achtergrond van de verkeersveiligheid* [Road design and road lighting against the background of traffic safety]. Preliminary advice congress day 6 December 1974. Den Haag, Het Nederlandse Wegencongres, 1974.

Asmussen, E. (1972). *Transportation research in general and travellers' decision making in particular as a tool for transportation management.* In: OECD (1972).

Blaser, P. (1990). Counterbeam lighting; a proven alternative for the lighting of the entrance zones of road tunnels. *Transp. Res. Record* **1287**, pp. 244–251.

Box, S. (1983). *Power, crime and mystification.* London, Tavistock, 1983 (cit. Hollin & Howells, 1992).

Brunia, C.H.M. (1979). 'Activation'. Chapter 9 in: Michon *et al.*, eds. (1979).

Broadbent, D.E. (1958). *Perception and communication.* London, Pergamon Press, 1958.

Brown, I.D. & Poulton, E.C. (1961). 'Measuring the spare "mental capacity" of car drivers by a subsidiary task'. *Ergonomics* **4** (1961), pp. 35–40.

Bunt, A.A. & Sanders, A.F. (1973). *Informatieverwerking in het functionele gezichtsveld; Een overzicht van de literatuur* [Information processing in the functional field of vision; An overview of the literature]. Rapport nr. IZF-1973 C-8. Soesterberg, IZF-TNO, 1973.

CBS (1989). *Statistiek van de ongevallen op de openbare weg 1988.* [Accident statistics on public roads 1988]. Den Haag, SDU-Uitgeverij, 1989.

CIE (1981). *An analytical model for describing the influence of lighting parameters upon visual performance. Summary and application guidelines.* Two volumes. Publication No. 19/21 and 19/22. Paris, CIE, 1981.

CIE (1990). *Calculation and measurement of luminance and illuminance in road lighting.* Publication No. 30/2. Paris, CIE, 1982 (reprinted 1990).

CIE (1992). *Fundamentals of the visual task of night driving.* Publication No. 100. Vienna, CIE, 1992.

De Boer, J.B., ed., (1967). *Public lighting.* Eindhoven, Centrex, 1967.

De Jong, P.T.V.M. (1995). 'Ergoftalmologie' [Ergophthalmology]. Chapter 20 in: Stilma & Voorn, eds., (1995).

Denker, R. (1967). *Agressie* [Aggression]. Amsterdam, Van Ditmar, 1967.

Dollard, J.; Doob, L.W.; Miller, N.E.; Mowrer, O.H. & Sears, R.R. (1939). *Frustration and aggression.* New Haven, Yale University Press, 1939 (cit. Hollin & Howells, 1992).

Freud, S. (1915). *Zeitgemässes über Krieg und Tod.* Cit.: Denker, 1967.

Griep, D.J. (1971). 'Analyse van de rijtaak' [Analysis of the driving task]. *Verkeerstechniek* **22** (1971) 303–306; 370–378; 423–427; 539–542.

Gundy, C.M. (1989). *Verkeersborden en verkeersveiligheid; Een literatuurstudie* [Traffic signs and traffic safety; A literature study]. R-89-29. Leidschendam, SWOV, 1989.

Hagiwara, T. & Zwahlen, H.T. (1995). *Proposed new driver eye scanning behavior recording and analysis system.* In: TRB, 1995.

Hollin, C.R. & Howells, K. (1992). *An introduction to concepts, models and techniques.* Chapter 1 in: Howells and Hollin, eds., (1992).

Howells, K. & Hollin, C.R., (eds). (1992). *Clinical approaches to violence* (reprinted). Chichester, John Wiley and Sons, 1992.

Janssen, S.T.M.C. (1979). *Categorisering van wegen buiten de bebouwde kom* [Classification of roads outside built-up areas]. R-79-43. Voorburg, SWOV, 1979.

Janssen, W.H. (1986). *Modellen van de rijtaak; De 'state-of-the-art in 1986'* [Models of the driving task; The state of the art in 1986]. Rapport nr. IZF 1986 C-7. Soesterberg, IZF-TNO, 1986.

Koornstra, M.J. et al, eds. (1992). *Naar een duurzaam veilig wegverkeer* [Towards a sustainably safe road traffic]. Leidschendam, SWOV, 1992.

Krech, D.; Crutchfield, R.S. & Livson, N. (1969). *Elements of psychology.* Second edition. New York, Alfred Knopf, 1969.

Laing, R.D. (1970). *Knots.* Harmondsworth, Penguin Books, 1970.

Lorenz, K. (1968). *Over agressie bij mens en dier* [On aggression in humans and animals]. Amsterdam, Ploegsma, 1968.

Maslow, A.H. (1954). *Motivation and Personality.* New York, Harper, 1954.

Michon, J.A. (1964). 'A note on the measurement of perceptual motor load.' *Ergonomics* **7** (1964), pp. 461–463.

Michon, J.A.; Eijkman, E.G.J.& De Klerk, L.F.W., (eds). (1979). *Handbook of psychonomics,* Vol. I. Amsterdam, North-Holland Publishing Company, 1979.

Mortimer, R.G. (1971). 'Hard braking is more common than you might think'. *Automotive Engng.,* 1971 (Aug.), page 32.

Norman, D.A. (ed.) (1976). *Memory and attention.* Second edition. New York, John Wiley & Sons Inc., 1976.

Novaco, R.W. (1978), 'Anger and coping with stress'. In: Foreyt, J.P. & Rathjen, D.P. (eds.). *Cognitive behavior therapy.* New York, Plenum Press, 1978 (cit. Hollin & Howells, 1992).

OECD (1972). *Symposium on road user perception and decision making.* Rome, OECD, 1972.

OECD (1990). *Behavioural adaptation to changes in the road transport system.* Paris, OECD, 1990.

OTA (1970). *Tenth International Study Week in Traffic and Safety Engineering.* Rotterdam, OTA, 1970.

Padmos, P. (1984). *Visually critical elements in night time driving in relation to public lighting.* In: TRB (1984).

Rockwell, T.H.; Ernst, R.L. & Rulon, M.J. (1967). *Research on visual requirements in night driving.* Final Report EES 254-1. NCHRP. Columbus, Ohio, Ohio State University, 1967.

Roszbach, R. (1972). *Verlichting en signalering aan de achterzijde van voertuigen* [Illumination and signals at the rear of vehicles]. Voorburg, SWOV, 1972.

Schreuder, D.A. (1964). *The lighting of vehicular traffic tunnels.* Eindhoven, Centrex, 1964.

Schreuder, D.A. (1970). 'A functional approach to lighting research'. In: OTA (1970).

Schreuder, D.A. (1972). 'The coding and transmission of information by means of road lighting'. In: SWOV (1972).

Schreuder, D.A. (1973). *De motivatie tot voertuiggebruik* [Motivation for using vehicles]. Haarlem, Internationale Faculteit, 1973.

Schreuder, D.A. (1974). 'De rol van functionele eisen bij de wegverlichting' [The role of functional requirements in road lighting]. In: Anon (1974).

Schreuder, D.A. (1981). *De verlichting van tunnelingangen; een probleemanalyse omtrent de verlichting overdag van lange tunnels* [Lighting in tunnel entrance zones; a problem analysis relating to lighting of long tunnels during the day]. R-81-26 I and II. Voorburg, SWOV, 1981.

Schreuder, D.A. (1985). *Fundamentele overwegingen omtrent visuele en verlichtingskundige aspecten van de verkeersveiligheid* [Fundamental considerations relating to visual and lighting aspects of traffic safety]. R-85-61. Leidschendam, SWOV, 1985.

Schreuder, D.A. (1991). *Visibility aspects of the driving task: Foresight in driving.* A theoretical note. R-91-71. Leidschendam, SWOV, 1991.

Schreuder, D.A. (1991a). *Motorway lighting under fog conditions.* R-91-72. Leidschendam, SWOV, 1991.

Schreuder, D.A. (1992). *De invloed van windturbineparken op de verkeersveiligheid; Advies uitgebracht aan de Nederlandse Maatschappij voor Energie en Milieu b,v. NOVEM.* [The effect of wind turbine parks on traffic safety; advice submitted to the Nederlandse Maatschappij voor Energie en Milieu b.v.]   R-92-74. Leidschendam, SWOV, 1992.

Schreuder, D.A. (1994). *Visual perception and lighting requirements for road tunnels at very high speeds.* Paper presented at Nihon Doro-Kodan, Japan Highway Public Corporation, Tokyo, Japan, July 19th, 1994. Leidschendam, Duco Schreuder Consultancies, 1994.

Stilma, J.S. & Voorn, Th. B., eds. (1995). *Praktische oogheelkunde* [Practical ophthalmology]. First edition, second imprint with corrections. Houten, Bohn Stafleu Van Loghum, 1995.

SWOV (1972). *Psychological Aspects of Driver Behaviour.* Symposium Noordwijkerhout, 2–6 August 1971. Voorburg, SWOV, 1972.

Theeuwes, J. (1992). *Selective attention in the visual field.* Ruinen, Bariet, 1992.

TRB (1984). *Providing visibility and visual guidance to the road user.* Symposium, July 30-August 1, 1984. TRB, 1984.

Verwey, W.B. (1995). *Effects of tunnel entrances on driver's physiological condition and performance.* Report TM 1995 C-19. Soesterberg, TNO/TM, 1995.

Verwey, W.B.; Alferdinck, J.E.A.M. & Theeuwes, J. (1995). *Quality of tunnel entrances in terms of safety and capacity.* Soesterberg, TNO/TM, 1995 (draft).

Vis, A.A. & Krabbendam, D.A. (1994). *Categorie-indeling van wegen binnen de bebouwde kom* [Classification of roads within build-up areas]. R-94-32. Leidschendam, SWOV, 1992.

Wilde, G.J.S. (1982). 'The theory of risk homeostasis; Implications for safety and health'. *Risk Analysis* **2** (1982), pp. 209–225. (Cit.: OECD, 1990).

Zwahlen, H.T. (1980). 'Driver eye scanning behaviour in rain and during an unexpected windshield wiper failure'. *Z.f. Verkehrssicherheit* **26** (1980), pp. 148–155.

9 Recommendations, standards and guidelines

Public lighting serves to render visually critical objects, relevant to traffic, visible. The sensitivity setting of the visual system of the observer/road user is essential here. Car drivers are concerned with detecting objects at a considerable distance in front of their vehicles; the state of adaptation is approached by road surface luminance. The distance leads to specific assumptions on the method of perception and on the description of the geometry. To slow traffic, pedestrians and cyclists, a completely different perception geometry applies; here the state of adaptation may be approximated by the illuminance on the road. The consequences of these assumptions for photometry were indicated in chapter 5. Such assumptions are used in the design of lighting installations. The standards are based on the same assumptions. As two approaches are currently used for adaptation, each for a different type of road, a classification of roads and streets is relevant. Most recommendations, standards and guidelines contain a classification system.

9.1 Luminance and illuminance

9.1.1 Adaptation condition

Public lighting serves to render visible objects relevant to traffic, i.e. the visually critical objects discussed in section 8.1.2. The visibility of an object depends principally on three things

- the observer (eyesight, age, attention, motivation etc.)
- the object (size, shape, colour, contrast in relation to the background, etc.)
- the adaptation condition (sensitivity setting of the visual system).

To the lighting expert, the observer is a person, over whom he or she has no influence. The objects are partly deliberately installed like road markings, etc.

and here some influence exists, but they are also partly there by chance, e.g. exhaust pipes. Those also are not affected by the lighting expert. Contrast, however, may be influenced; see section 10.1.2, where counterbeam lighting is discussed. The state of adaptation is difficult to describe and even more difficult to measure. It is essential to select an approximation for the state of adaptation. Two photometric variables are in contention, i.e. luminance and illuminance.

As indicated in section 3.2.3, roads belonging to the road network can be classified into three groups, from the point of view of sustainable safety

- roads with a flow function
- roads with an distribution function
- roads with a residential function.

The first two are in the first instance meant for fast traffic; they are therefore also called traffic roads. The third group is meant for mixed traffic, with the emphasis on slow traffic, i.e. cyclists and pedestrians. They are also called residential streets.

The state of adaptation mentioned above is best approached with road surface luminance in the case of traffic roads; for residential roads, illuminance would seem more appropriate. As luminance is indicated by L and the illuminance by E (see section 5.2) I will frequently refer to L-roads and E-street. In both cases this concerns an approach to the state of adaptation of the road user and not, as is sometimes thought, an independent quality criterion. The fact that two criteria are used, necessitates a classification of roads. See section 9.3

9.1.2   Road surface luminance
The quality of the lighting is expressed in road surface luminance for L-roads. As indicated in section 5.2.3, the luminance for a surface which does not emit any light itself is a type of tensor, a variable which is characterised by the scalar size itself, plus four angles. In some special cases, e.g. determination of the visibility of small objects in tunnels or in streets, where multiple reflection must be taken into account, all five variables appear in the calculations. However, this is too complicated for most situations in practice. In section 5.4.6 I indicated the method by which the standard direction is defined: straight ahead, and one degree downwards. As is shown in figures 5.4.7 and 5.4.9, a straight road resembles a trapezium in the perspective image, viewed from this direction. In reality the road looks the way it is pictured in figure 9.1.1.

The quality of the lighting for a traffic road is indicated by the following characteristics

- average road surface luminance, already mentioned
- luminance pattern, also called uniformity
- glare
- optical guidance.

Figure 9.1.1: *The perspective road image; an example of a Dutch road with a traffic function*

The order is not totally arbitrary. Looking in the first instance at the detection of objects, average luminance is the most important, as this represents the state of adaptation. This is the traditional method of approach; most research and nearly all standards and recommendations are based on this. See, e.g. CEN (1995); CIE (1992, 1995); De Boer, ed. (1967) and NSVV (1990). If the driving task, or more generally, the cognitive-psychological aspects are considered, optical guidance becomes most important, followed by uniformity. Uniformity and glare are the most important in the American approach, where the Small Target Visibility (STV, see section 9.2.2) is critical.

In practice this hardly matters. All recommendations are established in such a way that all requirements must be satisfied separately; there is no room for any form of trade-off between the criteria (Schreuder, 1988). For this a decision tree is required, and sufficient knowledge and experience are not available to set up such a 'tree'.

9.1.3 Uniformity

The second important quality criteria relating to road lighting is uniformity of the luminance pattern. The luminance pattern is characterised by two variables, which each characterise an aspect of the pattern. The first is absolute uniformity, U_o. This is defined as

> the ratio of the smallest luminance in the relevant part of the road surface to road surface luminance, to the average road surface luminance ($U_o = L_{min,\ abs}/L_{av}$) (NSVV, 1990, page 35).

The second measure is the lengthways uniformity U_l. This is defined as

> the ratio of the smallest and the largest luminance along the line through the location of perception above the road surface on a quarter of the road width, seen from the right hand edge line ($U_1 = L_{min}/L_{max}$) (NSVV, 1990, page 36).

Although in principle any line may be used, international agreement is for the middle of each lane (CIE, 1990). In the past other proposals for uniformity have been made, in particular S_{max} (De Boer & Knudsen, 1963). This definition is set up for right-hand traffic. CIE (1995) and CEN (1995a) give similar definitions that also refer to left-hand traffic.

When defining uniformity with these definitions, the result depends on the size of the area which can be considered as a point. As indicated in section 5.4.6 these matters are presently under discussion in CIE.

9.1.4   Illuminance

It was established earlier that the quality of lighting for E-streets is expressed in illuminance. The reason not to use luminance for these streets is based on the fact that it is not clear for which part of the field of vision luminance must be determined in many public areas. This can be explained with the aid of an example of a perspective road image of a residential street. See figure 9.1.2.

Figure 9.1.2: *The perspective road image; an example of a street with a residential function*

It is presently not clear which is the most relevant approach for the state of adaptation in streets with a residential function, and which is therefore the best measure to use in the design and in the recommendations. We should really have a type of general lighting, where being able to identify other road users is often much more important than being able to detect small obstacles. An example to illustrate this: it is not pleasant to tread in a dog's mess, but it is much worse to be attacked unexpectedly by a robber or a rapist. The emphasis in the example is on the word unexpectedly. The ability to identify other road users from a sufficient distance is essential. The concepts of 'detection' and 'identification' were explained in section 8.1.1.

Three variables are used as a measure for this general lighting, each with their own advantages and disadvantages. See section 5.2. for the photometric definitions. Most common is the average horizontal illumination E_{hor} on the road. This measure offers an overall picture of the lighting, and is a reasonable measure of detection, without being able to say much about the ability to identify. The advantage of this measure is that it is easy to calculate and to measure and that the product documentation contains the required information in nearly all cases. E_{hor} is therefore used in nearly all standards and recommendations to characterise the level of lighting in residential and public areas. Often vertical illumination E_v is used also, usually as a supplementary measure. However, it is not suitable as a general criterion. Finally, semicylindrical illuminance proves to be a good criterion (Van Bommel & Caminada, 1982). The concept of semicylindrical illuminance is explained in section 5.2.2. The research by Van Bommel & Caminada (1982) has been subsequently supplemented and extended. On the basis of this, semicylindrical illuminance has been included as an alternative or supplementary quality criterion in a number of recent recommendations and guidelines. See, e.g. CEN (1995), CIE (1992; 1995), NSVV (1990). The values resulting from the study by Van Bommel and Caminada, however, have been criticised: they often produce unacceptably strong glare. Nor are there any methods for the design of lighting installations based on the semicylindrical illuminance which are practicable. Finally, measuring semicylindrical illuminance is still very cumbersome in practice.

9.2   Visibility as a measure

9.2.1   The revealing power

When public lighting is considered as a means of reducing accidents, its quality should be expressed in a measure which can be related to the number or the seriousness of accidents. The fact that accidents can be considered to be failed evasive manoeuvres and that visual perception is essential for the selection of the correct manoeuvre, leads to the conclusion that visibility of the relevant visually critical objects may be taken as a criterion for safety.

The concept of 'revealing power' which is based on this idea, was introduced as early as the Thirties (Smith, 1938; Waldram, 1938). Revealing power was usually defined as the percentage of objects, a square foot in size, placed arbitrarily on the road, which can still be seen, where the diffuse reflection factor of the objects follows the statistical distribution of the clothes of pedestrians. As revealing power only applies to stationary objects and to a stationary observer, this is not a good measure for visibility. Moreover, application was impeded by practical problems in the design and the measurement of the lighting. The concept has therefore been forgotten, at least in Europe.

9.2.2 Small Target Visibility

Much research has been undertaken in North America during the last few years into the possibility of basing the lighting installation on visibility (see IES, 1988 and LRI, 1993). The principle is linked to the revealing power mentioned in section 9.2.1. It is based on research by Blackwell (1946), and the 'metrics' for perception, i.e. the visibility level VL (CIE, 1981). VL is defined as follows (see Enzmann, 1993)

$$VL = \frac{L_t - L_b}{\delta L_{th}}$$ [9.2.1]

in which

VL	is the visibility level
L_t	the luminance of the object (target)
L_b	the luminance of the background
δL_{th}	the threshold contrast associated with the adaptation condition in question

As indicated by Adrian (1993), VL is really what can be seen in 'supra-threshold' observation, i.e. $\delta L/\delta L_{th}$. The average of the VL for a large number of very small objects (10 cm) is chosen as a measure for visibility; hence the name 'Small Target Visibility' (STV) (Adrian, 1993). In a first draft for a CIE Technical Report, visibility STV is defined as the 'weighted average of the VL of objects with a reflection of 50%' (CIE, 1995a). However, the procedure has not yet been established.

Janoff has carried out research in relation to the visibility aspects of STV in practical traffic situations (Janoff, 1993). Experiments with unprepared and with prepared observers proves to offer comparable results. It is therefore possible to work with prepared observers, which simplifies the experiments considerably (Janoff, 1993a).

The STV approach allows for the interaction of public lighting and vehicle lighting to be taken into account. Moreover, the STV concept allows for some unevenness in the luminance pattern, which allows for cheaper installations with larger spacings between lamp posts (Keck, 1993). The latter would seem to be a sought after argument. An advantage of the STV approach is that only a single quality measurement is required. The visibility of small objects is also influenced by the uniformity of the luminance pattern and by glare – disability glare. These two influences can be directly included in the visibility. There is a trade-off between them. However, according to the CIE system, three variables are required (CIE, 1995; NSVV, 1990).

The main drawback is that the STV, like the revealing power mentioned in section 9.2.1, can only be defined for stationary objects and for a stationary observer. The significance in practice is therefore small. Moreover, the studies of the relation between STV and accidents are by no means conclusive. Critical comments are also emanating from the US; Eslinger concludes his contribution to the same conference as follows

> Only after adequate consideration [of the above factors] will it be reasonable for Public Agencies in the US to adopt and implement VL as a legal Standard for Design of Roadway Lighting Systems (Eslinger, 1993).

9.3   Classification of roads and streets

9.3.1   Principles
A CROW working party was established in The Netherlands in 1988 and charged with the task of setting up a classification system for roads within built-up areas. The 'SWOV philosophy' to be discussed in section 9.3.2 was used for this work. An interim report was published in 1992 (Slop, 1992). The basis for the CROW activities is the relation between the function, form and use of the road. See figure 9.3.1.

Figure 9.3.2 shows the relations between the functions for various types of roads.

9.3.2   The SWOV philosophy
As indicated in section 9.1.1 there are two measures for the approach of the adaptation condition, i.e. luminance and illuminance, and they are each used for different types of road. In addition to the reason relating to traffic, mentioned in section 2.4, a method is required to classify each road or street and I will follow the SWOV philosophy touched on in chapter 2. See Janssen (1979) and for results Dijkstra (1991), Janssen, ed. (1991) and Twisk (1991). The role of the road in the road network is central here. This philosophy also forms the basis for the classification used by NSVV, where the main categories are roads with a traffic function and a residential function (NSVV, 1990).

The philosophy is adapted for the application of the concept of sustainable safety. Three main categories have been introduced: roads with flow and distribution functions respectively and streets with a residential function. This

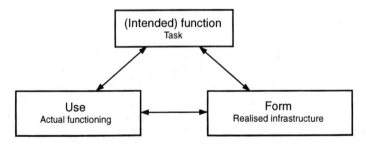

Figure 9.3.1: *The relation between the function, form and use of the road, after Slop, 1992*

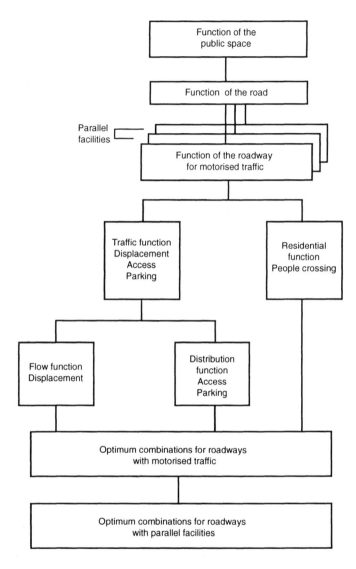

Figure 9.3.2: *Diagram of the function combination of a roadway with parallel facilities, after Slop, 1992*

classification is based on traffic characteristics, and on traffic safety in particular (Koornstra et al., eds., 1992). The difference between the old and the new philosophy lies mainly in the fact that the traffic function is divided into a flow function (purely traffic function) and a distribution function (traffic function plus 'something additional'). As far as the lighting is concerned, the flow function and the distribution function may be grouped together, which leads us back to the original traffic function. An application of these ideas can be found in Vis & Krabbendam (1994).

9.3.3   The NSVV classification

The classification introduced by NSVV links into the previously mentioned former SWOV philosophy. The classification of roads outside built-up areas corresponds to those of the well-known ROA (1990) and RONA (1990). An adaptation to the new philosophy is under consideration; the draft CEN guidelines are already in line with the new philosophy (CEN, 1995a; see also section 9.3.4).

The NSVV classification is based on two 'entries', i.e. the location of the road, within and outside the built-up area respectively, and the function of the road referred to above. In principle, all parameters of the classification can be established objectively by measurements or counts; qualitative characteristics such as 'district distribution roads' no longer appear. The class to which a particular road belongs can be found with the aid of a determination system. The determination occurs on the basis of tables which are included in the Recommendations. The lighting class follows directly from this. Other tables indicate the technical characteristics associated with each of the lighting classes. Details can be found in the original publication (NSVV, 1990). See also section 10.6.

The road network outside the built-up area comprises motorways, main roads and other roads. These remaining roads form a comparatively heterogeneous group. They include roads with access for cars, roads which are declared closed to certain categories of traffic, and roads for mixed traffic. The 'closed to' roads may prohibit all sorts of vehicles, e.g. tractors or cycles/mopeds. As most roads in this group have a speed limit of 80 km/h (50 miles per hour), they are often indicated by '80 km/h roads'.

Roads and streets in built-up areas are subdivided into roads with mainly a traffic function and roads with mainly a residential function. In addition, independent cycle paths have been included as a separate class. Roads with a residential function form a heterogeneous group. Further subdivisions relate to residential areas, footpaths, shopping centres, large parking areas and industrial estates/industry parks. The lighting requirements show considerable variations.

Streets and squares include the normal residential areas with a speed limit of 50 km/h (30 miles per hour), as well as the *woonerven*[1] with their characteristically restrictive traffic regulations for vehicles, and 30 km/h (20 miles per hour) zones which represent an intermediate form between residential streets and *woonerven*. Footpaths relate to paths which connect parts of residential areas. As far as shopping areas are concerned, a distinction is made between areas which are permanently occupied (shopping streets in town centres) and areas which are not occupied permanently (shopping centres and shopping malls). Important consequences for public lighting result from whether an area is occupied permanently or not. The classification is normally easily determined, based on the purpose stated in the plans.

---

[1] Residential areas in The Netherlands with severe restrictions on traffic speeds: everything has priority over vehicles (see Schreuder, 1979).

The Recommendations also take into consideration public safety. Residential areas and public spaces can be divided globally into two areas. Such a classification can only be qualitative; but an estimate can be given as to normal and unsafe areas within a district. This is incorporated in the specifications for public lighting.

The specifications with regard to lighting for a particular (existing or still to be designed) road or street can be found with the aid of determination tables as follows

1. determination as to whether the road is inside or outside built-up areas (build up area)
2. determination whether the road has mainly or exclusively a traffic function or has mainly or exclusively a residential function (traffic function)
3. determination of a number of characteristics of the street
   - constructional, relating to traffic (with crossings at street level or not at street level; one-way traffic or not; parking on the roadway or not)
   - trafficwise (traffic composition: mixed traffic, cyclists etc.)
   - geometrically (road width, number of lanes etc.)
   - technical (traffic intensity).

All these data are used to read off the class of lighting required for the road in question directly from one of the five tables in Part I of the Recommendations (tables 2, 3, 4, 5 and 5a). Subsequently it can be deduced from two further tables which lighting satisfies the respective lighting class (table 6 and 7). See also section 10.6.

9.3.4   The CEN classification

Previously I indicated that CEN has proposed a system which links into the classification of roads into three groups as used in the sustainable safety approach (CEN, 1995a). Highlight below are a number of points in the CEN proposal. It should be remembered that this is only a proposal; in view of the many interests represented in CEN, the final European Standard may vary considerably from the draft.

The CEN draft is based on four basic parameters

- B1: type of road user
- B2: separation of modes of traffic
- B3: relevant area (relating to types of traffic participation)
- B4: characteristic speed of main type of user.

In addition, three groups of specific parameters are included

- A: area (static geometry)
- T: traffic (dynamic use)
- E: environment and external effects (dynamic and static).

Each group comprises a number of parameters. The whole looks quite complex; this is in fact the case. The main problem is that we are not yet ready for a decision system (an 'expert system') at international level. The careful use of parameters results indeed in the fact, that roads can be distinguished by the following three main characteristics. The first entry is speed, the second the main category of traffic participants and the third is the environment.

Bibliography

Adrian, W. (1993). 'The physiological basis of the visibility concept'. In: LRI, 1993, pp. 17–30.

Blackwell, H.R. (1946). 'Contrast threshold of the human eye'. *J. Opt. Soc. Amer.* **36** (1946), p. 624.

CEN (1995). *Lighting applications and road equipment; road lighting, calculation of performance* (Draft 4, January 1995), CEN/TC 169/226 JWG "Road lighting", 1995.

CEN (1995a). *Lighting applications and road equipment. Part 1: Classification.* Draft 2.2, January 1995, CEN/TC 169 and TC 226, 1995.

CIE (1980) *Proceedings 22th Session, Kyoto, 1979.* Paris, CIE, 1980.

CIE (1981). *An analytic model for describing the influence of lighting parameters upon visual performance. Volume I: Technical foundations.* Publication No. 19/2. Paris, CIE, 1981.

CIE (1990). *Calculation and measurement of luminance and illuminance in road lighting.* Publication No. 30/2. Paris, CIE, 1982 (reprinted 1990).

CIE (1992). *Guide for the lighting of urban areas.* Publication No. 92. Paris, CIE, 1992.

CIE (1995). *Recommendations for the lighting of roads for motor and pedestrian traffic.* Technical Report. Publication No. 115-1995. Vienna, CIE, 1995.

CIE (1995a). *Technical report on design procedures for roadway lighting based on visibility concept.* Draft. CIE, 1995.

De Boer, J.B. & Knudsen, B. (1963). 'The pattern of road luminance in public lighting'. In: *Proceedings of the CIE Session 1963 in Vienna* (Vol. A, B, C, D). Publication No. 11, Vienna, CIE, 1963.

De Boer, J.B., ed. (1967). *Public lighting.* Eindhoven, Centrex, 1967.

Dijkstra, A. (1991). *Categorisering van wegen; Deel I: Verkeersplanologische gezichtspunten* [Classification of roads; part I: Traffic-planological aspects]. R-91-52. Leidschendam, SWOV, 1991.

Enzmann, J. (1993). 'Development and principles of the luminance and visibility calculations'. In: LRI, 1993, pp. 1–4.

Eslinger, G.A. (1993). 'Practical aspects of the application of VL in roadway design'. In: LRI, 1993, pp. 149–154.

IES (1988). *Annual Conference of the Illuminating Engineering Society of North America,* August 7–11, 1988. Minneapolis MN., 1988.

Janoff, M.S. (1993). 'The relationship between small target visibility and a dynamic measure of driver visual performance'. *J. IES* **22** (1993) no 1. p 104–112.

Janoff, M.S. (1993a). 'Visibility vs response distance: A comparison of two experiments and the implications of their results'. *J. IES* 22 (1993) no 1, p 3–9.

Janssen, S.T.M.C. (1979). *Categorisering van wegen buiten de bebouwde kom; Een discussienota* [Classification of roads outside built-up areas; A paper for discussion]. R-79-43. Voorburg, SWOV, 1979.

Janssen, S.T.M.C., red, (1991). *De categorie-indeling van wegen binnen de bebouwde kom; een neerslag van de overwegingen binnen de C.R.O.W.-werkgroep* [The classification of roads within built-up areas; reflection of considerations within the C.R.O.W. working party]. R-91-44. Leidschendam, SWOV, 1991.

Keck, M.E. (1993). 'Optimization of lighting parameters for maximum object visibility and its economic implications'. In: LRI, 1993, pp. 43–52.

Koornstra, M.J. et al. (eds.) (1992). Naar een duurzaam veilig wegverkeer [Towards a sustainably safe road traffic]. Leidschendam, SWOV, 1992.

LRI (1993). Visibility and luminance in roadway lighting. 2nd International Symposium. Orlando FL, October 26-27, 1993. New York, Lighting Research Institute LRI, 1993.

NSVV (1990). Aanbevelingen voor openbare verlichting; Deel I [Recommendations for public lighting; part I.] Arnhem, NSVV, 1990.

ROA (1990). Richtlijnen bij het ontwerpen van autosnelwegen (ROA). Hoofdstuk 6 'Verlichting' [Guidelines for the design of motorways (ROA). Chapter 6 'Lighting']. Rotterdam, Rijkswaterstaat, 1990.

RONA (1990). Richtlijnen bij het ontwerpen van niet-autosnelwegen (RONA). Hoofdstuk 6 'Verlichting' [Guidelines for the design of non-motorways (RONA). Chapter 6 'Lighting']. Rotterdam, Rijkswaterstaat, 1990.

Schreuder, D.A. (1979). 'The lighting of residential areas'. R-79-45. Voorburg, SWOV, 1979. In: CIE (1980).

Schreuder, D.A. (1988). 'Visual aspects of the driving task on lighted roads'. CIE-Journal 7 (1988), 1:15–20.

Slop, M. (1992). 'Categorie-indeling wegen binnen de bebouwde kom' [Classification of roads within built-up areas]. Verkeerskunde (1992) no. 3, pp. 33–37.

Smith, F.C. (1938). 'Reflection factors and revealing power'. Trans. Illum. Engin. Soc. (London), 3 (1938), pp. 196–200.

Twisk, D.A.M. (1991). Categorisering van wegen; Deel II: Psycho-ergonomische gezichtspunten [Classification of roads; part II: Psycho-ergonomical aspects]. R-91-53. Leidschendam, SWOV, 1991.

Van Bommel, W.J.M. & Caminada, J.F. (1982). Considerations for the lighting of residential areas for non-motorised traffic. Warwick, CIBS National Lighting Conference, 1982.

Vis, A.A. & Krabbendam, D.A. (1994). De categorie-indeling van wegen binnen de bebouwde kom [The classification of roads within built-up areas]. R-94-23. Leidschendam, SWOV, 1994.

Waldram, J.M. (1938). 'The revealing power of street lighting installations'. Trans. Illum. Engin. Soc. (London), 3 (1938), pp. 173–196.

10 Traffic roads and residential streets

Luminance in road lighting terms relates to the technique of illuminating roads which makes use of the luminance principle. This focuses on the detection of small objects. It also means that traffic safety is central, and that fast traffic receives more attention than slower traffic. In addition, this means that less consideration is given to subjective effects such as a sense of safety and travel comfort. The level of lighting in residential areas is characterised by illuminance; objective safety and crime are central here as well. Most recommendations, including those published by NSVV, are based on these aspects. A separate point, which is often forgotten, relates to tolerances in measuring and calculations.

10.1 The technology of lighting luminance roads

10.1.1 Luminance techniques in road lighting

As indicated in section 8.2.1, three categories of relevant objects must be perceived at the level of manoeuvres

- the course of the road, in particular road markings, etc.
- other participants in traffic (respectively, their signalling lights)
- dangerous obstacles.

The contrast must be sufficiently great to detect relevant objects. Usually this relates to the contrast between the object and the background, but often also contrasts between parts of the object are involved. It was noted earlier that a lower contrast threshold is associated with a high luminance level; that the luminance of the road surface may be used as a measure for adaptation and finally, that the road surface often forms the background for any objects to be detected in the perspective road image.

The road surface and, in particular, its luminance is therefore relevant to the detection of objects in traffic. The 'luminance technique in street lighting' is based on this conclusion. In order to ensure a large contrast, it is sufficient to ensure that the objects remain dark. A prerequisite for this is that they must have a low reflection; this is usually the case with most obstacles in practice such as stones, boxes and even pedestrians. Additionally, the illumination of objects as viewed from the direction of sight must be minimal. This leads to the principle of counterbeam lighting discussed in section 10.1.2. The light is aimed towards the direction of movement; the road surface becomes clear and the obstacles remain dark.

As mentioned above, the basic principle is that objects have a low reflection factor. In the past studies have been conducted into the reflection of clothing (Moon & Cittei, 1938; Smith, 1938). In general low values of at most a few percent were found, particularly in winter. The measurements, however, stem from the Thirties and Forties and it is questionable whether the results are still valid (Knudsen, 1968).

The luminance technique has been described by Schreuder (1964, 1967). Although this technique proves satisfactory in practice, it has a number of serious limitations which were partly discussed earlier

- motor vehicles are the main sources of danger on traffic roads, rather than stones or boxes (section 8.2.3)
- the main component of the driving task is following the road on traffic roads (section 9.1.2)
- the contrast between parts of the object, and in particular the visibility of signalling lights, is more important than the contrast between vehicle and road for the visibility of vehicles.

10.1.2   Counterbeam, pro-beam and symmetrical lighting

The light from luminaires above the roadway can be directed in three ways

1. counterbeam lighting (against the direction of movement of traffic)
2. pro-beam lighting
3. symmetrical lighting.

See figure 10.1.1.

All three methods of lighting are applied on a large scale. Public lighting, which is based on the application of luminance techniques, is a form of counterbeam lighting, although the light distribution of the luminaires is usually symmetrical. This is due to the reflection of the road surface (section 10.4). Vehicle lighting is pro-beam lighting; the interior lighting in traffic tunnels is commonly symmetrical lighting (section 15.4.6).

A number of aspects become clear when the three above-mentioned methods of lighting are compared. Usually counterbeam and pro-beam lighting are the extremes, while symmetrical lighting lies between these two.

- The reflective characteristics of road surfaces offer the highest luminance for counterbeam lighting at equal horizontal illuminance; for symmetrical lighting this is lower and it is lowest for pro-beam lighting. See under 'luminance yield', to be discussed in section 10.4.1.

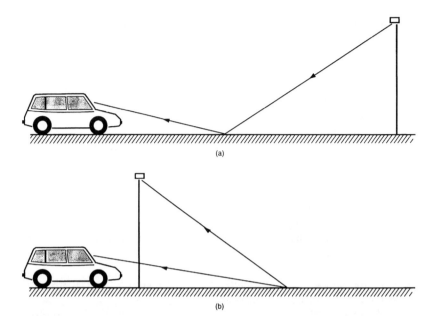

Figure 10.1.1: *(a) Counterbeam lighting; (b) pro-beam lighting; and (c) symmetrical lighting*

- Optical guidance is better for counterbeam lighting than for symmetrical and pro-beam lighting, as the light sources are more visible. Counterbeam lighting offers a greater risk of glare.
- Light distribution is more critical for counterbeam and pro-beam lighting than for symmetrical lighting. This sometimes results in a lower luminaire yield.
- The luminance pattern on the road surface is less even for counterbeam lighting than for other methods of lighting.

10.1.3   Supply and demand

The information required for decision making represents the demand; the environment provides the supply. The supply must, of course, cover the demand, in order to participate adequately in traffic (Schreuder, 1977). The demand as well as the supply may be expressed in terms of detectability, conspicuousness and identification discussed in section 8.1.1. Figure 10.1.2 shows the supply and demand in diagram form, with traffic safety as a central variable. A similar diagram may be produced for other functions of public lighting.

This diagram may be extended with the benefits on the side of the demand and the cost on the side of the supply. In this way the diagram may serve as a basis for a cost benefit analysis (Schreuder, 1993). See Figure 10.1.3.

When the demand exceeds supply, participation in traffic is not satisfactory. An attempt may be made to increase the supply or to reduce the demand. Starting with the latter: the demand for visual information may be reduced by opting for a lower speed. The principle of sustainably safe traffic

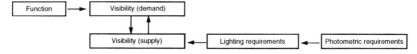

Figure 10.1.2: *Diagram showing supply and demand*

Figure 10.1.3: *Diagram showing supply and demand, extended with benefits and costs*

which has already been mentioned several times, can also be described in this sense. By rendering the environment more predictable, uncertainty is reduced and thus the need for information. The supply of visual information may be increased with the aid of a number of technical aids, such as lighting, signalling and markings.

10.2   Quality criteria for luminance roads

10.2.1   The quality criteria

Three criteria are traditionally used in public lighting to indicate the quality

- the level of illumination (average road surface luminance)
- uniformity (U_o and U_l)
- glare (threshold increment TI).

These criteria are based on the visibility of small, dark, diffuse reflecting, stationary objects. They are associated with the luminance principle. Previous chapters discussed how these measures are defined and measured; the design and the accompanying calculation of these measures will be further detailed in section 13.1.3. Sometimes psychological glare is used instead of, or in addition to, physiological glare.

As indicated in section 9.1.2, optical guidance is paramount in a functional approach. However, little attention is paid to guidance in standards and recommendations, partly because guidance is difficult to quantify. At most, some examples are cited (NSVV, 1957, 1974/75). Further details related to optical guidance and the methods for realising adequate guidance can be found in De Boer, ed. (1967), Springer & Huizinga (1975) and Van Bommel & De Boer (1980). The only serious studies relating to optical guidance were carried out for the design of tunnel entrances. Thus Boselie and Van Leeuwen submitted a proposal for the entrance of the Schiphol tunnel (Anon, 1987). Several studies were also carried out as a joint project between Norway and Japan (Narisada et al., 1977).

10.2.2   The relation between quality criteria

Quantitative demands are placed on each of the criteria listed in section 10.2.1, but little is known about the relative importance of these criteria. One of the advantages of the STV system described in section 9.2.2. is that a trade-off is possible between the criteria. Thus, the extent to which uniformity should be increased to compensate for a particular degree of glare can be checked.

Only a few exploratory studies have been conducted in this area, but research suggests that the level of luminance has a greater effect on the total quality level than uniformity or glare. Schreuder (1983) has given the following relation

$$AI = 0.6N + 0.2G + 0.2V \qquad\qquad [10.2.1]$$

in which AI is the general impression; N, G and V are the subjective evaluations relating to level, uniformity and glare. Cornwell (1973) has given comparable, albeit somewhat more complex, relations for dry and wet roads. For a dry road he found

$$AI = 0.55N + 0.04V + 0.14G + 0.54VG - 1.29 \qquad\qquad [10.2.2]$$

and for a wet road

$$AI = 0.36N + 0.10V + 0.40G + 0.23VG - 0.59 \qquad\qquad [10.2.3]$$

Here AI, N, G and V carry the same meaning as in formula 10.2.1. VG stands for visual (optical) guidance.

These relations are of little use as an aid to the design or to the evaluation of lighting installations, as they only offer relations between subjective experiences and not between objective photometric installation characteristics.

10.3   Drainage asphalt

During the past few years drainage asphalt has been applied on a large scale in The Netherlands. In Dutch, it is known as ZOAB; elsewhere, it is sometimes called porous asphalt or pervious asphalt. This type of road surface is characterised by a very high percentage of hollow spaces, up to 30% in volume. Even more interesting is the fact that the hollow spaces are linked with each other. See figure 10.3.1.

ZOAB has a number of properties which render it eminently suitable for application in roads for fast traffic

- Drainage ability. Rainwater can flow away along channels to the side of the road. Puddles cannot form, so that aquaplaning is nigh impossible. The skidding resistance also is not seriously reduced on wet roads. There is no question of splashing and spraying; visibility in rain is nearly as good as it is on a dry road.
- The noise level of the traffic is considerably lower.
- ZOAB shows a diffuse light reflection during the day and in darkness, as well as in dry and wet weather.

Surprisingly, the number of accidents do not bear out these advantages (Tromp, 1993). It is suspected that the improved vision incites a higher speed.

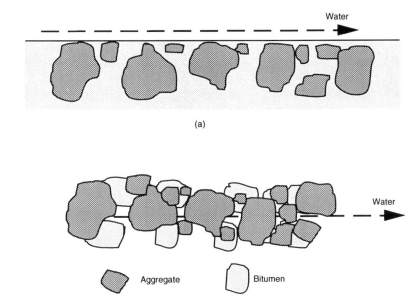

Figure 10.3.1 *The drainage properties of (a) closed asphalt and (b) ZOAB*

Reliable speed measurements, however, are not known. Although some people consider the risk homeostasis mentioned earlier to be a contributor, it may also be assumed that higher speed at equally safe conditions lead to less traffic-jams and queues.

A drawback relating to ZOAB is the fact that the drainage channels also drain salt faster; moreover, heat conduction of ZOAB is less than for coarse closed asphalt, so that ice will be formed earlier in unfavourable conditions. A number of places in The Netherlands experienced problems during the winter of 1995–1996.

Readers should refer to PIARC (1990), Schreuder (1988, 1990) and SCW (1977, 1985) for the construction and a number of physical aspects of ZOAB. See also Anon (1993) for details on the installation, maintenance and, in particular, on combating slipperiness with ZOAB.

10.4   Reflection in road surfaces

10.4.1   The description of the reflective properties

The method for describing reflection in road surfaces was mentioned in section 5.4.8, and it was shown how the measurements are carried out in principle. Sections 4.5.2 and 9.1.2 noted that we can speak of a single reflection factor only in the case of diffuse reflection. Four directions are relevant to road surfaces, in addition to the 'size', which is scalar. These flow from a number of assumptions and conventions described in section 5.4.6. Thus three variables suffice for an isotopic reflection, which has a rotational

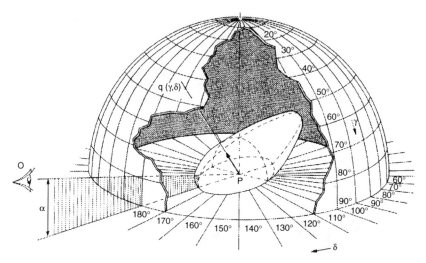

Figure 10.4.1 *The reflection indicatrix*

symmetry. The reflection may be presented in a 3D figure, the reflection indicatrix. See figure 10.4.1.

When, in addition, the observational direction is established, only two variables remain and the reflection characteristics may be portrayed in a table, as is explained in section 5.4.6. The form and the size of these R tables are standardised by CIE. These tables form the basis for the determination of luminance and luminance distribution, and therefore of the design of street lighting installations. An example of an R table is given in figure 10.4.2.

In particular, the top layer of the road is important in public lighting. The surface always has a texture which is usually divided into macro and micro texture (SCW, 1974). See figure 10.4.3.

Most traffic roads usually consist of several layers of asphalt, of which the top layer – which is subject to wear and tear – is normally approximately 4 cm thick (CROW, 1995). Roads made of cement concrete have a similar construction. The main difference is the binding medium; for asphalt roads this is bitumen and for concrete, cement. An important construction is the surface treatment. Here, a thin layer which essentially consists of chippings (aggregate) is 'stuck' onto the road with a thickness of approximately one stone chipping. Usually bitumen is used for the 'glue', but also, especially for bridge surfaces and suchlike, synthetic materials based on epoxy resins are used. A surface treatment is applied in three cases

- as repair or restoration of roads; this often allows for the reconstruction to be postponed for a number of years
- as an extra layer to increase the initial slipperiness on new roads, e.g. motorways
- as actual metalling for less important roads, such as rural roads.

The surface resembles a road with drainage asphalt (ZOAB, see section 10.3). This construction is relevant to public lighting as only one layer of chippings is

tg γ	0°	2°	5°	10°	15°	20°	25°	30°	35°	40°	45°	60°	75°	90°	105°	120°	135°	150°	165°	180°
0.00	10000	10000	10000	10000	10000	10000	10000	10000	10000	10000	10000	10000	10000	10000	10000	10000	10000	10000	10000	10000
0.00	9222	9199	9139	9222	9246	9222	9199	9199	9187	9151	9115	9199	9067	9115	9151	9270	9199	9402	9342	9390
0.00	7608	7560	7632	7548	7458	7488	7404	7368	7333	7225	7117	7022	6902	7069	7093	7297	7356	7620	7548	7656
0.75	6677	6065	6041	5909	5933	5789	5586	5455	5323	5179	5060	4976	4844	4988	5084	5347	5443	5682	5694	5778
1.00	4904	4833	4844	4713	4510	4294	4079	3888	3708	3541	3421	3373	3254	3445	3612	3828	3959	4127	4199	4270
1.25	4007	3947	3959	3708	3505	3170	2835	2644	2512	2404	2321	2249	2249	2380	2524	2691	2907	3074	3086	3182
1.50	3349	3301	3266	2978	2644	2309	2033	1854	1734	1663	1615	1555	1555	1711	1818	2010	2117	2297	2321	2392
1.75	2623	2775	2667	2368	1986	1675	1435	1304	1232	1172	1124	1089	1148	1268	1340	1507	1603	1734	1782	1794
2.00	2440	2356	2261	1842	1507	1232	1041	945	897	837	801	825	825	933	1017	1148	1232	1364	1400	1411
2.50	1890	1770	1567	1172	861	694	598	538	502	478	467	467	502	574	646	718	778	861	897	921
3.00	1531	1400	1124	742	538	419	359	335	323	299	287	299	323	359	407	478	538	586	610	658
3.50	1256	1124	837	502	335	263	239	215	203	191	191	203	227	251	299	347	395	431	455	478
4.00	1041	897	646	371	227	179	167	156	144	144	144	144	167	191	227	251	287	335	347	371
4.50	909	754	478	275	167	132	120	108	108	108	108	120	132	156	179	203	227	263	275	287
5.00	778	658	371	191	120	96	69	84	72	72	84	96	96	120	132	156	179	215	227	239
5.50	682	526	299	156	96	72	72	72	60	48										
6.00	622	467	251	108	72	60	60	60	60											
6.50	574	419	215	96	72	60	60	60												
7.00	526	359	179	84	60	48	48	48												
7.50	478	335	156	72	48	36	36													
8.00	443	299	144	60	48	36	36													
8.50	419	275	120	60	48	36	36													
9.00	383	251	108	48	48	36														
9.50	347	227	96	48	36	36														
10.00	335	203	84	36	36	36														
10.50	323	203	84	36	24	12														
11.00	299	191	72	36	24	12														
11.50	287	179	72	36	24															
12.00	275	179	60	36	24															

β

Figure 10.4.2: An example of an R table. Standard R table $c1.r \times 10^4$ $(cd.m^{-2} lux^{-1})$; $q_p = 0.084$ $cd.m^{-2} lux^{-1}$; $q_0 = 0.109$ $cd.m^{-2} lux^{-1}$

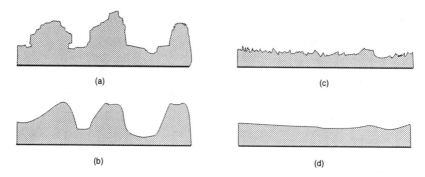

Figure 10.4.3: *The texture: macro and micro; coarse (a) and (b); and fine (c) and (d); smooth (b) and (d); and rough (a) and (c)*

involved. A cheap, lightly coloured road is possible when the latter is totally or partly replaced by a synthetic light producer (Schreuder & Tan, 1975; SCW, 1984). In some cases a double surface treatment is used.

Many streets in residential areas in The Netherlands are clinkered, i.e. the road surface consists of clinkers or concrete stones which resemble clinkers in outlook, but not in their properties, and which are laid directly onto a sandy bed. The reflection properties of clinkers and concrete stones will not be detailed further, as these are mostly used in streets with a residential function. Illuminance and not luminance is used as a criterion for these streets, so that light reflection is not so important. In other countries cobbles and stone paving may be found.

Colour is not taken into consideration for the calculation or for the measurement of luminance. This is justified for traffic roads, as nearly all asphalt and concrete roads are grey. A pronounced colour does not often occur. This is in contrast to roads and streets in residential areas and for cycle paths; colour may occur here. For these types of road, luminance is however not used as a criterion for the quality of the lighting.

Light which falls on the road surface against the direction of vision is usually reflected stronger than light which falls parallel to the direction of observation. Luminance which is the result of the incident light is called luminance yield (Schreuder, 1967; Knudsen 1968). Road surfaces show a type of reflection for which the luminance yield for counterbeam light is nearly always greater and usually much greater, than for pro-beam light.

10.4.2   Classification of the reflective properties of road surfaces

Although superficial observation shows that the reflective properties of road surfaces could vary significantly, a number of detailed studies have proven that road surfaces can be divided into a small number of classes based on a small number of characteristic reflection values. As already mentioned, the best known collection of R tables was published by the Technical University in Berlin (Erbay, 1974). See also Erbay (1973) and Erbay & Stolzenberg (1975).

CIE has published two systems for the classification of the characteristic reflection values. The first is the $q_o-\kappa_p$ classification (Westermann, 1963, 1964). This is based on two characteristic values

$$q_o = \frac{\int q\,d\Omega}{\int d\Omega} \qquad\qquad\qquad [10.4.1]$$

$$\kappa_p = \log\frac{q_o}{q_p} \qquad\qquad\qquad [10.4.2]$$

in which

q_o	is the lightness of the road surface
q	the reflection, to be derived from $q = L/E_h$ (see SCW 1974, page 25)
$d\Omega$	the solid angle
κ_p	the specular factor
q_p	q for vertical light incidence

The integral is taken over the solid angle which corresponds with the area of the R table. See figure 10.4.4.

A summary is given in SCW (1974). See also Schreuder (1967). The CIE classification is based on the values of κ_p (CIE, 1976, 1984). See table 10.4.1.

This system is called the R system. A standard R table has been defined for each of the R classes. Experience has shown that class V occurred with insufficient frequency to require a separate R class. Four classes remain therefore. The majority of all practical road surfaces turn out to fall into classes R_2 or R_3. Based on additional measurements from Denmark, the CIE system

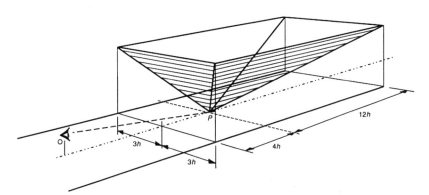

Figure 10.4.4: *The solid angle for the determination of q_o*

Table 10.4.1: *The CIE classification of road surfaces according to κ_p*

Class	κ_p
I	< 0.22
II	0.22–0.33
III	0.33–0.44
IV	0.44–0.55
V	> 0.55

was supplemented with four classes for wet roads, i.e. W_1 to W_4 (Sörensen, 1975; Sörensen & Nielsen, 1974). These classes are not used outside Denmark.

In order to facilitate the use of the numbers, the reduced luminance coefficient r was introduced

$$r = q \cos^3 \gamma \qquad\qquad\qquad\qquad [10.4.3]$$

For r the following notation was introduced: $r_{(x;y)}$ means the reduced luminance coefficient for a light source in the direction y at a distance x. This notation is explained later.

As in practice it proved difficult to determine κ_p, and as it was thought that one single value was not sufficient to represent the reflection characteristics of road surfaces, two reflective factors were introduced

$$S_1 = \frac{r_{(2;0)}}{r_{(0;0)}} \qquad\qquad\qquad\qquad [10.4.4]$$

$$S_2 = \frac{q_0}{r_{(0;0)}} \qquad\qquad\qquad\qquad [10.4.5]$$

From [10.4.5] it follows that

$$\kappa_p = \log S_2 \qquad\qquad\qquad\qquad [10.4.6]$$

See Erbay (1973) and Roch & Smiatek (1969). In this form the characteristic values for the reflection of road surfaces have been included in the CIE

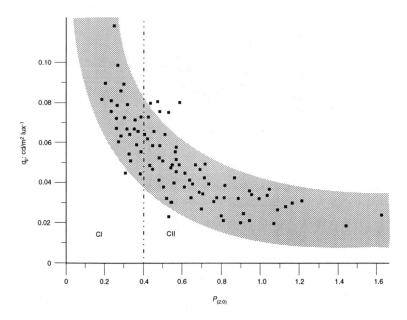

Figure 10.4.5: *The relation between* q_p *and* $P_{(2;0)}$ *for a large number of road samples* (after SCW (1974))

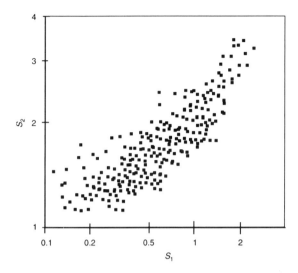

Figure 10.4.6: *The relation between S_1 and S_2 for a larger number of road samples (after Van Bommel & De Boer (1980) fig. 8.10)*

publications (CIE, 1984). The $q_o - \kappa_p$ classification, respectively the $q_o - S_1 - S_2$ classification, proved to have a number of drawbacks. Firstly, it became apparent that q_o and κ_p are not independent of each other. In mathematical terms this means that they are not orthogonal; statistically this means that they are covariant (see Schreuder, 1967, fig. 3.20.) Neither proved q_p and S_1 to be independent. The dependence is shown in figure 10.4.5. But S_1 and S_2 are not independent either. See figure 10.4.6.

A second problem was that q_o could not be measured in practice. The simple measuring instrument described by Schreuder (1967, section 9.5.1) turned out in practice not to be simple at all; even worse was the fact that the variable which was measured with it had little to do with q_o. So far all attempts to replace q_p with a variable which can be measured have led to nothing. This applies especially to q_D, the diffuse reflection factor, which is presently the subject of discussion at CIE (Sörensen, 1993). Although q_D can be measured reasonably easily, it is a bad predictor for q_o. However, q_D can be used to characterise the daylight situation (e.g. for an evaluation of the visibility of road markings).

A number of variants have been proposed over the years, which mainly boil down to the same thing. As these have not led to internationally accepted proposals, they will not be considered here. Refer to Hentschel (1994, section 7.3) for further details, as well as to the classic study by Bergmans (1937) who in many aspects laid the basis for all further studies in this area.

The Dutch SCW working party 'Wegverlichting en oppervlak-textuur' [Road lighting and surface texture] has carried out research since 1974, in order to end this unsatisfactory situation. But it is based on the same material as far as the reflection measurements used are concerned. The system consists of a number of steps. The first step is the characterisation of the road surface. Three reflection values are used for this, corresponding with the following light incidence directions

1. $r_{(0;0)}$:   vertical light incidence (sometimes indicated with q_p)
2. $r_{(2;0)}$:   light incidence 'straight ahead' with tangent 2
3. $r_{(1;90)}$:   light incidence 'crossways' with tangent 1.

Explanation: $r_{(0;0)}$ is sometimes given as q_p; $r_{(2;0)}$ equals, of course, the above-mentioned S_1. The account of these three characteristic values is written up in detail in SCW (1984). See also CIE (1984) and Burghout (1977; 1977a).

One road surface can also be compared with another one, using the same three reflection factors, as long as the two road surfaces have the same values for the three values in question. Finally, the three values, or at least two of these, are used for the classification according to the C_1–C_2 system. Here $r_{(2;0)}$ is divided into two classes. $r_{(2;0)} < 0.4$ applies to class C_1 and $r_{(02;0)} > 0.4$ applies to class C_2. $r(0;0)$ is used as scalar value.

A complete R table is required to calculate the luminance; the C_1–C_2 system therefore has two, a standard table for each class. These are presented in a relative measure with $r_{(0;0)} = 1$. Multiplication by the value of $r_{(0;0)}$, relevant for the respective road surface, produces the values of q for the calculation. According to SCW (1984), the variation between the values which have been calculated with the aid of the standard tables and the real R table are smaller than approximately 15% in the values of luminance or of uniformity.

There is fundamentally a clear difference between the q_o–κ_p and the C_1–C_2 systems. Reflection itself is used as the basis for the classification in the first system. In the second system, the classification is based on luminance and the luminance distribution of lighting installations which can be achieved when using the respective road surfaces.

The reflective properties of road surfaces play an important role in the energetic optimalisation of road lighting. A more precise knowledge of the reflective properties allows for a design which meets the specification more precisely. In those cases where an extra safety margin has been incorporated in the design, possible savings in energy and running costs are feasible in principle.

Measurements have been conducted with a prototype of a measuring instrument with which the three characteristic variables could be measured on the road, in a pilot study under the auspices of NOVEM at Sittard. (Schreuder, 1991). Based on the classes from the C_1–C_2 system determined with it, and the relevant value of $r_{(0;0)}$, a calculation was carried out relating to the installation, which would just meet the NSVV values for the road in question; this hypothetical installation was subsequently compared with the actual installation. The difference between these two represents the possible saving which can be made when the reflective properties of the road are known exactly. The results for five streets are shown in table 10.4.2.

Table 10.4.2: *Possible savings, expressed in the ratio between the installed power per unit of length (W/m)*

Street	Existing situation				Optimum situation				Ratio
	Lamp	W	s	R/m	Lamp	W	s	R/m	
B...singel	SON	70	27	2.593	SON-T	70	31	2.67	1.03
Pr. H...str	HPL	250	23	10.87	SON-T	70	31	2.26	0.21
N...singel	SOX	2×90	27	6.667	SOX-E	2×66	20	4.13	0.62
N...dijk	SON	70	25	2.8	SON-T	70	31	2.68	0.96
Z...weg	SON	70	22	3.182	SON-T	70	25	2.37	0.74

Table 10.4.2 shows that a considerable saving can be made in certain cases. In one case the saving is dramatic, but here inefficient mercury lamps were replaced by modern sodium lamps. The conclusion is that this approach can lead to results; more research is needed for a well-founded evaluation regarding possible savings. See Schreuder (1992).

10.5   Residential streets: illuminance as a criterion

The function of residential streets and residential areas is to enable the road user to start or end the journey. One might call it the function of a 'yard'. The facilities in residential areas are aimed more at slower traffic, in particular pedestrians and cyclists. Moreover, just being in the street or public area itself is an important function of residential areas and, e.g., shopping areas; particular standards are applied with regard to the aesthetic aspect. Also the sense of safety is an important aspect. In other public areas, such as industrial estates or parks and parking places, similar aspects play a role, albeit in a somewhat different ratio.

In the last instance, the specifications in respect of facilities in residential and public areas are based on three aspects, which follow below in the usual order of priority

1. promoting the quality of life
2. preventing and combating crime
3. promoting traffic safety, in particular with regard to slower traffic.

The quality of life is clearly less relevant to industrial estates and parking places.

Public lighting has an essential role in this; the specifications relating to lighting as regards the design must be based on these three aspects. As explained in section 9.1, usually illuminance is used as a measure for the general level of lighting in residential and public areas. Horizontal illuminance is normally used on the road surface, as the alternatives are less suitable and do not offer much additional information. As mentioned, semicylindrical illuminance is sometimes used as an additional criterion for guidelines and recommendations. Uniformity also is expressed in illuminance. As in luminance streets, glare plays a role; but not optical guidance, or only to a small extent. Conversely, the colour of light is important in residential and shopping areas, in respect of colour impression and reproduction. This has consequences for the choice of light sources and for the reflective characteristics of the surfaces which enter the range of vision.

10.6   The NSVV Recommendations for public lighting

10.6.1   The objective of the Recommendations

I have referred several times to the Recommendations, published by NSVV. They comprise four parts. The first part was published in 1990 and dealt with quality criteria and recommended values (NSVV, 1990). The second part, on measurements, the third part, on design and the fourth part, on financial aspects, were published more recently (NSVV 1993, 1995, 1997).

Part I gives an account of the objectives of the Recommendations and of the approach used. NSVV (1990) states

> In the approach of the present Recommendations we did not look for 'good' or 'just adequate' public lighting, in contrast to the previous publications. We have chosen for a technical and economical/energetic balance, i.e. for 'considered' lighting
> - considered in the light of the function of public lighting, i.e. contributing to traffic and public safety
> - considered in respect of energy consumption.

For roads in built-up areas, the emphasis in respect of functional requirements is on

> - the promotion of traffic safety and the flow of traffic
> - the promotion of public safety (in a social sense).
> As well as contributing to the promotion of traffic safety and public safety, public lighting forms an additional town planning element, which can contribute positively to the perceptive value of public spaces. The function of lighting outside built-up areas is to improve the quality of travel.

Finally, the Recommendations indicate a separate treatment for cyclists. This is dictated by a number of practical considerations.

The Recommendations link in with the Guidelines established by the Ministry of Transport (ROA, 1990 and RONA, 1990); they apply to new as well as to existing roads. The reservation, that the NSVV Recommendations ignore the question whether a particular road should or should not be lit, applies to roads outside built-up areas. For this ROA and RONA should be consulted.

It should be noted that the NSVV Recommendations are not based on criteria of visibility; in the first instance they are, like the earlier editions and like nearly all other current national and international recommendations, based on experience in practice. Also, they are based on the idea that public lighting serves to detect small objects in respect of traffic roads; the Recommendations often do not relate well to ideas with regard to the visual aspects of the driving task. Also, relatively greater attention is paid to fast than to slow traffic. However, the need to combat crime is well represented. Finally, objective safety (number of accidents and crime) is central. The subjective aspects of quality of life and travel comfort only play a secondary role; glare is characterised by disability glare and the colour of light is hardly or not at all referred to. Energy saving also only plays a small role, despite the introduction. Much is made of the financial aspects, in particular in Part IV (NSVV, 1995). All this means that there is a lot of scope for improvement despite the fact that the new Recommendations, like the earlier publications, represent a milestone in public lighting. This is evident from the fact that the Recommendations are generally complied with (CEN, 1995, 1995a; CIE, 1995).

10.6.2   The framework on which the NSVV Recommendations are based

As indicated in section 9.3.3, the classification used by NSVV corresponds to the former SWOV philosophy, where roads are classed into traffic and residential roads. We may expect that in the near future, in the light of the activities within CEN (section 9.3.4), that NSVV also will follow the ideas on sustainably safe traffic. This change will not have much effect on the contents, as far as the recommended values are concerned; I expect that the structure of the Recommendations in particular will be adapted.

The lighting class is determined with the aid of the determination system mentioned in section 9.3.3. Two tables were used, for clarity's sake: one for roads within, and one for roads outside built-up areas. The roads within built-up areas are again divided into two tables: one for traffic roads and one for residential roads. Apart from some supplementary information, the Recommendations consist basically of three tables. See figures 10.6.1, 10.6.2 and 10.6.3.

Other tables indicate the technical characteristics in relation to lighting which are associated with each of the lighting classes. Details can be found in the original publication (NSVV, 1990). The lighting specifications for a certain existing or still to be designed road or street can be found with the aid of these tables as follows

1. determination whether the road is in- or outside the built-up area
2. determination whether the road has mainly or exclusively a traffic function or a residential function (traffic function)
3. determination of a number of characteristics of the street
   - constructional (level intersections or not; one-way traffic or not; parking on the road or not)
   - trafficwise (traffic composition: mixed traffic, cyclists, etc.)
   - geometric (width of the road, number of lanes, etc.)
   - technical (traffic intensity)
   - public safety.

The Recommendations are intended for people who are professionally involved with the technical aspects of public lighting. In a supplement to the NSVV Recommendations a 'model policy plan' is set out for authorities who deal with policy planning and policy execution in regard to public lighting, in particular civil servants within local authorities (Anon, 1994). This model forms a framework for the policy plans to be established by local authorities and is based completely on the NSVV Recommendations; in addition, particular

Separated carriageway	Width of the carriageway	Level intersections	One-way traffic	Parking	Fast traffic — Traffic intensity			Mixed traffic (exc. cyclists and mopeds) — Traffic intensity			All types of traffic — Traffic intensity		
					High	Normal	Low	High	Normal	Low	High	Normal	Low
Yes	N/A	No	N/A	No	3A	4A	5A	#	#	#	#	#	#
		Yes	N/A	No	2A	2A	3A	2A	2A	3A	2A	2A	3A
				Yes	#	#	#	1A	2A	3A	1A	2A	3A
No	Wide (approx. 10-14 m)	Yes	No	No	2A	3A	3A	2A	2A	3A	1A	2A	3A
				Yes	#	#	#	1A	2A	3A	1A	2A	3A
			Yes	No	2B	3B	3B	2B	2B	3B	1B	2B	3B
				No	#	#	#	1B	2B	3B	1B	2B	3B
	Normal (approx. 7-8 m)	Yes	No	No	3B	4B	4B	2B	3B	4B	2B	3B	3B
				Yes	#	#	#	2B	3B	4B	2B	2B	3B
			Yes	No	3C	4C	4C	2C	3C	4C	2C	3C	3C
				Yes	#	#	#	2C	3C	4C	2C	2C	3C
	Narrow (approx. 5-6 m)	Yes	No	No	3C	4C	4C	2C	3C	4C	2C	3C	3C
			Yes	No	3C	4C	5C	3C	4C	5C	3C	3C	4C
				Yes	#	#	#	2C	2C	3C	2C	2C	3C

Figure 10.6.1: *Determination table for roads in built-up areas; traffic roads (after NSVV, 1990, table 2.) #: situation does not, or hardly, occurs*

			Unsafe	Public safety — Normal — Level of lighting environment				
				High Business		Low Business		
				Normal	Minimal	Normal	Minimal	
Residential area		Street/square	14K	15L	16L	16L	16L/17K	
		Yard	14K	15L	16L	16L	16L/17K	
		Path	14K	15L	16L	16L	16L/17K	
		Parking place	14K	15L	16L	16L	16L/17K	
Separate footpath			14K	16L	16L	16L	16L/17K	
Shopping area	Residential	Street/square	13K	15L	15L	15L	15L	
		Pedestrianised area/yard	13K	15L	15L	15L	15L	
	Non-residential	Street/square	13K	15L	16L	16L	16L	
		Pedestrianised area/yard	13K	15L	16L	16L	16L	
Parking place			13K	14K	15K	15K	16K	
Industrial area/harbour area			13K	14K	15K	15K	16K	

Figure 10.6.2: *Determination table for roads within built-up areas; residential and public areas (after NSVV, 1990, table 4)*

			Fast traffic			Mixed traffic closed to cycles and mopeds			Mixed traffic, all vehicles		
			Degree of difficulty			Degree of difficulty			Degree of difficulty		
Crossways profile	Width of carriageway/ width of roadway	Level intersections	High	Normal	Low	High	Normal	Low	High	Normal	Low
Dual carriageway	N/A	Yes	1B	2B	3B	2B	3B	3B	#	#	#
		No	2B	3B	4B	#	#	#	#	#	#
Single carriageway	Approx. 7 m	Yes	2B	3B	3B	2B	3B	4B	2B	3B	4B
		No	3B	3B	4B	2B	3B	4B	#	#	#
	Approx. 6 m	Yes	#	#	#	3B	4B	4B	4B	4C	5C
	Approx. 5 m	Yes	#	#	#	#	#	#	5C	Z	Z

Figure 10.6.3: *Determination table for roads outside built-up areas (after NSVV, 1990, table 5) z: orientation lighting*

attention is paid to the problems of responsibility and liability, as well as to the sometimes difficult relation between public lighting and open space planning. See also section 13.3.4.

On the initiative of NOVEM and NSVV, a course called 'Public Lighting' has been set up by PBNA, which is run by Elsevier in Zwijndrecht, for the same target group. So far the course has been run about 15 times.

In this context mention should be made of three more publications. The first is the brochure by SVEN (1981). This brochure was published to offer local authorities an aid in saving public lighting costs without impairing the function in respect of traffic safety and public security. This brochure used to be very influential but has now been overtaken by the NSVV Recommendations. Secondly, a brochure has been published in support of the NSVV Recommendations and the above-mentioned model policy plan (NOVEM, 1996). Finally, an article in a journal may be mentioned in which an overview is given of the principles of quality of living and public safety from the point of view of local government (Stroosnijder, 1995).

10.6.3   The recommended values

Tables 6 and 7 of the Recommendations give the conversion of the lighting classes in photometric specifications. These relate to the average road surface luminance for traffic roads and the average horizontal illuminance for residential areas; uniformity is also expressed respectively in luminance and illuminance. Glare is expressed as physiological glare (Threshold Increment TI, see section 7.3.2).

Experience shows that the lighting classes 2A, 2B, 3A and 3B for traffic roads, and for residential areas classes 13K, 14K, 15L and 16L occur most often. In order to give an idea of the general quality level used in the Recommendations, minimum values relating to lighting for these lighting classes are reproduced in table 10.6.1.

Table 10.6.1: *The minimum values relating to lighting for a number of frequently occurring lighting classes; after NSVV, 1990, tables 6 and 7*

Lighting class	Level L (cd/m^2)	Uniformity		Glare TI (%)
		U_o	U_l	
2A	1.5	0.4	0.7	10
2B	1.5	0.4	0.6	15
3A	1.0	0.4	0.7	10
3B	1.0	0.4	0.6	15
	E (lux)	U_h		
13K	10	0.3		
14K	7	0.3		
15L	5	0.2		
16L	3	0.2		

The values in the Recommendations are standard values: 'The lowest momentary value which is still acceptable' (NSVV, 1990, page 15). This means that immediate measures are necessary when the lighting level falls below the standard value. No limiting values for glare have been included for residential areas. The uniformity measures U_o and U_l were discussed in section 9.3.1. Uniformity measure U_h is defined as

$$U_h = \frac{E_{h,min}}{E_{h,av}}$$ [10.6.1]

(see NSVV, 1990, page 37).

All national and international recommendations will not be discussed here, as the recommended values are generally similar to those of the NSVV Recommendations. The considerable influence mentioned several times previously of The Netherlands as the 'land of lighting' is probably the cause of this. I will mention a Swiss publication, where special attention is paid to public safety and to the lighting of footpaths and cycle paths (Anon., 1993a). For footpaths the following is recommended: $E_{h,av} > 3...7$ lux; $E_{semicyl} > 0.8$ lux; $E_{h,min}/E_{h,av}$ better than 1:20; E_{min}/E_{max} better than 1:40. From this it can be determined that the darkest place should be at least $0.05 \times 3 ... 7 = 0.15 ... 0.35$ lux. For cycle paths, the following applies: $E_{h,av} > 3 ... 5$. Otherwise the same values as for footpaths apply. Finally, they give examples of 'creepy spaces' and of solutions. See also sections 11.4.1 and 15.6.

10.7   Tolerances in measurements and calculations

An aspect which is not or at most only referred to in passing, relates to tolerances in measurements and calculations. Measurements of phenomena in physics can never be absolutely accurate. Tolerances are always involved.

These cannot be avoided, but they are harmless when they lie below a certain maximum. In general, measurements are more expensive to the extent that tolerances are small: equipment is more expensive, as is the expertise and the measuring time involved.

Below some proposals for acceptable tolerances in measurements and calculations in respect of road lighting

- errors in input data in calculations (light distributions, etc.): less than 5%
- errors in calculations: no tolerances
- differences in calculation variants: less than 2%
- differences between calculation and measuring methods: less than 3%
- measuring errors (instrument errors)
    - horizontal illuminance: less than 3%
    - vertical illuminance (exclusive of multiple reflection): less than 5%
    - luminance factors: less than 5%
    - road surface luminances: less than 10%
    - point luminances: less than 15%
    - veil luminances: less than 25%
- technical (photometric) measurements
    - illuminance: cosine correction – better than 99%; colour correction – better than 95%; temperature correction – better than 99%
    - luminances: colour correction – better than 95%; temperature correction – better than 99%.

The above suggestions are taken from a paper which was compiled for the discussion (still ongoing) in a number of working parties in CIE and CEN (Schreuder, 1995). It is not at all certain that these working parties will include a proposal with regard to tolerances in measurements and calculations in their draft report.

Bibliography

Anon. (1987). Report of a plan for the new entrance for the Schiphol tunnel. No title, no author. Report of a proposal made by the University of Nijmegen, 1987 (year estimated).

Anon. (1993). *ZOAB; Zeer open asfaltbeton* [ZOAB; Very open asphalt concrete]. Gewijzigde herdruk. Breukelen, Vereniging tot Bevordering van Werken in Asfalt, 1993.

Anon. (1993a). *Sicherheit durch gute Beleuchtung von Rad- und Fusswegen; Information für Gemeinden, Elektrizitätswerke und Planer.* Bern, Schweizerische Lichttechnische Gesellschaft SLG, 1993 (year estimated).

Anon. (1994). *Model beleidsplan openbare verlichting* [Model policy plan public lighting]. Sittard/Arnhem, NOVEM/NSVV, 1994 (year estimated).

Burghout, F. (1977). 'Kenngrössen der Reflexionseigenschaften von trockner Fahrbahndecken'. *Lichttechnik* **29** (1977) 23.

Burghout, F. (1977a). 'Simple parameters significant of the reflection properties of dry road surfaces'. In: LITG (1977).

CEN (1995). *Lighting applications and road equipment; road lighting, calculation of performance* (Draft 4, January 1995), CEN/TC 169/226 JWG "Road lighting", 1995.

CEN (1995a). *Lighting applications and road equipment. Part 1: Classification.* (Draft 2.2, January 1995), CEN/TC 169 and TC 226, 1995.

CIE (1976). *Glare and uniformity in road lighting installations.* Publication No. 31. Paris, CIE, 1976.

CIE (1984). *Road surfaces and lighting.* Joint CIE/PIARC publication. Publication No. 66. Paris, CIE, 1984.

CIE (1991). *Proceedings 22th Session,* Melbourne, Australia, July 1991. Publication No. 91. Paris, CIE, 1992.

CIE (1995). *Recommendations for the lighting of roads for motor and pedestrian traffic.* Technical Report. Publication No. 115-1995. Vienna, CIE, 1995.

Cornwell, P.R. (1973). Appraisals of traffic route lighting installations. *Lighting Res. & Technol.* **5** (1973) 10-16.

CROW (1988). Wegbouwkundige Werkdagen [Road construction workshop] 1988, Ede, 26-27 May 1988. *Deel 2; Stroom II: Kwaliteit in meervoud; zitting II-1: Milieu en veiligheid* [Part 2; Stream II: Quality in the plural; session II-1: Environment and safety]. Publikatie 8-II. Ede, CROW, 1988.

CROW (1995). *Van A-nummer tot Zweepmast* [From A-number to Zweepmast]. Publikatie 91. Ede, CROW, 1995.

De Boer, J.B. (ed.) (1967). *Public lighting.* Centrex, Eindhoven, 1967.

Erbay, A. (1973). *Verfahren zur Kennzeichnung der Reflexionseigenschaften von Fahrbahndecken.* Dissertation Technische Universität Berlin, 1973.

Erbay, A. (1974). *Atlas for the reflection properties of road surfaces.* Published by Technische Universität Berlin, 1974.

Erbay, A. & Stolzenberg, K. (1975). 'Reflexionsdaten von allen praktisch vorkommenden trockenen Fahrbahnbelägen'. *Lichttechnik* **27** (1975) 58–61.

Knudsen, B. (1968). *Dangerous points in street lighting* (in Danish). Dansk Vejtidsskrift (1968) 8, pp. 153-164.

LITG (1977). *Measures of road lighting effectiveness.* Symposium, Karlsruhe, 5–6 July 1977. Berlin, LITG, 1977.

Moon, P. & Cittei, M.S. (1938). 'On the reflection factor of clothing'. *J. Opt. Soc. Amer.* **28** (1938) 277–299.

NOVEM (1996). *Dat licht zó!!!* [Shedding light] Sittard, NOVEM, 1996 (year estimated).

Narisada, K.; Inoue, T. & Björset, H.-H. (1977). *Tunnel lighting; Luminous intensity of luminaires to guide approaching drivers.* Draft, March 1977. (Ref.: CIE, 1984).

NSVV (1957). *Aanbevelingen voor openbare verlichting* [Recommendations for public lighting]. Den Haag, Moormans Periodieke Pers, 1957 (year estimated).

NSVV (1974/1974). 'Richtlijnen en aanbevelingen voor openbare verlichting' [Guidelines and recommendations for public lighting]. *Electrotechniek* **52** (1974) 15; 53 (1975) 2 and 5.

NSVV (1990). *Aanbevelingen voor openbare verlichting; Deel I* [Recommendations for public lighting; Part I]. Arnhem, NSVV, 1990.

NSVV (1993). *Aanbevelingen voor openbare verlichting; Deel II, Meten en berekenen* [Recommendations for public lighting; Part II, Measurements and calculations]. Arnhem, NSVV, 1993.

NSVV (1995). *Aanbevelingen voor openbare verlichting; Deel IV, Financiële aspecten* [Recommendations for public lighting; Part IV, Financial aspects]. Arnhem, NSVV, 1995.

NSVV (1997). *Aanbevelingen voor openbare verlichting. Deel III, Ontwerpen* [Recommendations for public lighting. Part III, Designs]. Arnhem, NSVV, 1997.

PIARC (1990). *Final report. PIARC, Working Group on Pervious Coated Macadam.* Draft, 1 October 1990. Paris, PIARC, 1990.

ROA (1990). *Richtlijnen bij het ontwerpen van autosnelwegen* (ROA). Hoofdstuk 6: 'Verlichting' [Guidelines for the design of motorways (ROA). Chapter 6: 'Lighting']. Rotterdam, Rijkswaterstaat, 1990.

Roch, J. & Smiatek, G. (1969). 'Die Reflexionseigenschaften von Strassendecken und ihre Kennzeichnung'. *Strasse und Autobahn* **20** (1969) 396–404.

RONA (1990) *Richtlijnen bij het ontwerpen van niet-autosnelwegen* (ROA). Hoofdstuk 6: 'Verlichting' [Guidelines for the design of non-motorways (ROA). Chapter 6: 'Lighting']. Rotterdam, Rijkswaterstaat, 1990.

Schreuder, D.A. (1964). 'De luminantietechniek in de straatverlichting' [Luminance technology in street lighting]. *De Ingenieur* **76** (1964) E89-E99.

Schreuder, D.A. (1967). 'Theoretical basis of road lighting design'. Chapter III in: De Boer (ed.) (1967).

Schreuder, D.A. (1977). 'The relation between lighting parameters and driving performance'. In: LITG (1977)

Schreuder, D.A. (1983). 'Glare in streeet lighting'. *CIE Journal* **2** (1983) 53–57.

Schreuder, D.A. (1988). 'Zeer open asfaltbeton en de verkeersveiligheid' [Drainage asphalt and traffic safety]. Bijdrage 27. In: CROW, (1988).

Schreuder, D.A. (1993). *Het niveau van de openbare verlichting op verschillende categorieën van wegen* [The level of public lighting in different categories of roads]. Leidschendam, Duco Schreuder Consultancies, 1993.

Schreuder, D.A. (1995). *Tolerances in the measurements.* Contribution to CEN/TC169/ WG6. Standard for the lighting of road traffic tunnels. Draft, 21 March 1995. Leidschendam, Duco Schreuder Consultancies, 1995.

Schreuder, D.A. & Tan, T.H. (1975). 'Waardering wegdekken' [Evaluation of road surfaces]. In: *Mexico '75, 15e International Wegencongres, De Nederlandse bijdrage*, pag. 137 t/m 140. Arnhem, SCW, 1975.

SCW (1974). *Wegverlichting en oppervlaktetextuur* [Road lighting and surface texture]. Mededeling nr. 34. Arnhem, SCW, 1974.

SCW (1977). *International Symposium on Porous Asphalt.* S.C.W. Record 2, Arnhem, SCW, 1977.

SCW (1984). Lichtreflectie van wegdekken [Light reflection of road surfaces]. Mededeling 53. Arnhem, SCW, 1984.

SCW (1985). *Zeer open asfalt* [Very open asphalt]. Mededeling 56. Arnhem, SCW, 1985.

Smith, F.C. (1938). 'Reflection factors and revealing power'. *Trans. Illum. Engng. Soc. (London)* **3** (1938) 196–200.

Springer, J.F. & Huizinga, K.E. (1974). *Het wegbeeld als toetssteen voor het wegontwerp* [The road image as touchstone for road design]. Two volumes. Rijkswaterstaat Serie nr. 15. Den Haag, 1974.

Stroosnijder, I. (1995). 'Goed licht maakt van stad een huiskamer' [Good light makes the city into a sitting room]. *NG Magazine* **49** (1995) 51/52 pp. 25–27.

SVEN (1981). *Besparing op energie en kosten bij openbare verlichting* [Cost and energy saving in public lighting]. Apeldoorn, SVEN, 1981.

Van Bommel, W.J.M. & De Boer, J.B. (1980). *Road lighting.* Kluwer, Deventer, 1980.

Westermann, H.-O. (1963). 'Reflexionskennwerte von Strassenbelägen'. *Lichttechnik* **15** (1963) 507-510.

Westermann, H.-O. (1964). 'Das Reflexionsverhalten bituminöser Strassendecken im Zusammenhang mit der Griffigkeit'. *Strasse u. Tiefbau* **18** (1964) 290–295.

11   Effectiveness of public lighting

Public lighting is functional and the effect of the lighting depends on the extent to which the task is fulfilled. This chapter deals with the effectiveness of lighting: the result of the effort. Effectiveness rating is based on the benefit. Should we wish to find out to what extent the benefits of lighting justify the costs, however, then we must consider the efficiency. This latter will be discussed in the next chapter.

Effectiveness must be determined separately for each function. Traffic safety is paramount on all roads; to this are added public safety and a feeling of safety for residential areas and public spaces. Public lighting serves additional functions: these are not discussed in this chapter, as no data, neither quantitative nor qualitative, are available.

The analysis offered in this chapter proves that the popular perception that lighting 'helps', is supported by objective data. Moreover, efficiency is often evident from the research. Increasing the level of lighting is not always an efficient measure.

11.1   Effects of the presence of public lighting on traffic safety

11.1.1   Roads within built-up areas

Nearly all roads within built-up areas have public lighting. Roads outside built-up areas, however, are mostly unlit. The first question relating to effectiveness – at least for roads outside built-up areas – is therefore: what are the benefits of public lighting?

Much research has been carried out into this subject in the past. This was usually based on before-and-after studies as described in section 7.1.3. The results are summarised in a number of reviews (CIE, 1968, 1992; OECD, 1972; Fischer, 1973; Schreuder, 1983). The main studies were conducted in Great Britain (Tanner, 1963). The result of these studies can be expressed in a single sentence: On urban main roads, with mainly a traffic function, a reduction in accidents involving injuries of approximately 30% can be expected at night, following an improvement in the lighting from very bad to good (Shreuder, 1988).

It is usually assumed that a similar result applies to other types of roads. However, fewer relevant data are available. The method of meta-analysis was mentioned in section 7.1.3. The result of the review conducted in Norway reads

> The best current estimate as regards the safety effects of road lighting ... is a 65% reduction in night-time injury accidents and a 15% reduction in night-time property-damage-only accidents. (Elvik, 1995, page 122.)

This conclusion was based on 142 studies. Most related to lighting within built-up areas; many of the studies were included in the earlier reviews. The more recent method of the meta-analysis would seem to lead to an estimation more favourable for lighting. Meta-analysis should be used on a larger scale.

11.1.2 Dutch research on non-motorways, outside built-up areas

A series of studies, carried out in The Netherlands during the last 10 to 15 years, investigated the relationship between public lighting and safety, including both traffic safety and public safety. This set of studies will be returned to more than once. Firstly, the effect of the presence of public lighting on traffic safety relating to non-motorways will be looked at.

The relationship between lighting and accidents on rural non-motorways – closed to cyclist – was researched between 1985 and 1990. The roads comprised 92 lit stretches with a total length of more than 7000 km, and 35 stretches without lighting. Crossroads were not included in the research. The data referred to 1622 injury accidents from 1984 to 1988. The results are given in BGC (1990) and Schreuder (1990), and are summarised in tables 11.1.1. and 11.1.2.

The length of the road stretches varied considerably. The saving per km can be deduced from table 11.1.2.

Table 11.1.1: *Accident totals (after BGC, 1990)*

	Number of accidents		n/d ratio
	Day	Night	
Lit	649	328	0.37
Unlit	215	136	0.63

Table 11.1.2: *Accident totals per km (after BGC, 1990, table 2.2)*

	Number of accidents per km over 5 years			per year Total
	Day	Night	Total	
Lit	8.01	3.02	11.03	2.206
Unlit	5.36	3.49	8.85	1.77

Based on the data from table 11.1.2, it is possible to estimate the number of accidents which would have been found at night-time on unlit roads, had these been lit. The expected number is

$$\frac{3.02}{8.01} \, 5.36 = 2.02$$

This applies to five years, so the annual total is 0.404. The actual total was 3.49 over five years, i.e. 0.698 annually. The saving per km per year is 0.698 − 0.404 = 0.294 or more than 42%. The savings are therefore higher than those found in the English research mentioned above. This saving applies to all lit roads from the sample. As shown in section 11.2.4, the level of lighting influences the result. This estimation is based on the assumption that traffic at night-time is a set fraction of traffic by day which does not depend on the type of road.

11.1.3 Dutch research into motorways outside built-up areas
A similar relationship applied to motorways was researched in another study (Vis, 1993, 1994). The results are summarised in table 11.1.3.

The expected total accidents which would have been found at night-time on unlit roads, had these been lit

$$\frac{9.06}{22.89} \, 6.58 = 2.60$$

This applies to three years, which is 0.869 annually. The actual number is 3.29 for three years, or 1.097 annually. The annual saving per km is 1.097 − 0.868 = 0.229 or approximately 21%. This is less than the saving found in the English study.

The following comments are worth noting

- The English study only applies to roads within built-up areas, so a difference in the results is not unlikely. The savings prove to be of the same order.
- Lit motorways prove to be more dangerous than unlit motorways, especially during the day. This results from the fact that only busy motorways are lit.
- Motorways prove to have not much more accidents per km annually than non-motorways; the saving in annual accidents per km would also

Table 11.1.3: *Accidents and accidents per km; motorways; 1989 − 1991 (data from Vis, 1993)*

	Length	Annual total accidents				
		Day	Night	Total	Annually	*n/d*
Lit	276.2 (14%)	6323	2502	8825		0.39
Per km		22.89	9.06	31.95	10.65	
Unlit	1588.5 (81%)	10460	5231	15691		0.50
Per km		6.58	3.29	9.87	3.29	

seem to be of the same order, despite the fact that motorways carry much more traffic. This relates to the fact that motorways are inherently much safer. See section 2.2.2.

- Traffic junctions, crossroads and slip roads are excluded from the study. There are indications from research in built-up areas, that the accident pattern at crossroads relates differently to lighting than is the case for other road stretches. See section 11.2.3.
- The estimation is based on the assumption that traffic at night is a set percentage of the traffic by day and does not depend on the type of road.
- The level of lighting influences the result. See section 11.2.4.

11.1.4   Other research into roads outside built-up areas

Schreuder (1983) gives a review of the literature relating to all main research concerning the relationship between lighting and accidents. Schreuder (1988) has an additional review. Nearly all studies relate to a change in public lighting. Most of the studies relate to roads within built-up areas. Only one study relates to the presence of lighting on motorways (Lamm et al., 1985). This research was carried out between 1972 and 1981 on a stretch of road with a length of 5.6 km. Section 1 (1.9 km long) and section 2 (3.7 km long) had been lit since December 1973. The level of lighting is not indicated but we may assume that the level is approximately 10 lux, based on the relevant German standard. The unlit section 3, 2.3 km long, served as a control. The first year comprised the preliminary period; all sections were unlit. Sections 1 and 2 were lit all night for five years (after period 1). During the following three years (after period 2), the lighting was usually extinguished in section 1 as well as in section 2 after 10 pm. The lighting remained lit in section 2 whenever required. The results, expressed in accident quotients, are shown in table 11.1.4.

Table 11.1.4: *The effects of the presence of lighting on accidents (per 10^6 vehicle kilometres (based on data from Lamm et al., 1985; see also Schreuder, 1988, table 2)*

| | Section 1 | | | Section 2 | | | Section 3 | | |
	d	n	n/d	d	n	n/d	d	n	n/d
Pre	2.03	4.28	2.11	1.8	3.33	1.82	1.41	1.85	1.31
After 1	0.88	1.97	2.24	1.08	1.66	1.54	1.13	2.98	1.84
After 2	0.62	1.76	2.84	0.90	2.18	2.42	0.93	1.89	2.03
After1/Pre	0.43	0.46	1.06	0.59	0.50	0.84	0.80	1.12	1.40
After 2/Pre	0.31	0.41	1.35	0.49	0.65	1.33	0.66	1.02	1.55

| | Section 1/Section 3 | | | Section 2/Section 3 | | | Average section 1:2 | n/d |
	d	n	n/d	d	n	n/d		
Pre	1.44	2.31	1.61	1.30	1.80	1.39		
After 1	0.78	0.95	1.22	0.96	0.80	0.84		
After 2	0.67	0.93	1.40	0.97	1.15	1.19		
After 1/Pre	0.54	0.41	0.76	0.74	0.44	0.60	0.68	
After 2/Pre	0.46	0.40	0.87	0.75	0.64	0.86	0.87	1.27

The data in table 11.1.4 enable us to compare unlit and lit stretches: section 3 in relation to sections 1 and 2. If the night/day ratios are compared after period 1 in relation to the before period, then 0.76 is found for section 1 and 0.60 for section 2. In both cases, a considerable improvement in the situation can be seen. According to Lamm et al. (1985) the effect is, however, not statistically significant. The individual values in table 11.1.4 do not mean much, probable as a result of the difference between the sections and between the years. Lamm et al. (1985) state, however, that the positive effect of the lighting is cancelled out by extinguishing the lighting between 10 pm and 5.30 am. This is backed up by the data in table 11.1.4. The average of the values for the after 1/before period is 0.68 in sections 1 and 2; the value for the after 2/before period − where the lighting was extinguised at night − is 0.87. The suggestion arises, that the introduction of an evening/night switch in this case led to a relative increase of 27% in the number of accidents (0.87 / 0.68 = 1.27). It is not possible, of course, to predict with any certainty what is to be expected on other roads.

11.2   The effect of the level of public lighting on traffic safety

11.2.1   Research on roads within built-up areas

Research was carried out in a number of countries into the effect of the level of public lighting on traffic safety. Here, a brief review of the results is offered: a detailed discussion can be found in Schreuder (1983, 1988, 1993). References to the original literature can also be found there.

The English study

One of the most important studies in this area was carried out in England. All relevant data relating to accidents and lighting were collected in relation to 70 urban arterial dual carriage roads with a speed limit of 40 miles per hour (Hargroves & Scott, 1979; Scott, 1980). A clear relationship was found between the risk, expressed in the night/day ratio for accidents, and the luminance level. See figure 11.2.1.

When the analysis was restricted to accidents with no pedestrians involved, there proved to be a relationship between the n/d ratio and the uniformity, in addition to the relation between the n/d ratio and the luminance level. See figure 11.2.2.

Figure 11.2.2 shows a peculiarity: the n/d ratio increased with increasing uniformity.

The American study

A study was conducted in Philadelphia (PA, USA), which was based on a different method. The research was part of a series of studies on the way in which the visibility principle can be applied in public lighting (See section 9.2.2; Gallagher et al., 1975). This study is based on a large sample of roads and streets. Few data were collected relating to the lighting, but there are many data relating to traffic, the function of the road in the road network, on town and country planning aspects and on the roadside development. However,

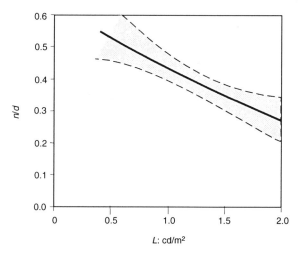

Figure 11.2.1: *The relationship between the n/d ratio and the luminance level (after Scott, 1980)*

insufficient account was taken of the close interdependency of these factors in the statistical analysis of the material. Apart from this accidents study, which produced few useful data, a study into the visibility of obstacles was carried out. A number of obstacles were placed on a normal road with variable lighting. The Visibility Index (VI) of each obstacle was determined (see section 9.2.2). The behaviour of naïve car drivers, who were not informed about the test, was recorded. The 'Time-To-Target' (TTT) was determined for each reaction. This represents the period of time it would have taken to hit the obstacle, had no reaction taken place. The results of these tests are shown in figure 11.2.3.

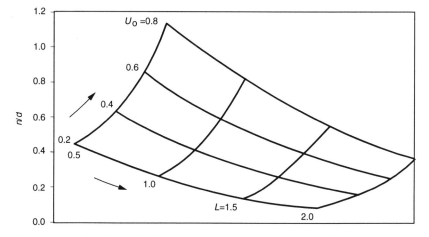

Figure 11.2.2: *The relationship between the n/d ratio, the luminance level and uniformity. Accidents involving pedestrations excluded (after Scott, 1980)*

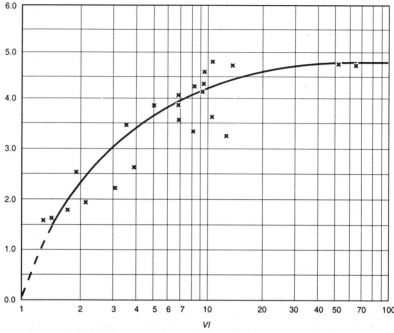

Figure 11.2.3: *The relation between the Visibility Index (VI) and the Time-To-Target (TTT); after Gallagher et al., 1975*

11.2.2   Research relating to roads outside built-up areas

A study carried out in Belgium relates to the evaluation of savings measures on motorways: the lighting was switched off between 12.30 and 5 am. Traffic and weather conditions permitting, the lighting was halved on a number of other roads, i.e. from approximately 2.5 cd/m^2 to approximately 1.3 cd/m^2. The number of accidents at different degrees of severity before and after the changes was compared, looking at the changes on treated roads and at the changes on untreated roads. The savings measures proved to have a clear negative effect on safety (De Clercq, 1985; 1985a).

A number of smaller studies were carried out in Germany. The first study relates to a stretch of motorway where public lighting was first halved and subsequently extinguished. The result is unclear; the day/night ratios relating to accidents increased when the lighting was halved and fell when the lighting was extinguished. No further conclusions can be drawn without further details relating to road length, number of accidents, traffic density and particularly to statistical significance.

A second study relates to a stretch of motorway 14.4 km long on the B 10 between Stuttgart and Esslingen. A comparison of the day and night-time accidents in the before and after periods of 11 months each, showed that extinguishing the lighting is correlated with a relative reduction in the number of accidents at night. Here, also, a definite conclusion cannot be drawn from the results without further data. But surprisingly these two studies in Germany do not show a positive effect produced by public lighting, in contrast to most other studies. See also Pfundt (1986) and Schreuder (1988).

11.2.3   Dutch research relating to roads within built-up areas

SWOV has carried out a series of studies into the relationship between level of lighting and traffic safety. The research was drawn up as a set of correllation

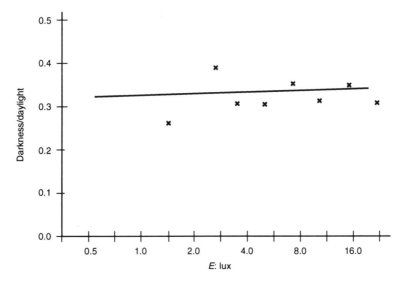

Figure 11.2.4: *The relationship between accidents during darkness and in daylight on roads with a traffic function (road stretches + crossroads)*

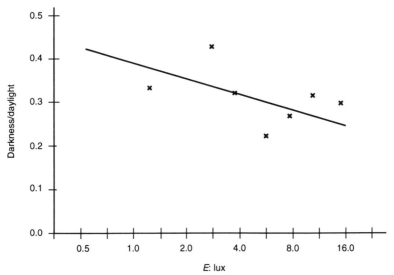

Figure 11.2.5: *Relationship between accidents during darkness and in daylaight on roads with a traffic function (road stretches)*

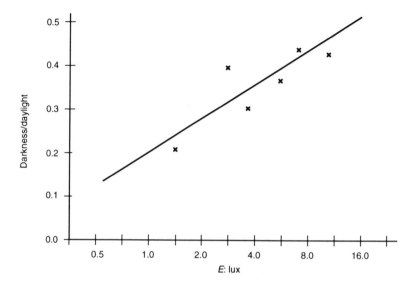

Figure 11.2.6: *Relationship between accidents during darkness and in daylight on roads with a traffic function (crossroads)*

studies. Data from Amsterdam (West), Leeuwarden, Utrecht, Oss and Barendrecht were used. Details can be found in Schreuder (1992). The method used here led to a considerable collection of data. The research related to a part of The Netherlands with a population of approximately 540,000 people. The accident records comprised 22,333 recorded accidents, of which 17,020 occurred during the day and 5,313 in darkness.

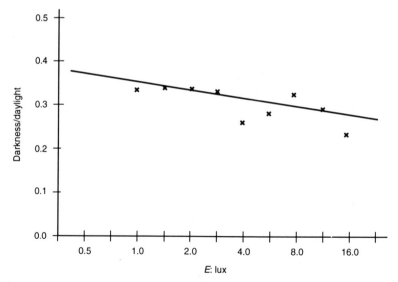

Figure 11.2.7: *Relationship between accidents during darkness and in daylight on roads with a residential function (road stretches and crossroads)*

The data for the various towns could be combined, following a correction for any evening and night switching. The results for the traffic roads – stretches and crossroads – are shown in figure 11.2.4.

A detailed analysis shows that road stretches become relatively safer when the level of lighting is increased, whereas crossroads become relatively more unsafe. The first corresponds to the expectation, but not the second. An explanation has not yet been found. See figure 11.2.5 for the results on stretches of road; for crossroads, see figure 11.2.6.

The results for residential roads – road stretches and cross-roads – are shown in figure 11.2.7.

11.2.4   Dutch research relating to non-motorways outside built-up areas

Research relating to non-motorways outside built-up areas also concerned the effects of the luminance level. A statistically significant relationship was found between the luminance level and the risk at night-time, expressed in accidents over 10^6 vehicle kilometres. See table 11.2.1.

Furthermore, a not insignificant trend was found indicating that accidents in daylight per vehicle kilometre also decrease when the luminance is increased. A combination of these data shows that the proportion of the night-time accidents also decreases to a considerable extent when the luminance is increased, although this is not significant at the 5% level. See table 11.2.2.

Table 11.2.1: *Relation between luminance level (cd/m^2) and risk at night-time (accidents per 10^6 vehicle kilometres); after BCG 1990*

Luminance	$L < 0.4$	$0.4 < L < 0.73$	$L > 0.73$
Risk	0.59	0.37	0.26

Table 11.2.2: *Relationship between the number of night-time acidents (the n/d ratio) and the luminance (in cd/m^2); after BCG 1990*

Luminance	$L < 0.4$	$0.4 < L < 0.73$	$L > 0.73$
Risk	0.33	0.27	0.23

11.2.5   Dutch research relating to motorways outside built-up areas

The above-mentioned SWOV research concerns the relationship between safety and the level of lighting, with the traffic density as a parameter (Vis, 1993). An important conclusion from this study is that night-time risks on lit roads are generally lower, in particular at relatively high luminance levels. The final conclusion is put very tentatively (Vis, 1993, page 5).

> In conclusion we can say that most trends point in the direction of a positive effect of public lighting

This of course leads to a recommendation for further research.

Table 11.2.3: *Risk on motorways (number of recorded accidents per million veh/km). Lighting in cd/m^2 (based on data from Vis, 1993, tables 5 and 6)*

Light	Luminance classes						Average lit	Vis table
	None	**0.5**	**0.7–0.9**	**0.9–1.1**	**1.1–1.3**	**1.5**		
Night	0.35	0.31	0.36	0.35	0.47	0.50	0.398	5
Day	0.24	0.28	0.27	0.27	0.43	0.45	0.34	6
n/d	1.458	1.107	1.333	1.296	1.093	1.111	1.170	

Table 11.2.4: *Lighting according to table 11.2.3 (based on data from Vis, 1993, tables 5 and 6)*

Luminance values given in cd/m^2	
Table 11.2.3	**Vis, 1993, tables 5 and 6**
0.5	<0.7
0.8	0.7–0.9
1.0	0.9–1.1
1.2	1.1–1.3
1.5	>1.3

The SWOV study data have been used for a more detailed analysis (Schreuder, 1993). Based on the data from tables 5 and 6 from the study by Vis (1993), table 11.2.3 was drawn up.

The lighting classes vary a little from Vis (1993). See table 11.2.4.

Table 11.2.3 shows that in all cases the night/day ratio is larger than 1. This means that motorways are relatively more dangerous in darkness than during the day. But the statistics also prove that this ratio is considerable lower for lit

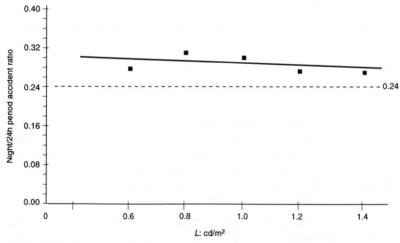

Figure 11.2.8: *The relationship between the ratio night-time accidents/accidents over 24 hours and luminance*

roads than for unlit roads. The ratio is 1.170 for all lit roads together, while for all unlit roads the ratio is 1.458. The ratio between these ratios is 0.802; this means that lit roads are relatively 19.8% safer than unlit roads.

In additon table 11.2.3 shows that the n/d ratio – the night-time risk – decreases when luminance is increased. See figure 11.2.8.

11.2.6   The general relationship between level of lighting and accidents

The relationship between the level of public lighting and traffic safety was discussed in the previous sections. In order to compare the results for the different types of road, lighting levels are standardised to the level which is recommended for these types of roads (NSVV, 1990, tables 1, 3 and 4; see tables 10.6.1 to 10.6.3). I have selected the following lighting classes with their accompanying lighting levels as standard

- rural motorways: class 2B (average road surface luminance 1.5 cd/m^2)
- rural non-motorway roads: class 3B (average road surface luminance 1.0 cd/m^2)
- urban main roads: class 2A (average road surface luminance 1.5 cd/m^2)
- urban roads with a flow function: class 3B (average road surface luminance 1.0 cd/m^2)
- urban roads with a distribution function: class 4C (average road surface luminance 0.7 cd/m^2) or class 5C (average road surface luminance 0.5 cd/m^2)
- urban streets with a residential function: class 16L (average illuminance 3 lux) or class 17K (average illuminance 2 lux)
- squares etc.: class 15L (average illuminance 5 lux).

The roads which appear in various studies are sometimes brighter or darker than the recommended values. The above-mentioned standard has been set to unity for each class of road. This becomes zero on the usual logarithmic scales. I used a scale where a factor two – a doubling or halving of the level – corresponds to a difference of two units on the scale. In Figure 11.2.9, the indication '−2' therefore means a halving of the level in relation to the NSVV Recommendations, etc.

The relationships between the darkness/daylight ratio and the level of light for the different types of road can be derived from the above-mentioned accident studies. In all cases the darkness/daylight ratio decreases when the level of lighting is increased: higher levels of light would seem to correlate with safer streets. The determination of the extent of this reduction at a doubling of the level of lighting is given in Schreuder (1993). The values for this decrease are weighted for the three main types of roads in accordance with the number of the accident records used. These weighted values are then averaged to determine a general relationship between the level of lighting and the number of accidents. See table 11.2.5.

Only few roads and streets appear in the sample where the level of lighting is higher than the NSVV recommended standard, but these few roads suggest that the n/d ratio rises again after a reough. See figure 11.2.9.

Table 11.2.5: *Weighted average reduction in accidents when the level of lighting is doubled*

Type of road	Accident records	Reduction	Weighted reduction
Motorway	28,664	5.8%	1662
Non-motorway	1.238	12.9%	160
Urban	22.333	4.4%	983
Total	53.235		2805
Average			5.37%

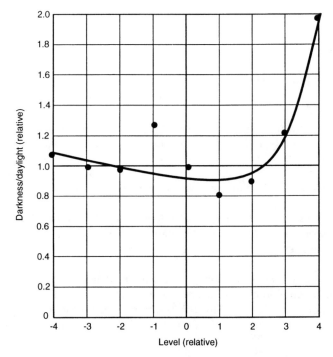

Figure 11.2.9: *A possible optimum level of lighting. The relative darkness/daylight ratio in relation to the relative level of lighting (0: corresponds to NSVV Recommendations)*

The data are too few and too uncertain with regard to accuracy to draw a definite conclusion, but the implications are interesting. This suggests an optimum level of lighting; that a further increase not only produces hardly or no increase in traffic safety, but also that it might be harmful to traffic safety.

11.3   The effects of public lighting on crime

11.3.1   A literature review of the relationship between crime and the level of lighting

Public safety, or the prevention or deterrence of crime, is traditionally one of the main reasons for installing public lighting in towns. A number of

Table 11.3.1: *The relationship between the level of lighting and street attacks; taken from Marinier, 1983*

Illuminance	Attacks	
(lux)	N	%
0–5	70	40.5
5–10	56	32.4
10–15	33	19.1
15–20	9	5.2
>20	5	2.8
Total	173	100

important studies will be briefly discussed; details can be found in Schreuder (1992, 1994).

One of the best known studies, which was carried out on a reasonable scale, stems from the USA (Tien, 1979). The research relates to a sample of 41 lighting projects. The study offers some useful suggestions for road network managers, but no research results. Another study, which drew a lot of attention, was published by Marinier (1983). Research in Lyon showed that considerbly more crime takes place in badly lit streets than in well-lit streets. See table 11.3.1.

An improvement in lighting led to a reduction or possibly a displacement of crime. As no data are supplied concerning the extent of the street network or the lighting, it is difficult to draw a conclusion.

Two reviews of the literature have been published in The Netherlands (Aelen & Van Oortmerssen, 1984 and Maas, 1986), which are partly overlapping. The publications give a review of the available international literature to approximately the year 1983. The summarised result boils down to an increase in criminality when the lighting is decreased and vice versa. Halving the lighting led to an increase of approximately 20% to more than 100% in crime of varying kinds (Anon, 1976), while an increase in the level of lighting led to reductions of 40 to 90% (Le Vere, 1977; Fisher, 1978).

A study in Eindhoven investigated whether dimmed lights were better for night time rather than switching off which may easily lead to dark spots on the road. Criminality was used as a criterion. There was evidence that crime in the test area was reduced more than in the rest of the town. This suggests that crime may be particularly deterred by eliminating very dark places on the road (see Nohlmans, 1987) and corresponds to subjective experience which is discussed in section 11.4.1.

The studies by Painter (1991, 1993) are more recent. An improvement in public lighting in an urban area in Great Britain led to a considerable fall in crime.

> According to survey data, the total number of criminal offences (excluding harassment) has been reduced by 27%. Personal offences were reduced by 35%; property offences by 25%. Sexual offences, which amount to 14% of the total, were reduced by 24%.

A problem is that no indication is given as to what is meant by an improvement in public lighting. Fear of crime also proved to have been diminished. Similar results are shown in Baldrey (1992).

In addition, the British Crime Prevention Unit has conducted some studies (Ramsey & Newton, 1991, and a follow up study, Atkins et al., 1991). Following an improvement in the lighting, a reduction of more than 6% was found; however, the results are not statistically significant (Atkins et al., 1991, table 3). Here, also, no indication is given as to the meaning of improved lighting.

The interest in the relationship between aspects of the built-up environment and crime has increased considerable in The Netherlands since the Commissie Roethof published their report (Anon., 1986). Lighting obviously plays an important role in these aspects of the built-up environment. Experience has shown here, also, that the distribution of the light is relevant, in addition to the level of lighting. I should mention the Safe Outside prize here ('Buiten Gewoon Veilig') (Anon., 1987, 1989; Hajonides et al., 1987).

The main points of these studies are the five criteria for public safety

1. The presence of social control. Local residents must be able to see the installation.
2. Absence of potential criminals. Areas where crime is concentrated must be avoided.
3. Visibility. Lighting should be sufficient, but the view must also be good. Bushes, columns, obscure nooks and crannies must be avoided, to aid surveillance and to assist visitors/users.
4. The situation must be clear. Visitors must be able to find what they are looking for without searching. Escape routes should be provided.
5. The environment must look attractive and cared for. Care for the surroundings suggests care for visitors also. The removal of graffiti is particular important.

These five criteria for public safety are discussed in detail in Anon. (1991, 1994).

Visibility is one of the most important criteria, which clearly points to lighting. See also Anon (1991, 1994). In general, little attention is paid to producing a theory. The direct applications of technical or administrative measures have primarily been considered. Thus, police in the Mid-Holland district produced suggestions for lighting roads, paths and back entrances of houses. They mean well, even if the values are not always realistic. For all sorts of applications a semicylindrical illuminance is recommended of not less than 1.5 lux, while the points of light must not be further removed from each other than 15 metres (Anon., 1995, part D16, page 45). The Dutch Ministry of Justice has published a brochure which deals in particular with lighting specially aimed at the prevention of crime (Anon., 1993).

11.3.2   The relationship between crime and the level of lighting
Data relating to crime have been collected on a small scale within the framework of the studies into the relationship between lighting and traffic safety (Schreuder, 1992, 1994). The relationship between the day/night-time

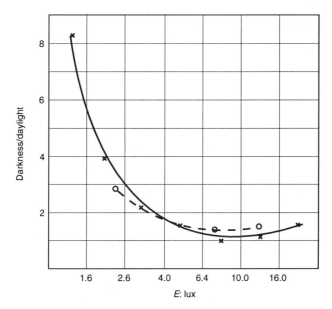

Figure 11.3.1: *The relationship between the darkness/daylight ratio of break-ins into cars and the level of lighting; x town O..; o town U..*

ratio of break-ins into cars and the level of lighting is determined. Figure 11.3.1 shows the available data for two towns in the Netherlands.

This figure shows a clear suggestion of an optimum level of lighting. It is not known whether this relates to the fact that roads and streets of different types appear in the records, or to a preference for certain levels of lighting on the part of criminals. Here, also, a better theory would be able to shed light on this.

11.4   Experience and perception

11.4.1   Subjective safety and the quality of life

Quality of life (amenity) is a concept which is difficult to describe. By quality of life we usually mean that road users, in particular children, women and older people, can use the streets with a sense of safety and even with enjoyment. Fear of fast traffic, fear of robberies and fear of sexual attacks interfere with a sense of quality of life, similarly excessive noise and smells. The concept therefore comprises aspects of subjective safety as well as aesthetic aspects. In practice, complaints about the lighting, in particular in residential areas, are nearly always related to the quality of life.

With the publication of the report by the Committee on Petty Crime in The Netherlands an interest arose into the subjective experience of the urban environment, apart from an interest in actual crime (Anon., 1986). Visibility, night-time conditions and thus lighting are included in the considerations in the subsequent elaboration (Anon., 1991, 1994). Before this, only fear of traffic was included in research into perception. Neither the night-time conditions, nor the fear of crime was given consideration in the extensive re-allocation projects of residential areas in Rijswijk and Eindhoven (Kraay, 1984; Janssen & Kraay, 1984).

Research into the contribution of public lighting to the quality of life in residential areas proved that the level of lighting at the darkest place on the road was more important than the average (Schreuder 1979). It was also shown that the horizontal illuminance is an insufficient measure for the description of the lighting level and the visual impression, in particular in relation to identifying people in pedestrianised areas (Van Bommel & Caminada, 1983).

Another aspect of the perception of lighting by car drivers was investigated by Van den Brink & Buijn (1987, 1990). See also Schreuder et al. (1991). Approximately 5,000 car drivers were questioned as to their opinion (subjective perception or appraisal) on the lighting after passing a lighting installation on straight, well-proportioned, relatively busy main roads outside built-up areas. The lighting was varied between 0.3 and 1.3 cd/m^2. Although the level of lighting has some influence on perception, even the lowest level, which only amounted to 0.3 cd/m^2, was generally perceived as satisfactory. The amount of oncoming traffic and the uniformity of the luminance pattern proved not to be relevant to perception. The lighting was generally even more appreciated in rain.

This corresponds with research into lighting in residential areas. Here, also, appraisal proves to depend only a little on the level of lighting and it is shown that a rather low level will be perceived as satisfactory (Van den Brink & Tan, 1979). A perception study in Schiedam showed that opinion regarding the quality of public lighting is exclusively determined by the lighting level and not by the colour of the lighting, and that opinions regarding the street in darkness and those regarding public lighting are very similar. But here, also, low levels are soon considered satisfactory. In order to be able to walk in safety, 1.7 lux proved to be too little; a level of 3 to 4 lux was judged satisfactory, provided the darkest places were not too dark (Schreuder, 1989 a,b; 1995).

11.4.2   Subjective perception of the colour of light

A separate question relates to the colour of the light in residential areas; in particular whether low-pressure sodium lamps (SOX) are acceptable in residential areas. There are cases where SOX lighting has given rise to protests (Anon., 1987a), as well as evidence that SOX lighting is also considered to be satisfactory by residents (Van den Brink & Tan, 1979). These complaints gave rise to the perception study in Schiedam mentioned in section 11.4.1. All streets in the district in question had SOX lighting. The colour of the lighting was judged to be negative: approximately two-thirds of the respondents thought the colour unpleasant (Schreuder, 1989b).

An extensive study was carried out in Utrecht. The results, however, have been published only in part (Anon., 1995b; see also Van Tilborg, 1991). An energy-saving lighting installation with compact fluorescence lamps was installed in a district, instead of an energy costly lighting. The old as well as the new lighting installation complied with the NSVV Recommendations (NSVV,

Table 11.4.1: *The opinion of residents on street lighting (after Van Tilborg, 1991)*

	Before period	After period
Number of questionnaires	1000	1000
Number of responses	198	145
Do you feel safe in your neighbourhood?	85%	92%
Do you avoid certain places?	52%	32%
What is your opinion of the street lighting?		
Good	47%	71%
Moderate	37%	11%
Bad	11%	6%
Is the lighting in your own street sufficient?		
Yes	51%	84%
No	39%	12%

Table 11.4.2: *The opinion of residents on the type of lamp (after Van Tilborg, 1991), expressed in 'marks out of ten'. TLC: compact fluorescence lamp; SON: high-pressure sodium lamp, SOX: low-pressure sodium lamp*

Type of lamp	TLC	SON	SOX
General opinion	6.67	5.94	5.96
Identification of persons	6.33	5.89	6.17
Identification of surroundings	6.13	5.61	6.13

1990). An opinion study was carried out among the residents before and after the change. Part of the responses are given in table 11.4.1.

Questions in relation to the type of lamp and the colour were also asked. See table 11.4.2.

It is striking that the opinion regarding the three types of lamp used was not much different, in contrast to what one might expect, although there is a large difference between the colour impression and the colour reproduction of these three types of lamp.

Bibliography

Aelen, J.D. & Van Oortmerssen, J.G.H. (1984). *De effecten van openbare verlichting op criminaliteit; Een literatuurstudie* [The effects of public lighting on crime; A literature study]. Interimrapport. Leiden, Rijksuniversiteit, 1984.

Anon. (1976). *Public lighting – the case against cuts*. Presented to Members of Parliament at the House of Commons. London, 1976 (cit. Aelen & Van Oortmerssen, 1984).

Anon. (1986). *Eindrapport Commissie Kleine Criminaliteit* [Final report, Committee Petty Crime]. Den Haag, Staatsuitgeverij, 1986.

Anon. (1987). *Juryrapportage Buiten Gewoon Veilig Prijs 1987* [Jury report, Safe Outside Prize 1987]. Rotterdam, Stichting Vrouwen Bouwen Wonen, 1987.

Anon. (1987a). *Jaarverslag 1986* [Annual Report 1986]. Bewonersvereniging Schiedam-Zuid (blz. 6). Schiedam, 1987.

Anon. (1989). *Juryrapportage Buiten Gewoon Veilig Prijs 1989* [Jury report, Safe Outside

Prize 1989]. Rotterdam, Stichting Vrouwen Bouwen Wonen, 1989.

Anon. (1991). *Scoren met sociale veiligheid; Handleiding sociale veiligheid in en om sportaccommodaties* [Scoring with public safety; Manual public safety in and around sports facilities]. Rijswijk, Ministerie van Welzijn, Volksgezondheid en Cultuur, 1991.

Anon. (1993). *Verlichting; Verlichtingstechniek als hulpmiddel bij de criminaliteitspreventie* [Lighting; Lighting technology as an aid in the prevention of crime] Derde druk. Den Haag, Ministerie van Justitie, Directie Criminaliteitspreventie, 1993.

Anon. (1994). *Zien en gezien worden; Voorbeeldprojecten 'sociale veiligheid'* [See and be seen; Good practice in public safety]. Rijswijk, Ministerie van Welzijn, Volksgezondheid en Cultuur, 1994.

Anon. (1995). *Politiekeurmerk veilig wonen; Inbraakpreventie en sociale veiligheid* [Police approval safe residences; preventing break-ins and public safety]. Zoetermeer, De Politie van Hollands Midden, 1995 (year estimated).

Anon. (1995a). *Symposium Openbare verlichting* [Symposium Public Lighting], 22 februari 1995, Utrecht.

Atkin, S.; Husain, S. & Storey, A. (1991). *The influence of street lighting on crime and fear of crime*. Crime Prevention Unit, Paper 28. London, Home Office, 1991.

Baldrey, P. (1992). 'Relighting Monsall: A successful crime prevention initiative'. The Lighting Journal 57 (1992) 169-170.

BGC (1990). *Verlichting op niet-autosnelwegen buiten de bebouwde kom; Effecten en niveaus* [Lighting on non-motorways outside built-up areas; Effects and levels]. RWE/917/09/Mn. Bureau Goudappel Coffeng, Deventer, 1990.

CIE (1968). *Road lighting and accidents*. Publication No. 8. Paris, CIE, 1968.

CIE (1980). *Proceedings 22nd Session*, Kyoto, 1979. Paris, CIE, 1980.

CIE (1992). *Road lighting as an accident countermeasure*. Publication No. 93. 1992.

CIE (1992a). *Proceedings 22nd Session*, Melbourne, Australia, July 1991. Publication No. 91. Paris, CIE, 1992.

De Clercq, G. (1985). 'Fifteen years of road lighting in Belgium'. *Intern. Lighting Rev.* (1985) no 1, pages 2–7.

De Clercq, G. (1985a). *Verlichting der autosnelwegen; Invloed van besparingsmaatregelen op de ongevallen* [Lighting of motorways; Effect of savings measures on accidents]. Brussel, Ministerie van Openbare Werken, Bestuur voor Elektriciteit en Electromechanica. 1985.

Elvik, R. (1995). *Meta-analysis of evaluations of public lighting as accident countermeasure*. TRB, Transportation Research Rec. No. 1485. (1995) 112–123.

Fisher, A. (1973). *A review of street lighting in relation to safety*. Dept. of Transport NR/18. Canberra, Governmental Publishing Service, 1973.

Fischer, S. (1978). 'Security lighting'. *Int. Lighting Rev.* (1978) 4 (Cit.: Aelen & Van Oortmerssen, 1984).

Gallagher, V.P.; Koth, B.W. & Freedman, M. (1975). *The specification of street lighting needs*. FHWA-RD-76-17. Philadelphia, Franklin Institute, 1975.

Hajonides, T. et al. (1987). *Buiten gewoon veilig* [Safe outside]. Rotterdam, Stichting Vrouwen Bouwen & Wonen, 1987.

Hargroves, R.A. & Scott, P.P. (1979). 'Measurements of road lighting and accidents; The results'. *Public Lighting* 44 (1979) 213–221.

Janssen, S.T.M.C. & Kraay, J.H. (1984). *Demonstratieproject Herindeling en herinrichting van stedelijke gebieden* [Demonstration project reallocation and redesigning urban areas]. R-84-29. Leidschendam, SWOV, 1984.

Kraay, J.H. (1984). *Beleving van de verkeersonveiligheid voor en na de invoering van verkeersmaatregelen* [Perception of unsafety in traffic before and after the introduction of traffic measures]. R-84-27. Leidschendam, SWOV, 1984.

Lamm, R.; Kloeckner, J.H. & Choueiri, E.M. (1985). *Freeway lighting and traffic safety; A long-term investigation.* TRB-1985-17. 64th TRB Annual Meeting. Washington, DC, Transportation Research Board TRB, 1985.

Le Vere, C.W. (1977). 'Street lighting as a crime deterrent'. *Lighting Design and Application* (1977) November.

Maas, C.J. (1986). 'De relatie tussen straatverlichting en criminaliteit' [Relationship between street lighting and crime]. *Tijdschrift voor de Politie* **48** (1986) 438-443.

Mariner, J.C. (1983). *Public lighting reduces the level of violence and the number of attacks* (in French). Lux (1983) 123 (June).

NEOM (1987). *Verslagen van de tweede en derde studiedag over energiebesparing openbare verlichting* [Reports on the second and third study day on energy saving public lighting]. Eindhoven, 24 november 1987. Sittard, NEOM, 1987.

Nohlmans, T. (1987). 'Motivatie en argumentatie voor de benadering van energiebesparing in het demonstratieproject Eindhoven' [Motivation and argumentation for the approach of energy saving in the Eindhoven demonstration project]. In: NEOM, 1987.

NSVV (1990). *Aanbevelingen voor openbare verlichting; Deel I* [Recommendations for public lighting; Part I]. Arnhem, NSVV, 1990.

NSVV (1990a). *Licht90. Tagungsberichte Gemeinschaftstagung,* Rotterdam, 21-23 Mai, 1990. NSVV, Arnhem, 1990.

OECD (1972). *Lighting, visibility and accidents.* OECD, Paris, 1972.

Painter, K. (1991). 'An evaluation of public lighting as a crime prevention strategy: The West Park Estate surveys'. *The Lighting Journal* **56** (1991) 228–232.

Painter, K. (1993). 'Street lighting and crime: A response to recent Home Office research'. *The Lighting Journal* **58** (1993) 229–231.

Pfundt, K. (1986). 'Verkehrssicherheit und Strassenbeleuchtung'. *Mitteilungen der Beratungsstelle für Schadenverhütung.* No. 28, pp. 30–38. Köln, HUK-Verband, 1986.

Ramsey, M. & Newton, R. (1991). *The effect of better street lighting on crime and fear: A review.* Crime Prevention Unit, Paper 29. London, Home Office, 1991.

Schreuder, D.A. (1979). 'The lighting of residential areas'. R-79-49. Voorburg, SWOV, 1979. In: CIE (1980).

Schreuder, D.A. (1983). *De relatie tussen verkeersongevallen en openbare verlichting* [The relationship between traffic accidents and public lighting]. R-83-12. Leidschendam, SWOV, 1983.

Schreuder, D.A. (1985). *Het effect van vermindering van de openbare verlichting op de verkeersveiligheid* [The effect of a reduction in public lighting on traffic safety]. R-85-58. Leidschendam, SWOV, 1985.

Schreuder, D.A. (1988). *De relatie tussen het niveau van de openbare verlichting en de verkeersveiligheid; Een aanvullende literatuurstudie* [The relationship between the level of public lighting and traffic safety; A supplementary literature study]. R-88-10. Leidschendam, SWOV, 1988.

Schreuder, D.A. (1989). *De relatie tussen het niveau van de openbare verlichting en de verkeersveiligheid; Een voorstudie* [The relationship between the level of public lighting and traffic safety; a preliminary study]. R-89-45. Leidschendam, SWOV, 1989.

Schreuder, D.A. (1989a). 'Enquête wijst uit: Straten zijn onveilig en licht is akelig' [Survey shows: Streets are unsafe and the lighting is miserable]. *De Gorzette* **17** (1989) 1:23–25.

Schreuder, D.A. (1989b). 'Bewoners oordelen over straatverlichting' [Residents judge street lighting]. *PT Elektronica-Elektrotechniek* **44** (1989) 5:60–64.

Schreuder, D.A. (1990). *De relatie tussen het niveau van de openbare verlichting en de verkeersveiligheid op niet-autosnelwegen buiten de bebouwde kom* [The relationship between the level of public lighting and traffic safety on non-motorways outside built-up areas]. R-90-45. Leidschendam, SWOV, 1990.

Schreuder, D.A. (1992). *De relatie tussen de veiligheid en het niveau van de openbare verlichting* [The relationship between safety and the level of public lighting]. R-92-39. Leidschendam, SWOV, 1992.

Schreuder, D.A. (1993). *Het niveau van de openbare verlichting op verschillende categoreën van wegen* [The level of public lighting on different road categories]. Leidschendam, Duco Schreuder Consultancies, 1993.

Schreuder, D.A. (1994). *Road lighting as a crime countermeasure.* Paper presented to the Kansai Lighting Engineers, Osaka, Friday, 22 July 1994. Leidschendam, Duco Schreuder Consultancies, 1994.

Schreuder, D.A. (1995). 'De relatie tussen de verkeersveiligheid, de criminaliteit en de openbare verlichting in stedeljke gebieden' [The relationship between traffic safety, crime and public lighting in urban areas]. In: Anon., 1995a).

Schreuder, D.A.; Buijn, H.R.; Van den Brink, T.D.J. (1991). 'Road lighting for road safety, public security and amenity'. In: CIE. (1992a).

Scott, P.P. (1980). *The relationship between road lighting quality and accident frequency.* Lab. Report LR 929. Crowthorne, TRRL, 1980.

Tanner, J.C. (1963). 'Lighting improvement on urban roads in Great Britain'. In: *Research on road safety.* Crowthorne, Road Research Laboratory, 1963 (Cit. CIE 1992).

Van Bommel, W.J.M. & Caminada, J.F. (1983). 'Openbare verlichting in woonwijken'. *Elektrotechniek* **38** (1983) no. 1.

Van den Brink, T.D.J. & Buijn, H.R. (1987). *De waardering van de verlichting van enkelbaanswegen buiten de bebouwde kom* [Evaluation of lighting single lane roads outside built-up areas]. Verkeerskundige Werkdagen, Deel 3, blz. 859-868. Driebergen, SVT, 1987.

Van den Brink, T.D.J. & Buijn, H.R. (1990). 'Die Bewertung öffentlicher Beleuchtung von Landstrassen'. In: NSVV, (1990a).

Van den Brink, T.D.J. & Tan, T.H. (1979). 'Openbare verlichting in woongebieden' [Public lighting in residential areas]. Verkeerskunde 30 (1979) 425–429.

Van Oortmerssen, J.G.H. (1987). 'De effecten van openbare verlichting op de criminaliteit' [The effects of public lighting on crime]. In: NEOM, 1987.

Van Tilborg, A.D.M. (1991). *Evaluatie van de verlichtingsproeven in Utrecht* [Evaluation of the lighting tests in Utrecht]. Utrecht Energiebedrijf, 1991 (unpublished; see also Anon., 1995a).

Vis, A.A. (1993). *Openbare verlichting en de verkeersveiligheid van autosnelwegen* [Public lighting and traffic safety on motorways]. R-93-19. Leidschendam, SWOV, 1993.

Vis, A.A. (1994). 'Street lighting and road safety on motorways'. In: *Road Safety in Europe and Strategic Highway Research Program (SHRP).* Lille, France, 26–28 September 1994.

12   Efficiency of public lighting

The effectiveness of lighting was discussed in chapter 11: the 'results' of effort. If results are compared with effort, then we arrive at efficiency. Like the effectiveness of lighting, efficiency can also be backed up by objective data. An increase in the level of lighting is not always an efficient measure.

12.1   Effectiveness and efficiency

In the past, efficacy of public lighting was almost exclusively the sole consideration. Efficiency hardly ever seemed to play a role in decisions relating to traffic safety in general and to lighting in particular. The unpublished small-scale study on a section of a road in Drenthe, The Netherlands (Planweg T.8) is an exception. Here the idea of efficacy is implicitly present, as limiting accidents is mentioned in the same breath as the cost of public lighting to be installed (Allewijn, 1982). However, the consideration of effectiveness is not sufficient when looking for a financially quantitative, acceptable method in responding to policy questions. Many effective measures can be thought of, but policy questions especially concern priorities among these possibilities; this requires an understanding of efficiency. Efficiency is characterised by the ratio between costs and benefits. We can also use the term cost-effectiveness.

In order to determine efficiency in public lighting, the costs as well as the benefits must be known; in addition, these must be expressed in the same unit of measure. Normally a monetary unit is used. Costs are discussed in section 12.3.1; here we start with the benefits. See also Schreuder (1993).

12.2   The benefits of public lighting

When considering lighting as a traffic safety measure, the benefits can be expressed in accidents saved. The monetary unit of measure is therefore the cost of accidents saved, quantified in money.

The cost of accidents is determined by the following factors

(a) costs relating to the victims
- cost of treatment and rehabilitation (medical as well as non-medical costs)
- cost of (lost) productivity
- human cost (effects relating to human suffering, pain, loss of loved ones, etc., which may be expressed in money)

(b) material cost (damage to vehicles and road furniture)

(c) costs which relate to the maintenance of traffic safety (in particular of road and traffic regulations)

(d) costs relating to the promotion of traffic safety (research, training, education, technical facilities relating to infrastructure and vehicles, etc.).

Little is known in The Netherlands as regards the cost of accidents. A study was carried out by McKinsey in 1983. This study, which was never published, was simple and limited in scope. Although the study was used in a number of policy papers (Anon., 1985), it was subject to a good deal of criticism, in particular from SWOV (Flury, 1990, 1995). The European Commission undertook an international study in 1994, the contribution from The Netherlands was based on the McKinsey data (COST, 1994). Most other countries contributed more complete and better specified data. These studies offer a better basis for the determination of efficiency in public lighting. There are, however, some limitations. The quantitative data of this international study only referred to victim-related costs, and not to material damage, apart from the problems which may be expected from aggregating data from very diverse sources. A conversion factor is therefore required. The costs mentioned above under (c) and (d) relating to the maintenance and promotion of traffic safety are not taken into account, as they cannot be separated from other costs.

A summary of the results of the quantitative analysis is offered here; for details refer to Schreuder (1994; 1995). The COST report provides the required information on methods used; the results are shown in a number of tables (relating to traffic fatalities, to seriously injured victims and to lightly injured persons). The data are expressed in ECU, with the reference year 1990, and are weighted according to the standard of living in the respective countries. The results are summarised in table 12.2.1.

Table 12.2.1: *Costs relating to victims; reference year 1990 (based on data from COST, 1994, tables 3, 8 and 9)*

Type	Amount (ECU)
Traffic fatalities	750,178
Seriously injured	53,059
Lightly injured	2995

Table 12.2.2: *Distribution of costs according to McKinsey (based on data from Flury, 1995, Appendix 2)*

	Guilders (millions)	Percentage
Medical costs	335	5.7
Loss of production	1936	32.6
Subtotal	2271	38.3
Material costs	3404	57.3
Other costs	260	4.4
Subtotal	3664	61.7
Total	5935	100

* Guilder = approx £3.2.

The material costs are not supplied in COST (1994). Based on the data from Flury (1995, Appendix 2), a conversion factor was established. This factor relates to the McKinsey study mentioned. See table 12.2.2.

The material costs and other costs together amounted to 61.7/38.3 = 1.61 times the total costs relating to victims. In order to determine the total costs, the costs per victim must be multiplied by the number of victims. See table 12.2.3.

The material costs amount to 8.417 million guilders and the total costs for traffic risks are 13,645 million guilders, using a factor of 1.61 (reference year 1990). This amount is considerably higher than the amount normally cited. The main reason is that data from the COST study have been used; as mentioned before, nearly all countries supplied a more realistic cost estimation.

The costs per recorded victim-accident amount to (in HFl)

$$\frac{13,645,000,000}{49,574} \approx 275,200$$

Table 12.2.3: *Costs relating to the victims per accident (reference year 1990)*

Type of victim	Costs per victim	Recorded number	Recorded percentage	Correction factor	Corrected amount	Total costs
Fatal	750,178	1253	100	1	1253	940
Hospital	53,059	11,648	70	1.43	16,657	884
No hospital	2995	36,673	25	4	146,692	439
Total		49,574				
In millions						
				ECU		2263
				Guilders		5228
				Sterling		1730

- Type: victim hospital: hospital admittance; no hospital: no hospital admittance
- Costs per victim: according to table 12.2.1
- Recorded number: number of recorded victims 1993 (CBS, 1994)
- Recorded percentage (Harris, 1989, 1989a)
- Guilder: exchange rate 1 ECU = HFl 2.31.

It should be remembered when using these figures, that the costs apply to 1990 and the accidents to the year 1993. For the costs per recorded accident – including accidents with only material damage – use is made of the records from the SWOV study relating to the lighting of motorways (Vis, 1993, page 17). See table 12.2.4.

Table 12.2.4: *Accident records of motorways (based on Vis, 1993, page 17)*

Type of accident	Number
Fatalities	177
Injury cases	3046
Total victim – accidents	3223
Only material damage – accidents	24,501
Total records	27,724

The costs per recorded accident (all accidents) are therefore (in HFl)

$$\frac{3223}{27,724} \times 275,200 = 31,993$$

As no other data are available, this approach is also used for non-motorways, as well as for roads in built-up areas.

12.3   Roads outside built-up areas

12.3.1   The cost of public lighting for roads outside built-up areas

In the past, efforts have been made to determine the costs of public lighting in general, under the auspices of NSVV (Van Os, 1989). Part IV of the NSVV Recommendations did not contain any costs, only a discussion on the methodology to determine the costs in specific cases (NSVV, 1995). It has proved possible, however, to determine the costs of lighting in specific cases.

Rijkswaterstaat and the Province of Noord-Holland supplied a number of data for this research which concerns motorways with two times three lanes and two-way, two-lane rural main roads. The luminance was not always the same; the costs are standardised for motorways to 0.75 and 1.5 cd/m^2 and for non-motorways to 0.5 and 1.0 cd/m^2. These values correspond with the main lighting classes according to the NSVV Recommendations (NSVV, 1990). This normalisation was arrived at by varying the light point distances; this means that the recommendations for uniformity are no longer met in all cases in the examples. Annual costs comprise the installation costs with a certain depreciation period, together with the running costs. The results are summarised in tables 12.3.1 and 12.3.2.

The difference between these two sets of data lies mainly in the fact that the cables are excluded from the costs quoted in the second case. In addition, there are other differences which are difficult to trace. It would seem that these at first sight quite small accounting discrepancies may have a

Table 12.3.1: *Annual costs per km in guilders in 1993 (data supplied by Rijkswaterstaat)*

Type of road	Number of lanes	Geometry	Type of lamp	Level (cd/m^2)	Total costs per year
Motorways	2 × 3	line	SOX	0.75	41,758
	2 × 3	line	SOX	1.5	55,892
	2 × 3	post	SON	0.75	17,776*
	2 × 3	post	SON	1.5	26,404*
Non-motorways	1 × 2	one-sided	SON	0.5	12,357
Non-motorways	1 × 2	one-sided	SON	1	16,862

* Experimental lighting for temporary works. The glare specifications were not always met.

Table 12.3.2: *Annual costs per km in guilders in 1995 (data supplied by the Province of Noord-Holland)*

Type of road	Number of lanes	Geometry	Type of lamp	Level (cd/m^2)	Total costs per year
Motorways	2 × 2	line	SOX	0.75	15,339
	2 × 2	line	SOX	1.5	30,667
	2 × 2	post	SOX	0.75	5599
	2 × 2	post	SOX	1.5	11,198
	2 × 2	post	SON	0.75	5355
	2 × 2	post	SON	1.5	10,709

considerable effect on the final result. It is striking that the costs of installations with low-pressure and high-pressure sodium lamps do not vary much, despite the considerable difference in specific luminous flux between the lamp types (section 13.3.1). In tables 12.3.1, 12.3.2 and 12.3.3 'line' means a lengthwise mounting of luminaires on span wires over the median (catenary lighting) and 'post' means twin bracket, median-mounted conventional mounting. The experimental lighting was on one side only.

12.3.2   The efficiency of public lighting on roads outside built-up areas
Based on earlier studies, it would seem that the night-time risk on lit motorways amounts to 0.40 (according to table 11.2.3, 0.398; number of recorded accidents per million vehicle km; all classes of lighting; taken from Vis, 1994). The lighting may also lead to a saving of 0.0988, again expressed in the number of recorded night-time accidents per million vehicle km, under certain conditions (see Schreuder, 1993). In order to determine the number of saved accidents per km annually, this number must be multiplied with the traffic on an annual basis. This amounts to 365 times n, in which n represents the traffic on a daytime basis (the 24-hour density). The costs are per recorded accident (in guilders from 1992 according to section 12.2) 31,993. The benefits therefore amount to

$$\frac{0.0988 \times 365 \times n \times 31.993}{1,000,000} = 11.538n$$

Table 12.3.3: *Minimum traffic density for efficient lighting (break-even point; cars per 24 hours) for different types of road, lighting geometry and levels of lighting. The percentage of the Dutch motorway network which corresponds to the break-even point is also shown (figure 12.3.1)*

Type of road	Number of lanes	Geometry	Type of lamp	Level (cd/m^2)	Break-even point	Road network (%)
Motorways	2 × 3	line	SOX	0.75	36,192	47
	2 × 3	line	SOX	1.5	48,442	27
	2 × 3	post	SON	0.75	15,406*	85
	2 × 3	post	SON	1.5	22,884*	76
	2 × 2	line	SOX	0.75	13,294	93
	2 × 2	line	SOX	1.5	26,588	65
	2 × 2	post	SOX	0.75	4853	97
	2 × 2	post	SOX	1.5	9705	94
	2 × 2	post	SON	0.75	4641	94
	2 × 2	post	SON	1.5	9282	97

* Experimental lighting

If these benefits are equalised to the costs as determined in section 10.5.3, then we get the break-even point, i.e. the minimum traffic density for efficient lighting. This is given in table 12.3.3.

The break-even values for the round the clock density seem to correspond to a rather small part of the Dutch motorway network in the assumptions by Rijkswaterstaat for line lighting. At lower luminances, however, and for cheaper installations, the lighting in a large part of the road network would

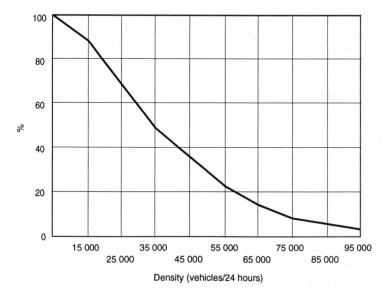

Figure 12.3.1: *Cumulative distribution of the 24-hour traffic density for the Dutch network (after Schreuder, 1993, fig. 3; based on data from Vis, 1993, fig. 3)*

seem to cover the costs; when using the assumptions by the Province of Noord-Holland, this applies even more. It should not be forgotten that a number of assumptions are not based on solid facts as far as the costs and the benefits are concerned. A study from Norway, which has not yet been published, however, would seem to produce similar results.

The same procedure can be implemented for non-motorways. Table 12.3.1 shows the total annual lighting costs on a non-motorway for two levels of lighting, namely 0.5 and 1 cd/m^2. The costs amount to HFl 12,357 and HFl 16,862 respectively.

The accidents are shown in table 10.1.2. Section 10.1.2 indicated that the prediction of the number of accidents over five years, which would have taken place at night-time on unlit roads, had they been lit, is: $(3.02/8.01) \times 5.36 = 2.02$, or 0.404 annually. However, the actual number was 3.49 over five years or 0.698 annually. The annual saving per km is therefore $0.698 - 0.404 = 0.294$ accidents per km annually. The cost per recorded accident amounts to HFl 31,993 (in guilders from 1992), according to section 12.2. The benefits therefore amount to $0.294 \times 31.993 = $ HFl 9406 per km annually.

It may be assumed, as a first approximation, that the benefits are proportional to traffic density n, and that the costs are independent of n. The class of road in the accident study corresponds with roads for mixed traffic with one lane, and which are closed to cyclists (see Janssen, 1988). There were 6537 km of these roads in The Netherlands in 1986. The average traffic amounted to 5186 vehicles per 24 hours. Assuming that these statistics can also be used for 1992, the break-even point n_{br} can then be determined as follows

- for 0.5 cd/m^2: $n_{br}/5186 = 12,357/9406$; $n_{br} = 6813$
- for 1 cd/m^2: $n_{br}/5186 = 16,862/9406$; $n_{br} = 9297$.

If the fact is taken into consideration that the sample of roads used in the accident study would seem to be much safer than the average road network, then the break-even point is considerably lower. Schreuder (1993) gives values of $n = 2352$ (vehicles per 24 hours). This round the clock density is exceeded in most of the Dutch road network and has resulted in the suggestion that public lighting is an efficient traffic safety measure for most single carriageway roads. It is interesting that the traffic density in question is close to the value of 3250 vehicles per 24 hours, which has been mentioned by Anderson et al. (1984) for the efficiency of lighting at crossroads outside built-up areas.

12.3.3   Increasing the level of lighting for roads outside built-up areas

The general relationship between the level of lighting and accidents was discussed in section 10.2.6. A doubling of the level of lighting generally produces a considerable, albeit not very large, saving in the number of accidents. This saving is not the same for different types of road. According to table 10.5.2, the saving for motorways is 5.8%, for non-motorways 12% and for roads and streets within built-up areas 4.4%. An increase in the level of lighting would therefore seem to be an effective traffic safety measure; the question remains whether it is also an efficient measure.

According to Vis (1993) 2502 accidents took place on 276.2 km of lit motorways in darkness over three years, or annually 3.02 accidents per km. A doubling of the level of lighting produces a saving of 5.4% or 0.163 accidents per km annually. The cost per accident amounts to HFl 31,993, so a doubling of the level produces a saving of 0.163 × HFl 31,993 = HFl 5215 per km annually.

Tables 12.3.1 and 12.3.2 show the differences in cost at a doubling of the level of lighting. See table 12.3.4.

If the data in table 12.3.4 are compared with the saving of HFl 5215 per km annually mentioned above, then a doubling of the lighting level from 0.75 to 1.5 cd/m^2 is not or hardly cost-effective. However, it is felt that halving, from 0.75 to 0.37 cd/m^2 cannot be recommended as a measure, from the point of view of efficiency.

According to table 10.2.1 the risk in darkness at a luminance of less than 0.4 cd/m^2 on lit non-motorways amounts to 0.59 and at a luminance of more than 0.73 cd/m^2 this amounts to 0.26, expressed in accidents per 10^6 vehicle kilometres. This corresponds to a reduction of 0.33 in the risk at an overall doubling of the luminance.

As indicated in section 12.3.2, traffic density on dual carriageways closed to slower traffic amounted to 5186 vehicles per 24 hours on average in 1986 (Janssen, 1988). This is a reduction of 0.6225 accidents per km annually, for a reduction in the risk of 0.33. The costs per accident amount to HFl31,993. A

Table 12.3.4: *Difference in annual costs per km at a doubling of the lighting level from 0.75 to 1.5 cd/m^2. RWS: assumptions Rijkswaterstaat; NH: assumptions Noord-Holland*

Type of road	Number of lanes	Geometry	Type of lamp	Level (cd/m^2)	Annual costs (in HFl)	Difference 1.5 and 0.75 (in HFl)
Motorway RWS	2 × 3	line	SOX	0.75	41,758	
Motorway RWS	2 × 3	line	SOX	1.5	55,892	14,134
Motorway RWS	2 × 3	post	SON	0.75	17,776	
Motorway RWS	2 × 3	post	SON	1.5	26,404	9628
Motorway NH	2 × 2	line	SOX	0.75	15,339	
Motorway NH	2 × 2	line	SOX	1.5	30,677	15,339
Motorway NH	2 × 2	post	SOX	0.75	5599	
Motorway NH	2 × 2	post	SOX	1.5	11,198	5599
Motorway NH	2 × 2	post	SON	0.75	5355	
Motorway NH	2 × 2	post	SON	1.5	10,709	5355

doubling in the level of lighting from 0.5 to 1.0 cd/m^2 produces a saving of 0.6225 × 31,993 = 19,915 per km annually. Table 12.3.1 shows that the costs for such a doubling amount to 12,357−16,862 = 4505 per km annually; a doubling of the luminance level on non-motorways would seem to be an efficient measure (costs in HFl).

12.4   Roads within built-up areas

As nearly all roads within built-up areas are lit, there is no point in studying the efficiency of the presence of lighting on roads within built-up areas. The effects of the level of lighting, however, are relevant. The additional costs for doubling the level of lighting on roads in built-up areas are determined on the basis of data from the Tanthof district in Delft (Steenks, 1994). The additional costs for an increase in the level of lighting, including 30% running costs, amount to 12%; the cost for investment may be ignored. Assuming that this also applies when the level of lighting is doubled, then the additional costs amount to 1/0.3 × 0.12 = 0.4. The annually running costs per kilometre were set at HFl 9436 for roads with a flow function; for distributor roads HFl 4833 and for residential streets HFl 3240 (Steenks, 1994). At a doubling of the level of lighting, an increase in costs of 3774, 1933 and 1296 respectively (in HFl) can be expected. This corresponds to a saving in accidents of 4.4%, according to table 11.2.5.

As no accident statistics are known for this district, I have used data from Utrecht for the cost/benefit analysis. The local authority has provided data on the areas of metalled roads which were in use during 1993. The statistics for annual accidents in darkness for the different types of road were derived from an earlier study (Schreuder, 1992, 1992a). From it the savings in accidents and in guilders per km annually can be determined. Above, the annual costs per km (for Delft) for these types of road was given. The pay-back period was derived from these. See table 12.4.1.

The pay-back period is short. For roads with a flow function and with a distribution function approximately six months; for residential areas a little longer, but no more than 18 months. An increase in the level of lighting in urban streets would therefore seem a very efficient traffic safety measure. I would point out again, however, that these analyses contain a number of assumptions which are difficult to test; the real results could very well turn out to be quite different!

Table 12.4.1: *The pay-back period for a doubling in the level of lighting on roads in built-up areas (data from Delft and from Utrecht)*

Type of	Length (km)	Accidents in darkness per km per year	Accidents per year	Saving	Saving HFl	Costs HFl	Pay-back year
Flow	30	152	5.067	0.223	7134	3774	0.53
Distribution	81	226	2.790	0.123	3935	1933	0.49
Residential	374	204	0.545	0.024	768	1296	1.69

Bibliography

Allewijn, P. (1982). *AVOV-Experiment openbare verlichting weggedeelte T 8 (Deurze-Rolde)* [Experiment public lighting road section T 8 (Deurze-Rolde)]. Brief DVV 1777/243/82 with Appendices. Den Haag, 1982 (unpublished).

Anderson, K.A.; Hoppe, W.J.; McCoy, P.T. & Price, R.E. (1984). *Cost-effective evaluation of rural intersection lighting levels.* TRB Annual 63rd Meeting, Washington DC, TRB, 1984.

CBS (1994). *Statistiek van de verkeersongevallen op de openbare weg over 1993* [Statistics of traffic accidents on public roads during 1993]. Den Haag, SDU, 1994.

COST (1994). *Socio-economic cost of road accidents.* COST 313. EUR 15464 EN. Brussels, Commission of the European Communities, 1994.

Flury, F.C. (1981), 'Cost/effectiveness aspects of road lighting'. *Lichtforschung* **3** (1981) no 1 p 37–41.

Flury, F.C. (1990). *De ontwikkeling van de verkeersonveiligheid tot en met 1988 en het beleid uit het Meerjarenplan Verkeersveiligheid 1987–1991* [The development of traffic risks up to 1988 and the policies from the Meerjarenplan Verkeersveiligheid 1987–1991]. R-90-28 Leidschendam, SWOV, 1990.

Flury, F.C. (1995). *Kosten ten gevolge van verkeersongevallen* [Costs resulting from traffic accidents]. R-95-27. Leidschendam, SWOV, 1995.

Harris, S. (1989). *Verkeersgewonden geteld en gemeten* [Injured victims of traffic accidents counted and measured]. R-89-13. Leidschendam, SWOV, 1989.

Harris, S. (1989a). *'Eerst meer, toen minder, een historisch overzicht'* [First of all more, then less, a historical review]. In: Voor alle veiligheid. Leidschendam, SWOV, 1989.

Janssen, S.T.M.C. (1998). *De verkeersonveiligheid van wegtypen in 1986 en 2010* [Traffic safety for types of roads in 1986 and 2010]. R-88-3. Leidschendam, SWOV, 1988.

Loos, W.A. (1982). *'Vergelijking van kostenaspecten bij openbare verlichting'* [Comparison of cost aspects in public lighting]. *Elektrotechniek* **60** (1982) no 9. 17-21.

NSVV (1990). *Aanbevelingen voor openbare verlichting, Deel 1* [Recommendations for public lighting, Part 1]. Arnhem, NSVV, 1990.

NSVV (1995). *Aanbevelingen voor openbare verlichting, Deel 4: Economische aspecten* [Recommendations for public lighting, Part 4; Economic aspects]. Arnhem, NSVV, 1995.

PAOVV (1994). *Cursus Openbare Verlichting* [Public Lighting Course]. Delft/Eindhoven, 1, 2 en 3 februari 1994. Rijswijk/Delft, PAOVV, 1994.

Schreuder, D.A. (1992). *De relatie tussen de veiligheid en het niveau van de openbare verlichting* [The relationship between safety and the level of public lighting]. R-92-39. Leidschendam, SWOV, 1992.

Schreuder, D.A. (1992a). *Openbare verlichting als verkeersveiligheidsmaatregel; Stand van zaken en toekomst* [Public lighting as a traffic safety measure; state of the art and the future]. R-92-64. Leidschendam, SWOV, 1992.

Schreuder, D.A. (1993). *Het niveau van de openbare verlichting op verschillende categorieën van wegen* [The level of public lighting at different categories of roads]. Leidschendam, Duco Schreuder Consultancies, 1993.

Schreuder, D.A. (1994). Kosten-Nutzen Ueberlegungen für Strassenbeleuchtung. LICHT94, Interlaken, 14.9-16.9.1994. Leidschendam, Duco Schreuder Consultancies, 1994.

Schreuder, D.A. (1995). *The cost/benefit aspects of the road lighting level.* Paper PS 161,

23rd Session of the CIE, 1-8 November 1995, New Delhi, India. Leidschendam, Duco Schreuder Consultancies, 1995.

Steenks, C. (1994). *Kostenaspecten* [Cost aspects]. In: PAOVV (1994).

Uschkamp, G. & Meseberg, H.-H. (1995). 'Zusammenhang zwischen dem Niveau der Strassenbeleuchtung und dem Verkehrsunfallgeschehen'. *Licht* (1995) No 7/8, pp. 631–638.

Van Os, J. (1989). 'Openbare verlichting en kosten' [Public lighting and costs]. *Elektrotechniek* **67** (1989) 731–732.

13   Design aspects of public lighting

The design of public lighting installations is rather a complex task. A number of different aspects are involved. Firstly, the purpose of the lighting must be determined; this can be deduced from the class of road and the nature of the traffic. Subsequently, a preliminary design must be produced. This is followed by the actual design, after the client's approval has been obtained. The design is based on a calculation of the luminance or the illuminance intensity, together with other technical characteristics relating to lighting. But economic factors are also relevant, while attention must be paid to the electrotechnical aspects of the lighting resources in relation to the characteristics of wiring. Often the design of the wiring is part of the lighting design. The mechanical aspects of lamps, luminaires and masts are very important too, while the environmental aspects must not be forgotten either. Finally, the lighting must fit in with the environment it is placed in; this usually produces some tension between lighting experts on the one hand and town and country planning experts and architects on the other. This often used to lead to conflict but more recently a solution is usually found which is acceptable to both sides.

This chapter deals with a number of aspects relating to design. The classification of roads and of traffic were discussed in chapter 9; the financial aspects in chapters 11 and 12, while the environmental aspects will be looked at in chapter 14. The design, which is complex, is a job for experts. In addition to a reasonable understanding of the technical and scientific fundamental aspects of lighting, an engineer's understanding and common sense are important, but in particular a good measure of practical experience. The basis for this is supplied in detail, accompanied by examples, in Part III of the NSVV Recommendations (NSVV, 1996).

13.1 The calculation of technical characteristics relating to lighting

13.1.1 The purpose of the calculations

Technical calculations relating to lighting are used at the design stage of public lighting. The design is based on a certain function of the (future) road. According to the NSVV Recommendations, the lighting characteristics, i.e. the level of lighting, the uniformity and glare control follow from these (NSVV, 1990). The lighting characteristics for traffic roads are expressed in luminances, and for residential and public areas in illuminances (section 9.1). The design amounts to the fact that an installation is selected which meets with the requirements. Presently this is a iterative process: an example is selected; this is calculated and checked as to whether the result comes anywhere near the requirement. If not, then the example is adapted. This is repeated until the result satisfies the requirements.

A careful design does justice to the technical aspects of lighting, as well as to other aspects such as maintenance, costs and environmental considerations. This makes the design part of a policy management plan for public lighting. Management plans are the subject of rapid development at present. Some information can be found in Guldemond (1994, 1994a), Steenks (1994), Meutzner (1996) and Zuring & Van de Holst (1996).

The installation is erected, following the design. It is important to check whether the realised installation actually meets with the specification; for this a test is required following completion. This test may consist of measuring the illuminance in streets where illuminance is the basis of the design. This is different for roads where luminance is the basis of the design. As indicated in section 5.4.7, there is presently no generally accepted, simple to apply method available with which to measure luminance on the road accurately. NSVV recommends measuring the horizontal illuminance as an intermediary step (NSVV, 1993). This is, of course, an unsatisfactory situation; a good method for measuring luminance on the road is urgently required.

This necessity is underlined by the recent developments relating to liability and responsibility. The new Dutch Civil Code as well as the European regulations shortly coming into force stipulate that the installation satisfy the requirements not only when new, but also during the whole of its service life (see section 3.4.3). Measurements during the service period of the installation are therefore paramount.

13.1.2 Calculating the illuminance

The calculation of the illuminance is, in principle, very simple. It is sufficent to have data relating to the geometry of the installation (method of installation, distance between masts, height of the light point, width of the road and outreach) as well as on the light emission of the luminaires to be used (the luminance intensity distribution, the I table). The illuminance is calculated at separate points of the road surface. The respective angles of the light incidence can be derived from the geometry for each separate luminaire. In this way the contribution by the luminaire to the illuminance at that point can be determined. Summing this for all luminaires in question produces the total illuminance at that point; the process is repeated for all points in the selected pattern. This method is similar for the horizontal and the vertical illuminance, as well as for the semicylindrical illuminance, provided the angles of incidence are adapted correspondingly.

13.1.3   Calculation of the luminance

De Boer published a method in 1952 to determine the luminance of a road when the reflection properties of the road surface and the luminous intensity of the luminaires are known (De Boer et al., 1952). This method is the EP diagram ('equivalent position diagram'). The idea was simple and at the same time elegant. The reflection properties of the road surface are drawn on a transparency in such a way that they are represented by lines of equal luminance and based on the assumption that the road surface is illuminated by a unit source of light – a source of light which emits a luminous intensity of 1 cd in all directions. This representation is called the iso-luminance diagram; the curves show the values of $q\cos^3\gamma$. In other words, they are lines of equal luminance if the road is illuminated by the unit source of light. An example of such a representation of the reflection is shown in figure 13.1.1.

The shape of the curves in this figure represents the fact that the road is seen by an observer under the given angle of 1° with the horizontal (see section 5.4.6). Subsequently, the luminous intensity of the luminaire was drawn on a second transparancy at the same scale. Now by overlaying a map of the road (also drawn to the same scale) with these two transparencies, the luminance at a point on the road can be determined by laying the origin of the iso-luminance diagram on the point in question. The value of $q\cos^3\gamma$ is read off and multiplied by the correponding I value from the luminous intensity table, which is also laid over the image of the road. This action is

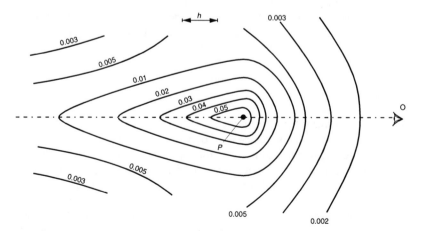

Figure 13.1.1: An EP diagram. The numbers relate to the value of $q\cos^3\gamma$ (after Schreuder, 1967, fig. 3.13)

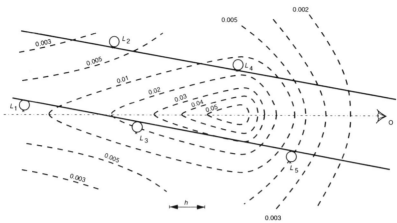

Figure 13.1.2: *Determination of the luminance with the EP diagrams (after Schreuder, 1967, fig. 3.14)*

repeated for all points for which the luminance is to be determined. The procedure is explained in figure 13.1.2.

Of course, working with EP diagrams was time-consuming; not much use was made of them therefore when designing lighting installations. However, the work by De Boer forms the basis for all further developments relating to the calculation of luminance. CIE established a system during the Sixties which is still used generally in the calculation of luminances (CIE, 1976, 1990). This system led to a computer program called LUCY. The CIE program was designed many years ago and is therefore not very up-to-date. However, the usefulness of its basis has not diminished (Rattunde, 1991). Many variants are used presently, which have in common that they are suitable for use with PCs; apart from that, there are quite a number of smaller differences between all these programs mainly pertaining to the display of the results.

Basically all programs are similar. They comprise the following framework

- The observation position is selected (according to certain rules).
- The horizontal illuminance is calculated per light point for each point of the road; for this the geometrics of the installation, the geometry of the observer and the road surface point, and the luminance intensity distribution (the *I* table) for the luminaire in question must be known.
- The luminance is determined for that point and for that luminaire; for this the characteristics of the road surface reflection (the *R* table) must be known; this calculation is quite complicated, as the *R* table must be interpolated for most points in the road surface.
- The luminance contributions from the separate luminaires are summed; there are certain rules regarding the number of luminaires to be included.
- The total procedure is repeated for other points on the road surface; there are certain rules relating to the number and the position of the points which are included.

Comparison of the CIE framework with the system relating to the EP diagrams described earlier, show clearly that the two systems are basically similar. At present a number of variants are used which are based on the same principle. See also Hentschel (1994, page 195).

This is, of course, rather a cumbersome method. A calculation system is urgently needed which works in reverse – i.e. where one starts with the specification and the installation is the outcome. These systems are sometimes called 'expert systems'; the reason for this is that a proper expert also works in this way. Di Fraia (1993) has made a start. Some commercially available computer programs have a module which points very generally to some design features. Methods which are useful in practice when designing lighting, however, do not yet exist.

13.2   Designing lighting as a 'project'

Working project-fashion is to systematise what comes 'naturally'. An overview is provided in an unpublished course by Bureau Zuidema (Zuidema, 1989). See also Wijnen et al. (1984) and NOVEM (1996). The characteristics of a project-fashion approach are

- there is a start, a middle and an end
- the work is phased (at least three phases: the start, the middle and the end)
- a phase is only started when the previous one is closed with an explicit decision.

The design and the realisation of a lighting installation as a a project is outlined in table 13.2.1.

Table 13.2.1: *Outline of the design and the implementation as a project*

Phase	Activity (project component)
Initiative	Policy plan local authority
	Decision: establish project
Definition	Road class, technical specification relating to lighting
	Decision: produce preliminary design
Design 1	Produce preliminary design, feasibility study, planning
	Decision: produce design
Design 2	Produce design (technical relating to lighting, electro technical, financial management)
	Decision: implementation
Preparation	Preparation, putting out to tender
	Decision: award
Realisation 1	Implementation
	Decision: first completion
Realisation 2	Test
	Decision: final completion
Service	Maintenance, management

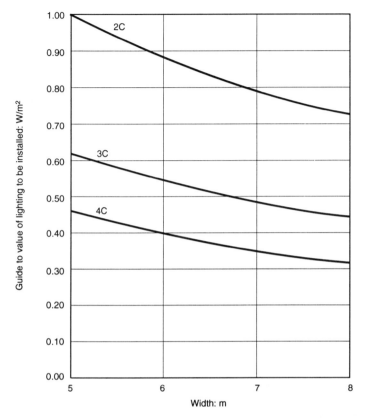

Figure 13.2.1: *The lighting to be installed in relation to the road width for the NSVV classes of lighting 2C, 3C and 4C (taken from NOVEM, 1996, fig. 14)*

An important part of the design is the preliminary design. Proposals for a method are given by Van der Lugt & Albers (1996) and Schreuder (1997, 1997a). The brochure published by NOVEM contains a number of illustrations which may be used when establishing a preliminary design (NOVEM, 1996). Figure 13.2.1 shows the overall relationship between the lighting to be installed and the road width for three classes of lighting which are used particularly for streets and opening up roads.

Figure 13.2.2 similarly shows the overall relationship between the lighting to be installed and the width of the area to be illuminated for five classes of lighting which are relevant in particular to residential areas.

13.3   Elements of the lighting design

13.3.1   Lamps

Only electrical sources of light are considered for modern public lighting, and in particular gas discharge lamps. Only two gasses, or rather vapours, are

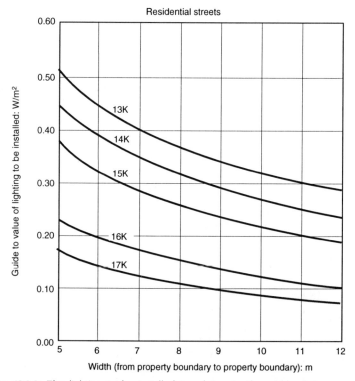

Figure 13.2.2: *The lighting to be installed in relation to the width of the area to be illuminated for the NSVV classes of lighting 13K, 14K, 15K and 17K (after NOVEM, 1996, fig. 12)*

considered: sodium and mercury. Both can be used at high and at low-pressure. There are therefore four families of lamps which are used in public lighting

- high-pressure sodium lamps
- low-pressure sodium lamps
- high-pressure mercury lamps
- low-pressure mercury lamps.

As indicated in section 4.3, all types of gas discharge lamps are based on the same principle: electrons are freed from the negatively charged cathode, and move to the positively charged anode. The vapour atoms are ionised or become excited, due to collisions. At recombination or when returning to the basic state, energy quanta are emitted which, directly or via adaptation by means of fluorescence, are perceived as light. Gas discharge lamps have a spectrum of lines or bands. A gas discharge lamp has a negative electrical resistance; external voltage restriction is therefore required for all gas discharge lamps. This voltage restriction is an important function of the ballasts. See also section 4.3; details can be found in the manuals by Elenbaas (1959, 1965), De Groot & Van Vliet (1986) and Meyer & Nienhuis (1988).

Table 13.3.1: *Overview of lamps for public lighting (after NSVV, 1996, sec.. 3.1.2); the data relating to metal halogenide lamps are from Anon. (1993a, page 44)*

Type of lamp	Specific luminous flux (lm/W)	Colour temperature (K)	Colour rendering index (Ra)
Low-pressure sodium	100–200	1800	(NA)
High-pressure sodium	68–150	1900–2150	26–60
High-pressure mercury	36–60	3300–4500	36–60
Low-pressure mercury	45–90	2700–7000	60–98
Metal halogenide	61–83	3000–5500	65–92

Designers should ensure that the characteristics suit the purpose of the lighting, when choosing a type of lamp for the design. This concerns the colour, the dimensions and the specific luminous flux. Table 13.3.1 gives an overview of the characteristics of the types of lamp suitable for public lighting. The NSVV Recommendations contain many data on the characteristics and the operation of the various types of lamps, with the emphasis on practical aspects which are directly relevant to the lighting design (NSVV, 1996, sec. 3.1.2; 3.1.3 and 3.1.4).

The metal halogenide lamps, mentioned in table 13.3.1, are high-pressure mercury lamps with the addition of halogen in the gas discharge. The colour rendering and the specific luminous flux are considerably better than those of the traditional high-pressure mercury lamps. The metal halogenide lamps are used in the lighting of sports fields and factory sites on a large scale and also for large traffic complexes. The application in normal street lighting is limited, especially as the luminous flux of even the smallest unit of 350 W is too great for optimum lighting of roads and streets. The new QL lamps are also mercury lamps; the excitation of the mercury atoms is not caused by a gas discharge, but by high frequency radiation. These lamps have a very long service life, but they are rather expensive. Application in public lighting is presently still of an experimental nature. Some data on this newest branch on the tree of the mercury lamps can be found in Anon. (1995, pages 3–24).

The development of new types of lamps and performance improvements of existing types continues apace. An overview is given in figure 13.3.1.

The new generation of low-pressure sodium lamps also deserves a mention. These are and remain monochromatic sources of light. The new developments relate mainly to two aspects, which both result in a higher lamp yield. This concerns measures which limit the sodium migration; i.e. the tendency for the sodium as a solid and therefore also as a vapour to become more and more concentrated during the life of the lamp. This simply means that only part of the lamp is effective as a source of light. The second is better heat isolation of the discharge tube. The tube stays warmer, which allows the specific luminous flux to increase. Conversely, the vapour pressure is reduced; a larger-sized lamp is required for the same luminous flux. As a result, two families or generations of SOX lamps are on the market. The characteristics are shown in

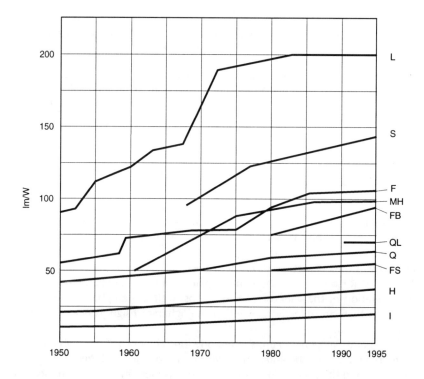

Figure 13.3.1: *The development of the luminous flux of the lamp over the years (after Anon., 1993a, fig. 1.85); see chapter 1 for the abbreviations of the types of lamps*

table 13.3.2. It is interesting that at the same constructional length the luminous flux is a little lower, whereas the wattage is considerably lower; the yield is higher.

Improvements have been introduced regularly in the field of fluorescent lamps also. Traditonal lamps used to be straight and were 38 mm in diameter. The specific luminous flux amounted to, at most, approximately 80 lm/W with the rather simple single fluorescence powders (De Boer & Fischer, 1981, page 151; Hentschel, 1994, page 152) and the colour rendering index amounted to approximately 80. Some decades ago, the triphosphor lamps, 26 mm in diameter, were introduced. These are now the standard lamps. The specific

Table 13.3.2: *The old and the new generation of SOX lamps (after NSVV, 1996 sec. 3.1.4)*

Old generation	Luminous flux	New generation	Luminous flux	Length of lamp
		18W	1800 lm	216 mm
36W	4550 lm	26W	3600 lm	310 mm
55W	7800 lm	36W	5800 lm	425 mm
90W	13,000 lm	66W	10,500 lm	528 mm
135W	22,500 lm	91W	17,000 lm	775 mm
180W	33,000 lm	131W	26,000 lm	1120 mm

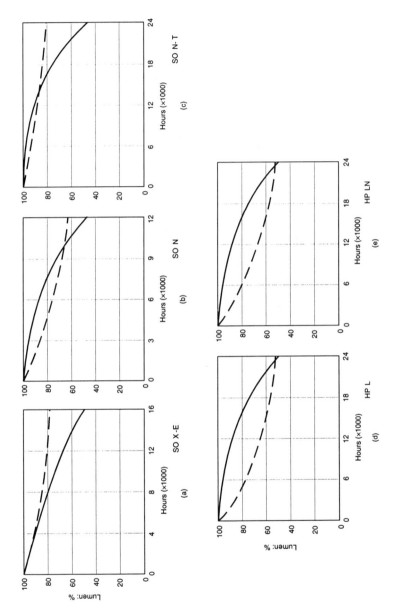

Figure 13.3.2: The light reduction and the failure rate of a number of lamp types (after Anon., 1993b, pages 6.2.12 and 6.2.13)

luminous flux for common light colour amounts to more than 90 lm/W and the colour rendering index is 85, some even considerably more (Anon., 1995, page 24). Recently, a new series of fluorescent lamps were introduced, the TL5 series by Philips. The lamps have a number of advantages (Anon. 1995a). They are 16 mm in diameter, which allows for smaller optics. The service life is longer and the lamp contains less mercury. The specific luminous flux can amount to 104 lm/W.

It is not known whether the TL5 lamp is also suitable for public lighting. This is, however, definitely the case for the compact fluorescence lamps; these are lamps where the discharge tube is folded, which can result in a very small lamp. I will return to the difference in the properties and, consequently, in the areas of application and also to the consequences of this development for the environment in section 14.2.4.

An important aspect of lamps is the reduction in luminous output and the related service life. The light yield decreases in nearly all cases with increased use. This is also the case for low-pressure sodium lamps, even if it cannot always be seen clearly, due to the increase of wattage. The luminous flux (lm) remains almost equal, but the specific luminous flux (lm/W) decreases. The extent to which the light yield is reduced depends closely on the type and size of lamp and on a number of external factors (switching schedule, temperature, variations in voltage, type of ballast, etc).

The light reduction in lamps is a factor which is important for the maintenance schedule of installations of public lighting. I will return to this in section 13.3.2. The service life of a lamp is defined in different ways. Sometimes the time, after which the light yield is reduced by – on average – 10%, is taken. The time, when a certain percentage of defective lamps is also used. As in both cases conditions have an significant effect on the result, the data can only be an approximation. In order to be able to compare lamps, standard conditions have been agreed. This allows the light reduction and the percentage of failure to be quoted. Some examples are given in figure 13.3.2.

13.3.2 Luminaires
All luminaires for public lighting, including the decorative luminaires, are functional lighting resources. They have a number of functions

- directing the light and protecting against glare
- attachment of the lamp (and often the ballast) and facilities for the electrical connections
- protection against touching, the effects of weather, climate and vandalism.

To this is sometimes added the contribution to the aesthetic aspect of the road.

The optical aspects of the luminaires were discussed in the previous chapters. These aspects concern directing the light and protection against glare. The attachment and the electrical connections speak for themselves. Here, a few comments will be made on the protection against touching and against the effects of weather and climate, in particular against the penetration of damp and dust. It is assumed that all luminaires for public

Table 13.3.3: *IP, first digit: protection against touching of charged parts and against penetration by objects and dust (after NSVV, 1997)*

Digit	Protection against:	
	accidental touching	penetration
0	None	None
1	By hand	Large objects > 50 mm
2	Fingers	Medium-sized objects > 12 mm
3	Wire > 2.5 mm	Small objects > 2.5 mm
4	Wire > 1 mm	Small objects > 1 mm
5	Impossible	Free of harmful dust deposits
6	Impossible	Completely dustproof

Table 13.3.4: *IP, second digit: protection against penetration by water (after NSVV, 1997)*

Digit	Protection against water penetration	CEE indication
0	None	
1	Drops falling straight down	
2	Drops falling max. 15° with the vertical	Dripping waterproof
3	Spray water max. 60° with the vertical	Rainproof
4	Splashing from all directions	Splash waterproof
5	Spraying from all directions	Water spray-proof
6	Waves, heavy seas	
7	Submersion (set pressure and time)	Waterproof
8	Submersion (set pressure and indefinitely)	Waterproof

lighting are closed; open luminaires are often seen in developing countries, but in the industrialised world luminaires in modern installations are almost always fitted with a transparent cover. This means that it is necessary to prevent damp and dust from penetrating the luminaires. The requirements relating to sealing luminaires will be commented on briefly. I will also supply some information on the requirements relating to intentional or unintentional touching of the charged parts (electrical insulation or protection against touching). A certain overlap exists between these two.

The sealing of luminaires is expressed in the two-digit IP classification. The first digit indicates the protection aginst touching charged parts and, at the same time, the risk of objects and dust penetrating the luminaire. The second digit indicates the extent of the sealing against penetration by water. See table 13.3.3 and table 13.3.4.

As far as the electrical insulation for luminaires is concerned, the usual EEC classes apply, see table 13.3.5.

Only classes I and II are used in public lighting in The Netherlands.

Section 10.6.3 indicated that the recommended values for lighting are required (or standard) values. A standard value is 'The lowest value which is acceptable at any moment in time' (NSVV, 1990, page 15). Figure 13.3.3 shows the relationship between the momentary value, the required value and the new value.

Table 13.3.5: *The classes for electrical insulation (after NSVV, 1997)*

Class	Insulation
0	Functional insulation, without earth facility
I	A facility for earthing of metal parts which can be touched, as well as functional insulation.
II	No exposed metal parts which may be charged (double or reinforced insulation). Luminaires class II must not be earthed.
III	Connected to a low voltage of 42V maximum.

The design should take into account the light reduction of the installation; the required value must be multiplied by the light reduction factor (maintenance factor) in order to find the design value (NSVV, 1997, sec. 4.4). Light reduction in lamps was discussed in section 13.3.1. This determines, together with the contamination and the age of the luminaires, the light reduction of the installation as a whole. In order to limit light reduction to an acceptable level, the installation must be maintained. Usually routine (periodic) maintenance is chosen. The optimum period depends on the circumstances and is determined on the basis of cost. As call-out charges form an important part of the maintenance costs, it is logical to combine the replacement of lamps and the cleaning of the luminaires; the period is therefore also determined by the service life of the lamps in use. Factors which influence the service life negatively must therefore be avoided on the basis of cost also. These include matters such as vibration and variations in voltage in the circuitry (NSVV, 1996). A number of factors are shown qualitatively in figure 13.3.4.

Much research has been conducted in the UK into light reduction. The results are summarised in table 13.3.6.

Table 13.3.6 shows the importance of a good seal in the luminaires, especially when there is considerable pollution and when the cleaning interval is large. See also Marsden (1993).

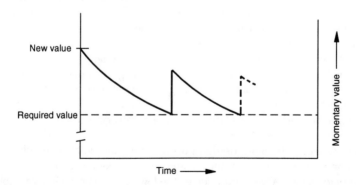

Figure 13.3.3: *The relationship between monetary value, required value and the new value (after NSVV, 1990, fig. 1)*

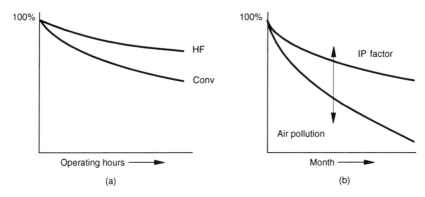

Figure 13.3.4: *(a) light reduction in lamps and luminaries; (b) light reduction is less when the IP factor is increased and more when air pollution increases (after Huenges Wajer, 1993). HF: high frequency supply; Conv: conventional supply*

Table 13.3.6: *The light reduction in luminaires; after NSVV, 1997, table 4.1; based on English data (BS 5489 Part 2, 1992)*

| Cleaning Interval (months) | Minimum extent of ingress protection | | | | | | | | |
| | IP 23 Pollution | | | IP 54 Pollution | | | IP 65 Pollution | | |
	high	av.	low	high	av.	low	high	av.	low
12	0.53	0.62	0.82	0.89	0.90	0.92	0.91	0.92	0.93
18	0.48	0.58	0.80	0.87	0.88	0.91	0.90	0.91	0.92
24	0.45	0.56	0.79	0.84	0.86	0.90	0.88	0.89	0.91
36	0.42	0.53	0.78	0.76	0.82	0.88	0.83	0.87	0.90

13.3.3 Lighting columns

Lighting columns form an essential part of public lighting. Luminaires are nearly always attached to lighting columns. Incandescent lamps often used to be attached to spans in streets in towns. Gas discharge lamps require larger and heavier luminaires, particularly when the ballast is built in. Moreover, it is difficult to attach luminares to spans, while finally cost plays a role. In many rural areas, particularly in developing countries, telephone poles are used to attach the luminaires.

Columns must comply with a number of regulations relating to strength, material and dimensions. These are discussed in detail in Anon. (1996, sec. 3.3). In addition, a number of recommendations are offered there relating to other aspects of columns, such as construction, preservation, etc. It is important to note that most are made of aluminium or steel. Polyester, concrete and wood are used also, sometimes on a large scale. The danger for traffic which columns can pose will be discussed in this section.

Although, as mentioned in section 7.2.3, more than two thirds of the accidents involving fast traffic concern collisions between vehicles participating in traffic, more than 20% of the accidents relate to collisions

Table 13.3.7: *Accidents (fatalities and hospital admissions) relating to various types of collisions (after CBS, 1992)*

Class	Number	Percentage	Percentage of category 9
Category 9 total	2041	17.94	100
911 Tree, fence, house	1198	10.53	58.70
912 Lamp post	235	2.07	11.54
913 + 921 Traffic sign	141	1.24	6.91
931 Crash barrier	199	1.75	9.75
941 Crossing animal	36	0.32	1.78
951 Loose object	64	0.56	3.12
0 Single car accidents	902	7.93	
Total, all accidents	11,374	100	

with stationary objects and single-car accidents. Collisions with lighting columns play a significant role. See CBS (1989).

The statistics shown in table 13.3.7 are more specific. These figures relate to collisions between a moving vehicle and an object or animal (category 9 according to CBS).

The data in table 13.3.7 relate to all accidents within and outside built-up areas involving fatalities or hospital admissions in 1991. The first percentage in the table relates to all accidents; the second to accidents in category 9: the collision between a moving vehicle and an object or an animal. The statistics are not complete; the figures for 911 to 951 inclusive do not produce exactly 100%. But they show that lighting columns amount to a little over 2% of the total number of accidents, and more than 11% of the accidents in category 9. This is approximately the same as the figure involving crash barriers: 2% and nearly 10% respectively.

In order to contain the seriousness of collisions with lighting columns, three possibilities are available

- keep the columns away from the road
- screen the columns
- render the columns pliable or fit them with a break-away construction.

Obstacle-free zones

The first method is, of course, best: here there is nothing to collide with. However, research has shown that the verge or central reservation must be quite wide in order to avoid collisions (Schreuder, 1992). Much research is based on collisions with trees; the reason for this is that trees alongside the road appear much more often in The Netherlands than lighting columns. A SWOV study has shown

- the number of tree accidents is reduced to 20% at a free verge width of approximately 4.5 metres and to 10% at approximately 6.5 metres on provincial single carriageway roads (usually 80 km/h roads)
- a reduction to 20% is achieved at approximately 7 metres and to 10% at more than 9 metres for single carriageway roads (usually main roads)

Table 13.3.8: *Width of obstacle-free zone for different classes of roads (categories in accordance with ROA/RONA; data taken from Van der Drift, 1987)*

Category of road	Required width of obstacle-free zone (m)
Motorways (cat. I and II)	10*
III	6.0
IV and V	4.5
VI	3.0
VII and parallel roads	2.0
VIII	1.5
Cycle paths	1.0

* Outside this an obstacle should be placed here only when absolutely necessary

- a reduction to 20% is achieved at more than 15 metres and 10% at 20 metres for dual carriage roads (usually motorways).

The dimensions of the obstacle-free zone for motorways are derived from the distance over which cars, having left the road with an empty verge, were found away from the edge of the road. It is questionable whether these numbers are of value, as there is not much need for corrective emergency manoeuvres on an empty verge. However, they are employed for lack of better evidence. An overview of the results pointed out the importance 'of an obstacle-free zone alongside the carriageway to prevent single-car accidents' (DHV, 1984, page 41). Most recommendations are based on research by Stonex (1964). This states that

> ... a relatively safe roadside can be developed by providing easy operation up to 25 ft from the edge of the pavement.

Table 13.3.8 shows the norms established in The Netherlands.

Screening construction

Screening would seem an effective solution, but screening in itself is a risk-carrying object. Table 13.3.7 shows that the numbers of victims in collisions with lighting columns and those with guard rails (crash barriers) are more or less similar. Guard rails are used frequently nowadays but they remain a risk, although this of course is not what is intended.

> The application of verge/central reservation protection constructions is aimed at creating facilities which produce less risk than the danger zone which is screened by the construction (SWOV, 1970, page 11).

Protective construction can be implemented continuously (guard rail construction) and intermittently (obstacle protection). Each has its own field of application. Continuous constructions are suitable for lighting columns. This is mostly a question of cost. A double expanded steel guide rail costs approximately HFl 75 per metre in materials plus installation, an obstacle protector of the RIMOB-type costs approximately HFl 15,000 each. In general, approximately 400 metres of guard rail can be installed for the cost of one set of RIMOBs. These figures are only rough, unpublished estimates. Guard rail construction is often more expensive with regard to installation costs than the lighting itself, expecially for central reservation lighting, as two guard rails are required, one on each side of the row of lamp posts (Schreuder, 1972).

A guard rail operates as follows: the colliding vehicle has its course corrected by the construction in such a way, that it is again parallel to the road axis. Rigid constructions usually affect the front wheel suspension. This creates a problem in that the course of a vehicle is difficult to predict when the front wheel suspension is completely deformed. However, penetration, even by very heavy trucks, no longer occurs. Rigid constructions are normally made of concrete (Heijer, 1992, page 23). Flexible constructions usually affect the bodywork. A flexible construction retards the vehicle in a crossways direction less abruptly, compared to a rigid construction. The risk of serious damage and of injuries is smaller. Flexible rail construction, however, is not always able to stop heavy trucks. Flexible constructions are mostly made of steel (Heijer, 1992, page 24). Information with regard to rail construction and obstacle protection can be found in the SWOV publications in question (Heijer, 1992; Schoon, 1982; Schoon & Bos, 1983; SWOV, 1976).

Non-aggressive construction
An obstacle is called 'non-aggessive' when the slowing down of the colliding vehicle is limited. This reduces the damage and also the risk of injury. In order to achieve that, the obstacle must be able to bend, give or break. In these cases we speak of flexible, shear and break-away constructions. The SWOV research in respect of this concerns lighting columns in particular (SWOV, 1976, 1976a).

Flexible construction is only used for columns which are not very tall (up to approximately 7 metres). The columns must be of aluminium. These bend after a collision. For higher columns, shear or break-away constructions can be used. This ensures that the column comes away from its foundation after a collision. These columns are usually made of steel. A problem is that one cannot predict beforehand where the column will land. This construction is seldom used in The Netherlands; in other countries, particularly in the US, shear and break-away constructions for columns up to 12 to 14 metres are used. The higher the column, the greater the windload and thus the necessity to attach them solidly. Shear and break-away constructions for columns of more than approximately 14 metres become so rigid that the column in fact becomes 'rigid'. Non-aggressive construction is therefore not used for columns which are higher than approximately 14 metres.

The fact that lighting columns with a height of over approximately 7 metres are produced as 'rigid' posts in The Netherlands means that the risk of collision can only be limited by the two methods mentioned earlier: by keeping the posts away from the road, or by screening them.

13.3.4   Other design aspects
Most design aspects were discussed in detail in Part III of the NSVV Recommendations (NSVV, 1996). A number of points will be touched on in this section which are dealt with less thoroughly in that part.

Method of switching on and off

In the past, switching on and off in the evening and in the morning was usually controlled by a switch clock. This method has been replaced in The Netherlands on a large scale by switching with the aid of a twilight switch. In other countries, switching is often done separately for each luminaire via an individual photocell. Each of these three methods has its own specific advantages and disadvantages. The switch clock is simple and always gives the same time, independent of the weather. In case of emergency, e.g. in sudden darkness or fog, manual switching can take over. The NSVV has carried out a study in which it was shown that it is better to link the times of switching on and off to the level of the horizontal illuminance in the free field (Anon., 1980). Twilight switching corresponds better to the visual task. In both cases, either a separate electricity network is required for the public lighting, or high frequency switches must be deployed. This is not necessary when each individual luminaire is switched on and off separately. However, the system is vulnerable and dependent on the sturdiness and the accuracy of the photocell. Although slightly more expensive, twilight switching is usually preferred. Central switching with the aid of modern computers is also easy to combine with the system for management, with defects reports, and also with possible dimming systems (Guldemond, 1994).

Evening and night switchings

Increasingly, the level of lighting is adapted to the density of the traffic. This used to be done by extinguishing a number of the lamps after a certain time during evening and night switching. This was easy when two-lamp luminaires were used, but the installation was not efficient. Switching off every other lamp is not recommended as the lighting becomes very uneven, and if one single lamp becomes defective a gap of 150 metres may be created. However, dimming is no problem with modern resources. See also section 14.2.3. More recently, dimming the whole installation, using traffic and/or weather data as an input, is extensively under study. A trial installation of about 10 km length is operational on the The Hague – Utrecht motorway in The Netherlands. See Dekker & Knol, 1997.

Time schedules for switching on and off

Public lighting used to be from half an hour after sunset to half an hour before sunrise when switch clocks were used generally, similar to the rules for cyclists (lighting-up time). During the energy crisis of 1972/1973, it was proposed to move the time of switching on in the evening to later, and to move the switching off in the morning to an earlier time. The NSVV study showed that the gain in time, and therefore in energy is minimal. See figure 13.3.5. The repercussions on traffic safety, however, may be considerable.

Illumination of dual carriageways

In most cases lighting from the central reservation is preferable for dual carriageways. There are a number of reasons for this

- the light which is emitted at the 'back' of luminaires contributes to the useful illumination

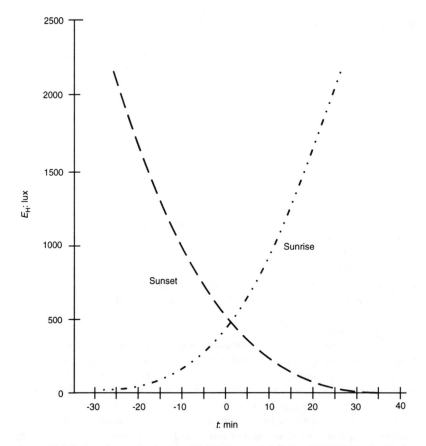

Figure 13.3.5: *Illuminance in the free field during twilight (after NSVV, 1980, fig. 3)*

- the level of light in the fast lane is usually a little higher than that in the slow lane. This corresponds to the relative difficulty of the visual task
- the optical guidance is usually better.

Global statements cannot be made in relation to the cost. Although it is said that central reservation lighting is cheaper, in practice this is not always so. Guard rails in the central reservation and/or on the verges must be taken into account for a cost comparison.

Two systems are suitable for central reservation lighting

- line or catenary lighting
- lighting with posts with a luminaire on each side, either with or without an arm (post lighting).

The advantages of line lighting compared with post lighting are

- superior optical guidance
- better glare limitation
- better lengthways uniformity, especially when the road is wet.

A disadvantage is the lower luminance yield. It would seem, however, that the difference is small for ZOAB-roads. The calculations in section 12.3.2 show that line lighting is usually considerably more expensive than post lighting. One suspects that this difference is the result of the considerably higher safety requirements which are set for line lighting, compared with those for post lighting.

Roundabouts

Roundabouts are implemented in The Netherlands on a large scale since the adaptation of the priority regulation. This achieves a dramatic reduction in accidents, and makes the traffic flow better (Van Minnen, 1990, 1991). Readers should refer to the respective reports (CROW, 1989; Van Minnen, 1989) on the characteristics of modern and old-fashioned' roundabouts — without adapted priority rule — such as curve radii, number of lanes and rounding curves.

There is evidence that the capacity of roundabouts, with only one lane on the feeder roads and on the roundabout itself, is relatively large. Depending on the density of cars and cyclists, 2000 to 2400 cars per hour can be processed (Van Minnen, 1991). The effects on traffic safety are spectacular. See table 13.3.9.

This table shows that the number of victims among cyclists and moped riders in the after period was reduced to about 8.5%. The reduction in the number of victims among drivers and passengers and pedestrians is much greater still, to about 1.5%!

As far as the lighting is concerned, roundabouts have a number of characteristics, as a result of which common practice cannot be applied without adaptation (Schreuder, 1992a). Based on research and on visual evaluations, NSVV has established recommendations (NSVV, 1993a). The main points include

- Feeder roads must be lit over approximately 100 metres (at least three posts) outside built-up areas.
- In order to mark the round shape of the roundabout, usually eight lamp posts are required. These should be placed on the outside of the roundabout.
- The siting of the lamp posts must take into account the manoeuvre

Table 13.3.9: *Accidents on roundabouts; summary of the results of 46 locations (after Van Minnen, 1991)*

Number of accidents/victims	Before period (crossing)	After period (roundabout)	After/ before (%)
All accidents	1061	159	14.98
Fatalities	7	0	0.00
Injured	310	14	4.52
Victims mopeds/cyclists	130	11	8.46
Other traffic participants	187	3	1.60

Figure 13.3.6: *An example of the siting of lamp posts on a roundabout in The Netherlands*

possibilities of trucks, free cycle paths, guard rails, traffic islands and pedestrian crossings.

- The central area must be marked clearly, preferably by means of lit signposts. Support via regular markings is desirable.
- The average horizontal illuminance on the road surface on the roundabout must be at least 1.5 times the level of the feeder roads and must be at least 10 lux.
- Lamps must be used on the roundabout itself which allow for a clear colour identification. Colour identification is important for supporting the visibility of participants in traffic on the roundabout, and of the marking, signalling and signs on the roundabout. As monochromatic sources of light are applied for feeder roads, the difference in the colour of lighting can support the perception of the presence of the roundabout.

An example, which does not conform to the recommendations in all aspects however, is given in figure 13.3.6.

13.4   Public lighting for developing countries

A subject which links in, to a certain extent, with what was said about the design of public lighting in the last section, is public lighting for developing countries. A separate workshop was conducted on this subjects during a recent CIE congress (Roy Chowdhury, 1995). Developing countries usually are not as advanced technologically as industrialised countries. The emphasis is on development of the electrification and of the infrastructure to support economic development. Public lighting is subject to a number of contradictions. On the one hand, high demands are placed on the lighting,

Table 13.4.1: *Minimum lighting for slight traffic; after Schreuder (1995)*

Method of transport	Speed (m/s)	Stopping distance (metres)	Minimum lighting
Pedestrians, handcarts	1	1	Moonlight
Pushbikes	3	4	Full moon
Bicycles	5–8	7–15	0.5 lux
Trucks, efficient brake	10–15	20–40	Dipped light
Trucks, inefficient brakes	10 -15	50–90	2–3 lux
Fast traffic	According to CIE recommendations		

Table 13.4.2: *Minimum lighting for busy traffic; taken from Schreuder 1995)*

Method of transport	Speed (m/s)	Stopping distance (m)	Type of road	Minimum lighting
Pedestrians, handcarts	1	1	Residential	1 lux
Pushbikes	3	4	Residential	1–2 lux
Cyclists	5–8	7–15	Distributor	2–3 lux
Trucks, efficient brakes	10–15	2–40	Flow	3–5 lux
Trucks, inefficient brakes	10–15	50–90	Flow	0.5 cd/m²
Faster speed	20	60	Main road	0.2–0.4 cd/²
Fast trucks	20	130	Motorway	0.2–04 cd/²
Fast traffic	30	120	Motorway	0.3–0.5 cd/²

due to the often bad condition of vehicles, particularly of trucks. Moreover, a large part of goods transport takes place by slowly moving vehicles pulled by oxen, donkeys or camels, as well as by handcarts and pushbikes (rickshaws), so that large differences in speed are involved. The demand for lighting and electricity is therefore higher than in the industrialised world. On the other hand, the supply is less, due to the economy being less advanced. Another problem for the lighting is that in most developing countries maintenance is at a low level.

The workshop in question concluded that it is not acceptable to have separate recommendations for developing countries. The level of lighting for developing countries may well be lower, by placing lower demands on visual comfort. Schreuder (1995) has given suggestions for future recommendations. See table 13.4.1 and 13.4.2.

Bibliography

AEC (1993). *Seminar Openbare verlichting; Besparing en kwaliteit* [Seminar public lighting; Savings and quality]. Zeist, 27 april 1993. Hilversum, Algemene Associatie van Energieconsulenten AEC, 1993.

Anon. (1980). 'Wijze van in- en uitschakelen van de openbare verlichting in het kader van doeltreffend energiegebruik' [Method of switching public lighting in the framework of effective energy consumption]. *Electrotechniek* **58** (1980) 371-373.

Anon. (1993). *Right Light 2. Second European Conference on Energy-Efficient Lighting*, 26–29 September 1993. Arnhem, NSVV, 1993.

Anon. (1993a). *Lighting manual.* Fifth edition. LIDAC. Eindhoven, Philips, 1993.

Anon. (1993b). *The comprehensive lighting catalogue.* Edition 3. Borehamwood, Herts, Thorn Lighting Limited, 1993.

Anon. (1993c). *Sicherheit durch gute Beleuchtung von Rad- und Fusswegen; Information für Gemeinden, Elektrizitätswerke und Planer.* Bern, Schweizerische Lichttechnische Gesellschaft SLG, 1993 (year estimated).

Anon (1994). *Model beleidsplan openbare verlichting* [Model policy plan public lighting]. Sittard/Arnhem, NOVEM/NSVV, 1994 (year estimated).

Anon. (1995). *Philips lichtcatalogus 1995/1996* [Philips light catalogue 1995/1996]. Eindhoven, Philips Lighting, 1995.

Anon. (1995a). *Philips TL5.* Eindhoven, Philips Lighting, 1995.

Anon. (1996). *Licht op de openbare weg* [Light on public roads]. NSVV/Uneto Congresdag 3 april 1996, RAI Amsterdam. Syllabus. Arnhem, NSVV, 1996.

CBS (1989) Statistiek van de ongevallen op de openbare weg 1988 [Statistics of public road accidents]. Den Haag, SDU, 1989.

CBS (1992). *Statistiek van de verkeersongevallen op de openbare weg* [Statistics of traffic accidents on public roads]. Den Haag, Centraal Bureau voor de Statistiek, 1992.

CIE (1976). *Glare and uniformity in road lighting installations.* Publication No. 31. Paris, CIE, 1976.

CIE (1990). *Calculation and measurement of luminance and illuminance in road lighting.* Publication No. 30/2. Paris, CIE, 1982 (reprinted 1990).

CIE (1995). *23rd Session of the CIE,* 1–8 November 1995, New Delhi, India. Volume 1. Publ No. 119. Vienna, CIE, 1995.

CROW (1989). *Verkeerspleinen* [Traffic squares]. Rapport van de werkgroep 'Rotondes'. Publikatie 24. Ede, Stichting C.R.O.W., 1989.

De Boer, J.B. & Fischer, D. (1981). *Interior lighting.* Second revised edition. Deventer, Kluwer, 1981.

De Boer, J.B.; Onate, V. & Oostrijck, A. (1952). 'Practical methods for measuring and calculating the luminance of road surfaces'. *Philips Research Records* **7** (1952) 46–76.

De Boer, J.B. (ed). (1967). *Public lighting.* Eindhoven, Centrex, 1967.

De Groot, J.J. & Van Vliet, J.A.J.M. (1986). *The high-pressure sodium lamp.* Deventer, Kluwer, 1986.

Dekker, G. & Knol, W. (1997). *DYNO geeft bij mist meer licht.* [DYNO offers more light in fog]. De Ingenieur (1997) No. 11, 16 juni 1997, pp. 28–29.

DHV (1984). *Literatuurstudie naar de effecten van dwarsprofielelementen op de verkeersveiligheid en de verkeersafwikkeling op wegen buiten de bebouwde kom* [Literature review into the effects of crosswise profile elements on traffic safety and the traffic flow on roads outside built-up areas]. Dossier 1-2896-05-28. Amersfoort, DHV Raadgevend Ingenieursbureau BV., 1984.

Di Fraia, L. (1993). 'Expert systems for automatic optimization of interior and road lighting systems'. In: Anon., 1993.

Elenbaas, W., (ed.) (1959). *Fluorescent lamps and lighting.* Eindhoven, Philips Technical Library, 1959.

Elenbaas, W., (ed.) (1965). *High-pressure mercury vapour lamps and their applications.* Eindhoven, Philips Technical Library, 1965.

Guldemond, L. (1994). 'Beheersplannen verlichting'. In: PAOVV (1994).

Guldemond, L. (1994a). 'Onderhoud; tarieven'. In: PAOVV (1994).

Heijer, T. (1992). De veiligheid van bermen en wegen; Een beschouwing over de stand van zaken [The safety of verges and roads; A consideration of the situation]. R-92-16. Leidschendam, SWOV, 1992.

Huenges Wajer, B.P.F. (1993). NOVEM: 'Een visie op openbare verlichting' [An opinion on public lighting]. In: AEC, 1993.

Marsden, A.M. (1993). 'The economics of outdoor lighting maintenance'. The Lighting Journal 58 (1993) March; 11–14.

Meutzner, H.J.J. (1996). 'Proefproject wegdimmen van de nieuwwaardefactor van fluorescentielampen in de Catharijnentunnel te Utrecht' [Trial study dimming the new value factor of fluorescent lamps away in the Catharijnentunnel in Utrecht]. In: Anon., (1996).

Meyer, Chr. & Nienhuis, H. (1988). Discharge lamps. Philips Technical Library. Deventer, Kluwer, 1988.

NOVEM (1996). Dat licht zo!!! [It's like that!!!] Sittard, NOVEM, 1996 (year estimated).

NSVV (1990). Aanbevelingen voor openbare verlichting; Deel I [Recommendations for public lighting. Part 1]. Arnhem, NSVV, 1990.

NSVV (1993). Aanbevelingen voor openbare verlichting; Deel I: Meten en berekenen [Recommendations for public lighting; Part 1: Measurements and calculations]. Arnhem, NSVV, 1993.

NSVV (1993a). Aanbevelingen voor de verlichting van minirotondes [Recommendations for lighting mini roundabouts]. Arnhem, NSVV, 1993.

NSVV (1997). Aanbevelingen voor openbare verlichting; Deel III: Richtlijnen voor het ontwerp van openbare verlichting [Recommendations for public lighting; Part III: Guidelines for the design of public lighting]. Arnhem, NSVV, 1997.

PAOVV (1994). Cursus Openbare Verlichting [Public lighting course]. Delft/Eindhoven, 1,2 en 3 februari 1994. Rijswijk/Delft, PAOVV, 1994.

Rattunde, R. (1991). 'Lichttechnische Berechnungsverfahren für die Strassenbeleuchtung'. Licht 43 (1991) 104–110.

Roy Chowdhury, S. (1995). 'Technology appropriate to developing countries'. Workshop, 23rd Session of the CIE, 1–8 November 1995, New Delhi, India. In: CIE, (1995).

Schoon, C.C. (1982). RIMOB: Obstakelbeveiliger met rimpelbuis [RIMOB: Obstacle protection with wrinkle tube]. R-82-30. Leidschendam, SWOV, 1982.

Schoon, C.C. & Bos, J.M.J. (1983). Boomongevallen; Een verkennend onderzoek naar de frequentie en ernst van botsingen tegen obstakels, in de relatie tot de breedte van de obstakelvrije zone [Tree accidents; An explorative study into the frequency and seriousness of collisions with obstacles, in relation to the width of the obstacle free zone]. R-83-23. Leidschendam, SWOV, 1983.

Schreuder, D.A. (1967). 'Theoretical basis of road-lighting design'. Chapter 3 in: De Boer, (ed.), (1967).

Schreuder, D.A. (1972). 'Safety barriers and lighting columns'. International Lighting Review 23 (1972) 1:20–21.

Schreuder, D.A. (1992). De invloed an windturbineparken op de verkeersveiligheid; Advies uitgebracht aan de Nederlandse Maatschappij voor Energie en Milieu b.v. NOVEM [The effect of wind turbine parks on traffic safety; Advice to the Nederlandse Maatschappij voor Energie en Milieu b.v. NOVEM]. R-92-74. Leidschendam, SWOV 1992.

Schreuder, D.A. (1992a). Overwegingen bij de verlichting van minirotondes; Bijdrage voor de NSVV-congresdag 'Licht op het verkeer' [Considerations for the lighting of mini

roundabouts; Contribution to the NSVV congress day 'Light shed on traffic'],
    Amsterdam, 13 april 1992. R-92-57. Leidschendam, SWOV, 1992.
Schreuder, D.A. (1995). 'Road lighting in developing countries'. Paper PP 160.
    Leidschendam, Duco Schreuder Consultancies, 1995. In: CIE (1995).
Schreuder, D.A. (1997). *Theory and background for road lighting in developing countries*.
    Paper presented at the Symposium on 'Road Lighting for Developing Countries'
    held in the SANCI-CIE International Conference on 'Lighting for Developing
    Countries'; Durban, South Africa, 1-3 September 1997. 1 Leidshendam, Duco
    Schreuder Consultancies, 1997.
Schreuder, D.A. (1997a). *The functional characteristics of road and tunnel lighting*. Paper
    presented to the Israel National Committee on Illumination on Tuesday, 25
    March 1997 at the Association of Engineers and Architects in Tel Aviv,
    Leidschendam, Duco Schreuder Consultancies, 1997.
Steenks, K. (1994). 'Beleidsaspecten gemeentewegen' [Policy aspects local authority
    roads]. In: PAOVV (1994).
Stonex, K.A. (1964). *The single-car accident problem*. Detroit, Michigan, Automotive
    Engineering Congres, 1964.
SWOV (1970). *Bermbeveiliging* [Verge protection]. Rapport 1970-1. Voorburg, SWOV,
    1970.
SWOV (1976). *Lichtmasten* [Lighting columns]. Pubicatie 1976-6N. Voorburg, SWOV,
    1976.
SWOV (1976a). *Gevaren bij het omvallen van lichtmasten* [Risks relating to lighting
    columns toppling]. Publicatie 1976-7N. Voorburg, SWOV, 1976.
Van der Drift, M.J.M. (1987). *Veiligheid bermen* [Safety verges]. Nota nr. 87-96. Den
    Haag, Dienst Verkeerskunde, Rijkswaterstaat, 1987.
Van der Lugt, D. B. & Albers, H. (1996). *The art of lighting*. Arnhem, NSVV, 1996 (year
    estimated).
Van Minnen, J. (1989). *Toepassing van rotondes; Informatie en aanbevelingen betreffende
    het toepassen van rotondes, in het bijzonder als alternatief voor kruispunten met
    verkeerslichtenregeling* [Application of roundabouts; Information and recom-
    mendations relating to the application of roundabouts, in particular as an
    alternative to crossroads with traffic lights]. R-89-56. Leidschendam, SWOV,
    1989.
Van Minnen, J. (1990). *Ongevallen op rotondes; Vergelijkende studie van de onveiligheid
    op een aantal locaties waar een kruispunt werd vervangen door een 'nieuwe'
    rotonde* [Accidents on roundabouts; Comparative study of the risks in a number
    of locations where a crossroad crossing was replaced by a 'new' roundabout]. R-
    90-47. Leidschendam, SWOV, 1990.
Van Minnen, J. (1991). 'Nieuwe rotondes ook veilig voor fietsers?' [New roundabouts safe
    for cyclists?] *Verkeerskunde* **42** (1991) no 10. blz 14-19.
Wijnen, G.; Renes, W. & Storm, P. (1984). *Projectmatig werken* [Working with projects].
    Utrecht, Marka, 1984.
Zuidema (1986). *Cursus projectmanagement* [Project management course], 15-17
    December 1986, Bureau Zuidema, 1986 (unpublished).
Zuring, J. & Van de Holst, P.M.J. (1996). 'Totaalbeheer van snelwegverlichting' [Total
    management of motorway lighting]. In: Anon., (1996).

14 Environmental aspects of public lighting

Environmental aspects increasingly play a role in policy decisions with a social character – such as public lighting. The benefits of public lighting are social and include the communication between people and particularly the promotion of safety, especially traffic safety and public safety. The costs too have social repercussions which relate to the expenditure of public financial resources, as well as to possibly harmful environmental effects. Environmental aspects especially must be included in a public discussion on lighting. A number of environmental aspects of public lighting are reviewed in this chapter. Energy consumption is another subject raised here, together with the associated characteristics of lighting resources. Finally, light pollution and the requirements for road lighting in nature reserves are also considered.

14.1 General aspects and opinions

14.1.1 Definition

The concept of environment is used in a number of very different ways; the concept may even be considered 'over defined' (Brouwer & Leroy, 1995, page 11). I will try to arrive at a definition useful for public lighting. By environment is meant 'the surroundings' of each individual separately, as well as of the population as a whole. This definition corresponds to definitions in sociology, chemistry and biology. Environmental problems signify a disruption of the harmony between people and their environment. This has a number of implications for environmental policy

- saving of irreplaceable resources, including energy
- prevention or limitation of pollution/emissions
- maintaining living nature, including non-human nature

- prevention or deterrence of violation of natural equilibria, including natural infringements and infringements resulting from human activities.

The concept of policy plays an important role. Usually this means establishing a number of policy objectives as well as a strategy to achieve these objectives. It is important to know during the implementation stage, that the policy is still on course. This could be called control. The input for control is the difference between the desired course and the actual course, the 'Sollwert' and the 'Istwert'. The optimum control strategy is aimed at reducing the difference between what is and what should be. In this case one speaks of a control or pro-active policy; this in contrast to the reactive policy discussed below (Schreuder, 1995).

The concept of feedback is relevant to control: the system output influences the input and therefore the operation of the system. Details are given in Amand & Zmood (1995). A distinction should be made between feedback and feedforward. Feedforward may reinforce the action, so that the output continues to increase. The system becomes evermore divorced from a state of equilibrium and the phenomenon is only stopped by external interference or by a catastrophe. By feedback is meant the phenomenon where the response is in a direction opposite to the direction of the action. This reduces or dampens the phenomenon. By these means a system can maintain an equilibrium, or an established course. The relationship between feedback and control is the basis for traditional information theory and for cybernetics, which is derived from it. See, e.g. also Bok (1958), Shannon & Weaver (1949) and Wiener (1950; 1954).

14.1.2   Dutch Government policy
The environmental policy strategies of most countries have much in common, even if they differ considerably in practical implication and, particularly, in the priorities for action and in the efforts to realise them. In this chapter, the situation in The Netherlands is described in some detail.

The basis for the policy by the Dutch Government is recorded in Anon., 1989 and 1990. Both these volumes continue to form the basis for the Dutch national environmental policy. The goal is

- A sustainable society in The Netherlands, even if sustainable relating to time is defined in rather a limited way.
- The polluter pays. All environmental effects must be allocated to the processes of production and consumption.
- Processes are viewed as a chain.
- All relevant environmental effects must be included in the policy considerations.

Table 14.1.1. gives an overview of the main environmental effects with regard to traffic. This table also shows the contributions by the different methods of transport. Light pollution is conspicuous by its absence.

Table 14.1.1: *Dominant environmental effects relating to methods of transport (after Van Wee, 1991)*

	Method of transport			
	Road	**Rail**	**Air**	**Water**
Change of climate	x	x	x	x
Energy consumption	x	x	x	x
Consumption of raw materials	x	x	x	x
Waste materials	x	x	x	x
Air pollution	x	x	x	x
Soil and water pollution	x			x
Fragmentation/occupation	x	x		
Obnoxious smells	x		x	
Noise pollution	x	x	x	
Violation of social environment	x			

14.1.3   Spearheads of the policy

So far, long-term policy has remained rather sketchy. The measures have an *ad hoc* character. Systematic prioritisation also leaves a lot to be desired. A few policy spearheads have been established. These played a role in the Traffic and Transport Structural Plan (Structuur schema Verkeer en Vervoer (Anon., 1990a)). This contains verifiable objectives which have been quantified for a number of cases. Thus, it was suggested that the railways will produce 15% less noise by the year 2000. The resources to achieve these objectives in the short term were also identified. The environmental measures are based on the idea that a sustainable society is endangered when

- it is polluted
- raw materials become scarce
- it is disrupted.

These three points apply to all social aspects and to all social activities. Traffic remains one of the main threats.

Pollution concerns emissions. By 'emission' one means everything relating to the creation of waste. The fight against waste is represented by a ladder. The waste ladder has rungs which become increasingly less desirable, less favourable from an environmental point of view from the top down. The rungs represent

- prevention
- reuse (recycling)
- useful application incineration
- dumping.

Raw materials become scarce when more is consumed than produced. Non-renewable materials (Meadows, 1972; see also Koumans, 1973) govern nearly all processes. Reuse or recycling could offer a solution. In some cases, recycling is not only introduced on a large scale, but is also economically advantageous.

Energy is also a type of raw material. Further details on energy and obtaining energy can be found in section 14.2.1. The problem is not so much the generation of energy as the emission accompanying the generation techniques. These include CO_2, NO_X, hydrocarbons, SO_2 and, not least, ozone. CO_2 or carbon dioxide is left after incineration of substances containing carbon: coal, lignite and hydrocarbons. NO_X is a collective name for several nitrogen oxides. The most common are NO and NO_2; the most harmful is N_2O. These usually appear mixed up, hence the collective name NO_X. Hydrocarbons are remnants of common fuels such as methane and petrol. SO_2 is sulphur dioxide which is released, particularly, during incineration of sulphur-rich soft coal and oil. Ozone is O_3, an unstable form of oxygen.

All these gas substances are harmful. CO_2 contributes quantitatively most to the greenhouse effect (see section 14.3) but NO_X and hydrocarbons also contribute. NO_X and SO_2, together with hydrocarbons, form the so-called photochemical smog when exposed to ultraviolet radiation from the sun; in combination with rainwater, acids are created, which fall on earth as acid rain. Ozone and carbon monoxide CO, which has not yet been mentioned, are noxious substances. A number of these gases are implicated in the greenhouse effect. See section 14.3.

Motorised road traffic is an important cause of environmental pollution and disruption, but not the only cause. Thus it is clear that the emission of SO_2 and of NO_X and the accompanying acid rain is partly caused by motorised traffic, but also by industry. Methane in the atmosphere results largely from the manure from pigs and cattle.

14.1.4   Zoning

An important expedient for establishing an environmental policy and for the implementation of environmental measures is zoning, in particular when dealing with distance-dependent effects (Brouwer & Klaver, 1995, page 209). The concept of zoning is defined here as

> the establishment of a spatial separation between environment-unfriendly and environment-friendly activities (Brouwer & Klaver, 1995, page 208, quoted from Brussaard et al., 1993).

In practice, this boils down to the fact that a country or a region is divided into zones. Classes are defined for all human activities (sectoral environmental quality classes). Conditions are imposed on noise, smells, hazards and air pollution. Requirements are then set for each environmental quality class. Finally, the purpose of the area in question is then linked to these, such as nature reserve, agriculture, residential and industrial. The methodology is rather complex; see Brouwer & Leroy, (red.) (1995) for a rather detailed discussion, as well as for relevant environmental questions. The need for this detailed approach is dictated by the fact that The Netherlands is 'full' and that there are many conflicting interests. The distribution of space is shown in figure 14.1.1 as an illustration.

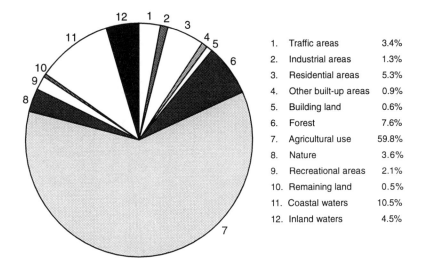

1.	Traffic areas	3.4%
2.	Industrial areas	1.3%
3.	Residential areas	5.3%
4.	Other built-up areas	0.9%
5.	Building land	0.6%
6.	Forest	7.6%
7.	Agricultural use	59.8%
8.	Nature	3.6%
9.	Recreational areas	2.1%
10.	Remaining land	0.5%
11.	Coastal waters	10.5%
12.	Inland waters	4.5%

Figure 14.1.1: *Use of land in The Netherlands (based on Brouwer & Leroy, (red.), 1995, fig. 3.2)*

Figure 14.1.1 shows that traffic areas occupy a significant fraction of the land in The Netherlands. Surprisingly, light pollution is not included in the list of environmentally-unfriendly factors, though traffic areas in particular must be lit in darkness. See also section 14.4.1.

14.2 Environmental aspects of lighting installations

14.2.1 Energy consumption

Industrialised societies guzzle energy. Approximately 8000 million tons of 'oil equivalent' (MTOE) was consumed worldwide as primary energy in 1994. North America accounted for nearly 2400 MTOE and Western Europe for more than 1400 MTOE, while Africa consumed a little over 200 and Central and South America consumed scarcely 300 MTOE. Total /energy consumption did not start to rise sharply until the end of the last century. The rise was spectacular, quantitatively spoken, during the first few decades following the Second World War. Electricity consumption in The Netherlands increased sixty-fold between 1920 and 1976 (Burghout, 1978; see also figure 14.2.1).

As far as public lighting is concerned, this relates almost exclusively to electrical energy. Electricity production in countries in the European Union is shown in table 14.2.1.

We see that the oil consumption is very large, but that it fell during 1980 and 1990; this also applies to hydro energy consumption. Nuclear energy, however, has increased sharply. Alternative sources of energy are not mentioned; they will be touched on briefly below. The distribution in relation to market segments is shown in table 14.2.2. Lost energy is also included in the table, for comparison.

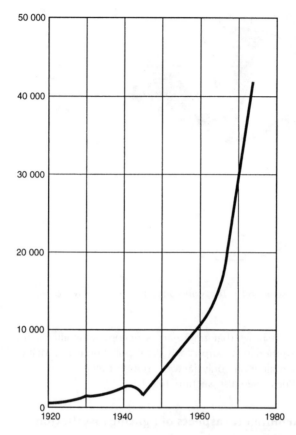

Figure 14.2.1: *Development of electricity consumption between 1920 and 1973 (after Burghout, 1978, afb. 4)*

Table 14.2.1: *Electricity production (in percentages; total in TWh) in the Member States of the European Union (after NOVEM, 1994, table 1.09)*

	Year	
Electricity source	1980	1990
Thermal power stations	75.8	56.9
Of which:		
– Natural gas	10.3	11.9
– Crude oil	28.7	17.7
– Coal	55.6	65.0
– Other	5.4	5.4
Hydropower	12.4	8.1
Nuclear energy	11.8	35.0
Total	100%	100%
	1403 TWh	1805 TWh

Table 14.2.2: *Energy consumption in 1983 (in millions of barrels of oil equivalent daily; after Anon, 1984)*

Areas of application	US region	Western Europe	Japan	Developing countries
Transport	8.7	4.6	1.3	4.5
Industry	5.1	5.1	1.8	4.5
Households	7.3	6.1	1.3	2.1
Loss	10.2	6.5	1.9	5.7
Total	31.3	22.3	6.3	17.0
Loss as a percentage	32.6	29.1	30.2	33.5
Index	112	100	110	115

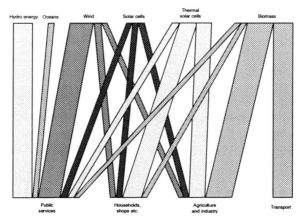

Figure 14.2.2: *The distribution of renewable energy in relation to sources and consumers (after Hoagland, 1995).*

The term alternative energy source is often used as a synonym for the term sustainable source of energy. Hoagland (1995) mentions in an article on solar energy that radiation from the sun which falls on earth represents approximately 15,000 times the consumption by all people. Predictions exist which say that the energy requirement world-wide in the year 2025 will increase by 30%, and the requirement for electrical energy by 265%. The authors of the predictions are not known. Energy from the sun could supply 60% of electricity and 40% of the fuel. An overview is given of the distribution of renewable energy for several sources and for several consumers (Hoagland, 1995). See figure 14.2.2.

14.2.2   Energy consumption in public lighting
A considerable amount of energy is required for public lighting. Table 14.2.3 shows some figures from EnergieNed.

These figures show that approximately 0.8% of the electrical energy in The Netherlands is used in public lighting, that is approximately 0.08% of the total

Table 14.2.3: *Energy consumption in The Netherlands, 1991*

Energy use in The Netherlands (1991)	
Total energy	$2{,}872 \ 10^{15}$ J
Electrical energy:	
Mains network	$246 \ 10^{15}$ J (68,340 GWh)
Proprietary generation	$36 \ 10^{15}$J (10,000 GWh)
Total	$282 \ 10^{15}$ J (78,340 GWh)
Consumed in public lighting	$2.29 \ 10^{15}$ J (635 GWh)

energy. That is not much, which is why it is sometimes said that energy saving is unnecessary in relation to public lighting. However, more than 600 GWh annually at a rate of HFl 0.25 per kWh equals nearly 20 million HFl. More significantly, a large amount of CO_2 is released in the generation of this energy. I will return to the associated greenhouse effect in section 14.3.

14.2.3   Energy saving in public lighting
Fernhout conducted a study, commissioned by NOVEM, into energy saving in public lighting (Fernhout, 1990). According to this study, the situation relating to public lighting in The Netherlands in 1991 was as shown in table 14.2.4.

The figures given by Fernhout vary approximately 10% from the figures from EnergieNed. This difference, probably the result of the data collection method, will be ignored.

Approximately 2,860,000 lamps were used in public lighting in The Netherlands in 1990, broken down into several types of lamps as shown in table 14.2.5.

The data in this table stem from 1990, or possibly earlier. Roadway lighting outside built-up areas and especially on motorways, has increased sharply. In addition, many high-pressure sodium lamps have been installed on motorways in recent years. And finally, the use of high-pressure mercury lamps has decreased still further. It is difficult to get hold of recent figures on a national scale in such a rapidly changing situation.

Fernhout estimated the effects of a number of possible savings measures, based on data from 1990. Taking into account the relevant lamp rating, replacement of the remaining incandescent lamps by more efficient sources of

Table 14.2.4: *The situation in relation to public lighting in The Netherlands in 1991 (after Fernhout, 1990)*

	Within built-up area	Outside built-up area	Motorways
Number of luminaires	2 million	331,000	29,000
Length illuminated (km)	41,000	10,000	875
Light yield (Mlm)	13,750		
Connection value (kW)	211,700		
Annual consumption (MWh)	712,600		

Table 14.2.5: *Numbers of lamps of different types in public lighting in The Netherlands in 1990 (after Fernhout, 1990)*

Lamps	Within built-up areas	Ouside built-up areas	Motorways	Total
Incandescent lamps	50,000	3000	–	53,000
Low-pressure mercury	1,225,000	116,000	–	1,341,000
High-pressure mercury	475,000	36,000	–	511,000
Low-pressure sodium	500,000	106,000	29,000	635,000
High-pressure sodium	250,000	70,000	–	320,000
Total	2,500,000	331,000	29,000	2,860,000

light may save 20,000 MWh annually. The replacement of high-pressure mercury lamps by partly high-pressure, partly low-pressure sodium lamps could save nearly 108,300 MWh annually. Finally, Fernhout indicates that improvements in the design and the management of installations for public lighting may save another 105,000 MWh annually. This amount is based on the idea that a reduction of 15% in energy consumption is thought to be feasible. These three measures together might therefore lead to a saving of 233,300 MWh annually. At an estimated consumption of 712,600 MWh annually for 1990, this would lead to a saving of 32.7%. Account has not been taken of the replacement of traditional tube-shaped low-pressure sodium lamps – the TL tubes – by compact fluorescent lamps. The design of the luminaires available in 1990 were not suitable for those lamps, but potentially considerable savings are cited. Thus Fernhout, for example, states that luminaires for 2 x 20 W TL can be converted for 18 W compact fluorescent lamps, provided they have good optics. Taking into account the additional losses in the ballasts, this may produce a saving of more than 50%.

In addition to the possibilities for energy saving known in 1990, Fernhout lists a number of possibilities for further savings (page numbers from Fernhout, 1990).

- Automatic adjustment of the level of lighting to weather and traffic conditions produces a saving of 35% (page 7).
- Adaptation of the lighting level produces an estimated reduction of 17,400 kWh/km annually to 12,500 kWh/km annually. This could lead to a saving of 28.2% (page 11). However, it is not known whether a satisfactory quality of the lighting would be maintained.
- The losses in the ballasts may be reduced by modern electronic control gear. According to Fernhout, this can lead to a saving of more than 20% (page 18).
- Switching on and off on an area or district basis during twilight can lead to a further, albeit limited, saving (page 18).
- According to Fernhout, further improvements in management are possible, which could lead to energy savings. At present quantitative figures are not available (page 19).
- The application of evening and night lighting (night switching) however, results in hardly any savings, according to Fernhout (page 12).

All these measures lead to a considerable potential energy saving. Energy consumption in the year 2000 can be reduced to 500,000 MWh annually, when use is made of the possibilities for saving (page 22); a saving of 33% in relation to 1988 and a saving of nearly 50% in relation to the 992,000 MWh annually estimated for an unchanged policy for the year 2000 (Fernhout, 1990, page 21).

This study is used a great deal in The Netherlands when establishing programmes relating to energy saving in public lighting. A few comments

- The road surface was not mentioned. From earlier studies (e.g. SCW, 1974, 1984) we know that the application of diffuse, light-coloured road surfaces requires less energy for the same luminance.
- Much progress has been made since 1990 related to the dimming of public lighting. This means that it is quite feasible nowadays to design evening and night switching, which allows for a considerable saving in energy. According to some estimates, a saving of approximately 20% is feasible (Anon., 1991).
- Many improvements have been introduced since 1990 in relation to ballasts. See, as an example, the High Efficiency Ballast, (HRV) outlined by De Wit (1995). In relation to existing electronic technology, a saving of 10% is claimed; in relation to conventional technologies, a saving of 30%. It should be remembered that the energy consumption of a ballast lies between 5% and 15% of the consumption of the lamp. Some dozens of percentage points in the ballast could therefore mean a few percentage points in the total.
- High frequency operation of gas discharge lamps is also applied in public lighting. In addition to a certain saving in energy, a reduction in the network contamination is of particular importance. It is said that the losses in the ballast could be reduced to nearly zero for low-pressure sodium lamps (NSVV, 1966).

As well as the important study by Fernhout, a study published in France in 1980 should also be mentioned, in which conditions for efficient energy use are described (Remande, 1980). Much of what is mentioned there is still valid today. The publication contains a number of recommendations, of which some have already been mentioned. The main recommendations include

- switching on and off with the aid of a combination clock-photocell. This will yield 5%
- keeping the network voltage uniform. An overvoltage of 10% between 10 pm. and 5 am. can lead to additional energy consumption of 16%
- replacement of high-pressure mercury lamps by high-pressure sodium lamps. This can lead to a saving in energy of 10 – 15%. This should be compared with an increase in cost of 3 – 7%
- replacing the remaining incandescent lamps with low-pressure sodium lamps outside built-up areas
- replacing the luminaires and the electrical appliances when replacing lamps; using the correct type of ballast instead of the old one can lead to a saving of 60% in energy consumption

- using high-pressure sodium lamps which are dimmed at night or switched down. A saving of approximately 27% energy can be made
- a good lighting design from a photometric point of view can save 30 – 35%.

14.2.4 Raw materials and waste

Besides a high specific luminous flux – including control gear – it is important from a environmental point of view that the lamps enjoy the longest possible useful service life; they should contain as few environment-unfriendly materials as possible, and as few as possible scarce resources, which must also be recyclable as much as possible. In fact, only gas discharge lamps can be considered for public lighting. There does not seem to be much difference in the use of scarce resources between the different types of lamps. Lamps mainly consist of glass. This is processed easily and can be partly reused. All sorts of metals in small quantities are used, which normally are not a problem in the processing of waste. This can partially be recycled.

As far as the 'gas' from gas discharge lamps is concerned – in fact a metal vapour, either sodium or mercury – a number of considerable differences do exist between the various types of lamps, in particular in relation to waste materials. Sodium is a relatively innocent material as far as the environment is concerned; mixing with water produces NaCl, or common kitchen salt. Mercury, however, is one of the most poisonous heavy metals. When using mercury lamps, effective measures must be taken to prevent mercury from escaping.

The combination of low specific luminous flux and high toxicity make the high-pressure mercury lamp an unfavourable type of lamp. They are therefore no longer used much in The Netherlands, particularly for new installations. The same applies to the traditional low-pressure mercury tubes. The low-pressure mercury lamp, however, is saved for application in public lighting by the compact fluorescent lamp. But the use of these lamps also has a disadvantage: not only do they contain mercury, but also some valuable raw materials are used in the built-in ballasts. As the service life is so long, it takes a number of years before the waste problem becomes acute. People are beginning to realise that waste disposal and the possible recycling of raw materials in these lamps is not a simple matter. A number of considerations are discussed in IAEEL (1993 and 1995).

14.3   The greenhouse effect

A greenhouse is a space which is enclosed by glass. If the sun shines on to this glass, then the larger part of the radiated energy is allowed to pass through. The greenhouse and its content are heated. This heating increases the energy radiation into the infrared as a result of Wien's law, mentioned in 4.2.2. The radiation cannot pass through the glass; the sun's radiation which has entered, cannot escape. The earth atmosphere has a number of characteristics in common with a greenhouse. There are a number of gases and vapours which appear naturally in the atmosphere, which show such an effect. The best-

Table 14.3.1: *The greenhouse effect of some gases, expressed in relation to CO_2 (after Kuhn 1990, Abb. 27)*

Gas	Name	Greenhouse effect
CO_2	Carbon dioxide	1
CH_4	Methane	30
N_2O	Nitrous oxide	150
O_3	Ozone	2000
CFC	Chlorofluorocarbons	15,000

known is the gas CO_2, carbon dioxide. As mentioned earlier, there are additional greenhouse gases, whose effect can be considerably greater. See table 14.3.1.

Obviously the contribution of each gas to the total greenhouse effect naturally depends on the concentration. The contribution by each of the gases is shown in table 14.3.2.

Table 14.3.2: *Greenhouse contribution of various gases (after Anon. 1990)*

Gas	Greenhouse contribution (%)
Carbon dioxide	55
Methane	15
Nitrous oxide	6
Chlorofluorocarbons	24

The concentration of CO_2 gas has changed considerably over the last hundred thousand years. This has led to considerable changes in temperature on earth, which among other things have led to the ice ages. The concentration of CO_2 has increased greatly during recent decades, as a result of burning fossil fuels (coal, lignite, oil, gas) but also due to deforestation in favour of agriculture. The increase of other greenhouse gases is linked even closer to human activities. See figure 14.3.1.

14.4   Obtrusive light as a result of public lighting

14.4.1   Light pollution

The regular changes between light and darkness form a natural rhythm for human beings. Many biological and psychological effects are associated with this. But since gas discharge lamps have appeared on the scene, darkness only happens when and for as long as people want it. Lighting contributes considerably to the spiritual and physical health of the population, in particular in respect of crime deterrence and the reduction in the number of traffic accidents.

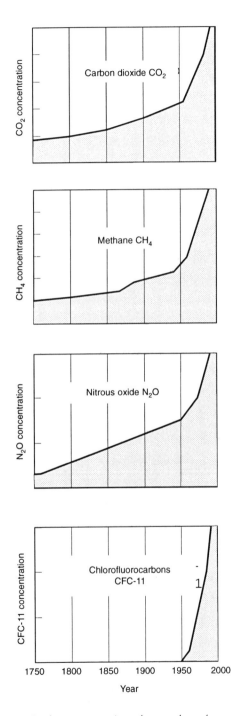

Figure 14.3.1: *Increase in the concentration of a number of greenhouse gases (after NOVEM, 1994)*

All this at a price. Outdoor lighting is usually designed in such a way that light falls where it is needed, but often we only partially succeed. In addition, a proportion of the light is always reflected. Part of the light in outside lighting is always directed upwards. This results in light pollution. See Gorter (1996).

14.4.2   Obtrusive light

Light which falls outside the area at which it is directed is spilled light. Spilled light always represents a cost, as light for which energy is consumed and money is expended is wasted. When spilled light falls on an area where other activities are taking place, these activities may be disrupted. We speak of obtrusive light in this case. Obtrusive light can be beamed directly from the source of light into the area where the activities take place. This is called light immission. Examples are the light from street lighting or from a sports field which enters bedrooms through the windows. This concerns direct disruption. The second form is the result of light which gets into the atmosphere. Part of this light arrives back on earth via scatter. This scattered light resembles a glow of light which can be seen, in particular, above large towns and above industrial centres. This is indirect disruption.

14.4.3   Determination of obtrusive light

Light immission is usually measured directly with the aid of a luxmeter at the place where we want to find out the extent of the obtrusive light. The luminance of the sky glow can be calculated and measured. Although astronomers are considerably hampered by the glow, no simple and reliable methods are available for the measurement. As a result, no guidelines or threshold values of tests have been established. And this, in turn, leads to the fact mentioned in section 14.1.4, that light pollution is not mentioned in environmental legislation. The methods available for calculating and measuring the luminance of the sky glow are described in CIE (1995, 1997). See also Schreuder (1995) and the textbooks in this field (Crawford, ed., 1991; McNally, ed., 1994; Schreuder, ed., 1993).

A simple method for determining the light glow across large areas is described by Isobe (see Kosai et al., 1994). Determination is based on a large number of straight-forward photographs of the zenith. The comparison with the track of certain stars, of which the brilliance or magnitude is known, and a part of the sky without stars, produces the luminance of the glow. In astronomy, it is usual to express luminance in magnitudes per square arc second (mag/arcsec^2). The conversion into more usual photometric units is '1nL (nanolambert) corresponds to 26.33 mag/arcsec^2' (according to Crawford, 1997). In comparison: the natural background radiation, a pitch-black sky, appears to amount to approximately 21.6 (mag/arcsec)^2 (CIE, 1997).

This method was used in The Netherlands on 7th February 1992 between 8 pm. and 10 pm. in more than 100 locations (Schreuder, 1994, 1995). Individual measurements varied from 20.97 to 17.2 mag/arcsec^2, which corresponds to nearly a factor of 100 in luminance. Even in the average values of large areas, the part in the North East of The Netherlands, compared with the Western –

densely-populated − part there was a difference of nearly 0.5 mag/arcsec^2. This difference corresponds to nearly a factor of two in luminance.

14.4.4   Threshold values of obtrusive light

The Commission International de l'Eclairage has established two working parties which are studying the problem of obtrusive light. Both have completed a draft report.The first group studied the direct obtrusive light (CIE, 1995), the second the indirect obtrusive light or sky glow (CIE, 1997). In both cases maximum threshold values are given for the light emission. Both also use zoning (see also section 14.1.4). Finally, both drafts contain a proposal to make the recommendations for the end of the night stricter than for the start; a sort of evening curfew.

Four zones have been proposed as threshold values for direct obtrusive light

(a) business and shopping areas (E_4)
(b) public/residential areas within a light environment (E_3)
(c) public/residential areas within a dark environment (E_2)
(d) dark outside areas, national parks. (E_1)

These zones are based on the zones proposed by the British Institution of Lighting Engineers ILE (ILE, 1994; see also Pollard, 1993). Threshold values have been proposed for the vertical illuminance at the site of terrain borders, for the luminous intensity of the luminaires, for minimisation of glare, for the upward lighting of façades, for each zone, and for the time periods before and after the evening curfew. Part of the recommendations is still under discussion. The main recommendations are listed in table 14.4.1.

Threshold values have also been established for indirect obtrusive light. The zones proposed by Murdin (1997) were used for this. In principle, these

Table 14.4.1: *Proposed threshold values for direct obtrusive light, based on CIE (1995)*

Area of application	Parameter	Zone			
		(a)	(b)	(c)	(d)
Area boundary (on the vertical plane at the site of the boundary)					
Before evening curfew	E_v (lux)	25	10	5	2
After evening curfew	E_v (lux)	4	2	1	0
Luminous intensity of luminaires (in directions where nuisance may occur)					
After evening curfew	I (cd)	2500	1000	500	0
Upwards luminous flux (% of total luminous flux)		25	15	5	0
Luminance of façades					
Before evening curfew	L (cd/m^2)	25	10	5	3
After evening curfew	L (cd/m^2)	5	5	3	0

Table 14.4.2: *Recommendations for the limitation of sky glow (after CIE, 1997, table 2)*

Zone	$ULOR_{inst}(\%)$
E_1	0
E_2	0–5
E_3	0–15
E_4	0–25

also resemble the ILE proposal, albeit that some zones have been divided into two for special cases. See table 14.4.2 where the sky glow limitation is expressed in $ULOR_{inst}$, the Upward Light Ratio of the luminaires as installed.

14.4.5   Remedies
A solution for the reduction of light pollution, which can often be applied, is a reduction in the amount of light. It is often possible to reduce street lighting after a certain time, e.g. 10 pm., by dimming lamps. In addition, this means that less electrical power is needed and the burden on the environment will therefore be reduced. See section 14.2.1.

Low-pressure sodium lamps are usually selected for areas close to astronomical observatories, because of the monochromatic light. This is easier to filter out, so that the nuisance for astrophotography is limited. A variant on this is reducing the spectral emission of lamps.

It is, of course, also important to direct the light carefully, so as to reduce obtrusive light. The interests of the economy and of astronomy can coincide: well directed light reduces waste and is therefore economical. Sometimes additional costs arising from the more expensive optics may be recouped within a couple of years.

Finally, obtrusive light can be limited by reducing the reflected or dispersed light. For this dark surfaces could be used. However, this does not apply to road surfaces on traffic roads, as we are not dealing with illuminance there, but with luminance. See section 9.1. It is also good to reduce air pollution. Aerosols often lead to an increase in light dispersion.

14.5   Roadway lighting in nature reserves

Sometimes it is not possible to avoid roads going through nature reserves. A number of specific problems may arise here, for which a number of specific remedies apply. Recent recommendations have been published by NSVV (1997).

14.5.1   The route
The selection of the road route concerns, of course, more than just a restriction of obtrusive light. There must be very good reasons to build a road, let alone a motorway, through a nature reserve. Being able to buy the land at a cheaper price, or more quickly, should hardly be an argument; when balancing the interests of nature with the interests of agriculture, trade, industry or construction, nature must weigh heavily.

14.5.2   Design of the road

It is often possible to select the road design in such a way that public lighting is superfluous for the expected traffic density. As an example let us take a road with an expected traffic density of 18,000 vehicles per 24 hours. According to the usual design criteria, a single carriage-way road is still just sufficient; a dual carriage road is not required. According to the criteria for the installation of public lighting, such a single carriage-way road must be lit, while a motorway may remain unlit. We can also think about the construction of unlit grade-separated junctions, instead of level intersections regulated by traffic lights, which must usually be lit. The extra costs incurred here must be balanced with the interests of nature.

14.5.3   The choice of road surface

Often the road surface, road markings and other guiding aids can postpone the installation of public lighting. If lighting is required, then it could be at a lower level. We could think of the use of very open asphalt concrete (ZOAB) or other drainage road surfaces, where the visibility of the road and of the other traffic as well as of the road markings is considerably better than for tradition road surfaces, especially during rain, so that road lighting is unnecessary for the amount of traffic expected. See also section 10.3. This also applies to the use of good road markings, especially raised pavement markers. The additional costs must be balanced against the interest of nature.

Road markings are an important aid to visibility, noticeably in darkness on roads without public lighting. Road markings have not been discussed in this book. A review is given in Schreuder & Schoon (1990). See also SCW (1982; 1987) and Schreuder (1978, 1980, 1985, 1986).

14.5.4   Adaptation of the installation criteria for public lighting

The lighting of motorways has, like the lighting of other roads, a number of functions, the most important of which is ensuring traffic safety. Enabling a higher speed and increasing driving comfort, two functions which may be important on other routes, must be accorded a low priority on roads through nature reserves. Legal or other measures to reduce speed and measures which lead to a different choice of route, all deserve attention. The decision to install public lighting must be taken on the basis of balancing the costs and benefits, and the benefits should be limited to a possible improvement in traffic safety.

14.5.5   Choice as regards the level of light

A number of specific studies has shown that traffic safety, measured in accidents per unit of traffic performance, is reduced when the level of light increases, but that this relationship is only weak. See section 11.2.6. A high level of light contributes especially to the driving comfort in rain. ZOAB can contribute just as much, or even more.

14.5.6   Choice as regards the colour of light

The possibility of using monochromatic light must be considered carefully. Traffic benefits by this and the nuisance to plants and animals is often less than with white light. Conversely, there is the aesthetic disadvantage, which is important, particularly in nature reserves. A general rule cannot be given. The advantages and disadvantages must be weighed up in each case.

14.5.7   The selection of lighting columns

The number and the height of the columns must be considered carefully in connection with the day aspect (horizon pollution). The higher the columns, the more they are visible; the greater the number, the more nuisance they cause. The way mounting height, the distance between columns, the width of the road and the requirements regarding uniformity are interdependent was discussed earlier. General rules cannot be given here either. The advantages and disadvantages must be weighed up in each case.

14.5.8   Selection of the luminaire

Finally, great care must be taken when choosing the luminaire. Not only the day aspect is important; the extent in which the light emission approaches the horizon or even exceeds it is especially relevant. A flat glass is required to ensure that the proportion of luminous flux above the horizon, which often contributes most to nuisance, is zero. This also means that the luminaires must be mounted exactly horizontal. The usual elevation of 5 to 10 degrees is unacceptable. In addition, a full cut-off light distribution must be chosen to limit obtrusive light still further. This means, of course, that the lighting installation must be designed with care and expertise. A cut-off light distribution requires small spacings between masts, or great mounting height, to satisfy the uniformity requirements.

Bibliography

Amand, D.K. & Zmood, R.B. (1995). *Introduction to control systems*. Third edition. Oxford, Butterworth-Heinemann, 1995.

Anon. (1984). *Energie in kort bestek* [Energy in short]. Shell Brochure Serie. Rotterdam, Shell Nederland B.V., 1984.

Anon. (1989). *Nationaal Milieubeleidsplan* [National environmental policy plan]. Tweede Kamer, Vergaderjaar 1988-1989, 21 137 nrs. 1-2. Den Haag, SDU, 1989.

Anon. (1990). *Nationaal Milieubeleidsplan-Plus* [National environmental policy plan-plus]. Tweede Kamer, Vergaderjaar 1989-1990, 21 137, nr. 20-21. Den Haag, SDU, 1990.

Anon. (1990a). *Tweede Structuurschema Verkeer en Vervoer* [Second structure plan traffic and transport]. Tweede Kamer Vergaderjaar 1989-1990, nrs. 15-16. Den Haag, SDU, 1990.

Anon. (1991). *Controlled road lighting*. Proposal submitted to the Commission of the European Communities, Promotion of Energy Technologies for Europe (THERMIE). Rotterdam, Rijkswaterstaat, June 1991 (unpublished).

Anon. (1994). *BP Statistical Review of World Energy*. London, British Petroleum Company, 1994.

Anon. (1996). *Licht op de openbare weg* [Light on public roads]. NSVV/Uneto Congresdag 3 april 1996, RAI, Amsterdam. Syllabus. Arnhem, NSVV, 1996.

Anon. (1997). *Control of light pollution; Measures, standards and practice*. Conference organised by Commission 590 of the International Astronomical Union and

Technical Committee 4.21 of the Commission Internationale de l'Eclairage. The Hague, 20 August 1994. The observatory, 117, 10-36, 1997.

Bok, S.T. (1958). Cybernetica (Stuurkunde). Utrecht, Prisma, Aula, 1958.

Brouwer, K. & Leroy, P. (red.) (1995). *Milieu en ruimte; Analyse en beleid* [Environment and space; analysis and policy]. Amsterdam, Boom, 1995.

Brouwer, K. & Klaver, J. (1995). *'Milieuzonering'* [Environmental zoning]. Hoofdstuk 10 in: Brouwer & Leroy, (red.) (1995).

Brouwer, K. & Leroy, P. (1995). 'Milieu en ruimte [Environment and space]'. Hoofdstuk 1 in: Brouwer & Leroy, (red.) (1995).

Brussaard, W.; Drupsteen, Th. G.; Gilhuis, F.C. & Koeman, N.S.J. (1993). *Mileurecht* [Environmental legislation]. Derde druk. Zwolle, 1993 (Cit. Brouwer & Klaver, 1995).

Burghout, F. (1978). 'Energiegebruik voor verlichting' [Energy consumption for lighting]. *Electrotechniek* **56** (1978), 885-890.

CIE (1995). *Guide on the limitation of the effect of obtrusive light from outdoor lighting installations.* Third Draft, August 1995. TC 5.12 Obtrusive Light. CIE, 1995.

CIE (1997). *Guidelines for minimising sky glow.* Publication No. 126. Vienna, CIE, 1997.

Crawford, D.L. (1997). 'Terminology and units in lighting and astronomy'. In: Anon. (1997).

Crawford, D.L., (ed.) (1991). *Light pollution, radio interference and space debris.* Proceedings of the International Astronomical Union colloquium 112, held 13 to 16 August, 1989, Washington DC. Astronomical Society of the Pacific Conference Series Volume 17. San Francisco, 1991.

De Wit, G. (1995). 'Energiebesparing in de openbare verlichting' [Energy savings in public lighting]. In: NSVV (1995).

Fernhout (1990). *Electriciteitsbesparing bij de openbare verlichting* [Electricity savings in public lighting]. Rapport 101-01-103. Castricum, Adviesbureau Fernhout voor Electrotechniek en Energie F.E.E., 1990.

Gorter, J. (1996). 'Licht in de duisternis [Light in the darkness]'. In: Anon. (1996).

Hoagland (1996). *Scientific American,* September 1995, page 138.

IAEEL (1993). Right Light II; 2nd European Conference on Energy-Efficient Lighting. Proceedings. Arnhem, International Association for Energy-Efficient Lighting IAEEL, 1993.

IAEEL (1995). *Right Light III;* 3rd European Conference on Energy-Efficient Lighting. Proceedings. Newcastle upon Tyne, International Association for Energy-Efficient Lighting IAEEL; 1995.

ILE (1994). *Guidance notes for the reduction of light pollution* (Revised). Rugby, The Institution of Lighting Engineers, 1994.

Kosai, H.; Isobe, S. & Nakayama, Y. (1994). 'A global network observation of night sky brightness in Japan – Method and some result'. In: McNally (ed.) (1994).

Koumans, W.A. (1973). 'Vervoer; Een wezenlijk welzijnselement' [Transport; a concrete component of well-being]. *De Ingenieur* **85** (1973) 461–467.

Kuhn, M. (1990). *Klimaänderungen: Treibhauseffekt und Ozon.* Thaur, Tirol (Austria), Kulturverlag, 1990.

McNally, D. (ed.), (1994). *Adverse environmental impacts on astronomy: An exposition.* Proceedings. IAU/ICSU/UNESCO Meeting, 30 June–2 July, 1992, Paris. Cambridge University Press, 1994.

Meadows, D.L. (1972). *De Club van Rome* [The club of Rome]. Utrecht, Spectrum, Aula 500, 1972.

Murdin, P. (1997). 'Zones of light pollution control'. In: Anon. (1997).

NOVEM (1994). *NOVEM Energiegids* [NOVEM energy guide]. Sittard, NOVEM, 1994 (year estimated).

NSVV (1995). *De NSVV op weg naar 2000* [NSVV on the road to 2000]. Congresdag 19 mei 1995. Arnhem, NSVV, 1995.

NSVV (1996). *Aanbevelingen voor openbare verlichting; Deel III: Ontwerpen* [Recommendations for public lighting; Part III: Designs]. Arnhem, NSVV, 1996.

NSVV (1997). *Richtlijn openbare verlichting natuurgebieden.* [Directive public lighting nature reserves]. Publicatie 112. Driebergen, CROW, 1997.

PAOVV (1991). *Verkeer en milieu; Van woorden (NEMP + SVV) naar daden (de uitvoering* [Traffic and the environment; from words (NEMP + SVV) to deeds (implementation)]. Course 16-18 april 1991. Delft, PAOVV, 1991.

Pollard, N.E. (1993). 'Sky glow conscious lighting design'. In: Schreuder, (ed.) (1993).

Remande, C. (1980). *Mieux utiliser l'Énergie en Élairage public.* Transport Environnement Circulation No 42, 1980, sept-oct, p. 33–35.

Schreuder, D.A. (1978). *Zichtbaarheid van wegmarkeringen op natte wegen; Een literatuurstudie* [Visibility of road markings on wet roads; a literature review]. Arnhem, SCW/SVT, 1978.

Schreuder, D.A. (1980). *Geprofileerde wegmarkeringen; Een literatuurstudie in opdracht van de Deutsche Studiengesellschaft der Hersteller von Markierungsglasperlen (DSGM)* [Profiled road markings; a literature review commisioned by DSGM]. Forschungsgesellschaft für Strassen- und Verkehrswesen e.V., Köln. R-80-51. Voorburg, SWOV, 1980.

Schreuder, D.A. (1985). *Regelen, beheersen en sturen ... bijvoorbeeld in het wegverkeer* [Control ... e.g. of road traffic]. R-85-27. Leidschendam, SWOV, 1985. Also in Wegen 59 (1985) 217–220.

Schreuder, D.A. (1985a). *De zichtbaarheid van wegmarkeringen op natte wegen. Een aanvullende literatuurstudie ten behoeve van de SCW/SVT-werkgroep E9 "Zichtbaarheid van wegmarkeringen op natte wegdekken"* [The visibility of road markings on wet roads. A supplementary literature review for the SCW/SVT working party E9 "Visibility of road markings on wet road surfaces"]. R-85-23. Leidschendam, SWOV, 1985.

Schreuder, D.A. (1986). *The function of road markings in relation to drivers' visual needs.* R-86-29. Leidschendam, SWOV, 1986.

Schreuder, D.A. (1994). Comments on CIE work on sky pollution. Paper presented at 1994 SANCI Congress, South African National Committee on Illumination, 7–9 November 1994, Capetown, South Africa.

Schreuder, D.A. (1995). *Quality lighting – The need to cry over spilled milk.* Paper presented at the 3rd European Conference on Energy-Efficient Lighting, 18th-21st June 1995, Newcastle upon Tyne, England. Leidschendam, Duco Schreuder Consultancies, 1995.

Schreuder, D.A. & Schoon, C.C. (1990). *De relatie tussen het koershouden van voertuigen en wegmarkeringen op 80 km/uur-wegen* [Relationship between steering and road markings on 80 km/hr roads]. R-90-54. Leidschendam, SWOV, 1990.

Schreuder, D.A. (ed) (1993). Urban sky glow, a worry for astronomy. Proceedings, Symposium, 3 April 1993, Edinburgh. Publication No. X008. Vienna, CIE, 1993.

SCW (1972). *Wegverlichting en oppervlaktetextuur* [Road lighting and surface texture]. Mededeling 32. Arnhem, SCW, 1972.

SCW (1982). *Zichtbaarheid's nachts van wegmarkeringen op droge en natte wegen* [Night-time visibility of road markings on dry and wet roads]. SCW Mededeling 52 /SVT Mededeling 17. Arnhem, SCW, 1982.

SCW (1984). *Wegverlichting en oppervlaktetextuur* [Road lighting and surface texture].

Mededeling 63. Arnhem, SCW, 1984.

SCW (1987). *Zicht op markeringen* [Detection of road markings]. Publicatie No. 2. Ede, CROW, 1987.

Shannon, C.E. & Weaver, W. (1949). *The Mathematical Theory of Communication.* University of Illinois, 1949.

Van Wee, G.P. (1991). 'De milieuproblematiek in het algemeen en de positie van het verkeer hierbinnen' [Environmental problems in general and the position of traffic]. In: PAOVV (1991).

Wiener, N. (1950). *Cybernetics, or control and communication in the anima and in the machine.* Eighth printing. New York, John Wiley & Sons, Inc., 1950.

Wiener, N. (1954). *The human use of human beings.* 2nd Edition. New York, Doubleday, 1954.

15 Tunnel lighting

In the case of cross river or canal connections, a choice must be made between high fixed bridges and tunnels. Economically, tunnels would seem the most sound choice for Dutch conditions. Traffic safety is a criterion for the lighting requirements for such tunnels. Short tunnels and tunnels for pedestrians and cyclists are relevant within built-up areas. Public safety is a criterion for lighting requirements for slow traffic. Mountain tunnels with little traffic are also discussed. The discussion on tunnel lighting is done on the basis of the existing recommendations by NSVV and CIE, as well as the CEN draft and also drafts by CIE. The perception of safety, which is important in tunnels for slow traffic, is also dealt with.

Visually speaking, vehicular tunnels have a special place in lighting theory. The reason is that it is not feasible to achieve a level of light with artificial light which even approaches the level at daylight, on economical and technical grounds. Tunnels are therefore always much darker than the open roads. In contrast to most areas of public lighting, temporal aspects of visual perception play a decisive role. Technical solutions for the lighting of tunnels concern mostly these two facts.

15.1 Tunnels for fast traffic and tunnels for slow traffic

15.1.1 General

Tunnels form important links in the road network, particularly for a smooth flow of motorised fast traffic. The lighting requirements follow from issues relating to traffic safety, characterised by the visibility of objects. There are, of course, many more tunnels in addition to tunnels which form part of main arterial roads. Short tunnels or underpasses and tunnels for slow traffic, pedestrians and cyclists, are also important. The lighting requirements for these last-mentioned are based on issues relating to public safety, and the perception of safety plays an important role. The lighting of these three types of tunnels will be considered in this chapter.

A completely different type of tunnel is seen in mountainous regions. Not only because of different characteristics in the subsoil, but also due to the different reasons for the construction of the tunnel from a traffic point of view. Thus, in mountain areas we often find tunnels which carry little traffic, but which serve as an access route to certain areas or valleys, even in bad weather or in snow. The lighting of these tunnels is also dealt with in this chapter.

15.1.2 Terminology

Before discussing the practical aspects of tunnel lighting, I will first say something on the terminology. This section is based on the NSVV Recommendations (NSVV, 1963, 1991).

- Each type of bridging of a road, irrespective of the length and the nature can be considered as a tunnel. Transparent or light-screening constructions are considered as part of the tunnel. For reasons explained later, tunnels are divided into long and short tunnels or underpasses, as far as their length is concerned.
- The access zone is the section of road situated immediately in front of the tunnel entrance. Vehicle drivers approaching the tunnel must be able to look into the tunnel. Figure 15.1.1 depicts an illustration of the situation as it may appear to a driver approaching a tunnel.
- The threshold zone is the first part of the tunnel. The visual problems of drivers approaching the tunnel are greatest when they are still outside

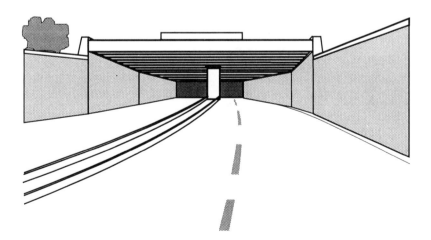

Figure 15.1.1: *The situation as it may appear to a driver approaching a tunnel*

the tunnel, but close enough to be able to look into the tunnel. Often these problems are termed the 'black hole' effect.

- The transition zone is the tunnel section following on the threshold zone. In the transition zone, luminance decreases from the level at the end of the threshold zone to the level in the central zone. This reduction must take place gradually to offer drivers the possibility of letting the eye adapt gradually to the lower level, or, more exactly, to avoid a large adaptation deficiency. Entrance zone means the combination of threshold and transition zones.

- The central zone or the tunnel interior is the tunnel section which follows the transition zone. The lighting is usually constant over the total length. In practice, an entrance zone of limited length is chosen, on grounds of cost; this means that the time is not sufficient to achieve a complete visual adaptation. Despite a gradual decrease in luminance in the transition zone, the luminance in the central zone must be higher during the day than that of an illuminated road at night, in order to ensure sufficient accuracy and comfort of visual perception.

Figure 15.1.2 shows a diagram illustrating a number of these terms. The remaining terms are self-evident

- The design speed is the speed used in the design of the tunnel. This speed is normative for the design and the design elements of the road, so that drivers of individual vehicles can drive safely at that speed, when not impeded by the other traffic. This description is based on Anon. (1986).

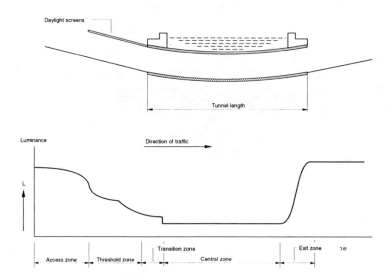

Figure 15.1.2: *Terminology for long tunnels*

- The stopping distance is the distance over which a road user must be able to view the road in order to be able to perceive any obstacles, identify them and stop the vehicle in good time, without endangering themselves, the object or the traffic from behind. This description is based on the concept of 'stopping sight distance' (03119) from Anon. (1986).

15.1.3 A historic review

Tunnels have been build for thousands of years. Historic reviews on the construction of tunnels, mainly those in The Netherlands, are given by Stiksma (1987), Vreugdenhil (1952) and Werkman (1959). The history of the lighting of traffic tunnels however, is much shorter. See, e.g. Schreuder (1964, 1981, 1989). The lighting in tunnels built before 1940 concerned primarily the interior of the tunnel. A threshold lighting of maybe 20 to 30 metres in length was installed at the entrance, to aid drivers entering the tunnel (Vreugdenhil, 1952, page 102). This is called the first generation of tunnel lighting. The lighting was based on practical experience; scientific research was hardly ever done. It was realised during the design of the Velser tunnel, that there was scope for improvement in the visual aspect of existing tunnels in The Netherlands and abroad. A number of model studies were conducted to arrive at a visually attractive design.

Towards the end of the Fifties, several new tunnels were designed: the Coen, the IJ, the Heinenoord, the Benelux and the Schiphol tunnels. These tunnels, plus many dozens of tunnels in other countries, built during the Sixties, represent the second generation. The lighting requirements were derived from the function of the tunnel: a rapid and safe flow of vehicles at high density and high speed. The necessity of extended entrance lighting with a very high level of light) followed from extensive theoretical research and research with models (Schreuder, 1964). Often a screeen in front of the closed tunnel was chosen, in order to reduce the daylight. The theory and practice of the second generation form the basis for the already mentioned NSVV Recommendations (1963) and those by CIE (1973). The CIE recommendations have been adopted by a great number of countries as their national codes or standards.

By making the surfaces in the neighbourhood of the tunnel entrance dark, the luminance in the open road, the access zone, could be reduced considerably. This also allowed for a lower luminance in the threshold zone. The ratio of L_2 and L_1 mentioned in section 15.4.4 could be considerably higher than 10:1, the value found for high luminances, at a lower luminance. Dark tunnel entrances lead therefore to a very considerable reduction in the extent of entrance lighting, in cost and in energy consumption. At the same time counterbeam lighting became popular in Alpine countries. See also section 10.1.2. The third generation comprises a collection of rules arising from practical experience with the construction, the fitting and the management of tunnels. Experience has shown that the luminance in the access zone can be kept to below 4000 cd/m^2 in nearly all cases. A long adaptation period is not necessary. Veiling luminance in particular is important. It has been shown that, beside stray light in the eye, we also must consider stray light on the windscreens of cars and in the atmosphere. See also section 15.4.3.

A fourth generation of tunnel lighting is being considered, which is based on the new understanding derived from the task analysis of drivers of motor vehicles. Perception in traffic is not based in the first instance on the detection of small objects, but rather on the identification of patterns in traffic and in the route of the road. This understanding is producing results in the design of some traffic safety measures.

It should be mentioned that reference is made in this chapter on several occasions to the draft recommendation of CIE (1995) and to the draft European Standard of CEN (1997). It must be stressed that in spite of the fact that they are often used in lighting design tenders and specifications, these are still drafts that may be changed considerably in the future.

15.2   The theory of tunnel lighting

15.2.1   Fundamental points relating to traffic and vision

Visually speaking, traffic tunnels have a special place in the theory of lighting. The reason for this is that it is not feasible to achieve a level with artificial light which can even approach the level during the day, on economical and on technical grounds. Tunnels are therefore often much darker than the open road. As the surroundings of the tunnel entrance works as a source of glare when illuminated by daylight, a driver who has approached the tunnel up to a distance equal to the preview distance (section 8.2.2) often cannot see into the tunnel. The tunnel entrance resembles a black hole. As will be seen in the next section, the only remedy is a considerable increase in the level of light in the first section of the tunnel – the threshold zone.

When drivers approach the tunnel, they need to adapt. See also section 15.2.3. The tunnel opening occupies such a large part of the field of vision that the adaptation situation of the visual system is affected. The point on the road where this takes place is also called the adaptation point (Schreuder, 1967). When the adaptation point has been passed, the adaptation of the visual system is affected by the tunnel itself. Here a number of completely different effects arise. The method of perception, in particular the pattern of eye movements, also changes. More fixations are directed at the tunnel entrance itself. Based on these results, Narisada introduced the fixation point (Narisada & Yoshikawa, 1974). There are also other characteristics which point to the approach and entering of a tunnel as being a situation which is accompanied by stress symptoms. A number of studies were recently carried out in this area, which have already been discussed in section 8.1.3 (Verwey, 1995; Verwey et al., 1995).

15.2.2 The black hole effect
Disability glare and the equivalent veil luminance

The black hole effect is actually a special case of disability glare, mentioned in section 7.3.2, where a strong source of light appears in the field of vision from a different direction than the object to be perceived. The light from the source of light causing the glare is dispersed in the eye media. This causes a veil of light which seems to occupy the whole field of vision. Most glare symptoms would seem to be cumulative and integratable. The practical determination of the veiling luminance is based on this.

The veil has a negative effect on the visibility of objects, as all contrasts in the field of vision are reduced. It was pointed out in section 7.2.2, that the contrast without glare amounts to

$$C = \frac{L_o - L_b}{L_b} \qquad\qquad [7.3.1]$$

and with a veiling luminance L_v is equal to

$$C' = \frac{(L_o + L_v) - (L_b + L_v)}{L_b + L_v} = \frac{L_o - L_b}{L_b + L_v} \qquad\qquad [7.3.2]$$

it follows from formulae 7.3.1 and 7.3.2 that

$$C' = C\frac{L_b}{L_b + L_v} \qquad\qquad [15.2.1]$$

and also

$$L_v = L_b\frac{C'}{C - C'} \qquad\qquad [15.2.2]$$

These calculations are important for determining the minimum lighting in the threshold zone of a tunnel. The relationship between contrast C' to be perceived and veiling luminance L_v follows from formula 15.2.1; the relationship between the luminance in threshold zone L_b and the veiling luminance follows from formula 15.2.2. As indicated in section 7.3.2, the veiling luminance may be determined with the aid of the formula stemming from Vos (Vos 1983; see also Vos & Padmos, 1983). This formula was given in section 7.3.2 (formula 7.3.4). A computer program called 'SNAEFELL' has been produced for the practical application of the formula for the design of tunnel lighting (Swart, 1994).

Empirical studies
In order to determine the effect of the black hole effect on perception in the tunnel entrance, two methods are followed – an empirical and a theoretical method. The empirical approach is based on measurements by Schreuder (1964). A clearly illuminated screen is offered to the observers. This screen represents the surroundings. An opening which can be closed with a shutter is situated in the screen. When the shutter is closed, the opening is invisible. When the shutter is open, a darker plane is presented, which represents the tunnel entrance. Simultaneously with the tunnel entrance, an object which is slightly darker is also presented, which represents a traffic obstacle. See figure 15.2.1.

The screen luminance (the surroundings) is called L_1, the tunnel entrance luminance is L_2 and the obstacle luminance is L_3. The shutter is opened for a short time for each perception. The time is so short that the adaptation situation does not change. The assumption is therefore, that L_1 represents not

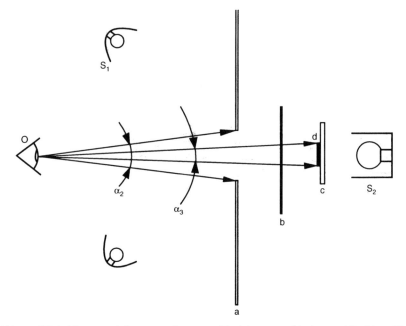

Figure 15.2.1: *Diagram of the measuring assembly; (a) screen, (b) shutter, (d) object, (S) source of light (after Schreuder, 1964)*

only the surroundings, but also the adaptation situation. A large number of measurements were taken, while L_1, L_2 and L_3 were varied. For each combination, the probability that the object was seen was determined. As a criterion the probability of perception p of 50% and 75% were used. The results are represented by the following formulae

$$\log L_2 = -1.04 + 0.50L_1^{0.2} + 39.1C^{-1.2} \text{ for } p = 50\% \qquad [15.2.3]$$

$$\log L_2 = -0.97 + 0.51L_1^{0.2} + 39.1C^{-1.2} \text{ for } p = 75\% \qquad [15.2.4]$$

The dimensions of the tunnel entrance, the dimensions of the obstacle and the perception time were also varied, but their effect proved to be relatively small. The results are summarised in figure 15.2.2. More recently, measurements in existing tunnels were conducted which led to similar results. See Anon (1995).

The following conclusion was drawn from the measurements: assuming that objects relevant to traffic safety have a contrast of 20% or higher in relation to their background, then the black hole effect can be avoided when the luminance of the threshold zone is not less than a tenth of the luminance of the open road. This is the rule on which most recommendations for tunnel lighting are based: $L_2 > 0.1L_1$. See CIE (1973, 1984, 1990); DIN (1987); NSVV (1963, 1991). Later studies and practical experience have shown that this value is a little high; in many cases the value can be considerably less than 0.1. This is also shown in figure 15.2.2.

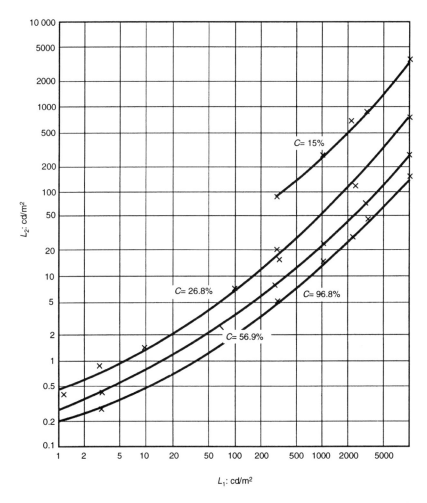

Figure 15.2.2: *Summary of measurements relating to the black hole effect (after Schreuder, 1964)*

The theoretical approach

The theoretical approach is based on the perception of contrast (Adrian, 1989, 1990). The basis is the earlier mentioned formula 15.2.2, which describes the relationship between L_b (or L_2) and L_v. If L_v is known, and assuming C and C', then L_2 can be calculated. The calculations are based on the CIE publication on contrast sensitivity (CIE, 1981), mentioned in section 7.2.2. A disadvantage is that the data used stem from the lab and not from the field. This relates to observers who were not concerned with a traffic task, the observers as well as the objects to be detected were stationary and small, sometimes very small objects were used. As already pointed out in section 9.2.2, these assumptions scarcely correspond to a realistic traffic situation. The same data are used in the studies discussed below relating to counterbeam lighting, so that the same reservations apply there (sections 10.1.2 and 15.4.4). Despite these reservations, the empirical and the theoretical approach lead to similar results. One of the reasons is that in the most common cases rather a close correlation exists between L_1 and L_v. When this correlation is not present, as in tunnels with conditions of sun on snow, or with a low sun which shines into the car and into the eyes of the observer, these two approaches lead to considerably different results. A further complication may occur, due to the fact that L_1 cannot usually be measured. Schreuder (1964) recommended an initial approach to account for the reflection of the surroundings. The highest value found, and which is feasible in practice, was 8000 cd/m^2. This value applies to a horizontal illuminance of 100,000 lux (a high but not an extreme value) and an average reflection of 20%. In practice however, it was shown that this assumption often led to unrealistically high demands for the lighting of the threshold zone. The easily measured L_{20} was therefore introduced. This is the average luminance within a solid angle which occupies $2 \times 10°$ on all sides of the direction of vision. Here also, in most cases, there is rather a close correlation between L_1 and L_{20}. But in the same cases (sun on snow, or low sun) the correlation does not apply. I will return to the method of determination of L_1 in section 15.4.3.

Obtrusive luminance
Obtrusive luminance L_d was discussed earlier in this chapter. This obtrusive luminance consists of four components which together produce obtrusive luminance L_d

$$L_d = L_{adef} + L_{seq} + L_{atm} + L_{ws} \qquad [15.2.5]$$

In which

L_{adef} is the component relating to the changes in brightness and the retardation in adaptation (the 'adaptation defect'; Schreuder & Oud, 1988)

L_{seq} is the contribution to the veil stemming from the light scattered in the eye (Vos, 1983; Vos & Padmos, 1983)

L_{atm} is the contribution to the veil stemming from the light scattered into the atmosphere (Padmos & Alferdinck 1983)

L_{ws} is the contribution to the veil stemming from the light scattered onto the windscreen (Padmos & Alferdinck, 1983a).

L_{adef} may be ignored for current conditions in The Netherlands. L_{sec}, L_{atm} and L_{ws} may have very different values in practice. In a clear atmosphere (visibility 20 km or more) and a clean windscreen, values of $L_{atm} = L_{ws} = 0.1 L_{seq}$ are possible. $L_d = $ then 1.2 L_{seq}. In an average murky atmosphere and with a normal dirty windscreen it often happens that L_{seq}, L_{atm} and L_{ws} are of approximately the same order (Vos & Padmos, 1983). In those conditions, L_d will be $3L_{seq}$. The lighting design of tunnels is usually based on this – rather rough – approach. A recent study showed that the approximation of the windscreen scatter by Padmos & Alferdinck (1983c) corresponds reasonably well with field measurements, as long as the windscreen veil is moderate. The closely-related reflection on the dashboard, however, proved to be more severe. Further studies are required. (Roovers & De Roo, 1996).

15.2.3   The adaptation

The state of adaptation was discussed in section 7.2.4 and the temporal adaptation process in section 7.2.5. It was pointed out there that for most practical cases, certainly when the starting level as well as the final level of the adaptation process is situated in the area of photoptic perception, adaptation of the sensitivity to the receptors is responsible for adaptation. The most important visual effect of adaptation is the disappearance of the after images. The speed of the processes in question can be seen from figures 7.2.8 and 7.2.9. If changes in luminance occur quickly, then adaptation cannot keep pace with it; an adaptation deficiency results. See Schreuder (1964). Readers should refer to Kabayama (1963), Ohayama (1995) and Schreuder (1964) for the

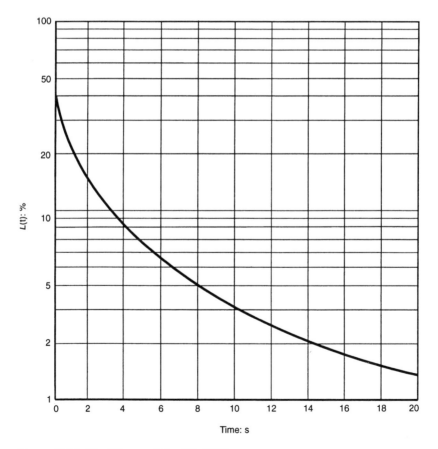

Figure 15.2.3: *The CIE curve (after CIE, 1990)*

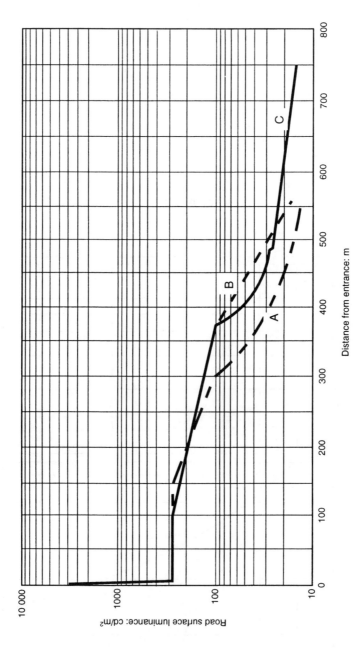

Figure 15.2.4: *The adaptation curve (after Ohayama, 1995). A: CIE curve. B: Curve according to Kabayama. C: Japanese proposal. Design speed 140 km/h; outside luminance 4000 cd/m²*

measurements in question. This has led to the 'CIE curve'. This curve is the basis for the requirements relating to lighting in the transition zone in tunnels (CEN, 1997; CIE, 1990; 1995, NSVV, 1991). See figure 15.2.3.

In view of the origin of the curve, a discussion relating to the accuracy and to the discrepancies between the graphical and the mathematical reproductions would seem rather meaningless. This concerns a partly subjectively determined curve, which is based partly on considerations of comfort, which are difficult to grasp. However, experience has taught us that the requirements based on the CIE curve are far from exaggerated. Based on practice, several countries (among others The Netherlands and the US) are pleading for a longer transition zone; at the end of the transition zone visibility problems often occur. During experiments relating to the light screens which are implemented in the Benelux tunnel, it was shown that often a new black hole effect occurred at the end of the transition zone, which is quite short in that tunnel. See Schreuder & Oud (1988) and Tan et al. (1983); Bourdy et al. (1987). More recent studies from Japan confirmed this. There also the CIE curve proved to fall too steeply at the end (Anon., 1993; Ohayama, 1995). See figure 15.2.4.

15.3   Classification of tunnels

15.3.1   Long and short tunnels
The lighting requirements for a tunnel depend closely on the type of tunnel. A classification system is required. The variables for such a classification are

- length
- speed (design speed)
- traffic density
- traffic composition (fast traffic, mixed traffic or slow traffic).

The main factor proves to be the length. Nearly all recommendations establish totally different lighting requirements for long tunnels and for short tunnels. In addition to the fact that in practice financial resources for the lighting of a short tunnel are usually very limited, there are also theoretical considerations. These relate to whether the exit is visible from a point in front of the entrance. In order to quantify this, the 'through view quotient' has been defined (Schreuder & Fournier, 1985). This through view quotient is usually defined as the ratio in solid angle between the two areas, usually rectangles, which comprise the visible section of the exit and the entrance respectively. See figure 15.3.1.

Based on the photographs, a visual evaluation has been conducted for a number of short tunnels. Here observers were asked if they had the impression that the tunnel was easy to drive through; this assessment was represented by marks ranging from 0 to 10. The evaluation was related to the through view quotient as described in figure 15.3.1 (Schreuder & Fournier, 1985). The results are shown in figure 15.3.2.

The results may be grouped into some three clusters. When the through view quotient is low, approximately two, then observers expect visual

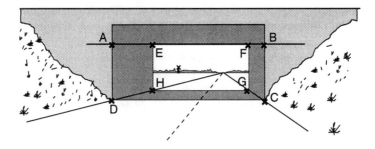

Figure 15.3.1: *Definition of the through view quotient* K = 10 *(EFGH)/(ABCD); after Schreuder & Fournier, 1985, afb. 1*

problems. A high through view quotient of approximately five does not seem to give rise to visual problems. As expected, the opinions are divided in the intermediate area. This classification has, however, never been tested in practice.

The Dutch recommendations only apply to long tunnels. The difference between long and short tunnels is indicated by the following characterisation

In general a tunnel or an underpass does not have to be illuminated during the day when the exit is illuminated by daylight and when it occupies a large part of the field of vision, seen from a point at a distance equal to the stopping distance

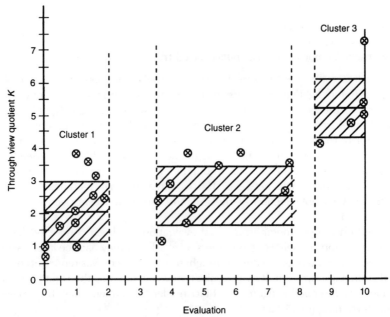

Figure 15.3.2: *The relationship between evaluation and through view quotient (After Schreuder & Fournier, 1985)*

associated with the design speed in front of the tunnel. Conversely, the tunnel must have additional lighting during the day when the exit can only be seen surrounded by a dark frame, in which objects of considerable dimensions may remain hidden. The problems of illuminating such tunnels, summarised in the term 'short tunnels', are not discussed in the present recommendations. NSVV will in time produce a separate publication on the lighting of short tunnels (NSVV, 1991).

In 1997, a first step has been made in the drafting of recommendations for the lighting of short tunnels.

The CIE recommendations (1984, 1990) offer a number of diagrams with which we can determine whether a tunnel must be considered to be long or short in relation to the lighting. These diagrams were adopted by CEN (1997). Consideration is given in the classification to the aspects mentioned above: the length, the design speed, traffic density and the composition of the traffic. However, the diagrams are not easy to work with; and some more fundamental reservations have been expressed. A better solution would be a decision tree which would also be used for determining the parameters relating to lighting in the tunnel. Such a decision tree, an expert system, however, is not yet available. As mentioned in section 13.1.3, some preliminary proposals were proposed for such systems relating to street lighting (Di Fraia, 1993).

The first publication of the NSVV Recommendations for tunnel lighting contains a brief chapter on short tunnels, which also contains a classification (NSVV, 1963). This subject will be further discussed in the lighting of short tunnels in section 15.5.

There is presently no completely satisfactory solution available. I will therefore adopt the current procedure and classify tunnels into long and short tunnels without entering in too great detail into the criteria set for them. The aspects relating to the design speed and the traffic density are relevant to the lighting requirements. As indicated in section 15.4, motorised fast traffic is especially interested in traffic safety and the accompanying visibility of objects. Finally, the assumption is, as far as the traffic composition is concerned, usually that most tunnels which are exclusively intended for slow traffic are short. The lighting requirements are primarily based on public safety.

15.3.2   Classification of long tunnels

A classification is also needed for long tunnels. The proposals by CEN and CIE contain a system of classification, which determine the tunnel class based on weight factors; subsequently the lighting class is derived from the tunnel class. See tables 15.3.1 and 15.3.2.

15.4   The lighting of long tunnels

15.4.1   Characteristics of long tunnels

As indicated in section 15.3, long tunnels are intended for fast or mixed traffic, according to the current classification. The lighting design is based on the

Table 15.3.1: *Classification of long tunnels based on weight factors, based on data from CIE (1995)*

Conditions			Weight factor
Traffic (vehicles per hour)*			
	Single direction	Two directions	
		> 1200	7
	>1200	650–1200	6
	650–1200	350–650	5
	350–650	180–350	4
	180–350	100–180	3
	100–180	60–100	2
	60–100	30–60	1
	<60	<30	0
Mixed traffic			2
Cars – percentage trucks >15			1
Exclusively cars			0
Bad optical guidance			2
Good optical guidance			0
High degree of comfort required			4
Medium degree of comfort required			2
Low degree of comfort required			0

* The actual flow of traffic, taking into account response time of the control system for the lighting

Table 15.3.2: *The lighting classes based on the weight factors from table 15.3.1; after CIE, 1995*

Sum of the weight factors	Lighting class
0–3	1
4–5	2
6–7	3
8–9	4
10–11	5
12–13	6
14–15	7

demands from motorised fast traffic. As mentioned earlier, this relates to traffic safety and the accompanying visibility of objects.

Tunnels are extremely costly constructions: a sizeable tunnel soon costs some hundreds of millions of guilders. It would therefore be economically expedient to realise the facilities in the tunnel with a quality which ensures optimal use of the tunnel. Tunnels serve to ensure the flow of traffic; in themselves they should therefore not impede the traffic. This concerns in the first instance the technical provisions relating directly to traffic and traffic participants, i.e. the lighting, traffic control and ventilation.

The long tunnels in The Netherlands are nearly always intended for very busy traffic: 120,000 vehicles per 24 hours is not exceptional. This means that most tunnels resemble motorways: separated carriageways, each with at least two, but often three or four lanes. Sometimes tunnel tubes for local or for slow traffic are added. The crossing of waterways leads to tunnels of average length: most Dutch tunnels are between 600 metres and 1 km long, in contrast to tunnels in mountainous countries, where tunnels of more than 10 km are not exceptional. This usually means a very wide but not very long tunnel for The Netherlands. This together with the subsoil in The Netherlands – more like a fluid with a high viscosity, rather than a solid – leads to the tunnel construction common in The Netherlands. Here tunnel sections are placed in a channel previously dredged into the river bed as sinkers. Drilled tunnels are commonplace in mountainous areas and in rocky subsoil. In The Netherlands these are an exception. The tunnels, including those for deep waterways, are not very deep below ground level: seldom more than 20 metres. It might be added that similar situations, and therefore similar tunnel construction methods, may be found in almost all coastal plains around the world.

All this determines to a large extent the constructional characteristics of tunnels of this type; it has also far-reaching consequences for the demands placed on the lighting, in particular for the entrance, but also in relation to the interior.

The situation in The Netherlands and other coastal plains can be summarised as follows

- flat land
- large traffic density
- wide flat tunnels of limited length
- soft soil.

In this connection one last remark: the Dutch daily traffic congestion radio announcements nearly all relate to river connections, especially to the tunnels. These messages are misleading: the tunnels themselves do not form the bottlenecks, but rather the feeder roads. This has given tunnels an undeserved bad name.

15.4.2   Recommendations and guidelines for the lighting of long tunnels

As pointed out earlier, the Dutch experience and the recommendations based on it, form the model for nearly all other national and international guidelines.

The first characteristic is that optimum lighting is sought; in addition to aspects of traffic safety and the accompanying visibility of objects much attention is paid to comfort. The reason is not the quest for luxury but the consideration that discomfort may lead to stress responses, which in turn endanger the flow of traffic and possibly even safety. This idea is supported by the recent study by Verwey (1995) and Verwey et al. (1995), mentioned in section 8.1.3. In international guidelines we find correctly that little or few comfort demands are made on tunnels with little traffic.

A second characteristic is that the recommendations are categorised according to the tunnel zone. There are requirements for the threshold zone which in first instance are derived from the conditions in the access zone. In the transition zone, requirements are derived from the design speed and in the interior the requirements are determined by the traffic density. The photometric characteristics are also largely based on Dutch research. The following sections, therefore, in which recommendations and guidelines, as well as installation characteristics are discussed, are based largely on the NSVV Recommendations and, as far as the latest developments are concerned, on the CEN and CIE drafts. As mentioned, these are also based largely on Dutch research (NSVV, 1991; CEN, 1997; CIE, 1995).

As well as the recommendations published by NSVV, the Rijkswaterstaat have also published their own guidelines for the design of tunnels, in which the lighting also – albeit only in passing – is mentioned (Anon., 1991). The publication concentrates on the tunnels which are important for the Rijkswaterstaat: 'traffic tunnels, aqueducts and dug road constructions in the national road network' (Anon., 1991, page 5). This means that in fact only tunnels below canals and rivers are concerned. This publication is particularly interesting as, in addition to a review of the general characteristics of Dutch tunnels, the emphasis is on the project-fashion approach (Anon., 1991, page 9; see also section 13.2).

15.4.3   The access zone

The requirements set for luminance in the threshold zone depend closely on the conditions in the access zone. The adaptation situation of the observer in the access zone is difficult to determine directly. There are a number of current approaches.

The equivalent veil luminance

The state of adaptation L_{ad} is determined by the luminance in the part of the field of vision at which the observer looks – usually the tunnel entrance with luminance L_2 – together with the obtrusive luminance L_d (CIE, 1984)

$$L_{ad} = L_2 + L_d \qquad [15.4.1]$$

Section 15.2.2 indicated that obtrusive luminance comprises four components

$$L_d = L_{adef} + L_{seq} + L_{atm} + L_{ws} \qquad [15.2.5]$$

and that L_{seq} can be determined with the aid of computer program SNAEFELL (Swart, 1994). This method lends itself very well to the production of a lighting design for a tunnel entrance by specialists; the system is less suitable for general easy application, as many data which might be difficult to access, must be available. Readers should refer to De Roo (1993) and Swart (1994) for the application of this system.

Determination with the aid of L_{20}

It was mentioned in section 15.2.2 that often L_{20} is used instead of the more difficult to determine L_{seq}. The use of L_{20} is accompanied by some disadvantages which have also been mentioned in section 15.2.2. Never-

Table 15.4.1: *Approximate values for L_{20}; after CIE, 1995, table 5. Note: (a) for E–W and W–E intermediate values must be taken; (b) in case of frequent snow L_{20} must be increased by 15%*

Design speed	Direction of traffic	Sky percentage in $2 \times 10°$ cone		
		15–25	5–15	0–5
<20 m/s	S to N	4000	2500	1500
	N to S	5000	3500	1500
20–30 m/s	S to N	4000	3000	2500
	N to S	6000	4500	2500

theless, the CEN as well as the CIE drafts are based on L_{20}. L_{20} can be measured in existing tunnels, but this is not usually possible at the design stage. A number of approaches have been listed for estimating L_{20} and the simplest is reproduced in table 15.4.1.

In addition to this approximation, the designs also indicate a graphic method (CIE, 1990, 1995), as well as a method of calculation which is based on the distribution of daylight during the day and during the year (Blaser & Dudli, 1993).

15.4.4 The luminance in the threshold zone

The luminance at the start of the threshold zone is indicated with L_{th}; sometimes the abbreviation L_2 which stems from the research, is used. This luminance is proportional to L_{20}; the proportional factor $k = L_2/L_{20}$. I indicated in section 15.2.2 that in the past it was often said that k should be at least 0.10. However, experience has shown that k can often be much lower. The recommended values for k in the proposals by CEN and CIE are shown in table 15.4.2, as well as the various values for the symmetrical and the counterbeam lighting to be discussed in section 15.4.5.

Table 15.4.2: *Minimum values for k; based on CEN (1997). Note: the values apply to new as well as to used condition; for intermediate values k must be interpolated; for a design speed above 30 m/s k must be determined by linear extrapolation*

	k-values for the threshold zone					
	Counterbeam lighting			Symmetrical lighting		
Design speed (m/s)	15	20	30	15	20	30
Lighting class						
7	40	50	70	50	60	100
6	35	45	60	40	55	80
5	30	40	55	35	50	65
4	25	35	45	30	40	50
3	20	30	40	25	35	45
2	15	20	35	15	25	40
1	5	10	*	5	10	*

* not relevant

Two methods are used for the lighting of the threshold zone: screened daylight and artificial light. In the first case exclusively 'sun-tight' daylight screens were used in the past (Schreuder, 1964, 1965). More recent research has shown that gratings which are not sun-tight can be used, as long as the flashing frequency (section 15.4.8) is high enough (Schreuder & Oud, 1988; Tan et al., 1983). In the last case, either symmetrical or counterbeam lighting is used (section 15.4.5).

The total length of the threshold zone must be at least equal to the stopping distance. The threshold zone is often divided into two sections, on practical grounds. The luminance must be constant over the first part of the threshold zone, viewed lengthways, and must be equal to the values of k shown in table 15.4.2. The luminance must remain constant over that part of the road which the driver must be able to view, as long as she is still outside the tunnel and as long as part of the sky is still included in the field of vision. When the point is passed where the sky can no longer be seen (disappearing behind the top edge of the windscreen), the luminance in the second part of the threshold zone may be gradually decreased to a value which is at least equal to 0.4 L_{th}. Usually the point where this decrease starts is chosen in such a way that it is midway in the threshold zone.

15.4.5   The lighting in the threshold zone: counterbeam lighting

Traditionally tunnels are illuminated in a symmetrical fashion. This means that the light is directed along the traffic flow in the same measure as against the direction of the traffic by the luminaires (Schreuder, 1967). See figure 15.4.1.

Counterbeam lighting contrasts with symmetrical lighting. Here the light is completely or mainly directed against the direction of the traffic. This method of lighting stems from Switzerland and is used frequently in the Alpine countries (Blaser, 1981; Blaser & Dudli, 1982). See figure 15.4.2.

Recently this system has become popular in The Netherlands also, due mainly to the economical and environmental advantages (Schreuder, 1991, 1993; Schreuder & Swart, 1993; Swart, 1994). It was mentioned in section 10.1.2 that certain aspects of countererbeam lighting can be recognised in street lighting also.

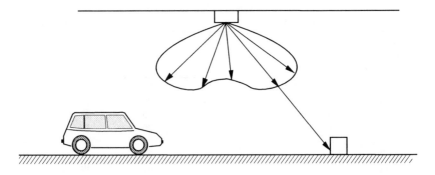

Figure 15.4.1: Symmetrical lighting

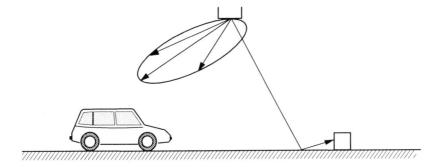

Figure 15.4.2: *Counterbeam lighting*

Table 15.4.3: *Comparison between counterbeam lighting and symmetrical lighting; after Schreuder & Swart, 1993. The q_o-correction after De Haan (1996).*

Aspect	Unit	Drecht tunnel symmetrical	Velser tunnel counterbeam
Length threshold zone	m	30	58
Width	m	8	8
Road surface q_o	–	0.098	0.075
Luminaires per row			
(SON 400 W)	each	10	52
(SON 250 W)	each	21	
Rows of light	each	2	1
Energy/capacity	W/m	616.67	358.62
	W/m^2	77.08	44.83
Luminance	cd/m^2	83	198
Yield	cd/W	2.27	4.42
Ratio counterbeam/symmetrical			1.95
Ratio counterbeam/symmetrical			
corrected for the q_o			2.44

Measurements undertaken in the Velser tunnel have shown that counterbeam lighting offers considerable economic advantages (see table 15.4.3). There is similar evidence from tests in Belgium (Dijon & Winkin, 1991). It is likely that this system will be a future standard in The Netherlands (Schreuder, 1997).

15.4.6   The transition zone

The average luminance may decrease gradually from the end of the threshold zone. See section 15.2.3. The permitted degree of decrease is given in figure 15.2.3, the frequently mentioned CIE curve. As the adaptation is a temporal effect, the CIE curve can be quoted in length or time units as required; the link between them is the design speed.

In practice, the luminance may decrease in steps. The luminance must not decrease more than a ratio of 3:1 for each step. The luminance level must, however, never be lower than the level which corresponds to the gradual curve as shown in figure 15.2.3. As the luminance may decrease in steps in the ratio 3:1, it is usually assumed that the end of the transition zone is reached when the luminance amounts to three times the luminance chosen for the central zone in the tunnel. However, as indicated above, this may lead to too short a transition zone, at least according to oft heard opinions in The Netherlands, Japan and in the US.

15.4.7   The central zone of the tunnel

According to the drafts by CEN (1997) and CIE (1995) mentioned earlier, the luminance level in the interior (the central zone) of a long tunnel must be at least equal to the values shown in table 15.4.4. during the day.

The average luminance of the road surface is determined across the lanes. Emergency lanes may have a lower luminance but not lower than 50% of the lanes. In case special difficulties relating to traffic are to be expected, e.g. lane changes, the luminance must be one step higher.

The walls in tunnels of lighting classes 3 – 7 must have the same luminance as the adjacent or emergency lanes, to a height of at least 2 metres. Twenty-five percent is sufficient for classes 1 and 2.

The requirements stipulated in table 15.4.5 apply to the uniformity of the luminance pattern.

Table 15.4.4: *The minimum luminance level in the central zone of a long tunnel during the day, depending on the design speed and the lighting class (after CEN, 1997)*

	Central zone – luminances in cd/m^2		
Design speed (m/s)	**15**	**20**	**30**
Lighting class			
7	3	6	10
6	3	5	8
5	2	4	6
4	2	3	6
3	1.5	2	4
2	1	1.5	*
1	0.5	1.5	*

* no requirements

Table 15.4.5: *Requirements relating to uniformity in the central zone of long tunnels, after CEN, 1997; definition of U_o and U_1 according to CIE, 1976*

Lighting class	U_o	U_1
6 and 7	0.4	0.7
4 and 5	0.4	0.6
2 and 3	0.3	0.5
1	0.2	0.4

15.4.8   Other lighting characteristics of long tunnels

Eye adaptation to the daylight outside is very rapid at the end of the tunnel, and additional exit lighting to facilitate this adaptation is in most cases not necessary. However, additional lighting at the exit may be useful to render small vehicles close to the exit visible when they are close behind a larger vehicle. (Schreuder, 1964).

The luminance level in the access zone varies with the daylight. In order to avoid a black hole appearing at the start of the tunnel in all relevant circumstances, the luminance in the first part of the threshold zone must under all circumstances comply with the demands. This requires a facility to adapt the lighting in the threshold zone to changes in the level in the access zone. Automatic adaptation is usually chosen, which is controlled by the luminance in the access zone. At present, the adaptation of the artificial light in the threshold zone to variations in daylight usually takes place in steps. The steps must be smaller than a factor of five, for reasons of visibility. Steps of, at most, a factor of three are recommended, for reasons of driving comfort and also of running costs. Dimming installations are recommended on the grounds of driving comfort and of energy savings.

Visibility in tunnels may be influenced negatively by glare, similar to road lighting. In tunnels only the physiological glare (disability glare) is relevant. Glare from the lighting luminaires in the tunnel must be limited in such a way that the threshold value increase TI amounts to less than 15% for all zones and all switchings in the tunnel. Readers should refer to CIE (1976) for the calculation of TI. See also section 7.3.2.

Flicker interrupts the driving comfort as a result of periodical changes in luminance in the field of vision. Flicker may stem from luminaires in the tunnel or from the components in the daylight screens. The seriousness of the nuisance depends mainly on the following factors: the number of changes in luminance per second (the flicker frequency), the luminance of the sources of light (luminaires or screen elements) in relation to the background (the contrast), the total duration of the flicker effect, and the sharpness of the luminous intensity distribution of the light sources. Nuisance is therefore dependent on the driving speed and on the distance between the sources of light, their luminous intensity and their luminous intensity distribution. See, for details on the research, Schreuder (1964).

In general, there is no nuisance as a result of flicker in the central zone of a tunnel which is illuminated by artificial lighting, when the frequency is lower than 2.5 Hz or higher than 15 Hz. If the distance between the extremities of the luminaires is less than the length of the luminaires, then there is no risk of nuisance, as the pattern is perceived as an uninterrupted line.

The same frequencies apply in fact for the entrance zone; here, however, there is no risk of flicker nuisance, due to the short length. Experience has shown that nuisance due to flicker effect is always present at daylight screens, as a result of the very high luminances which the sunlit components may have, as long as the frequency is lower than the flicker fusion frequency. This may be set to approximately 50 Hz for the conditions which appear in tunnels. This effect is especially relevant for screens which are non sun-tight, and where the cars (the windscreens, but also parts of the car interior) are lit by the sun. It is not possible to quantify this nuisance in general terms; the specific characteristics of the screen design are usually decisive. See Tan et al. (1983) for details.

15.5   Short tunnels and underpasses

As indicated in section 15.3.1, lighting requirements for a tunnel depend closely on the type of tunnel and that the length proves to be the main factor. I also pointed out that visual problems in short tunnels mainly depend on whether one is able to look through the tunnel (the through view quotient). When we can see through the tunnel, we no longer have a black hole, but we have a black frame. See figure 15.5.1

Objects in the tunnel can be seen when they stick out from the frame. See figure 15.5.2.

The frame is usually narrower than the tunnel is long, as most road surfaces have a specular reflection.

It is often useful to incorporate the black frame idea into the lighting of short tunnels. When the frame is narrow, the tunnel can remain unlit during the day. A tunnel with a very wide frame must be illuminated as a long tunnel, even if the exit is more or less visible. These are tunnels with a small through view quotient (section 15.3.1). Tunnels of medium length may be split into two short tunnels by applying an illuminated crossways band. See figure 15.5.3.

This is difficult to achieve with artificial light, but it is easily done with daylight. An opening of 1 to 2 metres is usually sufficient to admit a considerable amount of light (Schreuder, 1964, pages 36–37). See figure 15.5.4.

The classification of short tunnels, given in the first edition of the NSVV Recommendations (NSVV, 1963), was mentioned in section 15.3.1. See table 15.5.1.

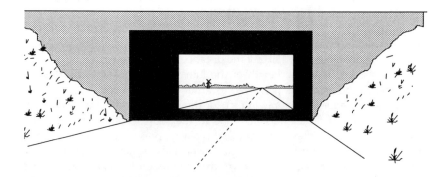

Figure 15.5.1: A black frame in a short tunnel

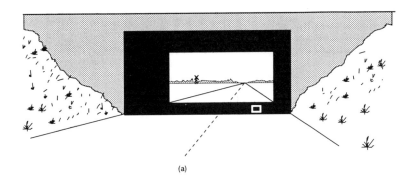

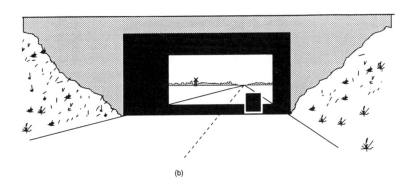

Figure 15.5.2: *A black frame with an object in a short tunnel*

Figure 15.5.3: *A medium-sized long tunnel split into two shorter tunnels*

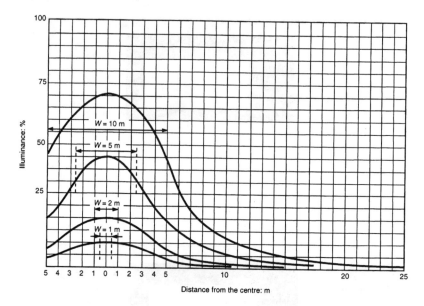

Figure 15.5.4: *The amount of light admitted (E_{hor}) through a gap in the tunnel; tunnel height 5 metres. Based on data from Higbie, 1934*

Table 15.5.1: *Recommendations for short tunnels; based on NSVV, 1963. After Schreuder, 1964, table 15*

	Favourable	Unfavourable
No lighting	0–50 m	0–25 m
Crossways band lighting *	50–80 metres	25–40 metres
Total length lighting *	80–100 metres	40–100 metres
Long tunnels	>100 metres	> 100 metres

Notes: (1) 'favourable' means no bends, moderate traffic, only motor vehicles; 'unfavourable' means bends and/or busy traffic and/or mixed traffic

(2) The value of 800 cd/m² is recommended for the luminances indicated with * in the original figures from NSVV (1963) and by Schreuder (1964). This value would seem to be too high in most cases. The CEN (1997) draft has the same principle, but the luminance values must be equal to the *k* values which apply to the lighting of the threshold zone (CIE, 1996, art. 7.3).

15.6   Tunnels for cyclists and pedestrians

As indicated in section 15.3.1, most tunnels which are intended exclusively for slow traffic are short. The lighting requirements are based on public safety. The requirements for slow traffic in respect to tunnel lighting relate to safety, similar to other facilities

- objectively: stumbling, robberies and sexual attacks
- subjectively: fear of fast traffic and fear of crime.

Table 15.6.1: *Lighting for pedestrian/cyclist tunnels in various countries based on data from De Groot & De Vlieger, 1994*

Country	Standard	Illuminance (lux)
UK	BS 5489	250–300
Belgium	BSN	200
Norway	N	50
Germany	FSV	50–120
Germany	DIN 67 528	200
The Netherlands	NEN 1890	100 (very rough details) 200 (rough details)

Table 15.6.2: *Suggestions for the lighting of pedestrian/cyclist tunnels after De Groot & De Vlieger, 1994*

Tunnel size	Time	Illuminance (lux)	
		Entrance	Interior
Length < 10 × height	Daytime	None	None
10 < length < 20	Daytime	Depends on circumstances	
Length > 20 × height	Daytime	250	50
All lengths	Night-time	15	15

The victims are mainly women and older people, but also disabled people and children.

A number of countries have recommendations or guidelines for pedestrian tunnels; an overview is given in table 15.6.1. The values relate to the average illuminance in the interior of pedestrian tunnels. The data are from De Groot & De Vlieger (1994).

De Groot & De Vlieger (1994) also offered some suggestions for the lighting of pedestrian tunnels. See table 15.6.2. These suggestions are presently being discussed in NSVV.

Much is known about the contribution which lighting can offer with regard to these problems. The knowledge is usually only based on practical experience. Little theory has been developed. The experience especially relates to scary places in public areas (sports complexes, shopping centres). Data are also known in relation to tunnels. The experience was mainly gathered in cities. Public safety in the built-up area has generally been researched extensively. See section 11.3.1. This has led to the five criteria for public safety (public control; absence of potential criminals; possibilities for visibility; overview and attractive surroundings). See, e.g. Anon. (1991, 1993, 1994) and Hajonides et al. (1987).

Bibliography

Adrian, W. (1989). 'Visibility of targets: Model for calculation'. *Lighting Res. Technol.* **21** (1989) 181–188.

Adrian, W. (1990). 'A method for the design of tunnel entrance lights.' *Journal IES* (1990) (winter), pp. 125–133.

Anon. (1986). *RAW/SCW/SVT; Nomenclatuur van weg en verkeer* [Classification of roads and traffic]. SCW-Mededeling 58/SVT-Mededeling 41. Driebergen, SCW/SVT, 1986.

Anon. (1991). *Scoren met sociale veiligheid; Handleiding sociale veiligheid in en om sportaccommodaties* [Scoring with public safety; Guide for public safety in and around sports facilities]. Rijswijk, Ministerie van Welzijn, Volksgezondheid en Cultuur, 1991.

Anon. (1992). *ARTO, Algemene Richtlijnen Tunnel Ontwerp* [ARTO, General guidelines tunnel design]. Utrecht, Rijkwaterstaat, Bouwdienst, 1992.

Anon. (1993). *Verlichting; Verlichtingstechniek als hulpmiddel bij de criminaliteitspreventie* [Lighting; Lighting techniques as an aid to crime prevention]. Derde druk. Den Haag, Ministerie van Justitie, Directie Criminaliteitspreventie, 1993.

Anon. (1993a). *State of the road tunnel equipment technology in Japan; Ventilation, lighting, safety equipment.* Technical Note of Public works Research Institute, Vol. 61. Asahi, Ministry of Construction, 1993.

Anon. (1993b). *Right Light II.* Second European Conference on Energy-Efficient Lighting, 26–29 September 1993. Arnhem, NSVV, 1993.

Anon. (1994). *Zien en gzien worden; Voorbeeldprojecten 'sociale veiligheid'* [Seeing and be seen; good practice projects 'public safety']. Rijswijk, Ministerie van Welzijn, Volksgezondheid en Cultuur, 1993.

Anon. (1995). Symposium on tunnel and motorway lighting, Amsterdam, 25 september 1995. Express Highway Research Foundation of Japan, Amsterdam, 1995.

Anon. (1995a). *Metingen van het drempelcontrast bij tunnelingangen; Meetrapport* [Measurements of the threshold contrast in tunnel entrances; Measurement report]. Gouda, Transpute, 1995.

Blaser, P. (1981). 'Die Gegenstrahlbeleuchtung in der Einfahrzone von Strassentunneln'. *Bull. SEV* **72** (1981) 991–996.

Blaser, P. & Dudli, H. (1982). 'Die Sichtverhältnisse in der Einfahrzone von Strassentunneln mit Gegenstrahlbeleuchtung'. In SLG (1982), pp 417–421.

Blaser, O. & Dudli, H. (1993), *Lighting Res. Technol.* **25** (1993) 25-30.

Bourdy, C.; Chiron, A.; Cottin, C. & Monot, A. (1987). 'Visibility at a tunnel entrance: Effect of temporal adaptation'. *Lighting Res. Technol.* **19** (1987) 35–44.

CEN (1997). *Standard for the lighting of road traffic tunnels*, CEN/TC169/WG6, 10th draft.

CIE (1973). *International recommendations for tunnel lighting.* Publication No. 26. Paris, CIE 1973.

CIE (1976). *Glare and uniformity in street lighting.* Publication No. 31. Paris, CIE, 1976.

CIE (1981). *An analytic model for describing the influence of lighting parameters upon visual performance.* Publication No. 19/2 (two volumes). Paris, CIE, 1981.

CIE (1984). *Tunnel entrance lighting.* Publication No. 61. Paris, CIE, 1984.

CIE (1990). *Guide for the lighting of road tunnels and underpasses.* Publication No. 88. Paris, CIE, 1990.

CIE (1995). *Tunnel lighting; A design guide.* Revision of CIE Documents No. 61 and No 88. First draft, 1995.

De Boer, J.B., (ed.) (1967). *Public lighting.* Eindhoven, Centrex, 1967.

De Groot, W.A.G. & De Vlieger, (1994). *Verlichten van onderdoorgangen en korte tunnels* [The lighting of underpasses and short tunnels]. Congresdag 12 april 1994. Amsterdam, NSVV, 1994.

De Haan, H.G. (1996). *Tegenstraal verlichting Velsertunnel, Eindrapportage* [Counterbeam lighting Velser tunnel, Final Report]. Utrecht, Bouwdienst Rijkswaterstaat, 1996.

De Roo, F. (1993). *Veiling luminance calculations on several Norwegian tunnels.* Utrecht, Bouwdienst Rijkswaterstaat, 1993 (unpublished).

Dijon, J.M. & Winkin, P. (1991). *Comparison and tests, Wevelgem Tunnel.* Symposium on Visibility; National Research Council, 1991 (year estimated).

Di Fraia, L. (1993). 'Expert systems for automatic optimisation of interior and road lighting systems'. In: Anon. (1993).

DIN (1987). *Beleuchtung von Strassentunneln und Unterführungen. Algemeine Gütemerkmale und Richtwerte.* Din 67 524 Teil 1/05.87. Berlin, DIN, 1987 (year estimated).

Hajonides, T. et al. (1987). *Buiten gewoon veilig* [Safety outside]. Rotterdam, Stichting Vrouwen Bouwen & Wonen, 1987.

Higbie, H.H., (1934). *Lighting calculations.* New York, John Wiley, 1934.

Kabayama, H. (1963). 'Study on adaptive illumination for sudden change of brightness'. *J. Illum. Engn. Inst. Japan.* **47** (1963) 488–496 (in Japanese).

Narisada, K. & Yoshikawa, K. (1974). 'Tunnel entrance lighting; Effect of fixation point and other factors on the determination of requirements'. *Lighting Res. Technol.* **6** (1974) 9–11.

NSVV (1963). 'Aanbevelingen voor tunnelverlichting' [Recommendations for tunnel lighting]. *Electrotechiek.* **41** (1963), 23; 46.

NSVV (1991). *Aanbevelingen voor de verlichting van lange tunnels voor het gemotoriseerde verkeer* [Recommendations for the lighting of long tunnels for motorised traffic]. Arnhem, NSVV, 1991.

Ohayama, T. (1995). 'Studies in lighting curves for dimmed tunnel entrances'. In: Anon. (1995).

Padmos, P. & Alferdinck, J.W.A.M. (1983). *Verblinding bij tunnelingangen II: De invloed van atmosferisch strooilicht* [Glare in tunnel entrances II: the effect of atmospheric stray light]. IZF 1983 C-9. Soesterberg, IZF-TNO, 1983.

Padmos, P. & Alferdinck, J.W.A.M. (1983a). *Verblinding bij tunnelingangen III: De invloed van strooilicht van de autovoorruit* [Glare in tunnel entrances III: the effect of stray light on the windscreen]. IZF 1983 C-10, Soesterberg, IZF-TNO, 1983.

Roovers, D.A.C.M. & De Roo, F. (1996). *Verstrooiing en reflectie van licht aan de voorruit en het dashboard van een auto.* [Scattering and reflection of light on the windscreen and the car dashboard]. Utrecht, Rijkswaterstaat, 1996.

Schreuder, D.A. (1964). The lighting of vehicular traffic tunnels. Eindhoven, Centrex, 1964.

Schreuder, D.A. (1965). 'Über die Beleuchtung von Verkehrstunneln'. Lichttechnik 17 (1965) 12: 145A-149A.

Schreuder, D.A. (1967). 'Tunnel lighting'. Chapter IV. In: De Boer, (ed.) (1967).

Schreuder, D.A. (1981). *De verlichting van tunnelingangen: De derde generatie* [The lighting of tunnel entrances: the third generation]. R-81-21. Voorburg, SWOV, 1981.

Schreuder, D.A. (1989). *Tunnelverlichting; 25 Jaar theorie en praktijk* [Tunnel lighting: 25 years of theory and practice]. Leidschendam, SWOV, 1989.

Schreuder, D.A. (1991). *Tegenstraalverlichting in tunnels; Een overzicht van de beschikbare literatuur* [Counterbeam lighting in tunnels: a review of the available literature]. R-91-96. Leidschendam, SWOV, 1991.

Schreuder, D.A. (1993). *Contrastwaarnemingen in tunnels – Een meetmethode* [Contrast perception in tunnels – a measuring method]. R-93-36. Leidschendam, SWOV, 1993.

Schreuder, D.A. (1997). *Recent developments in traffic tunnel lightinh in The Netherlands.* Washington, D.C. Transportation Research Board 76th Annual Meeting in January 1997. Leidschendam, Duco Schreuder Consultancies, 1997.

Schreuder, D.A. & Fournier, P. (1985). *Een systeem voor classificatie van korte tunnels* [A system for the classification of short tunnels]. R-85-59. Leidschendam, SWOV, 1985.

Schreuder, D.A. & Oud, H.J.C. (1988). *The predetermination of the luminance in tunnel entrances at day.* Leidschendam, SWOV, 1988.

Schreuder, D.A. & Swart, L. (1993). *Energy saving in tunnel entrance lighting.* Paper 2nd European Conference on Energy-Efficient Lighting, 1993, Arnhem, 1993.

SLG (1982). *Bericht Lichttechnische Gemeinschaftstagung Licht82.* Dok.No.500/82. SLG, Zürich, 1982.

Stiksma, K., (ed.) (1987). *Tunnels in the Netherlands; Underground transport connections.* Illustra, 1987.

Swart, L. (1994). *Tegenstraalverlichting in tunnels – wat is daar tegen?* [Counterbeam lighting in tunnels – what is there against it]? Congresdag 12 april 1994. Amsterdam, NSVV, 1994.

Tan, T.H.; van den Brink, T.D.J. & Swart, L. (1983). 'Tunnelingangsverlichting'. *Electrotechniek* **61** (1983) 669–675.

Verwey, W.B. (1995). *Effects of tunnel entrances on drivers' physiological condition and performance.* Report TM 1995 C-19. Soesterberg, TNO/TM, 1995.

Verwey, W.B.; Alferdinck, J.W.A.M. & Theeuwes, J. (1995). *Quality of tunnel entrances in terms of safety and capacity.* Soesterberg, TNO/TM, 1995 (draft).

Vos, J.J. (1983). *Verblinding bij tunnelingangen I: De invloed van strooilicht in het oog* [Glare in tunnel entrances I: the effect of stray light in the eye]. IZF 1983 C-8. Soesterberg, IZF-TNO, 1983.

Vos, J.J. & Padmos, P. (1983). *Straylight, contrast sensitivity and the critical object in relation to tunnel entrance lighting.* Amsterdam, CIE, 1983.

Vreugdenhil, A.C. (1952). *De Maastunnel.* Tweede druk. Haarlem, Stam, 1952.

Werkman, E. (1959). *Tunnels.* Bilthoven, H. Nelissen, 1959.

Index

observation position, 66–69, 217
obstacle protection, 229–230
obtrusive light, 252
older people, 103, 125, 128, 144, 197, 285
optical axis, 76
optical nerve, 82, 87
overload, 5, 136

paradigm, 90, 95
pedestrians, 6, 11, 141, 144, 148–149, 153, 161, 173, 186, 233, 260, 284
periphery, 80, 100, 105, 107, 126, 136
phenomenological description, 21
phosphorescence, 32
photocell, 58–59, 61–63, 71, 231, 248
photodiodes, 58
photometer, see flickering photometer
photometric threshold distance, 51–54, 72
photon model, 23
photons, 21, 23, 41, 58
photoreceptors, 23, 42, 75, 78–80, 104, 126
phototransistors, 58
physiological glare, see glare
physiology, 2, 75, 90–91, 133
point measurements, 62, 65, 70
polar diagrams, 60
policy, 13, 15, 175, 203–204, 215, 239–242, 248
  aims, 15
presbyopia, 76, 125
preview, 65, 138–139
  distance, 264
profit principle, 9
prognoses, 12–13
project, 163, 195, 198, 218
project-fashion, 218, 276
propagation speed, 22
protanopes, 115, 127
psychological glare, see glare
psychology, 86, 90–91, 97, 133, 142
pupil, 75–76, 78, 103
Purkinje effect, 44, 78, 82–83

$q_o - \kappa_p$ classification, 168
quantified (energy), 23
quantum mechanics, 23

radiation standard, 24
radiometry, 42

random, 35, 142
raw materials, 9, 241, 249
recombination, 29, 220
rectifiers 58
recycling, 241, 249
reduced luminance coefficient, 170
reduction in luminous output, 224
reflection indicatrix, 166
reflection, 25, 33–38, 49, 57, 61–62, 66, 71, 120, 149, 153, 161, 164–165, 268–269, 282
  regular, 35
  retro, 35–36
  total, 38–39
reflectors, 5, 34, 36, 140
reflexes, 138, 143
refraction, 24, 33–34, 36–37, 39
  defect, 123, 125
  double, 35, 39
  law, 38–39
refractors, 34
regular reflection, see reflection
response, 42, 82, 199, 275
retina, 43, 48, 75–76, 78–80, 83, 85, 87, 115, 123
revealing power, 152–154
rhodopsin, 79
risk, 1, 5–6, 12, 14–15, 17, 46, 93, 102, 122, 127, 135, 140, 142, 162, 186, 191, 193, 205, 207, 210, 225, 229–230, 281
  homeostasis, 142, 165
  reliability, 17
road,
  design, 255
  surface, 33, 35, 47, 78, 83, 112, 148–151, 193, 215–217, 234, 280, 282
rods, 42–44, 79–80, 82, 105, 107

sample, 72, 91, 184, 186, 193, 195, 209
saturation, 119
scalar, 36, 149, 165, 172
sealing of luminaires, 225
search behaviour, 137
sensitivity, 30, 42, 44–45, 70, 78, 97, 103, 125–126, 144, 269
  contrast, 97–100, 111, 128, 267
  eye curve, 63, 78–80, 115–116
  of the visual system, 102, 107, 148
service life, 17, 29, 62, 215, 221, 224, 226, 249